National Socialist Rule in Germany

National Socialist Rule in Germany

The Führer State 1933–1945

NORBERT FREI

Translated by Simon B. Steyne

BLACKWELL
Oxford UK & Cambridge USA

Copyright © Deutscher Taschenbuch Verlag GmbH & Co. KG, Munich 1987

English translation copyright © Basil Blackwell Ltd 1993

The right of Norbert Frei to be identified as author of this work has been asserted in accordance with the Copyright, Designs and Patents Act 1988.

First published in English 1993

Blackwell Publishers
108 Cowley Road
Oxford OX4 1JF, UK

238 Main Street, Suite 501
Cambridge, Massachusetts 02142, USA

British Library Cataloguing in Publication Data

A CIP catalogue record for this book is available from the British Library.

Library of Congress Cataloging-in-Publication Data

Frei, Norbert.
  [Führerstaat. English]
  National socialist rule in Germany : the Führer State 1933–1945 Norbert Frei: translated by Simon B. Steyne.
    p. cm.
  Translation of: Führerstaat.
  Includes bibliographical references and index.
  ISBN 0-631-16858-3. – ISBN 0-631-18507-0 (pbk.)
  1. Germany – Politics and government – 2. National socialism.
I. Title.
DD256.5.F7335713   1993
943.086—dc20   92-23312
                                                                            CIP

Typeset in Garamond on 10/12pt
by Graphicraft Typesetters Ltd, Hong Kong
Printed in Great Britain by TJ Press Ltd., Padstow, Cornwall

This book is printed on acid-free paper

Contents

Foreword to the English edition   vii
Introduction   1

Part I The Regime in Crisis, Spring 1934   3
The SA in the crossfire   9
Criticism from the right   15
Hitler's double coup   18
The consequences of 30 June   23

Part II The Internal Development of the Third Reich   29
1 Regimentation and Coordination, 1933–1934   31
From the assumption of power to the March elections   32
The conquest of the *Länder* and the Enabling Law   39
The elimination of the labour movement and agreement
    with industry   49
The end of the parties and the coordination of society   57
2 Consolidation, 1935–1938   70
The Nazi economic miracle   71
The workers and the 'national community'   77
Ideological mobilization   83
Culture and everyday life   91
The systematization of terror and the rise of the SS   99
3 Radicalization, 1938–1945   109
The Germans and the beginning of war   111
Cure, exploit, exterminate   120

The genocide of the Jews   128
Total war and the disintegration of Nazi rule   136
4   The 'Führer State': Impact and Consequences   149

Documents   156
1   Observations of a senior lecturer. On the sociology of the
    National Socialist Revolution   156
2   Potatoes instead of pork: Rudolf Hess on the 'fats crisis' of
    1936   163
3   Joseph Goebbels: 'The Führer is very happy'   166
4   The 'Führer' on the 'Führer State': 'The best type of
    democracy'   170
5   Heinrich Himmler: Smoking ban and 'special treatment'   175
6   Robert Ley: The Reich Vocational Contest and tiredness
    as *passé*   180
7   The regime and 'community aliens'   181
8   A euthanasia doctor writes to his wife: 'Work is going
    very smoothly'   186
9   Adolf Eichmann: The Wannsee Conference   190
10 Land of the East, land of illusion: Nazi melodies and songs
    to boost morale   192
11 Count Helmuth James von Moltke: Re-establishing the
    picture of man   194
12 The end of the 'Führer State': The Germans give up   195

Notes and References   204
Sources, review of research and bibliography   216
Appendix 1: Chronology 1933–1945   232
Appendix 2: Organization and leadership of the NSDAP,
    November 1936   244
Abbreviations and glossary   247
Index   254

Foreword to the English edition

An interpretation of the internal history of the Third Reich which opens with an outline of the situation in Germany one whole year after Adolf Hitler had become Reich Chancellor requires, perhaps, some words of explanation, for few readers of this book are likely to be familiar with the basis upon which the paperback series in which its original German edition appeared in 1987 was structured. One of the particular successes of this series, 'German History of the Recent Past' ('Deutsche Geschichte der neuesten Zeit'), is that the individual volumes do not begin with a systematic, historical description, but rather, after a summary of the subject, with a descriptive account of one of the most important events of the particular historical theme, intended to catch the reader's attention.

In our case we start with the events which culminated on 30 June 1934 – the day on which Hitler settled a bloody account with his critics inside his own movement and amongst the conservatives and ensured his unlimited monopoly of power. It was the day upon which his 'Führer State' was almost completed.

The reader is, of course, not obliged to comply with this approach. Those who are less familiar with German history and prefer to gain their information by following events in chronological order might be better advised to begin with part II, chapter 1, and to turn to part I afterwards.

Since, unlike the German edition, this English edition is not complemented by several volumes on adjacent themes, some sections of the present book have been extended. The reader must decide whether the end product, although certainly extremely brief, has turned out to be the reasonably rounded, comprehensive overview of the development of internal politics and society in Germany in the years between 1933 and 1945 that I had intended.

Those who are conversant with the historiography of the Third Reich will have little difficulty in recognizing how much this book owes to the insight and stimulus of Martin Broszat, the late Director of the Institute of Contemporary History in Munich, who died in the autumn of 1989. Being able to work with and learn from this great historian and fascinating man for an entire decade was a unique opportunity for which I will always be grateful.

N.F.
Munich, spring 1991

Introduction

The appointment of Hitler as Reich Chancellor on 30 January 1933 marks a break in German history. But were the destruction of the German Reich and the division of Europe already determined by the events of that day? Was the fate of the 'Führer State' sealed already, even before its foundations had been laid? With the benefit of hindsight we can now argue that the path to catastrophe was not inevitable. Even in the Third Reich there were turning points and alternatives, and in the final analysis its history was no more predetermined than any other.

One of the moments of lasting importance was 30 June 1934, the culmination of months of severe internal crisis. In a bloody double coup, Hitler eliminated not only the SA (*Sturmabteilung*, Stormtroopers) as a hotbed of unrest within his own 'movement', but also his critics and original coalition partners of the right. Only then was his claim to sole political power confirmed and the formative phase of the 'Führer State' concluded.

The claims of the regime to be restructuring Germany benefited from the now unfolding 'Führer' myth, and found wide acceptance in German society. It was no longer the political terror of the early days, but rather the economic and soon also the foreign policy successes of the National Socialists, that determined this middle phase in the consciousness of a 'national community' (*Volksgemeinschaft*) which, to a certain extent, had come to exist. The continuing socio-psychological binding power of the regime lasted long into wartime and can hardly be explained without taking into full historical account the 'good years' which many Germans experienced despite the increased pressure at work and the relentless ideological mobilization. For this reason this book concentrates on the general political, social and economic development of the Third Reich.

The war, conducted in the East from the beginning as an ideological struggle, also brought about a radicalization on the home front. After a phase in which state power expanded, the ideological dynamic of the 'movement' itself ushered in a new epoch. This radicalization found its expression in the monstrous projects of social and racial purification of German society, undertaken in the name of modernization.

Regimentation and coordination, consolidation and radicalization; the transitions between these phases of National Socialist rule were certainly fluid. But as lines of demarcation in the internal development of the Third Reich they are useful, not only on analytical grounds, but also to make it easier to assign both political and moral responsibility.

PART I

THE REGIME IN CRISIS, SPRING 1934

In the spring of 1934, many believed that the days of Hitler's government were numbered. The so-called 'seizure of power' had taken place only twelve months earlier, but there was not a trace left of the 'national uprising'. The wave of enthusiasm with which the new rulers had initially been met had left little more than a mood akin to a severe political hangover. The resurgence seemed to be stuck half-way up the slope. Everywhere – in the state and the Party, the economy and the administration, the Reichswehr and the SA, in town and countryside – there was widespread disillusionment. Still worse, the number of those who clearly articulated their dissatisfaction grew daily. Criticism came from all sides, and sprang from quite different motives.

Dissent was particularly great in the petit bourgeois business world, amongst small tradespeople. 'What did you lot promise us all before? You were going to close the department stores and abolish retail chains. Nothing has happened, we have been cheated and lied to.'[1] The furious shopkeeper who made this complaint at a meeting in Görlitz of the Nazi Craft, Trade and Commerce Organization (Nationalsozialistische Handwerks-, Handels- und Gewerbeorganisation – NS-Hago), was arrested the following day. The decree against 'malicious practices' (*Heimtückeverordnung*), promulgated as early as March 1933, had indeed made possible the punishment of even merely spoken criticism, but could do little to combat a growing sense of disappointment, embitterment and helplessness. Nevertheless, press censorship and fear of reprisals prevented the public from gaining as clear an impression of the extent of the crisis as the regime enjoyed. Tens of thousands of local Party functionaries had their ears to the ground, and the traditional reports of the domestic administration, which began at the basic level of rural police (*Gendarmerie*) stations, served as a substitute for the distorted account of reality to be found in the newspapers.

Only one group of organized opponents had an overview to compare with that of the Nazi leadership. This was the *Sopade*, the exiled SPD executive based in Prague, which was regularly furnished with information by agents throughout the Reich. A report from western Saxony stated:

> The miserable mood in the business world, which has already been reported, has become even worse. Today it is primarily these circles who swear like troopers, so long as they know that no-one is present who will denounce them. And amongst them are many people who only a year ago could not shout loudly enough their joy that Adolf was now Chancellor and who voted solidly for Hitler in the years before. Today they say with dismay that they had not imagined things would turn out as they have.[2]

Discontent about unfulfilled material expectations was not characteristic of the *Mittelstand* (the petit bourgeoisie) alone. The extreme frugality of working-class and white-collar families – the main complaint of the retail trade – did not exist by chance. Alongside exorbitant increases in the price of food, its origins were partly to be found in drastic wage cuts. In the porcelain and glass industry in the upper Palatinate, for example, wages sank by up to 50 per cent within a single year.[3] The fear of unemployment also remained present, for after the rapid initial successes which followed January 1933, when the six million-strong army of the unemployed had shrunk by more than a third within twelve months, further reductions were an uphill struggle. Some who had originally found employment thanks to the state 'work creation programme' – often in road building, where heavy work was performed by poorly-paid human labour instead of modern machinery – soon once again found themselves standing in front of the employment exchange. And many of the long-term unemployed must have discovered that the impressive official figures were based on biting reductions in social expenditure and massaged statistics. Local welfare support was often cut or made conditional on the fulfilment of utterly unreasonable requirements: for example, having to prove that one had unsuccessfully applied for work, in person, at twenty-five firms each and every week. In the 'works council' (*Vertrauensräte* – literally 'Councils of Trust') elections of March and April 1934, the Nazi Factory Cell Organization (Nationalsozialistische Betriebszellenorganisation – NSBO) slate received such a decisive defeat that in many workplaces the results were not announced.

A less uniform mood prevailed amongst the workers than among the *Mittelstand*. Those who were still unemployed remained more sceptical than people who, in the meanwhile, had found work. The massive propaganda campaign concerning the 'Arbeitsschlacht' (the 'battle for jobs'), Labour Service, and the agricultural auxiliary labour scheme (Landhilfe), none the less created the impression that, under National Socialism, something was being done:

> The worker complains about poor wages. At the same time, however, many are happy just to have jobs again. The worker forms his opinions, and they are not favourable towards those in power. But he keeps them to himself. Viewed overall, the working class seems at present to be waiting with uncertainty about what the future will hold. It lacks faith.[4]

With the exception of parts of the north German Protestant agricultural labour force, it was the peasants, having long given the Nazis the cold shoulder, who were particularly disillusioned. The newly centralized marketing of produce through the 'Reich Food Estate' (Reichsnährstand) which was intended to increase profits, led to considerable unrest in rural areas. In the Catholic-agrarian milieu of southern Germany Nazi agricultural policy, an inefficient mish-mash of aspirations to autarky and 'blood and soil' (Blut und Boden) ideology, met with clear and concrete rejection:

> Eggs, butter and fat have to be handed over to the central purchasing points. But the central purchasing points function badly. Commercial nous is what is most lacking . . . A short while ago, in the town of Cham, where there is such a district egg collection point, a whole truckload of eggs went rotten in the extreme heat. The manager of the egg collection point was only prepared to let the truck move off when it had a full load . . . The farmers know all about this and are becoming enraged about these useless big shots [Bonzen] 'who only know how to drive'.[5]

The Reich Entailed Farm Law (Reichserbhofsgesetz) met with an even more negative response than the Reich Food Estate, which in many respects simply continued to perform the tasks of the earlier agricultural cooperatives. Some farmers felt that it curtailed their property rights and freedom to make decisions. As a report from Brandenburg put it:

> According to this law, you may no longer use land as security against a loan, not even for the division of inheritance or for a dowry. In the district of one lawyer alone, 20 engagements have been broken off as a result of this law . . . In one case the son was forbidden to finish his almost completed studies because of the law, as the farm could not meet the cost without going into debt. Where the right of the eldest to inherit applies, the

eldest sons return from the city, drive out their younger brothers and sisters and run the farm alone.[6]

In the view of the Reich Food Estate functionaries these were transitional difficulties, for which Richard Walter Darré, the Reich Peasants' Leader (*Reichsbauernführer*) rather meekly begged understanding at the first Bavarian peasants' convention in Munich in mid-April 1934 – in front of barely a third of the expected 50,000 visitors. Nevertheless, the distrust amongst the farming community remained. It is certainly true that farmers profited from the increased allocation of agricultural auxiliaries (the selection and distribution of the unemployed driven into the villages by the lorry load reminded one *Sopade* observer of a slave-market), but such minor benefits did nothing to reduce the sense of alienation from the regime:

> The peasants, to a man, are angry about the Hitler system. Market days in the towns . . . almost assume the character of political meetings. Only a chairman is missing. Everything is discussed and grumbled about . . . about the 'pigsty', about the 'big-shot economy' [*Bonzenwirtschaft*], about the betrayal of the people . . . The gendarmes behave as though they had not heard the market-goers. If known Nazi informers turn up, the most that happens is that people move along a bit and talk more quietly, but the informers can sense the mood of the peasants perfectly well. For a long while it has been impossible to speak of the peasants fearing the Nazis. On the contrary, known Nazis avoid the peasants, so as not to be called to account about when they finally intend to start turning their promises into reality.[7]

It was not just the middle classes, workers and peasants who were angry. In the spring of 1934 the stylized image of the Nazi movement as dynamic and accustomed to success was showing clear signs of wear and tear in the eyes of all sections of the population. Housewives grumbled about the bottle-necks in the supply of dairy products, eggs and fat; it was precisely the cheap brands of margarine that were often totally unavailable. Instead there were recipes for making it yourself – and in one of the many ministerial discussions on the subject of the fats crisis, the 'Führer's' advice to plant soya beans. (Backe, the State Secretary for Food, suggested 'lupins with their bitterness removed' instead.) Industry lacked rubber and fuel oil, but instead of scarce foreign exchange reserves they received recommendations to choose substitute materials and to intensify their efforts in the production of synthetics. Hitler's opinion was that 'We should have already begun to find a solution to the raw materials issue in 1933.'[8]

The Reich Chancellor was not just fearful for his ambitious plans for autarky, he was worried about political and economic development as a whole. In a meeting with the Reich Governors (*Reichsstatthalter*) on 22 March 1934 he panicked openly. In front of these supposed 'viceroys of the Reich' (whose – as yet undecided – position within the Nazi state also stood on the agenda), Reich ministers and high-ranking Party comrades (*Parteigenossen*) such as Goering, Frick, Hess, Funk and Bormann, Hitler opined, with regard to the lamentable foreign exchange situation, that what was at stake was 'to avoid a catastrophe'. The Chancellor illustrated his – grotesque – demand, that all raw materials should be ordered only with the approval of the Reich Economics Minister, with the example of a German Labour Front (Deutsche Arbeitsfront – DAF] order for 'millions of uniforms' made out of imported cotton: 'If such an experiment were to be made five times, all the foreign currency reserves would be used up.' Finally he complained about 'intervention in the economy . . . by Party or SA authorities'. He commented on the latest boycott of department stores organized by the NS-Hago with the declaration that 'the closure of the department stores would lead to a banking crash [and] deliver a fatal blow to economic reconstruction.' The minute-taker, probably Bavaria's *Statthalter*, Franz Ritter von Epp, captured Hitler's gloomy mood when he reported phrases such as: 'Every grenade requires a copper ring – we have no copper in Germany – imagine what that means.'[9]

The Führer himself was complaining and high-ranking Nazis were using 'the present doubtlessly existing ill humor amongst the broad mass of the people' as a springboard for their own discontent (thus Bavaria's interior minister, Adolf Wagner, who complained that reform of the Reich – from which he personally expected even more power – had come to a standstill).[10] At such a juncture a leading figure in the economy such as the steel magnate Fritz Thyssen also believed he could lodge his own complaints about the organizational mess of the Labour Front and the 'disastrous perpetuation of the ideological struggle'. As one of Hitler's earliest supporters from the ranks of industry, he was now none the less remarking upon the disadvantages of 'journalistic monotony': there was 'not a single word' to be found in the Nazi press regarding the widespread criticism of Robert Ley's DAF, and the bourgeois press 'naturally' lacked 'the courage' to report it.[11]

Like industry, the civil service too complained about the disruptive intervention of Party groups and SA commissars, who certainly had political power at their disposal, but not the relevant specialized knowledge. Hitler's coalition partners on the old right had at first been quite prepared to turn a blind eye to unpleasant 'side-effects' of the 'national revolution', especially to the brutal destruction of the labour movement and the left-liberal cultural and intellectual world during the first months after the 'seizure of power'. Now, however, in the eyes of civil servants, churchmen, lawyers, right-wing intellectuals, indeed of almost the whole bourgeois establishment, developments appeared to be taking a threatening turn. Some had meanwhile already recognized that the more firmly the regime held the reins, the more certain it was that it would turn its totalitarian demands against their own interests.

Simpler souls were asking themselves just what had improved under the new regime. Fewer and fewer believed that the 'Hitler movement' was unique, more and more held the NSDAP to be a 'typical political party', as useless as all the others. The decline in willingness to denounce others and make donations, the ever more sparse display of flags on private houses on state holidays, whispered grumbling, the frankness of the jokes cracked about 'them up there' and the critical tone struck by pronouncements from church pulpits – all these were signs of a dramatic change of mood, which Goebbels attempted to overcome with a campaign of mass rallies and meetings.

On 11 May 1934 at the Berlin Sportpalast, the Minister of Propaganda and Reich Propaganda Leader of the NSDAP initiated the 'struggle against verminous enemies of the state' (*Staatsschädlinge*).[12] Full of indignation, he stated that there were 'people who cannot stand themselves, and get angry just by looking in the mirror. They find fault with everything.' But even epithets such as 'alarmists' and 'carpers' could not disguise the noticeably defensive tone of the speech: it had always been clear 'that National Socialism could only be realized step by step', and that 'symptoms of crisis' had simply to be overcome. Responsibility for this was born by grumbling 'reactionaries', the Jews ('We have baulked at nothing in order to free the German people from this vermin') and the previous governments from whom 'we uncomplainingly took over the legacy of Marxism'.[13] French criticism of the status of the SA, which was seen as a paramilitary force and therefore as a breach of the Versailles Treaty, occasioned him to defend the Party army:

> And when they ask why the SA continues to exist in Germany, I say just this: that, in the final analysis, the SA also delivered France from Bolshevism . . . The SA is not a force for war but a force for peace, a force of order and discipline, which makes young Germans into citizens of the state, and which guarantees that domestic and foreign-political tensions will be defeated by the steadfast German people.[14]

Such phrases betrayed Goebbels' own uncertainty about the future course, and what he kept silent about was no less revealing. No mention of the discontent in sections of the 'movement' and particularly in the SA, nor of the otherwise so enthusiastically praised genius of the 'Führer'. Hitler, meanwhile, kept himself aloof from the unpopular measures of his government, and Goebbels had to respect this, if only because one development could not be kept secret from the Propaganda Minister: the *Sopade* report for May/June 1934 recorded the attitude of the 'easy-going Munich petit-bourgeois man in the street' thus: 'Oh yes, our little Adolf, he is alright, but the cronies round him, they're just a bunch of good-for-nothing big-shots!' ('Ja, ja, unser Adoifi war schon recht, aber de um ean uma, de san lauter Bazi!')[15]

Expressed in standard German and applicable to people in all walks of life, this widespread opinion was revealed in the stereotyped adage: 'If only the Führer knew what was going on!' This was a crucial socio-psychological element of the 'Führer myth', which was soon to reach almost unbelievable proportions. For now, for the first time, popular opinion was coming perilously close to a global condemnation of the regime, in which the willingness to differentiate between the 'Führer' and the fallible rest of the 'movement', a willingness which was important for Hitler's very existence, threatened to disappear. The 'campaign against grumblers and alarmists' had proved an obvious failure. The *Sopade* reported from south-west Germany: 'If public confidence continues to dwindle at the current rate for only a few more weeks, something must happen. What this will be is open to question. In any event, the final barrier has now been reached. Even Hitler himself is now the subject of criticism.'[16]

The SA in the crossfire

In the three years since Ernst Röhm, Reichswehr captain (retired), had been recalled by Hitler from his role as military adviser in Bolivia and had resumed leadership of the SA, it had expanded to become a gigantic brown Party army. As early as 1931, its total strength was comparable to that of the 100,000 strong state army, the Reichswehr. Now, in the spring of 1934, the Stormtroopers numbered almost three million men, not including the members of the veterans' and regimental associations and those members of the 'coordinated' (*gleichgeschaltet*) German nationalist Stahlhelm who were over forty-five years old. These ranked as the SA second reserve. But the SA's power had not grown with the size of its membership; rather, the opposite had occurred. Hitler had already proclaimed the end of the National Socialist 'revolution' at the beginning of July 1933 and had announced 'evolution' for the future. Consequently, the Brownshirts were forced out of many of the positions they had assumed. Their despotic role as auxiliary police and 'special commissars' or 'special commissioners' in the economy and administration was no longer required. The largest organization of the NSDAP had, in effect, become politically obsolete.

Certainly the terror and the sheer physical presence of an organized Party army had rendered inestimable service during the 'period of struggle' [the 'Kampfzeit'] and then during 1933 as political power was monopolized. The smashing of the trade unions and the Gleichschaltung ('coordination') of associations and federations could simply not have been carried out without the SA. Now, however, its aimless revolutionary behaviour, its tendency to violence, well practised since the Freikorps period, and its primitive mob radicalism were simply damaging, as was the gnawing dissatisfaction of its leaders, who had drawn the short straw in the distribution of official posts. The SA could contribute nothing more to aid the penetration and development of Nazi power on a social level.

Just like the Nazi movement as a whole, the SA was also not an immutable, homogeneous block. The mass of Stormtroopers were between eighteen and thirty years old – too young to have already laid the foundations of a solid working life before the beginning of the economic crisis. Meanwhile it was young workers, journeymen, schoolboys and students, none of whom had done military service, who determined the image it presented; by the time of the assumption of power those left over from the Freikorps, the socially stranded front-line soldiers of the First World War, were already in the minority. The high level of turnover was remarkable: almost half those who had been members of the SA in 1931 had left again by the beginning of 1934.[17] Tens of thousands of young people had sought in the SA that which bourgeois society, at least in times of crisis, could not give them: security, solidarity, comradeship, trust and hope in a better future. In the atmosphere of the SA pubs and field kitchens, in the street fights with the 'reds', martial sports and mass marches, their desire to belong seemed fulfilled, at least for the present. But although they found the paramilitary drill and sense of adventure in this male community rather attractive, the long-term goal of the majority of SA members remained that of a secure civilian existence, not the life of a soldier.

Convinced that capitalism had nothing to offer them, and at the same time united in a common hatred of the 'Marxists', many of these people who had 'fallen between classes' projected their vague longings onto a 'National Socialism' which the NSDAP did more than pursue in words alone. Fewer and fewer new SA members, however, also joined the Party. After the elimination of the left wing around Otto Strasser in 1930/

31 and the resignation of his brother Gregor at the end of 1932, this served to heighten the impression that the anti-capitalist and revolutionary components of the Nazi movement lived on particularly in Röhm's batallions. In popular parlance, the SA was compared to a beefsteak: 'brown on the outside, red inside'. This juicy image was not only a consequence of the massive influx of former followers of the workers' parties, who, in the summer of 1933, had obviously not all intended to join the SA for conspiratorial reasons. Its size and composition had turned the SA, as if of its own accord, into a reservoir of proletarian interests and revolutionary hopes.

It is indeed true that, in many respects, the Brownshirts already stood opposed to the ideological (war) aims of Hitler and the inner circles of the Nazi leadership. But what the NSDAP Party Organization (PO) registered as particularly negative was the unease caused by the continuous revolutionary talk. In a situation in which an enduring dearth of genuinely popular successes, above all in foreign policy, had still to be overcome, this seemed simply dangerous. Long-existing mutual resentments intensified: NSDAP officials, already occasionally smeared as 'Party *Bonzen*' or 'careerists' by disaffected SA men, inveighed for their part against the 'undisciplined hordes', and often shared the aversion which the debauched life of the leading clique of the SA – compensating for frustration and boredom – produced amongst many 'upright citizens'. In addition to this was the undisguised enmity, bordering on murderous intent, felt by Martin Bormann and some others for the homosexual Röhm. As early as 1932 this hatred was expressed in the following terms: 'May God have mercy on my own brother, if he does even a fraction of what the Chief of Staff has done against the movement.'[18]

The taunts of high-ranking Party comrades against the SA became more common as the situation in spring 1934 continued to deteriorate. Goering, who had been battling for months in Prussia to incorporate the 'unofficial' (*wilde*) concentration camps of the SA into the Gestapo's sphere of influence, contributed to this when, in the company of the Reich Governors, he reported in detail on 'events' and on the 'secret camps in the hands of the SA'. Fritz Sauckel, Gauleiter (regional Party leader) and Reich Governor of Thuringia, seconded with sinister remarks on the subject of the 'SA and a second revolution' and claimed that SA leaders had used phrases such as 'cowards and quitters who must be defeated' to refer to the 'leaders of the political organization of the Party'.[19]

But declared opponents of the SA were by no means to be found solely in Party offices. The differences between the SA and the Army had at least as long a tradition as the tensions between the SA and the NSDAP. The main reason for this was Röhm's military ambitions. His completely public and constantly repeated demand for a brown 'people's militia' could not leave the Reichswehr officers unmoved. In the final analysis it was not just a question of the monopoly of arms. If Röhm's most remarkable speeches are to be believed, what was at issue was the continued existence of the 'grey rocks' of the Army, which the SA Chief of Staff wished to see 'sunk in the brown tide'. Friction and clashes became ever more commonplace. Consequently, by mid-January 1934, this had become a central theme of discussions amongst Army commanders. Under the motto 'Avoid incidents, but stand no nonsense!', the commander of the Stuttgart Defence District (*Wehrkreis*) discussed examples of the apparent lack of self-confidence on the part of members of the armed forces:

> a) An officer of the Defence District dressed in civilian clothes crossed the road with a girl and in so doing failed to salute an SA flag. The leader of the SA section attacked him and boxed his ears. The officer did not defend himself. This was wrong. Even if his opponents had been there in greatly superior numbers, he should have defended himself, even if he were beaten to a pulp . . . b) At an airfield outside the Defence District two young officers jokingly made derogatory remarks about the Minister for Aviation. They were beaten up by an SA leader, without having defended themselves. Both officers were discharged from the Army. c) In a garrison bar the Reich Sport Commissar seized an officer cadet by the collar for allegedly failing to stand up when he entered; and yelled at him, 'You ladle of snot, can't you stand up when the Reich Sport Commissar walks in?' This cadet too, should have immediately punched the Reich Sport Commissar in the face.[20]

The generals' discussion of 'incidents' during these weeks did not simply serve to clarify 'discipline, comradeship, propriety of thought and conduct'. The distinction between the SA leadership and the troops was already being rehearsed:

> The superiority of the Army officer and the regular soldier is acknowledged on all sides, and to a certain extent not without envy. Many leaders of the SA and the PO clearly recognize that, though they may indeed be good fighters, in the long term they are no leaders, and that the role of leadership automatically reverts to the Army. Amongst these persons we see, in many cases, the originators of the agitation against the Army. The young SA-man recognizes the superiority of the Army plainly and clearly, and envies the Army with all his heart.[21]

Since the beginning of 1934, the Army command had been purposefully and resolutely working towards a solution of the conflict with the SA. Comparable resolve was not to be found in the SA. Regardless of the proven ability of Röhm and his leading clique to cast terror across the land and not to shrink from murder in so doing, from early on the SA had lacked the specific power to assert itself against the leadership of the Party. This was particularly true of the relationship between Hitler and Röhm. An example was Röhm's never-ending struggle for a separate SA jurisdiction, with which he hoped not only to settle deftly the problem of the thousands of unpunished criminal cases from the time of the seizure of power[22] but also to develop a parallel status with the Reichswehr. At the end of July 1933 the Chief of Staff had given notice in a circular of the 'imminent' creation of an SA judiciary: 'Endeavouring, in every respect, to secure and defend the rights of the SA as the troops of the nat. soc. [sic] revolution, recognized as such by the state.' Even in the then prevailing conditions the order contained outrageous passages:

> I will happily cover and take responsibility for any action by SA men, which although it may not correspond to prevailing legal provisions none the less serves the exclusive interests of the SA. Within this falls, for example, that as atonement for the murder of an SA man, up to 12 members of the enemy organization which initiated the murder may be sentenced to death by the SA leader with jurisdiction over the case.[23]

Even without this passage, which remained secret, the opponents of the SA knew how to quote the so-called 'Discipline Circular' to effect. After all, it threatened with internal justice those 'rogues' within its own ranks, who disgraced the 'honourable uniform of the SA' through 'the satisfaction of personal desire for revenge, unlawful maltreatment, robbery, theft and looting'.

But as far as Röhm was concerned, criticism was like water off a duck's back. According to all that is known about his opinions and his behaviour towards the 'Führer', the Chief of Staff never abandoned the belief that 'in the final analysis' he could count Hitler on his side. This was partly due to Röhm's completely naïve self-confidence and lack of will, but also to his incapacity for tactical caution. Superfluous threatening gestures and unnecessary provocation of the Reichswehr, even in his very last days, illustrate how far removed the SA boss was from a realistic assessment of the configuration of power and the position of Hitler. Röhm's most serious and ultimately fatal error doubtlessly lay in this renunciation of objective analysis.

Hitler was certainly never prepared to allow the extent of his own power to be endangered by any ambitions the SA might have. As early as the summer of 1933 he had unambiguously renounced all speculation of a 'second revolution': 'We leave no doubt about the fact, that if necessary, we would drown such an attempt in blood.'[24] Of course Hitler strove for the integration of the Party army, for example with the 'Law to Secure the Unity of the Party and the State', which Röhm (and Hess) commended to Reich ministers without portfolio on 1 December 1933. In the context of the many negotiations, copious correspondence and the conspicuous ceremony of reconciliation between the Reichswehr and the SA on 28 February 1934, Hitler's New Year letter of thanks to his 'dear Chief of Staff' (Röhm was one of a very few who was still permitted to address the 'Führer' with the informal *Du*) also helped to obscure the gravity of the situation. But during the course of 1933, careful listeners could have already heard Hitler's priorities even in his public speeches. In numerous addresses the supreme SA leader had paid homage to 'his' Brownshirts, but had simultaneously attempted to clarify, set limits and leave no doubt about who, under emergency conditions, was to be controlled by whom.

Hitler's great speech of thanks to the SA of 8 April 1933 already expressed this. By means of 'collective reception' (*Gemeinschaftsempfang*), 600,000 SA men heard their 'Führer' in a radio broadcast from the Berlin Sportpalast:

> Through your courage and your steadfastness, you have today the right to consider yourselves the saviour of the *Volk* and the Fatherland. But now, today, you must also be the unshakeable fighting force of the national revolution. You must also arm yourselves with those virtues which you have had for these 13 or 14 years . . . If in the future you stand behind me as one man in loyalty and obedience, no power on earth will be able to break this movement. If in the future too, you keep the same discipline and the same obedience, the same comradeship and the same unlimited loyalty, it will continue on its triumphal march.'[25]

Only a month later in Kiel, on the occasion of a mass procession of the 'Nordmark' SA, Hitler turned to the subject of the relationship between the SA and the Reichswehr:

> If the Army is the nation's bearer of arms, then you must be the bearer of the German nation's political will. If the Army is the military academy of the German people, then in you must be found the political academy, so that one day, from both of these components, the creation of political will and the defence of the Fatherland, a great complementary whole will develop. It is your duty not to present some sort of competition to the other great institution.[26]

'Discipline', 'inviolable comradeship', 'unbreakable loyalty' – hardly a single one of Hitler's speeches to 'his SA' lacked such rhetoric. Yet what now came increasingly to the fore was the demand for unconditional allegiance: '. . . I believe that we are as one. Just as I am yours, so you are mine! . . . Thus your will must fuse with mine.'[27]

At the celebration of the 'covenant of loyalty' between the Stahlhelm and the SA at the end of September 1933, Hitler hardly still mentioned the specific merits of the SA, but did indeed speak of those of the Reichswehr, 'for we all know full well, that if the Army had not stood at our side during the days of the revolution, then we wouldn't be stood here today [sic].'[28] During Christmas celebrations 'in the company of his SA and SS men', the 'Führer' found 'serious words', as the *Völkischer Beobachter* reported, '. . . for his old fellow-combatants of the SA and SS and exhorted them also to stand behind him as loyally and steadfastly now as they had in the early years of the struggle.'[29]

Within a few months, Hitler's tone with regard to the Party army had undergone a marked change. His growing unease, which since the assumption of power had effectively caused him to avoid the question of what was to become of the SA, was noticeable. Recently the main problem had been the internal dynamics of the 'movement', to which its 'Führer' by his own hand now had to put a decisive end. Otherwise he himself ran the risk of being overrun by an alliance of opposition forces. For beside the widespread economic and social discontent and the uncertainty about the attitude of the Reichswehr to Röhm's continuing adherence to the idea of a militia, a coalition of political opponents, though certainly hard to define, had meanwhile built up. In June 1934 in Berlin it was no longer possible to hide, even from outside observers, just how precarious the situation for Hitler had already become:

> The atmosphere in political circles is such that one wonders how long Hitler will last, what chances he still has? The regime is an invincible fortress no longer. Fewer jokes are being cracked about it; rather people are more serious and are examining the regime's prospects . . . The fear of informers and spies has subsided. The end of the regime and its transformation into a military dictatorship with or without Hitler is expected within a short time.[30]

Criticism from the right

Catholic-conservatives, monarchists, ideologues of the 'conservative revolution' and representatives of the right who were bitter that their attempts to 'contain' Hitler had failed, believed once more that their time would come. They hoped that if the domestic political situation were to deteriorate further, they would be able to persuade the Army to intervene. The centre of these efforts was to be found in Franz von Papen's Vice-Chancellery.[31] There, Herbert von Bose, Baron Wilhelm von Ketteler, Friedrich Carl von Savigny, Count Hans Reinhard von Kageneck and Fritz Günther von Tschirschky und Boegendorff (all self-styled 'young conservatives' aged between thirty and forty) conducted the business of what became known as the 'Reich Complaints Office' (Reichsbeschwerdestelle). The submissions, complaints and requests for help concerning arbitrary acts by the Nazis which were received at von Papen's office (the network of informal contacts amongst the landed gentry from east of the Elbe and the Catholic bourgeoisie was still quite intact) provided an impressive picture of the political situation. Under the dominant influence of the Munich lawyer Edgar Julius Jung, the circle of friends became increasingly convinced that it was necessary to put a stop to the disastrous way in which things were developing. In 1927, Jung had been promoted as a leading prophet of the 'conservative revolution' with his anti-democratic bestseller '*The Rule of the Inferior*' (Die Herrschaft der Minderwertigen), and in 1932 rose to the position of von Papen's ghost-writer. The group around him became the 'vanguard of the conservative resistance'[32] against the Nazis.

Of course the chances of the right-wing opposition were poor from the start, and by no means simply because Goering's Gestapo were, on the whole, well informed about the activities of the 'reactionaries'. The central weakness of these opponents of Hitler lay in the esoteric nature of their own 'revolutionary' vision of the future, which prevented wide sections of its potential audience from perceiving any clear distinction between them and the Nazis. However, this was not a flaw in their ideas but a consequence of them: in the summer of 1933 Jung still formulated 'the aim of the German revolution' as 'the depoliticization of the masses, their exclusion from the running of the state'.[33] To him, the 'popular movement' (*Volksbewegung*) of National Socialism seemed to be an avoidable, perhaps damaging 'detour' on the way to the 'anti-democratic principle of government' of the longed-for 'New Reich'. Added to the difficulty of explaining what was an extremely elitist and subtle critique (not to mention then maintaining the support of its adherents), was the fact that, in the event of emergency, von Papen himself could not definitely be relied upon. With regard to this latter point, Jung, who held nobility to be a 'spiritual challenge', was certainly a realist. He had no illusions about the nature of the Vice-Chancellor's character and also knew very well that not all of Hitler's 1933 coalition partners were disappointed with the new regime and were consequently not disposed towards concerted opposition.

This was also precisely the case with the Army, which had been allocated a central role in the plans of Jung and his allies. The military's attack on the SA, which was considered to be both inevitable and imminent, was to widen into a revolution, and was possibly even to end in the restoration of the monarchy. The hope was that to this end the elderly *Ersatz*-Kaiser, Reich President Hindenburg, could be won over.

Apart from Hindenburg, the Reichswehr leadership remained the only independent power group, but they had little interest in such far-reaching reform of the state. The Reichswehr Minister Blomberg and in particular General Walter von Reichenau, the head of the Ministerial Office, said that they had recognized the value of cooperation with Hitler. Only at the end of February he had demonstratively reassured them of his esteem and strongly rejected Röhm's idea of a militia. The generals knew that Hitler needed a modern, easily armed war machine for his plans of conquest, and conversely, it was clear to Hitler just how painstaking and time-consuming it would be to bring the SA up to such a standard. Above all, however (and not simply because he would then have to reckon with the opposition of the Reichswehr), the latter option would have been the more risky of the two. For with a strengthened SA it would be even harder to effect a political consolidation on the domestic front, and Hitler's concept of totalitarian efficiency and Führer absolutism would be put in question for the immediate future and perhaps in the long term too. In this respect the diffuse, but deeply anchored, anti-capitalist sentiment in the SA again played a specific role. This was not the Reichswehr's main objection to it, but none the less the officers could only welcome the simultaneous elimination of both the SA as a military rival and of its demands for social and political reform, which irritated the bourgeoisie as a whole. For Hitler, the ultimate priority was to make a speedy decision about an arrangement with the Reichswehr at the expense of the SA, which would place the former under an obligation to him at the time of Hindenburg's imminent demise. The 'statesmanlike' renunciation of a brown 'people's militia' could only yield additional trust in him.

The strategists in the Vice-Chancellery clearly believed that the 'Führer' did not possess the audacity to act simultaneously against the 'revolutionaries' of both the right and the left (essentially Hitler's only remaining choice in the spring of 1934). On 17 June, after preparations lasting several weeks, they sent their chief to a meeting of the Marburg University League.[34] In the main lecture theatre von Papen assumed a sensationally acerbic position against 'the talk of the second wave which will complete the revolution'. Was it coincidence or with intent that von Papen repeated, in parts almost word for word, what Hitler had preached to the Reich Governors twelve months earlier? The Vice-Chancellor warned: 'Whoever toys irresponsibly with such ideas should not deceive himself that a second wave cannot easily be followed by a third, that whoever threatens to use the guillotine is himself the likeliest to fall under the executioner's axe.' Two-thirds of Papen's speaking time was given over to a presentation of Edgar Jung's political creed. But in the last pages of the manuscript the critique developed into an unmistakeable attack on 'all the selfishness, arrogance, and lack of character, sincerity and chivalry which aims to expand under cover of the German revolution.'[35]

Of course Goebbels immediately forbade any reports by the press, but the team at the Vice-Chancellery had already sent offprints both to its supporters and abroad. The speech was broadcast on the national broadcasting station in Frankfurt, before the Propaganda Minister's interdiction arrived.[36] Those who were interested found the opportunity to study the text and could point to passages such as this:

> No people which would stand the test of history can afford a continuous rebellion from below. At some time the movement must come to an end; one day a solid social structure, held together by an unbiased administration of justice and the undisputed power of the state, must arise. With never ending conflict nothing can be built. Germany must not become a train on a mystery tour, with nobody knowing where or when it will end.[37]

The harshness of this attack was no less unexpected than were the ensuing results. From the moment of von Papen's speech, the countdown against the SA had begun. But the initiative did not lie with the Reichswehr as the young conservatives had hoped, but with Hitler, Himmler, Heydrich and Goering. And what the rightists did not suspect was that the 'Führer' was preparing to strike on two fronts.

Hitler's double coup

For months Hitler had been carefully holding back. The matter was to be allowed to 'come to a head'. Now he allowed his coup to be prepared: systematically, by a variety of people and on various levels, without external signs of any hectic activity. Heydrich composed lists of the names of the intended victims. In the last week of June, together with Himmler, the SD-Chief informed the SS and SD Oberabschnittsführer who had been ordered to Berlin, about the 'imminent revolt of the SA'. On 21 June, Hitler (without the usual company of von Papen), visited the Reich President at Neudeck and convinced himself of Hindenburg's physical and mental decrepitude. Four days later (during that evening the Gestapo was to arrest Edgar Jung on the orders of the 'Führer') Rudolf Hess once again administered a sharp rebuke to all those who sympathized with a 'second revolution'. As opposed to his speech in January, which had really been intended to offer a further warning to Röhm, the words of the 'Führer's Deputy' now provided direct justification for the impending events:

> Responsible, genuine National Socialists must prevent our people, together with the genuine revolutionaries, from suffering severe damage . . . They who believe they are the chosen, that they should help the Führer in a revolutionary manner through agitation from below, are pitiable . . . Adolf Hitler is the great strategist of the revolution. He knows the boundaries of what can be presently achieved, with present methods and under the present circumstances. He acts only after ice-cold deliberation, often apparently only serving the needs of the moment and yet looking far ahead to the pursuit of the distant aims of the revolution . . . Woe betide him who crudely blunders between the fine threads of his strategic plans, in the mad delusion that he could do it more quickly. He is an enemy of the revolution, even if he believes he is acting for the best.[38]

Both Goering and Goebbels expressed their opinions publicly on several occasions during these days. Like Hess, they not only criticized the SA but also condemned the conservatives and monarchists. 'Reactionaries at work everywhere' was the reason Goebbels gave in his travelling diary for his self-diagnosed melancholy ('ever more depression').[39] The date was Thursday, 28 June 1934.

On 29 June the Reichswehr Minister von Blomberg joined the propaganda battle and announced in the *Völkischer Beobachter* that 'Army and state have become as one.' This was the final link in a chain of extremely clear signals. Four days earlier the Reich Association of German Officers had expelled Röhm from its ranks. Meanwhile the Defence District Commands were put on increased alert; of course, not everyone realized that the rumours of a *putsch* were being spread intentionally and that the SS was readily being supplied with weapons and vehicles. But besides Blomberg and Reichenau, Chief of the Ministerial Office, the Chief of the Army High Command, General Werner von Fritsch, was also aware of the situation. The Reichswehr awaited its orders.[40]

For two days Hitler mentally prepared himself to execute the murderous plan, the actual performance of which was partially influenced by his own paranoid and self-deluding obsession with his perceived enemies. On 28 June, in the company of some trusted followers, he travelled to Essen to attend the wedding of Gauleiter Joseph Terboven. In the evening he telephoned his old friend Röhm, who was taking the cure for his rheumatism at Bad Wiessee, and arranged to meet him and the most important leaders of the SA on Saturday 30 June. The Chief of Staff clearly suspected nothing: he had sent the whole SA on a month's furlough from 1 July.

An extended 'inspection trip' by the 'Führer' through Westphalia was planned for 29 June, during which the activities of the Reich Labour Service were to be visited. But at midday Hitler prematurely departed from the programme – precisely in line with the real programme, as Goebbels' diary reveals: 'Phone call this morning from the Führer. Fly immediately to Godesberg. So it's starting then.'[41] The former Nazi leftist, fixated on driving out the 'reactionaries', was clearly still unaware of just how all-embracing a blow the 'boss' had up his sleeve.

In the Rheinhotel Dreesen in Bad Godesberg, Hitler was awaiting his moment. In the late evening the desired news of SA parades in Munich finally arrived and also of plans for the next day in Berlin (presumably under Himmler's direction). The 'Führer' needed both these communications to reassure himself of his own plans. Meanwhile Goebbels had arrived. He, together with Hitler's entourage of subalterns, formed the audience for the 'Führer's' explosive hysterical outburst and for the staged drama of a rushed night flight to Munich.

At dawn the 'Führer'-aeroplane landed at the Oberwiesenfeld airfield. Throughout the night, inhaling his image of the 'traitor Röhm' like a narcotic, Hitler had worked himself into a rage. In the Bavarian Ministry of the Interior he tore the insignia from the uniforms of the SA leader Wilhelm Schmid and August Schneidhuber, the Munich Chief of Police. The SS and the Bavarian political police were guarding the main station in order to intercept the leaders of the SA, who were arriving for the conference at the Tegernsee lake. The Nineteenth Infantry Regiment was put on alert, the 'Brown House' in the Briener Strasse was surrounded by the police and SS. Later it was also secured by heavily armed Reichswehr troops.

At about half past five in the morning, Hitler left for Bad Wiessee in a convoy of three cars. From Kaufering, thirty-five army lorries with 1,300 men of the SS *Leibstandarte* ('Bodyguard Regiment') set off in the same direction. The task force under the leadership of Sepp Dietrich, which had been despatched from Berlin the previous evening, was joined by sections of the guard from the concentration camp at Dachau. But the column was still *en route* as Hitler's convoy drove up to the front of the Hanselbauer guest-house. The peace of early morning in summer hung over the valley. The 'conspirators' were still asleep. Armed police and SS men stormed the unguarded guest-house and moments later Röhm found himself confronted by his 'Führer' in full flow, shouting and fumbling with a pistol, and announcing that he was under arrest. The Chief of Staff's designated successor, Viktor Lutze, was a witness to the operation, as was Goebbels, who sneered hypocritically at the 'most disgusting and almost nauseating scenes'. Here the Minister was alluding to the long-known fact that the SA Obergruppenführer and Breslau Chief of Police Edmund Heines, Röhm himself and other prominent SA figures were homosexuals. During the following days this was to spice up his propaganda to great effect.

The Mafia-style attack was over in a matter of minutes. On the way back to Munich, Hitler ordered suspect cars travelling in the opposite direction to be stopped. In this manner the Pomeranian SA leader, Peter von Heydebreck, was arrested and transported to Stadelheim with the other prisoners. At Munich's main station, where numerous arrests were taking place, Hitler met Hess, who had been ordered to Munich, and at 10 am Goebbels gave the password 'Kolibri' ('humming bird') to Goering in Berlin. There too the snatch squads now went into action. The second phase of the coup had begun.

In conjunction with Himmler and Heydrich, Goering, who had executive power in Prussia, pursued the specific elimination of the conservative opposition. That same morning the head of their organization, Herbert von Bose, died in the offices of the Vice-Chancellery in a hail of SS submachine-gun fire. Shortly after the murder, von Papen, who had already been summoned by Goering early that morning, arrived at his office. The fact that one of his closest advisors had been murdered, and countless others arrested, made clear to the Vice-Chancellor the gravity of the situation and his own privileged position: he was merely under house arrest.

Just like von Bose, Erich Klausener, a senior official in the Ministry of Transport and leader of 'Catholic Action', who was in loose contact with the group in the Vice-Chancellery, was killed in his office by an SS squad. Edgar Jung was taken by Heydrich's henchmen from his cell in the basement of the Gestapo Headquarters in the Prinz-Albrecht-Strasse; he died in a small wood near Oranienburg. Around noon, a red-brown limousine with six youngish men on board drove up to a villa in Neubabelsberg. Two members of the Gestapo pushed past the housekeeper and into the library of the master of the house. He had hardly had time to identify himself before several shots were fired. Kurt von Schleicher, the last chancellor before Hitler, was dead. Seconds later the intruders gunned down the General's wife, who had witnessed the murder; she died in hospital from her wounds.[42] Hours later, General Ferdinand von Bredow, Schleicher's former influential and knowledgeable collaborator, was also liquidated.

The situation was no longer being determined by Hitler alone and some old scores were settled: Gregor Strasser met his death in the cellar of the Gestapo headquarters; a similar fate befell both Hitler's opponent of 9 November 1923, the former General State Commissar Gustav von Kahr, and Dr Fritz Gerlich, an ardent anti-Nazi and managing editor of the Catholic periodical *The Straight Path* (Der gerade Weg). Father Bernard Stempfle, an early supporter of Hitler who had distanced himself in the intervening period and who probably knew too much, was also shot there. Dr Willi Schmid, the music critic of the *Münchener Neueste Nachrichten*, fell victim to the confusion of his name with that of one of Strasser's friends. The homosexual landlord of one of Röhm's favourite pubs in the centre of Munich, the Bratwurst-Glöckl by the cathedral, was abducted by SS men and murdered.

That same morning, Hitler described Röhm's and Schleicher's alleged plans for a *putsch*, which he claimed to have just thwarted, to angry SA leaders who had been intercepted *en route* to the conference at Bad Wiessee and meanwhile assembled in the 'Brown House'. The hysteria into which the 'Führer' had increasingly slipped since his departure from Godesberg gave credence to his ranting monologue. Furthermore it helped to obscure the fact that he was also not least concerned to justify the coup and secure a form of retrospective insurance. But no resistance worth mentioning emerged amongst the *Alte Kämpfer* ('Old Fighters'), even during the hours which followed. On the contrary, one after another offered to wipe out the 'Röhm-clique'. Hess told Hitler: 'My Führer, it is my duty to shoot Röhm!'[43] Reich Governor Epp, who would have preferred to see his former staff-officer Röhm brought before a military court, received a taste of Hitler's wrath. Later, the Bavarian Justice Minister, Hans Frank, who, having been alerted by the director of the prison, tried to prevent the summary shootings in Stadelheim, received a taste of the same.

By this time Hitler had already left Munich. Further suprises were not to be feared; he knew that in leaving his commands for the murders with Sepp Dietrich he had placed them in reliable hands. Six times in Stadelheim Prison the peace of the summer's Saturday evening was shattered by volleys of rifle fire: for August Schneidhuber, Wilhelm Schmid, Peter von Heydebreck, Edmund Heines and also for the Dresden SA Gruppenführer Hans Hayn and the Munich SA Standartenführer Count Hans Joachim von Spreti-Weilbach. Hitler had still not crossed Röhm's name off the death list.

At Tempelhof airport in Berlin, Goering and Himmler were awaiting the Chancellor. An honour-guard had fallen in as Hitler, 'wearing the most sombre of expressions', climbed out of the aeroplane: 'a chalk-white, unshaven face that had clearly been up all night and which seemed at once both sunken and puffy'.[44] Heydrich's machinery was still running at full tilt. Between then and the following Monday more SA leaders were to die in many locations throughout the Reich as well as other opponents of the regime and yet others who had incurred the displeasure of one or another of the main actors in the drama. Apart from at Dachau concentration camp and the Lichterfelde cadet school near Berlin, where the firing squads were still being mustered against high-ranking Brownshirts, it was primarily in Silesia that a whole series of murders were committed. There the SS Obergruppenführer Udo von Woyrsch allowed his men to create a bloodbath amongst the SA in the area formerly controlled by Edmund Heines and, moreover, to launch a full-scale military campaign against their personal private enemies.

Ernst Röhm survived until the late afternoon of 1 July. For a few hours it seemed as if Hitler was hesitating to eliminate physically his last real rival. Röhm was the only one who, for more than a decade, had stood in close and naïve friendship with him. Only during the course of the Sunday, whilst giving a tea party for members of the cabinet and their families in the garden of the Reich Chancellery, did Hitler give the order. Theodor Eicke, the camp commandant of Dachau, now handed Röhm a pistol in his cell, together with a special edition of the *Völkischer Beobachter*. The distracted Röhm was able to glean from the Party organ that the removal of his power was being celebrated as a victory by Hitler over extravagance, homosexuality and disloyalty. An averted *putsch* was not yet being mentioned: the use of this terminology was first approached in the reports of the following day's edition, when Röhm's demise was pithily referred to: 'The former Chief of Staff Röhm was given the opportunity to draw the conclusions of his treacherous action. He did not do so and was therefore shot.'

On 2 July the massacre came to an end and the following day Hitler had it 'legalized' by the judiciary with a single phrase: 'The measures taken on 30 June, 1 and 2 July 1934, in order to defeat high treason and treason [*hoch- und landesverräterische Angriffe*], were legally justified in the interests of state security.'[45] Thus the threat of punishment for the cold-blooded murder of a total of 89 people was removed and non-Nazi German Nationalists such as Justice Minister Gürtner were hoping that they could thereby commit Hitler to maintaining the judicial system. The new law, argued Gürtner in the cabinet, created no new precedent, it simply reaffirmed 'already existing statutes'.[46]

The consequences of 30 June

It almost seems as though Hitler awaited the reaction to his coup in the days which followed with a degree of uncertainty. After the cabinet meeting on 3 July, at which Blomberg thanked him demonstratively 'for his decisive and courageous action', the Führer relaxed on the Baltic coast and in Berchtesgaden in the company of the Goebbels family. Not until 13 July was he seen in public. The intervening two weeks, in which the population was dependent on inconsistent radio reports and, at times, contradictory newspaper articles, had proved fertile soil for the most diverse rumours. Precisely for this reason the painfully long Reichstag speech, which was broadcast on the radio, met with a great deal of interest. Hitler only managed to overcome the tone of justification towards the end:

> If anyone reproaches me and asks why we did not call upon the regular courts to pass sentence, then I can tell him only this: In that hour, I was responsible for the fate of the German Nation and was therefore the highest judge of the German *Volk*. In every epoch mutinous divisions have been called back to order by the process of decimation . . . I gave the order to shoot the main culprits in this treason, and furthermore I gave the order to cauterize the abcess of intrigue, both at home and abroad, right down to the raw flesh. The Nation must know that no threat to its existence will go unpunished. And every man should know, and for all time, that if he raises his hand to strike at the state, his fate will be certain death.[47]

In their monthly reports, principal officers of Rural District Offices (*Bezirksamtsvorsteher*) in Bavaria remarked that Hitler's address had been 'received with the greatest acclaim by all "national comrades" [*Volksgenossen*], including those who still stand apart'. This was by no means untypical. Not only Goebbels' press, but the people too, were full of 'admiration and gratitude', of 'respect', 'sympathy' and 'trust in the Führer' who 'only wanted the best for his people'. Critical voices were few and far between, and when they did articulate themselves, as for example in Kempten, they specifically excluded the 'Führer':

> The suppression of the Röhm revolt has been like a purifying thunderstorm. The nightmare which has burdened the people has been followed by a liberating sigh of relief . . . Wide sections of the population, however, have been deeply shocked by the shooting of persons completely unconnected with the Röhm revolt. It is realized that these were excesses, which took place without the knowledge and against the will of the Führer and leading figures. It is feared, however, that such transgressions could repeat themselves in other circumstances and that therefore the life of everyone who is not a Party comrade could be at risk.[48]

Since the public remained in the dark about the unscrupulous way in which the assassinations were staged, anything more than half-hearted criticism such as this was hardly to be expected. It was only with difficulty that details about the crimes managed to spread beyond the immediate locality; even newspaper announcements of the deaths of the victims were forbidden. The struggle of the bereaved for pension payments and insurance claims (a delicate problem, particularly in the case of Gregor Strasser, who officially had committed 'suicide') assumed the nature of a minor backstage war between the Gestapo, SS and state bureaucracy.[49] Neither from the Catholic Church (nor from the Protestant), nor from the Reichswehr, came any protests, not even about their 'own' people. Considering this background, occasional reports of 'disquiet following the shooting of Dr Klausener', such as the president of the local government of the Catholic Münsterland telegraphed to Berlin,[50] are doubly remarkable.

The Reichswehr savoured their apparent total triumph. The military ignored with frightening stubbornness the fact that in the long term it was also being weakened because it had not only accepted the violent methods of the Nazi leadership, but had helped to bring them about:

It was an unavoidable necessity that, accompanying the blow against the mutineers of the SA, a blow would also be struck against those circles which are today usually designated 'the reactionaries'. This 'blow to the right' was also necessary in the interests of the armed forces. According to the wishes of these circles, we, the armed forces, should be pushed into an untenable position. This blow was struck most decisively against Schleicher and his agents. There was also a victim [von Bose] who was associated with von Papen.[51]

The Reichswehr Minister could hardly have expressed himself more unambiguously to his commanding officers on 5 July 1934. Blomberg added enthusiastically:

The purge is by no means concluded. The Führer will continue the process of purification regardless and with an iron will. He is fighting against corruption, against perverted morality, criminal ambition and for the state and the *Volk*. For the Führer the most obvious expression of the state is the armed forces. It was not least in their interest that he acted as he did, and it is the duty of the armed forces to thank him wherever possible through still greater loyalty and devotion.[52]

For a considerable period, the rhetoric of the 'purge' became the tried and tested crux of the argument of all those who now devoted themselves to filling the power vacuum created by the removal of the SA. But it was not only the SA which was to come under attack. Goering, who at the end of August 1934 provided the 'Party Minister' Hess with a 90-page catalogue of deficiencies distilled from the situation reports of the presidents of the Prussian administrative districts, held the 'freeing of the Party apparatus from elements to which the *Volk* quite rightly takes offence' to be urgently required. Indeed, it did already appear that 'amongst wide sections of the *Volk* the concern is arising that following the completion of the action of 30 June, everything will remain as it was.'[53] Himmler, too, argued along similar lines. He chose a meeting in the area under the power of his SS Obergruppenführer in Breslau, Woyrsch, to announce 'that furthermore, 1935 must be the year of purification of the movement and the state'. This would mean that the 'hardest task' would fall to the SS, just as in the 'terrible two days' in the summer: 'to carry out this operation on the orders of the Führer' and (here the parallel with Himmler's infamous Posen speech of 4 October 1943 is striking) 'to be absolutely pure ourselves'.[54]

Apart from the Führer, in the long term it was really only Himmler and Heydrich who profited from the changes in the structure of power brought about on 30 June. On 20 July 1934, the SS, which until that date had been formally commanded as a section of the SA, became independent, its 'Reichsführer' was henceforth under Hitler's 'personal and direct' command. The background report of 'someone who knows the situation' was accurately introduced by the *Neue Zürcher Zeitung*: 'The events of 30 June have shown the black '*Schutzstaffeln*' to be the ruthless and most effective instrument of the National Socialist dictatorship. The significance of the SS and its Reichsführer Himmler can hardly be over-estimated.'[55]

Abroad there was shock at the bloodbath which had been planned at the behest of the Reich Chancellor. Meanwhile the German bourgeoisie (with its diminished political and cultural breadth after the events of 1933) had clearly lost the moral high ground, precisely by failing to reject in principle the methods of organized gangsterism as a political expedient. They had given their agreement to the establishment of a Führer absolutism, in which everything was subordinate to the will of that 'Führer': justice, law, morality, the state itself. With his essay 'The Führer protects the law', the renowned teacher of constitutional law, Carl Schmitt, provided the 'academic' underpinning of this departure from every tradition of modern legal and constitutional statecraft: 'The true Führer is always also judge. The status of judge flows from the status of Führer . . . The Führer's deed was, in truth, the genuine exercise of justice. It is not subordinate to justice, rather it was itself supreme justice.'[56]

Sooner than expected, only a month after the series of murders, the final building brick in the construction of the 'Führer state' could be put in place. On the evening of 1 August 1934, without waiting for Hindenburg's death, Hitler had passed the 'Law concerning the Head of State of the German Reich', which merged the offices of President of the Reich and Reich Chancellor from the moment the news of the death came from Neudeck. On 2 August the Field Marshal died. On the very same day, the Reichswehr, whose supreme command had hitherto lain with the President of the Reich, was sworn on oath to the 'Führer and Reich Chancellor'. In accordance with Hitler's wishes, the title 'Reich President' was to exist no more nor 'for all eternity'.[57]

In only a few weeks, Hitler had successfully disposed of all opposition and, moreover, had stabilized his rule in a way that, in the spring of 1934, almost no one would have believed possible. If every single action against the SA or the conservatives had become virtually impossible, or at the very least highly dangerous for him, now both hotbeds of unrest had been eliminated in one fell swoop. Much to the satisfaction of the Reichswehr and the bourgeoisie, a new solid equilibrium had apparently been created under the now totally undisputed leadership of 'Caesar Hitler',[58] as the *Deutschland-Berichte* of the *Sopade* commented.

On 19 August 1934, there was a retrospective referendum on Hitler's new position of omnipotence as Head of State, Chief of Government, Supreme Leader of the Party and Supreme Commander. With an 89.9 per cent yes vote (out of a turnout of 95.7 per cent) its results already intimated the nature of the impetus which the regime, lent speed by growing domestic and foreign political successes, was now soon to take. In the following years the power of the 'Führer' myth as a force for social integration grew to fantastic proportions. Germany looked to a future with Hitler.

PART II

THE INTERNAL DEVELOPMENT OF
THE THIRD REICH

1

Regimentation and Coordination, 1933–1934

We've done it. We're installed in the Wilhelmstrasse. Hitler is Reich Chancellor. It's like a fairy tale! . . . We all have tears in our eyes. We shake Hitler's hand. He's earned it. (Joseph Goebbels, Diary, 31 January 1993[1])

Hitler became Chancellor at a time when the NSDAP was declining and the economy was already beginning to recover. The events of 30 January 1933 came not as the end of triumphant electoral progress by the National Socialists, nor as a result of the severe economic crisis which had taken hold of Germany since 1929. Hitler's success was not a coincidence, but neither was it inevitable. He was wanted. The coalition of power groups and interests which brought him to power had as many disparate elements as the Nazi movement itself and was no less ambivalent. Despite the many predictions, the question of where Hitler's appointment would lead remained open.

Hindenburg, the tired old Reich President, was surrounded by many trusted faces as he swore in Hitler as his seventh chancellor on the morning of 30 January. Hitler behaved modestly. Apart from Hitler himself, the Nazi Party was represented by only two other members of the new presidential cabinet: Wilhelm Frick, who since 1930 had been gathering experience of government in Thuringia, became Reich Minister of the Interior; Hermann Goering as Minister without Portfolio assumed the duties of Reich Commissar for Aviation and of acting Minister of the Interior for Prussia. Alfred Hugenberg as Reich Minister for Industry, Food and Agriculture, and Fritz Gürtner as Reich Justice Minister (from 1 February), represented the German National People's Party, DNVP (Deutschnationale Volkspartei). All the others were right-wing conservatives without party affiliation, amongst them, as in the cabinet of the outgoing Chancellor Kurt von Schleicher, Foreign Minister Baron von Neurath, Finance Minister Count Schwerin von Krosigk, and Transport and Post Minister Baron Eltz von Rübenach. The Stahlhelm leader Franz Seldte was promoted to Minister of Labour. Franz von Papen assumed the function of Vice-Chancellor and Reich Commissar for Prussia, where, during his former chancellorship, the legal Social Democratic government had been deposed in July 1932. General von Blomberg became Minister for the Armed Forces, and he, like the new head of the Ministerial Office General von Reichenau, had made his sympathy for Hitler clearly known.

The negotiations over the formation of the government had been dramatic, but in comparison the result was, at first glance, rather less spectacular. It could almost have been interpreted as the beginning of a process of normalization, since the attempt was no longer being made to form a minority government. But the NSDAP, which had won almost exactly one-third of the votes in the Reichstag elections in November 1932, had not set out to assume joint political responsibility for the state. Its declared aim was to overcome the Republic and to erect a 'Führer state,' more or less comparable with that of Fascist Italy.

Neither the opponents of the NSDAP nor its sympathizers could be in any doubt about this, for Hitler had repeatedly emphasized that his party would win power through legal means in order then to abolish parliamentary democracy. This knowledge, and fear of the socially revolutionary potential and the violence and dynamics of the Nazi movement, also explains why the old right marked time for so long before a coalition of the most diverse forces from the German nationalist bourgeoisie – the big estate owners, industry, the bureaucracy and the armed forces – finally felt ready to accept the risks entailed in Hitler's participation in government for the sake of a definitive restructuring of society and the state. During this final stage in the dissolution of the Weimar Republic, and with a lack of foresight which is hardly commensurate with the high-flown rhetoric of the concept of keeping Hitler under control (*Zähmungskonzept*), the sceptics were assured that within two months Hitler would be pushed so tightly into the corner 'that he would squeak' (Franz von Papen). What sort of a Reich Chancellor could Hitler be, if it were possible for such a fate to befall him?

From the assumption of power to the March elections

The declared common intention of the coalition was to free German politics from 'Marxism'. The Communists (KPD), who had achieved their best result ever in the previous election with almost 17 per cent, were to be eliminated, and the Social Democrats (SPD) (last result 20 per cent), and with them the trade unions, were at the very least to be divested of any political relevance. The reactionary right had had their fill of parliamentary democracy. Their concern was to establish an enduring, authoritarian, presidential regime. In this respect absolute unity also seemed to exist in the new cabinet, as was demonstrated in the discussion about the proclamation of new elections. The Vice-Chancellor could be sure of Hitler's agreement when during the second meeting of the cabinet on 31 January he declared that 'it would be best to establish now that the impending elections to the Reichstag will be the last and that a return to the parliamentary system should be for ever avoided.'[2]

Von Papen's contribution was preceded by Hitler's report on the talks he had had that morning with the prelate Dr Kaas and Dr Perlitius of the Catholic Centre Party. Its participation in the government would have provided a parliamentary majority and thus an important argument against the dissolution of the Reichstag. Precisely for this reason Hitler had ensured that the negotiations had quickly failed;[3] he wanted neither an enlargement of the coalition, nor the toleration of his government by the Centre Party, nor even a long-term self-imposed recess of parliament. The Chancellor wanted new elections. In order to achieve this he was even prepared to give a guarantee of continued existence to the DNVP. He promised Hugenburg, who (with good reason) was afraid of losing his electoral base, that the result of the election was not intended to have any influence on the composition of the government. Barely forty-eight hours after the government was formed, the Reich President signed the decree dissolving the Reichstag, which had been elected only on 6 November the previous year. The people, according to Hindenburg, should express their opinion on the 'Government of National Concentration'.[4]

Hitler was doubtless expecting considerable gains for the NSDAP in the new elections. On the day before Hindenburg's decision, Hitler's ministers were told he believed that 51 per cent was possible for the government coalition. The 'Führer' was attracted by the opportunity of leading an election campaign for the first time from a position of governmental responsibility. After the setback of the previous autumn and the subsequent crisis within the Party which had led to the resignation of Gregor Strasser, the last important representative of the Nazi left, a resounding success at the polls would do the NSDAP good. But the main motive lay elsewhere: Hitler was seeking the agreement of the Germans for a policy of anti-parliamentary and anti-Marxist alignment. The monopolization of political power was to be introduced with the retrospective mandate of a plebiscite.

Of course, in the election campaign which immediately began, this did not appear so clear and calculated. Beside the massive propaganda, which made unrestrained use of all the technological means available to a Weimar government, including its direct grip on broadcasting, stood terror. State intervention in the freedom of the press and of assembly, which the Reich President made possible with the emergency decree 'For the Protection of the German People', was flanked by increasing acts of violence by grass-roots Nazis against the meetings and offices and other premises of the KPD and SPD, and occasionally against those of the Centre Party. After the torch-lit parade through the government quarter of Berlin on the evening of 30 January, the Brownshirts ruled the streets. Nevertheless, the bitter animosity on the left between Communists and Social Democrats persisted. An ideologically and theoretically based policy of 'wait and see' (*vis-à-vis* monopoly capital's experiment with Fascism, which it was believed would 'necessarily' lead to Communism) began to be mixed with resignation. The 'united front from the trade unions to the KPD against the present Government', about which Hitler warned his ministerial colleagues,[5] remained a chimera.

What could be observed, in fact, was a further rapid decline of political and cultural self-confidence and, above all, of critical reason amongst the liberal-democratic bourgeoisie and the intelligentsia. Many no longer resisted the 'fascist infiltration of public life',[6] which had already begun in the early 1930s with the removal of the SPD from governmental responsibility. A process of political desensitization had been set in train: even liberal intellectuals were barely able to react when, for example, an event such as the congress of 'The Free Word', at which Thomas Mann's profession of his opposition to National Socialism had been read out, was closed by the police. And it meant too that the withdrawal of Heinrich Mann and Käthe Kollwitz from the Prussian Academy of Arts, which was really an act of self-denial in order to save an institution which had fallen into political danger, could be interpreted as an act of confession and resignation.[7] The youthful, dynamic 'movement of renewal' which after years of 'struggle' had finally 'wrested' power, exerted a strong pull. Individuals and organizations which on the whole had previously assumed a distanced stance of 'wait and see', no longer wished to hang back. The often-heard Nazi call 'no longer to stand on the sidelines' was taken very seriously in such circles, and not always for opportunistic reasons. Even before Joseph Goebbels could establish his system of censorship, important organs of public opinion were swinging round to a position of ostentatious goodwill towards Hitler's government.[8]

Without a doubt there was a hankering for political authoritarianism, and Hitler corresponded to the dominant *Zeitgeist*. But this cannot explain the extent of the political changes which occurred even before the election on 5 March 1933. They were the result of shrewd tactics, political skill – and coincidence.

Despite the fact that the number of Nazi members of the government was only very small, Hitler's paladins Goering and Frick were able to take all the steps necessary for the 'assault against Marxism', which Hitler had issued as his 'election slogan' in the cabinet.[9] The most important next step was to establish control of the police – especially, of course, in the capital of the Reich and in Prussia. On 7 February, only a day after Hindenburg had decreed the dissolution of the Prussian State Parliament, Goering, in his capacity as acting Prussian Minister of the Interior, named SS-Gruppenführer Kurt Daluege as 'Commissar with Special Duties'. The political purge in the Ministry of the Interior and in the Berlin police apparatus, which Daluege prepared, in effect as a private individual, became the pattern for later actions in the *Länder*.

Whilst the public was experiencing a hectic winter election campaign, in Prussia the goalposts were being moved to enable the Nazis to penetrate and usurp the internal state administration. The operation was conducted under Goering's rigorous direction. His so-called 'Shooting Decree' (*Schiesserlass*) of 17 February directed police officers, under threat of disciplinary action, to 'combat the activities of organizations hostile to the state with the severest means . . . and if necessary to make use of firearms without regard for the consequences.'[10] Conversely, it now became the duty of civil servants to support the 'national associations' and their propaganda. This restricted still further the room for political manoeuvre available to the parties of the left and opened up new space for terrorist acts by the SA and SS. Attacks on opposition election meetings were now often left unmentioned in police reports, and in street fights the police did not intervene, so long as it was only the 'Marxists' who were coming off worst. In the weeks leading up to the election there were 69 political murders in Germany; 18 of the victims were Nazis.[11] When, on Goering's directions, the SA, SS and Stahlhelm were able to recruit approximately 50,000 men as 'auxiliary police' (supposedly to curb the increasing excesses of the Communists), terror by the Brownshirts escalated so much that Hitler and Goering urged them to be more disciplined.

In the preceding few years, large cities like Berlin and Hamburg and the Ruhr region had had repeated experience of conflicts between right and left-wing radicals on a par with civil war, and not solely during election campaigns. But considered as a whole the political climate had now become even more violent. To the aggressive nature of the Nazi grassroots was now added the opportunity of 'fighting the enemy' with the means of state power. Thus, with the help of the emergency decree of 4 February, it was made possible virtually to silence Communist publications and to hamper severely the Prussian Social Democrats. The brazen manner in which this was undertaken put in the shade the banning of newspapers by previous governments which had been made possible by the Law for the Protection of the Republic passed in 1930. Even the Supreme Court, which lifted several bans on SPD leaflets, was of the opinion that Goering was taking his methods too far. At the same time Reich Interior Minister Frick was to discover that *Länder* outside Prussia were repeatedly opposing banning attempts, though not, however, when they were directed against organs of the KPD. Then, on 27 February 1933, when the Reichstag went up in flames, the political fate of the Communists was sealed. The fire gave the government the unhoped for reason and justification, even before the election, for an all-embracing blow against the KPD – and for the final invalidation of the constitutional state.

Hitler's immediate reaction at the site of the fire during the night seems to have differed little from Goering's, who instantly interpreted the conflagration as the start of an attempted Communist revolution. And he persisted excitedly in this interpretation, even when the arrested sole culprit, a Dutch syndicalist named Marinus van der Lubbe, provided absolutely no evidence for it. During the assessment of the situation which took place the following morning in cabinet, Goering confirmed his theory. The Chancellor, on the other hand, as was so often the case during these weeks, played the role of the superior statesman. According to the minutes, he stated that 'the psychologically correct moment for the showdown had now arrived. It was pointless to wait any longer. The KPD was completely decided. The struggle against it should not be made dependent on juridical considerations.'[12] The last sentence was directed at those hesitant conservatives whose support for the destruction of the KPD was not at all in doubt, but who were likely to vote against too far-reaching abrogations of the law. In case this were to occur, the possibility was indicated of the alternative to a quasi-legal anti-Communist pogrom: terrorist SA violence. But Hitler got the 'legal' basis for action which he had suggested, packaged in a whole catalogue of banalities (like the vote of thanks to the men of the fire brigade). On the afternoon of 28 February the cabinet met again and hurriedly ratified the draft of a decree introduced by Frick 'For the Protection of the People and the State'. The Reich President put his signature to it the very same day.

Invoking Article 48 of the Weimar Constitution (which gave the President the right to rule by decree in an emergency), basic civil rights were thereby suspended. At a single stroke the freedom of the individual, of opinion, the press, association and assembly, the secrecy of postal and telephone communications and the inviolability of property and the home were abolished. Moreover, the Reich government was now empowered, 'in order to re-establish public safety and order', to 'temporarily attend' to the responsibilities of the highest state offices of the *Länder*. So, even before the election, the basic framework had been created for the legal justification of the Nazi conquest of the *Länder* which was to take place immediately it was over. By furnishing the possibility of an effectively limitless expansion of its original justification – the 'defence against Communist acts of violence which endanger the state' – the Reichstag Fire Decree fulfilled a central role in the process by which Nazi rule developed. Political prisoners could now be held at will for unlimited periods without legal examination of their cases. This undeclared state of emergency was to remain in force until the end of Nazi rule. For this reason, Ernst Fraenkel called the decree of 28 February the 'constitutional charter' of the Third Reich.[13]

The systematic persecution of the Communists began during the very night of the fire. During the following days in Prussia, which had already been brought into step or 'coordinated' by the Nazis, the KPD Reichstag deputies and many KPD functionaries were arrested. Amongst them was their chairman, Ernst Thälmann. It is true that since Hitler had been named Chancellor and since the unsuccessful call for a general strike on 31 January, preparations for continuing Communist Party work underground had been made. But the Communists had underestimated the pace of political change and also probably the extent of surveillance by the political police.[14] The measures were, of course, extended to KPD offices, which were occupied, destroyed or closed, and to the Communist newspapers, which were banned. Now the SPD press too was forbidden to publish for a period of two weeks and thus disappeared *de facto* for ever.

Despite the possibilities for intervention and attack which had been opened up by the Reichstag Fire Decree, for the moment, outside Prussia, Hitler's government held back. Certainly, from the Nazi perspective, the manner in which the southern German *Länder* proceeded against the Communists was anything but satisfactory. However, an open controversy between the Reich and the *Länder* only a few days before the election would only have damaged the prestige of the new government, which had earned so much praise amongst the bourgeoisie and the peasantry for its 'decisive intervention'. Thus the prevailing political conditions under which people voted on 5 March remained non-uniform. In Prussia the political obstacles faced by the KPD extended to the SPD and even to the Centre Party, whilst in the non-Nazi *Länder* in which the Centre participated in coalition governments it was able to complete its election campaign in a semi-normal fashion. The democratic opposition parties, however, did not know how to combat the suggestive power of Hitler's propaganda. Nobody expected anything other than an electoral victory by the right-wing coalition. Even before the Reichstag fire, a local authority official in Upper Bavaria summed up the popular mood in this regard:

> Hitler's clearing up nicely in Prussia. He's throwing the parasites and spongers on the people straight out on their ear. He should follow it up in Bavaria, too, especially in Munich . . . If Hitler carries on the work he has done so far, he'll have the trust of the majority of the German people at the coming Reichstag election.[15]

All the more amazing was just how accurate Hitler had been with his cautious forecast of 51 per cent; the actual result, only 0.9 per cent higher, was sufficient for the coalition to gain an absolute majority, but as far as the NSDAP itself was concerned it still remained far from a triumphal victory. That was true even in comparison with its poor result in the previous November, compared to which it had improved its vote by 10.8 to a total of 43.9 per cent. There was no sense in which enthusiasm for Hitler had been transformed into votes for the NSDAP. Its strongest bastions continued to be found in the agricultural regions of northern and eastern Germany. But the Nazis had made particular gains in Catholic Bavaria and Württemberg, where they had almost reached the national average by soaking up the votes of the anti-clerical and middle-class parties. But by no means did the NSDAP make the lion's share of its gains at the expense of the other parties, but rather from the reservoir of previous non-voters. One of the most remarkable results of 5 March was, above all, the 88.7 per cent turnout, which was extremely high by Weimar standards. The mobilization of additional voters provided the Nazis with about half of their increase of five-and-a-half million votes. Altogether, approximately 17.3 million Germans voted for Hitler.[16]

Even if the NSDAP had not reached its actual election target, it had nevertheless achieved the purpose for which it had striven: both in percentage and political terms all the other parties looked like losers. This was true even in the case of the German Nationalists (who now went under the name of 'Combat-Front Black-White-Red' (Kampffront Schwarz-Weiss-Rot) and the Centre. While the latter had won around 200,000 additional votes, it had not kept pace proportionately with the increase in the overall number of participating voters. In terms of the absolute number of votes cast, the SPD maintained an almost constant position. The KPD, on the other hand, lost more than 1.1 million votes. The Centre and SPD results demonstrated for the last time the high degree of unity of ideological blocs, which even the most massive propaganda campaign was barely able to touch. But the drop in the Communist vote suggests considerable movement of voters on the margins of politics, in which a certain 'subliminal affinity'[17] of the extremist parties became apparent, as did also a common recruiting base in that constituency comprised of those who were suffering most as a result of the economic crisis. Given the already far advanced suppression of the KPD, especially in Prussia, it could have appeared to those who were primarily protest voters and not firmly anchored in a specific ideology that a change from the Communists to the Nazis was a pragmatic choice for the more effective force. One 'argument' was certainly the influence over the allocation of jobs which the SA already enjoyed in many firms.

The tactics adopted against the Communists and their election results both showed just how careful Hitler had been during the first weeks of his chancellorship and how much he had taken his conservative partners into consideration. With a complete ban on the KPD before the election, the NSDAP would probably have won an absolute majority and consequently would have had no further need of the DNVP. The 'interlacing' (*Verschränkung*)[18] of the Nazi movement with the established groups of the ruling elite, however, needed to be demonstrated for the foreseeable future, precisely in order to be able to translate the electoral success into corresponding influence in the state and in society without irritating business and the military. The process of monopolization of political power lasted longer than the continued existence of the parties, which was limited to only a few more months.

The conquest of the *Länder* and the Enabling Law

Hitler's reaction to the election results at the first cabinet meeting two days later was similar to that of the Nazi press, which celebrated the outcome in a manner both triumphant and threatening. The Chancellor noted for the minutes that 'he regarded the events of 5 March as a revolution. In the end Marxism would no longer exist in Germany.' He made a rather more dutiful denial that 'many Communists had moved over to the National Socialists'. He was not interested in analytical descriptions of the election, but rather in the conclusions which were to be drawn from it: 'At this stage a large-scale campaign of propaganda and enlightenment had to be launched so that political lethargy would not emerge.' Also necessary was 'a courageous tackling of the problem of the relationship between the Reich and the *Länder*'.[19] The first point gave notice of the establishment of a Reich Ministry of Popular Enlightenment and Propaganda, the second referred to the coordination (*Gleichschaltung*) of those *Länder* not governed by the Nazis. In fact, this had already begun.

In the Free Hanseatic City of Hamburg events had already been set in motion on election day when Nazi police officers hoisted the first swastika flags on public buildings. The double act which now developed between the Nazi regional leadership (*Gauleitung*) and the Reich Ministry of the Interior became characteristic of a process of *Gleichschaltung* which ran a similar course throughout Germany.[20] The local Party leaders gave specific permission for their Stormtroopers to demonstrate the 'indignation of the population' at 'untenable political circumstances' through threats, marches and the occupation of municipal offices. In so doing they created the opportunity for the Nazi Reich Minister of the Interior to intervene. Referring to the Reichstag Fire Decree, Frick ordered, mostly by telegraph, the appointment of so-called police commissars. In Hamburg this had already taken place on the evening of 5 March. There the bourgeois-Social Democratic coalition in the senate had already disintegrated over the issue of the banning of an SPD paper which had been demanded by the Reich government.

The next day brought similar events in Lübeck, Bremen and Hessen. In Baden, Württemberg, Saxony and Schaumburg-Lippe (where the government had resigned the previous day), the Reich Commissars assumed control over the police on 8 March. Finally, on 9 March, Frick named a commissar for Bavaria, equipped with plenipotentiary Reich powers: the former Freikorps leader, Franz Xaver Ritter von Epp. The transfer of power was toughest in Munich, not least because the Catholic BVP (Bayerische Volkspartei – Bavarian People's Party) controlled government had been seeking moral support from the Reich President for several weeks. At the same time there had been separatist rumours and the threat that a Reich Commissar would be arrested as soon as he crossed the river Main. If nothing of the sort occurred then it was for one reason: because Catholic-conservatives, monarchists, separatists, federalists and anticlericalists proved themselves to be incapable of cooperation, particularly with the Bavarian Social Democrats. The other reason was because the foe came not from outside, from Prussia, but was already ensconced in the 'capital of the movement', Munich itself.

The events in Bavaria and elsewhere demonstrated anew the difference between the traditional parties with their leading class, which in many respects had become immobile, and the dynamic power of the Hitler movement. The politicians of the Weimar Republic, '*Systempolitiker*', despite individual cases of personal courage, were simply no match for the Nazis' radical forms of action. This was true too of the Bavarian Minister-President Heinrich Held, who allowed himself to be assured by Hindenburg, even on 8 March – at a time when the Brownshirts had already long dominated the outward image of the Bavarian capital – that there would be no Reich Commissar in Bavaria. Even then, Held continued to oppose the demands of the leading figures of the Munich Nazi Party – Adolf Wagner, Ernst Röhm and Heinrich Himmler – who issued an ultimatum demanding Epp's appointment as General State Commissar and threatened an SA uprising. But when the relevant instruction from the Reich Minister of the Interior arrived the following evening, the state government gave in. A contributory factor had been the refusal of the Ministry of Defence (to be expected given the circumstances) to guarantee, if necessary, support for the already mobilized Bavarian *Land* police. Reich Commissar Epp appointed Röhm and Hermann Esser as State Commissars with special duties, Wagner as his 'deputy' in the Ministry of the Interior and the SS-Reichsführer Himmler as acting head of the Munich police headquarters. On 16 March, Held's cabinet formally resigned as the last of the coordinated state governments. It was replaced by an almost completely Nazi administration.[21]

The reorganization of the *Länder* parliaments was followed at the end of March by the transformation of the *Länder* governments. An 'Interim Law for the Coordination of the *Länder* with the Reich' (*Vorläufiges Gesetz zur Gleichschaltung der Länder mit dem Reich*) decreed that the division of seats in the *Länder* parliaments should be altered to correspond with the results of the Reichstag elections (except in Prussia, where a new election to the *Länder* parliament had been held at the same time). As the Communists' seats were not to be taken into account, the government coalition or the NSDAP therefore gained a simple majority everywhere. But henceforth the *Länder* parliaments were politically insignificant anyway, for the *Gleichschaltung* law empowered the *Länder* governments to decree even laws which altered the constitution without the participation of the parliament.

A week later, a 'Second Law for the Coordination of the *Länder*' presented the newly strengthened *Länder* governments with the new institution of the Reich Governor. This did not represent the introduction of a Reich reform, long discussed during Weimar, and which the Nazi regime was hardly expected to enact, but was effectively the final blow to the sovereignty of the *Länder*. The eleven Reich Governors, appointed by the Reich President at the suggestion of the Chancellor, were supposed to guarantee 'the observance of the political guidelines drawn up by the Reich Chancellor'. An exception to this was Prussia, where the function of the Reich Governor was assumed by the Reich Chancellor. In so doing, he appeared to have re-established the constitutional situation as it had existed under Bismarck. Indeed, in this way, Hitler went even further in ditching his Vice-Chancellor, for von Papen now had to resign his office as Prussian Reich Commissar. Thus the path was cleared for Goering to become Minister-President of Prussia.

In the other *Länder* the actual power of the Reich Governors was, to a great extent, determined by their previous strength as Gauleiter or SA leaders. This is particularly clear in the special case of Bavaria, where Hitler did not have any of the six Gauleiter appointed, but rather Epp, who until then had been Reich Commissar and had enjoyed little influence within the Nazi Party. As was to be expected, the 'Blessed Virgin General' (*Muttergottes-General*) did not succeed in laying the foundations of a genuine position of power. But in choosing Epp, Hitler had avoided the preferential promotion of any one Gauleiter, and thus also the premature development of a clear dominance such as that later achieved by Adolf Wagner. This was not a bad move considering the power which the concentration of *Alte Kämpfer* in Bavaria still represented in the spring of 1933. It was there that strongly revolutionary streams of opinion within the Nazi Party, dissatisfied with the earlier progress of the seizure of power and directed against Berlin, would have been most likely to have been able to flow together.

While, up until the election, the brown grass-roots had primarily provided the mass effect at Hitler's public appearances, an active political role first fell to them with the conquest of the *Länder*. This was obvious: without the pressure from the Party's grass-roots it would hardly have taken only four days for the whole process to reach the point where the provincial governments were all brought into step. From this success there flowed demands. Henceforth it was no longer just the Reich Chancellor, who had come to power through behind-the-scenes manoeuvres, and a few ministers who would embody the position of state power enjoyed by the NSDAP. Now Nazi Reich Commissars, Minister-Presidents, Gauleiter and SA leaders also laid claim to direct political influence. This effected the first major push in the Nazi penetration of the state arena right down to the level of the local authority.

The special commissars and representatives of the SA, and of the SA and SS auxiliary police which had now been established outside Prussia, became the symbol of this 'Party revolution from below'.[22] In Bavaria the SA Chief Röhm, in his capacity as State Commissar with special duties, suceeded in permeating the whole of the internal administration with SA commissars. Rabid Nazi Gauleiter boasted that they would thus bind a 'decaying' bureaucracy to the political will of the Party. The target of the terror from below no longer lay solely in the 'Marxist' milieu, where workers' functionaries were being arrested and maltreated and where party offices, publishing presses, consumer cooperatives and trade union buildings were falling victim to unrestrained destruction. In towns and villages the 'reckoning' with individual bourgeois opponents and Jewish business people also began. Prompted by the events at the *Land* level, district and local group leaders of the Nazi Party laid claim to local political leadership, and with the 'purging' of local government the SA leaders often took over the control of the local police. 'Undesirable' local government officers were sacked. The 'movement' controlled the streets and increasingly the public arena too. But its power derived from the chaos which had been created and from the general intimidation, not from a particular unfolding of events according to a specific plan. Much was determined far less by calculation than by the wild determination of countless 'little Hitlers' to play their part in the 'national uprising' – and to profit from it personally too.

The seizure of power from below was not part of a classic revolution. And thus, despite all the arrests, torture and political murders, there was no 'night of the long knives'. This assertion in no way diminishes the brutality of the events. In Berlin alone, SA troops held political victims in 50 so-called 'bunkers'. In comparison with these anonymous prisoners, the 25,000 or so prisoners in 'protective custody' (*Schutzhaft*) who were held in Prussian prisons in March and April 1933 could feel almost safe. The situation was characterized by the simultaneous existence of open terrorist violence and a perverted, but also, in some areas, unchanged and functioning, constitutional order. Within an already partially dismantled 'normative state' (*Normenstaat*), the beginnings of a 'prerogative state' (*Massnahmenstaat*) (Fraenkel) could be discerned.

The less the Weimar constitution was abrogated the less need there was to forego the formal legality of illegal actions. Even the establishment of the concentration camps was 'legally' based on the decree 'For the Protection of the People and the State', and Himmler announced the opening of the first of these in a former munitions factory on the outskirts of the town of Dachau near Munich at a press conference on 20 March 1933.[23]

The 'dual state' embodying prerogatives and norms was an expression of fascist rule, not a specific ploy aimed at disguising it. In retrospect the majority opinion in the population would have given little cause for one. Even the German Nationalists in the government continued to set aside their own emerging concerns with the proverb that omelettes are not made without breaking eggs. After all, had not Hitler demanded, in his broadcast on 12 March, 'the strictest and blindest discipline' and warned against 'disrupting our administration or economic life'?[24] Could it not be expected, therefore, that the 'excesses' against the bourgeois camp would disappear only when the so ardently desired reckoning with 'Marxism' had been completed and the labour movement brought to heel?

Such expectations were fostered by 'Potsdam Day'. Under Goebbels' masterly direction the opening of the new Reichstag in the Garrison Church at Potsdam was turned into a meeting of the 'old Germany' with the 'new'. A million times over the mass media reproduced that which seemed to be embodied in the joint appearance at the grave of Frederick the Great of the elderly symbol of the nation, Hindenburg, and the youthful 'People's Chancellor', Hitler: 'national resurgence', the 'unification' of Prussianism and National Socialism, the fusion of political tradition and 'revolutionary' dynamism. This was no 'sentimental melodrama',[25] as a disillusioned bourgeoisie was later wont to explain, but rather one more of those populist stimulants that the Nazi regime needed at regular short intervals after the elections of 5 March. The failure to estimate accurately the effect of political symbolism led many contemporary opponents of Hitler to fail to recognize the genuine extent of the support which Nazi rule already enjoyed.

The suggestive effects of the national celebrations had hardly begun to wear off when, two days later, the Reichstag met again in the Kroll Opera House. In the shadow of the Garrison Church, German parliamentary history experienced its darkest day. The passing of the so-called Enabling Law achieved what Hitler and his coalition partners had mutually agreed in January: that parliamentarism should be eliminated indefinitely.

However, because this unconstitutional plan was also supposed to be achieved by a process which appeared at least semi-legal, the 'double two-thirds majority' required to change the constitution was necessary. This meant that two-thirds of the 647 members of the Reichstag had to be present and two-thirds of those present had to vote in favour. The NSDAP and the Kampffront Schwarz-Weiss-Rot had between them won 340 seats on 5 March and therefore still had fewer than the required number of votes, even if the mandates of the 81 KPD deputies who had been arrested or gone underground were simply subtracted from the total number of those elected. On the assumption that the SPD would reject the 'Law for the Relief of the Suffering of the People and the Reich', it therefore seemed to depend on the support of at least a section of the Catholic Centre Party and BVP. It was also conceivable that the Social Democrats would stay away from the Reichstag. In that case not only the votes of the Catholic conservatives would have been necessary, but also their actual presence in order to avoid inquoracy. In this unclear situation[26] the Nazis were able to evade any risk of defeat through a sleight of hand. Immediately before the decisive vote, a change in the standing orders was put into effect with the agreement of the Centre Party. As a result it was left to the judgement of the President of the Reichstag (Goering) to establish the 'presence' of deputies absent without valid excuse. Thus the number of those present and eligible to vote could be determined according to requirements, and in simple terms of voting strength even the votes of the Centre Party were now no longer required. Hitler had of course already procured its favour by a string of promises relating to cultural and church policies which culminated in the agreement of the Reich Concordat. Apart from this, the Chancellor, in discussions with Prelate Kaas and two further Centre politicians, had given his agreement to the establishment of a 'small committee' that would be kept continually informed of the measures the Reich government was taking on the basis of the Enabling Law. Four days later Hitler made it unequivocally clear that the committee would only convene 'if it appeared appropriate to the Reich government'.[27]

Of course, at this juncture the Enabling Law had already been passed; parliament had granted the government the competence to make laws and even the right to change the constitution. This divestment of its own powers was to remain in force for four years, until 1 April 1937.

The bourgeois opposition parties had all been moved to agree by a series of factors: a mixture of a mood of resignation, a sense of 'national duty', illusory hopes that their readiness to conform and to cooperate might be recognized at a later stage, and tactical considerations to save their own respective organizations. In the Centre Party and the German State Party (Deutsche Staatspartei) there were differences of opinion between internal factions, but in the end all those present, apart from the Social Democrats, voted in favour. The SPD Party leader Otto Wels defended the no-vote of his fraction, which had already lost 26 deputies as a result of arrests and of others going underground. It was the last speech sustained by the spirit of democracy to be delivered in a theatre packed with SA men and bedecked with swastikas. Never before had a Reichstag been excluded from the control of public affairs to the degree that was already the case and which was to be worsened further as a result of the Enabling Law:

> We Social Democrats know that it is not possible to defeat the realities of power politics simply through legal protests. We see the political reality of the power of your present rule. But the people's sense of justice is also a political force and we will not cease to appeal to this sense of justice.

Wels concluded with a restrained greeting to the 'persecuted and oppressed'. The implication was clear: it was recognized that the labour movement had missed the moment for an open struggle against the regime. Hitler savoured the fact in his reply: 'I don't in the slightest want you to vote in favour! Germany shall become free, but not through you!'[28]

Table 1 The growth in membership of the NSDAP

End of 1925	27,000
September 1930	130,000
January 1933	850,000
May 1935	2,500,000
1939	5,300,000
1942	7,100,000
1945	8,500,000

In comparison with the Reichstag Fire Decree, the Enabling Law was of lesser importance in the actual process of the establishment of Nazi power. However, it brought the process of political (self-)exclusion of the parties to an interim conclusion and the act of legislation itself once again underlined, before the nation and the world, the 'legal course' being steered by the new masters. 'The acceptance of the Enabling Law by the Centre', Hitler had already prophesied to the cabinet in the run-up to the legislation, would 'mean a strengthening of our prestige abroad'.[29]

In contrast to the situation in Germany, where the number of the 'March fallen' ran into the hundreds of thousands, and where, at the beginning of May, the NSDAP attempted to defend itself against the uncontrollable flood of Hitler enthusiasts and opportunists into the Party with a moratorium on new membership,[30] there were indeed problems with public opinion abroad. The American press in particular, represented in Berlin by a very active corps of correspondents, had reported extensively, and consequently in hardly flattering terms, about the 'revolutionary' events in Germany. The arrest of thousands of political opponents and the increasing number of outrages against Jewish doctors, civil and public servants and business people were described quite appropriately by the journalists as an expression of a prevailing state of siege. Public statements by socialist and Jewish emigrés tarnished the image of the Hitler government still further. At the end of March the German consul-general in New York sent a telegram to Berlin, reporting that a 'mass meeting against supposed German atrocities' was being planned, to take place in Madison Square Gardens.[31] While Foreign Minister Neurath tried, not without success, to keep the Catholic clergy in the USA from participating in protest rallies scheduled in other towns, Goering took responsibility for informing the foreign press about the true 'state of affairs in Germany': there was 'not a single person who had had a finger-nail or an earlobe cut off or had their eyes put out. The number of deaths each day had been no higher than during the political upheavals of the previous years.' It was true that in a few isolated cases Jews had been arrested and beaten, but 'a whole string of members of nationalist associations who had got on the wrong side of the law had [also] been punished and dismissed.' Of course this was a complete fabrication and Goering's assurance that 'neither I nor the Government ever tolerate persecution of someone simply because he is a Jew' was nothing more than propaganda. In the same breath the Prussian Minister-President announced 'measures against encroachment by the Jewish elements' and pointed out that 'a strong anti-Semitic mood exists amongst the people. But if, despite this, the shops are open, then this is proof of the iron discipline by which the national uprising has been accompanied.'[32]

Goebbels and Hitler shared this logic. A few days later, in the ministerial circle, the Chancellor, in a similar inversion of cause and effect, established the need for 'defensive measures' against the negative echo from abroad, the preparation for which had already been begun with an expressly created NSDAP 'Central Commitee for the countering of the Jewish atrocity and boycott campaign' under the leadership of Julius Streicher, the Nuremberg Gauleiter and publisher of the infamous anti-Semitic *Stürmer*. On 31 March, ignoring a declaration of loyalty by the Jewish Community of Berlin and the Reich Representatives of Jews in Germany, the Nazi leadership gave the starting signal for the boycott. The next morning SA and SS pickets were posted in front of Jewish shops and medical and legal practices. The idea of the organizers was that the action should 'be carried forward into the smallest country village, in order that Jewish merchants should be affected, particularly in the flat lands'.[33]

The campaign was a failure in two respects. The independent foreign press did not allow itself to be silenced as a result, nor did the silent majority of Germans identify with it. American newspapers naturally also reported the new discrimination fully and German housewives completed their purchases in Jewish department stores and textile shops before the boycott began, just in case. Both of these responses were to be predicted, and thus the question of the deeper reasons for the action remains. The decisive clue was provided by one of its main organizers, Joseph Goebbels, in his speech broadcast on the evening of 1 April. In it, the newly created Propaganda Minister justified the centrally planned action with the advice that otherwise they would have had to reckon with an outbreak of uncontrollable 'popular rage'. This was the height of cynicism – but there was an element of truth in it.

For indeed, in deciding in favour of the action, Hitler met genuine needs of his Party members. The old radical anti-Semitic camp, embodied in Streicher as leader of the Boycott Committee, was to be satisfied, the 'revolutionary' pressure for action from the SA was to be granted a sphere of activity, and at the same time something was to be done for the traditional Party clientele in the Nazi alliance – the commercial middle classes, whose economic discontent was directed primarily at the competition from Jewish department stores. The need of thoroughly heterogeneous forces within the Nazi movement to have a taste of power and violence was specifically allowed some leeway in the first days of April 1933. However, the claim of the Party leadership to central direction was thereby simultaneously underpinned, as it could now not only lay claim to state authority, but also had to exercise it.

In a similar fashion such a dual function was attributed to the 'Law on the Restoration of the Professional Civil Service',[34] promulgated a few days later. This provided the 'legal' grounds for the 'purging' of the administration of politically 'unreliable elements.' An 'Aryan paragraph' specifically made possible the dismissal of Jewish officials and employees in the public services. The application and time limitations of the law show that in the first instance it was intended to fulfil 'practical' aims. Actually it concerned a relatively small number of officials, whose exclusion continued the reversal by the von Papen government of the 'republicanization' of the bureaucracy initiated cautiously during the Weimar Republic. However, the loyalty of the majority of *Beamten* towards the 'new State' was not to be challenged. The law and its later enforcement orders directed the purge with maximum harshness into state legal channels, developed criteria for the treatment of Jewish war veterans (as a result of Hindenburg's intervention they were not retired) and regulated pension claims. In fact, however, it also restricted the influence of the grass roots of the Party and the SA, which, as a result of the excesses of the preceding days and weeks, had given rise to great insecurity and, in parts, to chaotic conditions.

Beyond the immediate tactical-political motives, the Professional Civil Service Law and the April boycott, for the first time since the assumption of power, brought clear elements of a specifically Nazi racist anti-Semitism to the fore. These were also followed by further 'constriction of the Jewish realm of life',[35] but it was the 'Nuremberg Laws' of September 1935 which first made into a reality constitutional discrimination against German Jews which corresponded to Nazi ideology on race. Just as in the period in which the NSDAP rose to become a mass party from 1929/30, during the early years of the Third Reich racist anti-Semitism did not stand in the foreground of policies and propaganda. The regime did not enjoy rising popularity because of, but rather in spite of the anti-Jewish elements in its policies, which had little success in inflaming the widespread 'traditional' popular anti-Semitism. Nevertheless, the first measures against the Jews – like those against the 'Marxists' – were widely welcomed as a sign of a determined 'tidying up'. They resulted in both a further dulling of political morality and a regimentation of society based on intimidation.

But in its twelve-year history, the regime only rarely ruled by repression and terror alone. Ideology and propaganda may have made it possible to bridge difficult periods, but they were no substitute for tangible political successes (or for what could be presented as such). Hitler knew this better than most.

The elimination of the labour movement and agreement with industry

By the beginning of 1933 experts could recognize that the downward trend of the economy was coming to an end. When political change followed the economic turn-round, the German Council of Industry and Commerce (DHI – Deutscher Industrie- und Handelstag) hastened to make clear to the Chancellor that the '*question of confidence*' was 'of the greatest importance'. According to the memorandum of 1 February, it was absolutely vital 'that under a strong government, and alongside state policy, the bridging of party differences and the rallying of all forces committed to reconstruction, an economic programme with clear aims should be pursued, which corresponds to the needs of private business'.[36] But it never entered Hitler's head that he should allow himself to be put under pressure from experts, either on the programme or the time-table. In the weeks leading up to the March elections little happened on the economic policy front, and deliberately so. The 'economic dictator' Hugenberg may well have been able to undertake some measures which favoured agriculture; but when the Reich Finance Minister announced that he was considering the introduction of a tax on department stores (which was popular, specifically in Nazi circles, as an anti-Jewish measure), Hitler reprimanded him for going too far. During the election campaign 'all exact details regarding an economic programme were to be avoided'. The Chancellor's justification according to the cabinet minutes, was that 'The Reich government had to gather 18–19 million votes behind it. Nowhere in the whole world did there exist an economic programme which could find the agreement of a mass of voters of this size.'[37]

Hitler's reticence in economic policy was certainly not based on tactical considerations alone. A certain helplessness was also discernible, but above all the primacy of politics: everything was to be subordinated to the extension of power in the realm of the state. Hitler made no bones about this, even with regard to big business, with which increasingly close contacts had existed since the beginning of the 1930s. On 20 February 1933, before an illustrious audience of top industrial managers (IG Farben, Krupp, Vereinigte Stahlwerk, AEG, Siemens, Opel and others), Hitler, seconded by Goering and in the presence of Schacht, President of the Reichsbank, promised a 'peaceful future', rearmament, and for the 'next ten, yes perhaps one hundred years', no more elections. For the managers concerned this was clearly quite adequate as a 'concept' of economic policy, for at the end of the secret meeting the election campaign fund of the NSDAP was richer to the tune of a least three million Reichsmarks.[38]

It is true that mass unemployment did play a certain role in Nazi election propaganda, but in fact the coalition government remained inactive in the field of employment policy for months. No progress was made even with the voluntary Labour Service (*Arbeitsdienst*), whose 'development' had been recommended by the Council of Industry and Commerce 'on state-moral, social and economic grounds.'[39] Only the public spending package totalling 600 million marks and already agreed by the Schleicher Cabinet was carried out (not without the interference of Hitler, who demanded that public investment should, in the first place, benefit the Reichswehr, although its procurement plans were not, in the short term, to be extended correspondingly). The fact that the unemployment figures were now clearly falling anyway – in the first year of the Hitler government from 6 to 3.7 million – also, of course, made further state employment-creation initiatives seem less urgent. The political structure had priority. However, this could cause ripples in the economy if, for example, what the DHI memorandum genteelly described as the 'relaxation of the nature of collective wage agreements' were to succeed. In essence this was a demand for effective repression of the employees' side, a demand which had been on industry's economic policy shopping-list for years. Under Hitler this was translated into a fatal blow against the trade unions.

Despite the level of aggression with which the Nazis, after the March election, persecuted the Social Democrats and the Free Trade Unions which were politically allied to them, at first only pessimists believed that the aim could be the total destruction of the German trade union movement. The mere existence of the Nazis' own quasi-trade union arm, the National Socialist Factory Cell Organization – the NSBO – seemed to suggest the contrary. The fact, too, that until Gregor Strasser's resignation in December 1932 the left wing of the NSDAP had seriously participated in negotiations concerning a government of a 'trade union axis' aspired to by von Schleicher, nourished hopes that the Nazi struggle against 'Marxism' would not be directed with absolute vigour against the organized working class.

If the Nazi leadership, even after the assumption of power, had considered conceding a right of existence to a depoliticized General Federation of German Trade Unions (Allgemeiner Deutscher Gewerkschaftsbund – ADGB), the turning point came for them with the disappointing results of the works council elections in March 1933. The NSBO, which in comparison to the Free Trade Unions had hitherto occupied only a peripheral position, certainly closed the gap considerably. Nonetheless, an average of roughly one-quarter of the elected officials could hardly be interpreted as a triumphal advance. Enthusiasm for Hitler still stopped at the factory gate. The regime reacted with a hastily enacted 'Workplace Representation Law' (*Betriebsvertretungsgesetz*), which authorized employers to dismiss employees summarily, even if there was only a suspicion of 'activities hostile to the state'; all those works council elections still pending were suspended for six months. Moreover, it was also intended that 'Reich Commissioners' (*Reichsbeauftragte*) should be installed in the *Land* employment offices, thus further curtailing the rights of the trade unions. However, in the cabinet debate on 31 March the relevant article was deferred until the so-called 'envisaged reconstruction of the trade unions on new lines'.[40] This already sounded like a countdown.

In fact the impotent opportunism displayed by the ADGB after the change in government produced growing resolve on the part of the Nazis. In the hope that an acceptance of political neutrality and a self-imposed restriction to economic and social issues would be accorded due recognition, the Trade Union Federation, under the leadership of the veteran Social Democrat Theodor Leipart, publicly distanced itself from the SPD. In vain, Leipart implored Hindenburg's protection ('in the certainty that today you remain the guardian and guarantor of the rights of the people anchored in the constitution') against the 'terrorist acts' by 'supporters of the ruling parties', which were threatening the 'life and property of the German working class'.[41] The erosion of the political power of the trade unions, which had begun under the pressure of mass unemployment, also continued, in a fashion which could be recognized by opponents and supporters alike as a decay of their institutional self-confidence. This was a substantial reason why the ADGB leaders chose to forgo a mobilization of its four million members. On 'Potsdam Day' the Trade Union Federation pointedly declared its readiness to cooperate 'regardless of the type of state regime'.[42] The intention was that trade union organization and their social institutions should be saved, almost at any price.

But this was a fatal miscalculation. While the ADGB was seeking to prove its 'patriotic reliability', a Nazi 'Action Committee for the Defence of German Labour' was planning, in total secrecy, the decisive blow to be struck on 'Tuesday, 2 May 1933 at 10 am'. But this was only to be the second half of a carefully staged coup. This bold stroke against the trade unions was preceded by individual acts which appeared to benefit the working class. Hitler had hitherto rarely applied the principle of stick and carrot more perfectly.

What the Republic had failed to provide for the workers, the new regime now offered with an ostentatious gesture: without formal procedures, as was now possible, it proclaimed the heavily symbolic 1 May a public holiday. As with 'Potsdam Day', the 'Führer' placed the preparation of the 'premiere' in the hands of his congenial Propaganda Minister; significantly, Labour Minister Seldte remained in the wings. More or less overnight the international day of struggle of the labour movement was turned into the 'Day of National Labour' (*Tag der nationalen Arbeit*) and its purpose was formulated precisely by Goebbels before an audience of hundreds of thousands at the Berlin Tempelhof Airfield: 'This evening, transcending classes, rank and confessional differences, the whole German *Volk* finds itself united to destroy finally the ideology of class struggle and to clear the path for the new ideas of solidarity and national community.'[43]

Hitler expanded on these thoughts in his keynote speech, in unusually mild and flowery language. In contrast to the vocabulary of internecine warfare and murder, hatred, misery and discord, he spoke of reconciliation, introspection, coming together, revival: 'The German *Volk* must once again get to know one another! The millions of people who are torn apart in professions and trades, held apart in artificial classes, who, infected with the arrogance of status and the madness of class, learned to cease to understand one another; they must find one another again!'[44] Effectively equipped with an assurance of non-objection from the ADGB, which had called for participation in the nationwide festivities, the Chancellor considered concrete explanations of future labour policy unnecessary. 'Honour work and respect the worker!' was the motto of the day, and Hitler left it at that, for he knew that anything other than this sort of wooing of support would only detract from the emotional appeal of the broadcast mass rally. This was an accurate appraisal: the French Ambassador François-Poncet noted, 'Yes, it really is a beautiful, wonderful festival! A breath of reconciliation and unity [is wafting] over the Third Reich.'[45]

Less than twelve hours later this newly postulated social consensus was put to a severe test which demonstrated the usefulness of skilfully manipulated political symbolism. On the morning of 2 May 1933, SA and SS auxiliary police, led by NSBO functionaries, occupied the offices and institutions of the Free Trade Unions throughout the Reich. They met hardly any opposition. The senior leaders of the ADGB, caught totally unaware, and the leading functionaries of the individual unions were taken into protective custody, but so too were the directors of the trade union bank and the editors of the trade union press. In contrast, most of the middle- and lower-ranking trade union employees were allowed to remain in their posts, under NSBO direction. Simply for practical reasons it was necessary to limit the extent of the action, and its aim was in any case less the institutional than the final political destruction of the trade unions. The old organizational framework could perfectly well be used in setting up the 'German Labour Front' (Deutsche Arbeitsfront – DAF) announced by Robert Ley.

The Hirsch-Dunckersche Trade Union Ring (Hirsch-Dunkerscher Gewerk-schaftsring) and the German National Clerical Association (Deutsch-nationaler Handlungsgehilfen-Verband), intimidated by the action against the Free Trade Unions, joined Ley's Action Committee. After only three days almost all the blue- and white-collar workers' associations (with a total of eight million employees) had subordinated themselves to the Committee; only the Christian trade unions enjoyed a reprieve until the summer.

In contrast to the thorough planning of the events of 2 May, the future of the DAF at the time of its foundation was somewhat hazy; however, divergent interests rapidly emerged.[46] Thus the assertion, common at the outset, that the aim of the DAF was to realize the old dream of a single united trade union, had staunch advocates within the NSBO, whose leading personalities around Walter Schumann held important positions within the Labour Front. But even after Ley, mainly for reasons of power politics and in the wake of 30 June 1934, had eliminated these NSBO 'leftists', certain trade union tendencies remained intact within the Labour Front. The DAF was soon advancing interests relating to social and wages policy, especially in those industries benefiting from the rearmament boom.

At first and above all, however, the DAF was an instrument for the regimentation of the workers. This was demonstrated only nine days after its official foundation, when on 19 May the 'Law on Trustees of Labour' (*Gesetz über Treuhänder der Arbeit*) substituted state compulsion for the hitherto existing autonomy in negotiating wage rates. Formally it placed similar restrictions on both capital and labour, but in reality the law meant a strengthening of the employers, for the 13 senior officials who henceforth acted as 'Reich Trustees of Labour' (*Reichstreuhänder der*

Arbeit) were, for the most part, nearer to industry than to the employee side or the NSBO. Indeed, regional conflict with the NSBO arose on more than one occasion in the following months.[47]

The 'Law on the Regulation of National Labour' (*Gesetz zur Ordnung der nationalen Arbeit*) of 20 January 1934, confirmed the role of the Reich Trustees and shifted the balance of power further in favour of the employers. Subsequently the DAF participated only in an advisory capacity in wage negotiations and the formulation of employment contracts; the previously existing employee codetermination was abolished. Drawing an analogy with the 'national community' (*Volksgemeinschaft*), the law posited the 'works community' (*Betriebsgemeinschaft*) which allocated the role of 'leader' (*Führer*) to the employer and merely that of 'retinue' (*Gefolgschaft*) to the employees. In future, conflicts were supposed to be resolved by 'social courts of honour'. Works councils (*Betriebsräte*) were replaced with powerless 'consultative councils of trust' (*Vertrauensräte*), which were to be 'elected' from a single list drawn up by the *Betriebsführer* and the NSBO shop steward; the workers reacted to this farce in April 1934 and again in the following spring with less than 50 per cent of votes in favour in some places, after which no more elections took place.

The Nazis undoubtedly pursued further aims with the DAF than simply the elimination of trade union power so welcomed by industry. Besides the satisfaction of the desire for social and political compulsion, there was also the conscription and control of the workers and ultimately the ideological penetration of every aspect of the world of work. But the DAF was not the cutting edge of Nazi social policy which the ideologists of 'national community' may have had in mind. For the present it remained above all an organizational juggernaut with the – eminently political – function of a 'kind of no-interest group'.[48]

This was clearly expressed in the autumn of 1933 by the 'Appeal to all working Germans', in which the DAF leader Ley, together with the Reich Ministers for Labour and Industry and the industrial commissioners of the NSDAP, posited 'the integration of all persons involved in working life regardless of their economic standing'. In the DAF 'the worker' was supposed to 'stand alongside the entrepreneur, no longer divided by groups and associations which serve to protect specific economic or social strata and interests.' Once again the DAF was denied any competence in questions of labour or social policy: 'In accordance with the will of our Führer, Adolf Hitler, the German Labour Front is not the place for deciding material questions of daily working life, or for reconciling the natural differences of interest between individual working men.'[49] Thus the misgivings from the employers' camp that the Labour Front could become too powerful were taken into account. Gustav Krupp von

Bohlen und Halbach, the 'Führer' of the newly established 'Reich Estate of German Industry' (Reichsstand der Deutschen Industrie) was able to recommend entry into the DAF to his fellow employers with an easy conscience.

In any case, the Nazi *Gleichschaltung* of the industrial organizations had remained cosmetic. Of course, the Party Commissioner for Economic Matters, Otto Wagener, forced the resignation of the managing director and several Jewish board members of the Reich Confederation of German Industry (Reichsverband der Deutschen Industrie – RDI), but it escaped a long-term presence of Nazi commissars. For this it was sufficient for Krupp to promise the Chancellor that, as the new boss of the Confederation, he would make sure there was a tight central organization.[50] Hopes and expectations were great on both sides; each in turn believed itself to be indispensable. In no other sphere did Hitler repress the 'Party revolution' so clearly as in the industrial arena – or at least, he allowed Schacht free rein in this regard. The leaders of industry reciprocated by remaining silent about the discrimination against their Jewish colleagues. In 1932, the RDI board member Paul Silverberg had himself argued for the participation of the Nazis in the government, but when he was forced to leave, it was only Hitler's old supporter, Emil Kirdorf, who spoke openly of a 'stab in the back'.

However, events such as these did not detract from the honeymoon between the Nazi leadership and big business, as was proved on 1 June 1933 by the delivery – at Krupp's suggestion – of a nice little wedding cake with the sobriquet of the 'Adolf Hitler Donation of German Industry': companies were, in future, to pay over to the NSDAP a contribution at the rate of five thousandths of their total annual wages and salaries. This was intended as a mark of gratitude for the elimination of the trade unions, the prospect of a rearmament-led boom and the departure into economic autarky, which promised big business outstanding profits and possibilities for development. At the same time, however, with this self-imposed levy, big business protected itself from excessive demands by the Party and put up a clear marker of its independence.

The move not only succeeded in keeping the ideological old-style Nazi out of the boardrooms; in order not to endanger the willingness of private business to cooperate, the regime was even prepared to make concessions on the political front. In July 1933, Hitler appointed the chairman of the board of the Allianz insurance company and representative of big business, Kurt Schmitt, Alfred Hugenberg's successor as Reich Economics Minister, and a short while later he jettisoned some corporatist ballast by replacing his Economic Commissioner Wagener with the chemicals manufacturer Wilhelm Keppler. Keppler, who had served as a successful NSDAP contact with big business since 1932, had an office in the Reich Chancellory itself. In the first years of the Third Reich at least, private big business penetrated the political system rather than the other way round.

For the small businesses of the lower middle class other rules applied.[51] The NSDAP possessed traditional target groups in craft, trade and small businesses and for a while after the assumption of power Hitler gave the 'League of Struggle for the Commercial Middle Class' (Kampfbund für den gewerblichen Mittelstand), founded only in 1932, free rein to take over guilds and professional associations. Despite this, all the substantial political expectations of the Nazi *Mittelstand* politicians remained unfulfilled. This was demonstrated as early as the summer of 1933, when the Party leadership, after protests from business and in order to protect jobs, began to prohibit the resentment-laden actions of the Kampfbund against Jewish department store chains and against those consumer co-operatives previously owned by the trade unions and now incorporated into the DAF. The incorporation of the Kampfbund into the NS-Hago in August 1933 marked the end of the romantic petit-bourgeois dreams which the Nazi Party programme had promised to fulfil. In modern industrial society, even of the Nazi type, they had no place. The bogus designations of the new 'Reich Estate of German Commerce' (Reichsstand des Deutschen Handels) and the 'Reich Estate of German Craft' (Reichsstand des Deutschen Handwerks) were unable to obscure this fact for long. Instead of the hoped-for financial improvement, the *Mittelstand* experienced strict organization by the state. In later years this did, however, also facilitate economically sensible measures for structural adjustment.

The Nazi policy of *Gleichschaltung* in agriculture proceeded more quickly than in the organizations of the *Mittelstand* and more effectively than in any other economic sector. A major reason for this was certainly the greater practical commitment which the NSDAP had brought to this field for years through its 'Agricultural Policy Unit' under the leadership of Richard Walter Darré. The change in direction towards the 'soil' had not been an electoral tactic. It was one of the basic ideological elements of National Socialism and to this extent was more authentic than, for example, the canvassing of the *Mittelstand*, which had been made susceptible to radical sloganizing during the economic crisis. Darré's rapid organizational successes in the spring of 1933 were, however, also helped by the fact that, for a long time, efforts had been made to unify the widely compartmentalized system of agricultural associations. The pointed respect of the new Reich government for 'blood and soil' *(Blut und Boden)* and the policy of generous subsidy of agriculture which Hugenberg pursued – purely to the benefit of the big landowners – provided the Nazi supporters of centralization with strong arguments.

Even so, additional pressure was necessary. The Nazi agricultural strategists achieved this in a fashion already often proven in other areas: Andreas Hermes, the President of the Christian farmers' unions, who was opposed to both the Nazis and the amalgamation of the agricultural associations, was arrested on charges of alleged embezzlement. Meanwhile, in the big landowners' Reich Land League (Reichslandbund), two members of the 'Agricultural Policy Unit' were preparing the ground for negotiations on a merger with the Farmers' Unions, and only a fortnight after Hermes' arrest Darré was 'invited' to take over the leadership of the new 'Community of Reich Leaders' (*Reichsführergemeinschaft*). After a further two weeks this fully qualified agriculturalist secured for himself the chair of the Union of Agricultural Cooperatives (*Raiffeisenverband*), and on Hitler's birthday on 20 April reported to his 'Führer' 'the assumption by me of the leadership of 40,000 rural cooperatives'.[52] Shortly afterwards, alongside the German Agricultural Council (Deutscher Landwirtschaftsrat), which, with complete confidence in the promises of an autarkic economy, had already sworn its allegiance to the new government on several occa-sions, the Council of Chief Executives of the Chambers of Agriculture (*Landwirtschaftskammern*) also subordinated itself to Darré's command. By the end of May 1933 the 'blood and soil' ideologue, barely 38 years old, had won control of all the agricultural organizations. His new official title of 'Reich Peasants' Leader' (*Reichsbauernführer*) was intended to give expression to this. After this success it was hardly surprising that the position of Reich Agriculture Minister also fell to him when Hugenberg relinquished all his official posts at the end of June. Thus, in the agricultural sector, there came about the concentration of state, corporate and official Nazi Party power in one pair of hands. Such a power of command did not exist in any other area of the economy. It stood alone even in the Nazi system.

The end of the parties and the coordination of society

The internal inability of the bourgeois parties to withstand the wake of Nazi alignment policy had become so obvious as a result of their un-animous approval of the Enabling Law that it was bound to have consequences.[53] From all of them, from the Centre Party to the German Nationalists, members left in droves, partly through disappointment, partly through fear of reprisals, but also often in order to seek membership of the NSDAP. Increasing pressure by the 'movement' strengthened this process, and in the meanwhile it had gripped the only party which, while stressing its patriotism, still declared its opposition – the SPD.

After the *de facto*, though never *de jure*, banning of the KPD and the far-reaching elimination of the 'Reichsbanner' – the Social Democratic paramilitary organization – as early as March 1933, fear grew in the ranks of the SPD of the destruction of the party machine and of the growing terror against its members. The action taken against the Free Trade Unions on 2 May could only fuel this apprehension. There were, though, differing points of view within the SPD leadership as to what awaited Social Democracy in the intermediate term. This now manifested itself when a section of the Executive, as a 'Representation Abroad', moved first to the Saarland, which was administered by the League of Nations, to prepare for eventual exile, and then at the end of May to Prague. Optimists, meanwhile, hoped to be able to save the Party through consistent adherence to a 'course of legality'. The latter group believed the situation could be compared with the period of Bismarck's anti-socialist laws, when the SPD suffered internal political repression but retained its parliamentary presence and in the end emerged organizationally strengthened.

The controversy within the SPD became public as a result of the summoning of the Reichstag, at Hitler's behest, for 17 May. Both Friedrich Stampfer, the Editor in Chief of the main SPD party newspaper *Vorwärts*, and Otto Wels could now be counted amongst the majority of the Executive. Ignoring their warnings and despite the sequestration of party assets, which had occurred only a week earlier, half the parliamentary fraction participated in the Reichstag session. Hitler intended to make a showcase speech on foreign policy before the plenum. Just beforehand, Reich Interior Minister Frick had made it clear, with a threat against the lives of Social Democratic concentration camp prisoners, that anything other than agreement would be out of the question. Indeed, the 'Führer's' declaration gave little grounds for rejection: before the eyes of world public opinion, which was expecting aggressive demands, Hitler acknowledged the right of all peoples to self-determination and committed himself to a peaceful policy of treaties. As a sign of their approval the deputies were to rise to their feet at the end of the 'Führer's' speech; no-one refused to make this spectacular gesture. Germany, so it appeared, stood loyal and united behind Hitler.

The critique by the leading emigré members of the SPD, which demanded determined preparation for illegality, was rooted in this impression, which threatened to obscure the courageous position of the Party on the vote on the Enabling Law. The first edition of *Neuer Vorwärts*, published in Prague on 18 June, called for the overthrow of the Hitler regime. It is true that the Berlin leadership immediately contested the right of the emigrés to speak in the name of the SPD, but they did not bow to the regime's demands that the Prague group should be expelled from the Party. And so Frick possessed a welcome reason to reverse his decision. On 22 June 1933, invoking the Reichstag Fire Decree, he declared the SPD to be an 'organization hostile to the people and the state' – also because it had failed to 'discard' its emigré Executive members 'in the light of their treasonable behaviour'. The response from Prague displayed little more than helpless anger: 'Banning clears the way!' was *Neuer Vorwärts*' headline for the report; the 'remaining semblance of democratic legality' had now been 'destroyed'.[54]

These were feeble words, which, if anything, minimized the gravity of the situation. Yet the Nazis had already been able to alter far too much of the political reality of Germany in the preceding months without encountering opposition to have to reckon with resistance now. With the SPD the last institution of the German left was defeated by decree, and the absolute nature of its elimination strongly suggested that there was still more to come in the process of political regimentation and coordination.

The representatives of the bourgeois parties now found themselves confronted with the hitherto suppressed realization that in voting for the Enabling Law they had not only repudiated their political function but also their institutional right to exist. The DNVP (German National People's Party), in January Hitler's enablers and by June his prisoners, were at least still able, with the self-imposed dissolution of their organization, to buy the acceptance of their deputies into the NSDAP fractions of the Reichstag, the *Land* parliaments and local authorities. Similarly, a formal agreement was concluded for the incorporation of their paramilitary organization, the Stahlhelm, into the SA. This was no mean achievement, considering that on 26 June, after serious blunders at the London World Economic Conference and having been under fire from Nazi critics for weeks, the DNVP leader Hugenberg relinquished all his ministerial posts. The *Zähmungskonzept* had failed miserably, at least at the level of national politics. The German State Party (Deutsche Staatspartei – DSP), had had its Prussian *Landtag* seats removed because of a joint list it had put up with the SPD before the last election. On 27 June, it decided to dissolve itself. Twenty-four hours later the German People's Party (Deutsche Volkspartei – DVP) took the same step.

Propaganda Minister Goebbels now brazenly demanded that the Centre Party should 'shut up shop'. In actual fact the Catholic party did accept the inevitable consequences of the Vatican's agreement to Hitler's demand that in future all party political activity by clerics be forbidden – even before the Reich Concordat, which the former Centre leader Prelate Kaas was helping to prepare, was signed. For the sake of a – never clearly defined – guarantee of continued existence for church institutions, the

Vatican had thus abandoned political Catholicism, for the clergy had traditionally held a substantial proportion of posts in the leadership of both the Centre Party and the BVP. The BVP dissolved itself on 4 July. At the end of June, despite the still continuing negotiations on the Concordat, it had been struck with a wave of arrests by Himmler's Bavarian Political Police. On the following day the Centre was the final party to follow suit. Even before it had been enacted, the Concordat had borne fruit both bitter and sweet: on the one hand was the dismay of the Centre's leadership at the Vatican's policy, while on the other was the sharp rise in the regime's popularity in ecclesiastical circles and a growth in its prestige abroad.

Even Hitler himself seemed surprised by the lack of drama which accompanied the end of the multi-party state. 'We are witnessing the slow completion of the totalitarian state' was his comment on the events of the last few days at a conference with the Reich Governors on 6 July.[55] What mattered now was that the already existing situation should be embodied in law. 'An attempt to alter it, for example by the re-establishment of parties, must be seen by us simply as an attack on the essence of the present state and treated as high treason.' The 'prospects for such a counter-attack' were of course slim. 'The members of those parties which had disappeared', according to Hitler, in a realistic ap-praisal of the situation, 'were not capable of any specific activity.'[56]

None the less, on the agenda of the next cabinet meeting on July 14 stood a 'Law against the Establishment of Political Parties'. Following exactly the implications of the 'Führer's' comments to the Reich Gover-nors, it threatened with punishment befitting 'treason against Germany and high treason,' those who engaged in the maintenance or establishment of a party. But missing from the draft, as the Reich Justice Minister re-marked, was a concrete penalty. It also seemed doubtful to Gürtner 'if the present point in time was psychologically correct for the adoption of the law'.[57] Hitler remained unimpressed by this and the law was passed, with Frick and Gürtner being assigned to append the punishment. The final version referred to a maximum of three years' imprisonment. One-party rule was sealed.

A cabinet meeting in which 43 points of agenda and no less than 38 laws were discussed (some with the gravest of consequences, such as the 'Law to Prevent Progeny with Hereditary Diseases') could, and in-deed was intended to, create a public impression of efficiency and com-petence. On the other hand, there was now a growing development which finally led to the complete break-up of normal governmental activity: the frequency of ministerial meetings, which in the spring of 1933 had taken place twice weekly on average, diminished drastically.

Dictatorial revelation of the 'will of the Führer' replaced discussion amongst colleagues, and increasingly often draft laws were now simply hurriedly passed in cabinet. Where internal clarification still occurred it took place in an overgrown jungle of competing authorities. The 'Führer State' began to assume its contours. Also symbolic of this was the 'Heil Hitler' salute, which Frick now made obligatory for all civil servants: 'Since the multi-party state has been overcome and the entire administration of the Third Reich is under the control of the Reich Chancellor Adolf Hitler, it would appear appropriate to use the greeting introduced by him as the normal German greeting. The affinity of the entire German *Volk* with its Führer will thereby assume a clear outward manifestation. Here too, civil and public servants must be in the vanguard of the German *Volk*.'[58]

On the governmental, parliamentary and party level the process of Nazi monopolization of power could be considered to have been concluded in July 1933. In barely five months the Nazi movement had totally altered the existing balance of political power. But the constitutional reality of the Third Reich was still not that of the indisputable dictatorship of the 'Führer'. There were still many open questions, amongst them that of the status of the NSDAP in Hitler's state. Neither the completion of the one-party state nor the 'Law to Secure the Unity of the Party and the State' promulgated on 1 December 1933 provided any clarification on this issue. Although it is true that the law did elevate the NSDAP to the status of 'representative of the German state idea', it did not establish an autonomous pre-eminence of the Party over the state administration. The 'Führer' retained the right to decide in conflicts between the Party and the state bureaucracy, and it gradually became clear that the ever-present right of intervention and decision counted amongst the basic principles of the 'Führer State' of the Hitlerite type.

Awe-inspiring mass rallies, like the 'Party Victory Congress' in Nuremberg in early September, were able only temporarily to conceal the fact that, as a result of the conclusion of the process of political regimentation and coordination, the grass-roots of the Party (and in particular the SA) had lost their role. In the summer of 1933 there were already rumours in the 'movement' of what Hitler acknowledged to the Reich Governors. He gave them an urgent warning against seeing the 'revolution' as a 'permanent situation'. The willingness of specialist professionals to perform well, vital to overcome the economic crisis, was in danger of being crippled – particularly in business and the administration – by the unbridled lust for power on the part of lower-ranking Party and SA leaders. According to the published summary of the 'Führer's' position, 'in the economy only ability may be the deciding factor'. Hitler now tried to steer those forces in the movement that were pressing for more far-reaching change by impregnating society with the 'National Socialist concept of the state': 'The attainment of external power must be followed by the inner education of each individual.'[59]

In so saying, the 'Führer' confirmed the totalitarian claims of his movement, while taking account of tactical requirements. Hitler knew that the social reality of Germany could not be changed as quickly or as radically as its political constitution without endangering the gains already made. Social hegemony was not necessarily inherent in the political monopoly already established, even if as a result of their unscrupulous display of energy the Nazis had succeeded, to an astonishing degree, in putting into question old, basic convictions and certainties about social relationships of both the bourgeoisie and the working class. Those social traditions and intellectual currents which were out of favour could not simply be forbidden like parties and trade unions, but state power was wielded with sufficient vigour to create an atmosphere of uncertainty and intimidation in which cultural life could also be regimented.

Perhaps the most spectacular example of this was provided by the book burnings of 10 May 1933.[60] That evening, bonfires were built by activists of the German Students' Association (Deutsche Studentenschaft) and the Nazi Students League, with the support of many academic teaching staff, on the Opera House Square in Berlin and in most university cities. The Nazis had gained a particularly firm foothold in the universities very early on, and it was obvious that there the eagerness finally to strike a blow against everything 'un-German' and 'corrupting' would concentrate on literature and teaching. For weeks there had existed a list with the names of leftist, democratic-pacifist and Jewish authors whose work was no longer to be tolerated in public libraries and university seminars. The 'excommunication' hit contemporary authors and publicists such as Erich Maria Remarque, Alfred Döblin, Kurt Tucholsky, Carl von Ossietzky, Heinrich Mann and Ernst Glaeser, and in addition to socialist theoreticians, scientists like Albert Einstein, Sigmund Freud and Magnus Hirschfeld were also affected. A selection of the forbidden books was 'committed' to the flames accompanied by ritualistic 'epigrams of fire'. Undesirable writings disappeared by the ton into police custody. On his way into exile – a path taken in the following years by some 5,000 writers, scientists and other prominent figures in the cultural sphere – Oskar Maria Graf called upon the Nazis to burn his books too; Erich Kästner, who witnessed the spectacle from the anonymity of the crowd, did well to remain silent when his name was called out.

If, simply because of their lack of knowledge, the *auto-da-fé* left many Germans unmoved, amongst the educated middle classes it signalled assent to a policy which could be interpreted as the 'purification of the

German spirit'. The 'classics', of course, were left untouched (with the exception of Heinrich Heine, whose dark prophecy that the burning of books would be followed by the burning of people was familiar only to a few). That second-rate intellectuals and writers expected to benefit from the exclusion of those who had dominated the literary and intellectual discourse of the Weimar Republic was hardly surprising; but this must have been outweighed by the fact that amongst those of the first rank who were not affected – that is amongst those who were not Jews or leftists – there was little evidence of solidarity, but instead several rather obvious sighs of relief. They were sighs of relief at the assumed end of Modernism.

There was little about the revolt against modern literature and intellectual development – which included the fine arts, painting and music – that was specifically Nazi; the sense of unease about the technological-industrial world and its cultural products was as old as that world itself and had always given rise to yearnings for the simple life. What was new was the decisiveness with which the regime's denunciations linked political opposition and aesthetic nonconformity. Hand in hand with the destruction of the political system of Weimar, announced Goebbels in the light of the flames of the burning books, should go the elimination of the 'intellectual basis of the November Republic'.

The banning of newspapers and self-censorship by journalists had already crippled public opinion extensively, even before Goebbels, immediately on his appointment as Propaganda Minister, was able to begin the regimentation and coordination of the 'consciousness industry' at an institutional level. The *Gleichschaltung* of broadcasting proceeded smoothly because of its close structural alignment to the state, and Nazi Party members rapidly moved in to replace those editors and other programme-makers decried as 'cultural and salon Bolsheviks'. In no other area of culture and mass communications was the the grip of the new rulers comparably efficient. The radical purge of the personnel of the new medium of broadcasting led to such a degree of uniformity that, in spring 1934, Goebbels felt obliged to take steps against an over-'energetic politicization'. None the less, the Nazis were right to congratulate themselves on being the first to understand how to make use of the enormous posibilities offered by radio. With the production of cheap wireless receivers (*Volksempfänger*) and small radios and the promotion of reception via communal loudspeakers (*Gemeinschaftsempfang*), they developed broadcasting into a central instrument of ideological and political indoctrination.

From the very beginning, especially in respect of journalism and publishing, the Nazi regime laid claim to totalitarian control and direction which distinguished it like little else from a 'normal' one-party dictatorship. Amongst those who felt it particularly quickly were the Berlin newspaper correspondents to whom, at daily press conferences, Goebbels pronounced his – compulsory – version of reality. Characteristically, the Nazis did not restrict themselves to regulating the media solely in terms of content and personnel, but also pursued their nationalization (news agencies, film) or takeover into Party ownership (the press). After the banning of all Communist and Social Democratic publications, whose publishing houses and printingworks had immediately become the victims of parasitic seizure by the Nazi papers, began the economic conquest of the bourgeois press. Besides Max Amann, the Nazi Party Reich Leader (NSDAP-Reichsleiter) for the Press, the various Gauleiter and Kreisleiter (Regional and District Leaders) often played an important role in this process.[61]

The Law on Editors (*Schriftleitergesetz*) of October 1933 removed editors from much of the control of their publishers and bound them in duty to the state (it included an 'Aryan paragraph', of course). The subsequent establishment of a Reich Chamber of Culture sealed the regimentation and coordination of intellectual and cultural life.[62] At the head of this corporation under public law stood Joseph Goebbels. Membership of one of the seven individual chambers for film, music, theatre, press, broadcasting, literature and fine arts was obligatory for the respective professional groups.

The Reichskulturkammer belonged to the German Labour Front as a corporate member. In material terms, its most important function was the coordinated representation of the social and economic interests of all 'those engaged in the cultural sector'. Many members of the free artistic professions were totally and resolutely opposed to the idea, but the Third Reich appeared thus to be taking up demands that had long been raised by the professional associations in many branches, for example in journalism (protection of professional title, regulated old age pensions etc.). Some may also have been attracted to the new organization by one of the numerous and prestigious official titles which were now to be assigned; they stretched from President of the Reich Chamber of Music, a post first held by Richard Strauss, to 'Commissioner for Artistic Modelling' in the Reich Chamber of Fine Arts, a position occupied by the well-known Nazi caricaturist Hans Schweitzer ('Mjölnir').

At first, the regime's specific purpose in founding the Reich Chamber of Culture found only vague expression in the provision that it should 'promote German culture for the benefit of the *Volk* and the Reich'. But in the area of culture and the media, as in other spheres, it was not least a matter of restraining a 'revolutionary' activism which threatened to get out of control. Throughout the summer the 'League of Struggle for German Culture' had pursued the 'cleansing' and *Gleichschaltung* of academics, museums and other cultural institutions. Given the chaotic conditions which resulted, the assumption by a central authority of responsibility for the control both of personnel and to a certain extent, content, could almost appear as a return to normality. The various Chambers made decisions on prohibitions to practise professionally (*Berufsverbote*), ordered the closure of newspapers and journals, controlled theatre programmes, examined film scripts and granted or denied permission for art exhibitions.

The nature and extent of the control was not uniform in all areas of culture and there were also variations over time. The range of persons and issues tolerated in cultural life in the first years of the Third Reich was different from that of the war years, but the latter was not necessarily narrower. The varying extent of cultural tolerance of which the Nazi regime was capable or to which it was forced was particularly clearly demonstrated by the example of the Churches. Here, after only a few months, the Nazis came up against the limits of their power to regiment society in every area. Nevertheless, their policy towards the Churches had already made a hopeful start, in respect of Protestants and Catholics alike.[63]

At the end of March 1933, Hitler having just promised to recognize the *Länder* Concordats, the Catholic bishops rescinded their prohibitions and warnings against the Nazi movement which had been in force for years. The conclusion and ratification of the Reich Concordat in the summer then led, for a while, to surprisingly amicable relations between espiscopate and Reich government. In the Catholic lay movement, however, the bishops' praise for the confessional freedom now guaranteed by treaty found only a muted echo. The disappointment in the Centre Party and BVP milieu that Rome had abandoned political Catholicism and had not unequivocally protected the dense network of Catholic organizations, had not yet been overcome. Many believers neither could nor wanted to forget all at once their long-rehearsed, deep mistrust against the totalitarian ideological claims and the blatant animosity towards the Church of sections of the Nazi movement at least – all the less, the more vigorously it was necessary to continue arguing with local Nazis about the right of religious associations, Catholic kindergartens, social provision or youth groups to exist. Some parish priests may have tried to talk this away with pious speeches, but by agreeing to the Concordat the curia and the episcopate had distanced themselves from the congregation and the lower echelons of the clergy. Unintentionally the official Church had thereby dismantled the remaining barriers in the way of the incorporation of faithful Catholic Germany into Hitler's *Volksgemeinschaft*. The bishops' subsequent political tactics further weakened the ability of the Catholic milieu to resist. This was to show itself in the Reichstag elections in November 1933.

At precisely this juncture, Nazi Church policy towards Protestantism underwent its first change of direction. Because of the fragmentation into independent *Land* Churches the starting point here was in many respects more complicated, but in one also much simpler: there had hardly ever been principled objections to National Socialism on the part of the Evangelical (that is, Protestant) Church; on the contrary, there had been strong evidence of an affinity. For years the strongholds of Protestantism had also been strongholds of the NSDAP. The prevailing underlying mood of anti-republicanism and German nationalism found expression in the desire for a unified Protestant 'Reich Church' with a 'Reich Bishop' at its head. The movement of the 'German Christians' was close to Nazism. In the spring of 1933, it strove, not alone but with particular vehemence, for a change in the constitution of the Church. Conflict developed when the conservative majority of the *Land* Church representatives failed to nominate Hitler's 'Plenipotentiary in the Affairs of the Evangelical Church' – the former Königsberg Defence District Chaplain Ludwig Müller – for the office of Reich Bishop and instead named the leader of the Bethel Institute (a home for people with physical and mental disabilities), Friedrich von Bodelschwingh. Thereupon the German Christians initiated a campaign of protest and propaganda, in the course of which the 'Führer' also finally declared himself clearly for Müller. The internal strife within the Church had already led to the appointment of a Church Commissar in Prussia, and in order to overcome it general Church elections took place in July. The German Christians, vigorously supported by the Party machine, walked away with a two-thirds majority. At the General Synod, held in Wittenberg at the end of September 1933, the 'Stormtroopers of Jesus Christ' chose Müller to be Reich Bishop.

Shortly before, however, a Pastors' Emergency League had been established. This took a stand against German Christian 'theology', which, *inter alia*, demanded an Aryan paragraph for the Church. The rise of the Confessing Opposition, which in only a week was joined by 2,000 and in a few months by almost half of all Evangelical pastors, already marked the beginning of the decline of the German Christians. As a result of this new movement Reich Bishop Müller took pains to steer a conciliatory course; Hitler's Party Deputy Hess urged the NSDAP to adopt a neutral stance on Church matters. The regime was anxious to avoid an intensification of the conflict. When the German Christians inflamed the dispute none the less, with demands that extended to an absurd nazification of

Protestant theology, the Reich Bishop withdrew his patronage from them. Subsequently, the German Christians and ultimately the Reich Bishop soon lost influence, whilst from the Pastors' Emergency League emerged the Confessing Church.

These early experiences were to be of lasting importance for the development of the relationship of the Protestant Church and the Nazi regime. Despite considerable patriotic common ground, the attempt at a complete *Gleichschaltung*, embracing the constitution of the Church and theology, had foundered. Moreover, it had provoked a lasting opposition. The 'Church Struggle' did indeed continue for years, but there was no further attempt at a frontal assault. Just as with the Catholic Church, where such an assault was never tried, the regime henceforth restricted itself to measures aimed at neutralizing its influence on social policy. This did not exclude occasional attempts at a more aggressive course, but did rule out the total confrontation striven for by Party ideologues such as Alfred Rosenberg and, later, Martin Bormann. Hitler postponed hopes of a 'great day of reckoning' until the period after the war. The ability of the regime to keep its claim to power within specific limits, precisely not to give free rein to its totalitarian ambitions, constituted one of the pre-conditions for Hitler's success in the elections of November 1933.

In the middle of October, the 'Führer' had unexpectedly announced Germany's withdrawal from the League of Nations and in so doing had given the signal for the beginning of a foreign policy which was no longer linked to the disarmament negotiations taking place in Geneva. This posited the end of previous revisionist diplomacy. Hitler was seeking freedom of action for the radical struggle against the system of the Versailles Treaty. In an 'Appeal to the German People' and a half-hour broadcast address, the Chancellor explained that the step had been necessary for reasons of national honour, for the aim of the disarmament conference had been to deprive Germany of the right to military parity. At the same time he gave notice of the first of those plebiscites for which the legal basis had been created in July (together with the law on the monopoly of the NSDAP).

On 12 November, after a mobilization campaign which, though brief, pulled out all the stops and skilfully exploited the support of the bishops of both confessions and other prominent public figures, 45 million Germans had the opportunity to answer the question: 'Do you, German man, and you, German woman, agree to this policy of your Reich Government, and are you prepared to declare it to be the expression of your own opinion and your own will and to accept it solemnly?' 40.6 million (95.1 per cent) voted yes, barely three million said no or returned spoilt ballot papers.

Simultaneously with the plebiscite there took place a new election to the Reichstag. No-one dared to criticize publicly the inconsistency of renewed parliamentary elections which, only in the spring, Hitler had promised sympathetic interlocutors he would abolish. The course of events served to get rid of troublesome DNVP or Centre Party Reichstag deputies, who, after the dissolution of their own parties had gone over to the NSDAP fraction as 'novices'. Mainly veteran Party comrades stood on the unity 'list of the Führer' (the designation, like the wording of the plebiscite, an indication of its pointed emotionalization). With the double ballot Hitler did on the domestic front what was to become the rule in his foreign policy: he put all his money on one horse and scored a triumphant success. On a turnout of 92.5 per cent, on average across the Reich 92.2 per cent of the voters approved the unity list; in one Protestant, small-holding constituency in Kurhessen it gained 99.8 per cent of the vote. Even the worst result, which was reported from Hamburg, stood at 78.1 per cent.[64]

In spite of repeated warnings to Party organizations to avoid anything that could be presented by 'anti-German propaganda' as 'cases of "electoral terror"',[65] there were breaches of the secret ballot and acts of violent coercion against individual voters in many places. But there was no systematic manipulation of the election results. Despite a widely perceived atmosphere of psychological pressure, the result, in the main, reflected the mood really prevailing in Germany at the time. The politics of the 'national uprising', with the unswervingly propounded aim of pacification on the home front and the foreign policy goal of 'making Germany fit for war', the beginning of economic improvement and the general impression of a dynamic and decisive mastering of the future had all won the 'Führer' considerable prestige; now the incursion into the Catholic milieu and the Social Democratic working class had succeeded. The confessional differences still clearly apparent at the Reichstag election in March 1933, which had delivered results of 90 per cent for the NSDAP in Protestant parishes in the small mixed area of Central Franconia (Mittelfranken), but as before a BVP majority in neighbouring Catholic parishes, were now evened out. With the plebiscite the retrospective underpinning of the policy of regimentation and coordination was complete.

Two days after the triumph, Hitler's cabinet paid its tribute. Vice-Chancellor von Papen admitted they were in a daze:

We, your nearest and most intimate colleagues, are still spellbound by the unparalleled, most overwhelming recognition a nation had ever rendered its leader. In nine months the genius of your leadership and the ideals

which you newly placed before us have succeeded in creating, from a
people internally torn and without hope, a Reich united in hope and faith
in its future. Even those who hitherto stood apart have now unequivocally
professed their loyalty to you . . .[66]

Hitler's former coalition partners had every reason to rub their eyes:
at a tempo thought possible by only a few – and least of all by them –
a tempo that itself constituted part of the success, the Nazi process of
regimentation and coordination had succeeded. It had not only changed
the political system from top to bottom, but also left hardly a single area
of the economy, culture and social life untouched. Essential characteristics of Nazi rule were now developed. Democracy and the constitutional
state were set aside, parliamentarism, parties and trade unions defeated,
the *Länder* and most social organizations had been subjected to *Gleichschaltung*, discrimination against Jews established, the spirit of leftism
and left-liberalism quashed, public opinion and culture censored. But the
one-party state was not based on force and repression alone – it was
supported by the agreement of broad strata in society. Both totalitarian
and populist traits united the regime, and from this characteristic mixture
it drew its ability to stabilize itself.

The master and medium of this display of power based on dictatorship
and plebiscites was Hitler. He balanced coercion and terror with individual
populist measures, suggestive rhetoric and vast social and political promises. The 'Führer' myth which grew from this constituted the strength
of Hitler's rule, but it also revealed its weak point: only through the
continual renewal of the enthusiasm for Hitler could the heterogeneous
forces of the movement be held together and the unsolved economic
and political problems, which determined the situation until the end of
1933, be obscured.

According to Hitler's own claim, Nazi hegemony could not be considered to have been attained completely so long as there remained
particular areas of policy in which he was not independent. The
Reichswehr and the Reich President still had to be considered as independent power factors, as had the SA. That remained unchanged until
the double coup of 30 June 1934, which ended the process of regimentation and coordination and marked the beginning of the years of consolidated rule.

2

Consolidation, 1935–1938

Destruction marked the beginning of the Nazi era and self-destruction its end. If 1933 symbolizes the parasitic undermining on the domestic front of forms of state and social order handed down from the Weimar Republic, then 1945 symbolizes a political destructiveness, directed both outward and inward, of world-historic proportions. But it would be misleading to consider Hitler's rule only from the perspective of these key dates – if only because no understanding is to be gained from them alone about the ability of National Socialism to achieve a certain consolidation, the realization of which only then permits us to speak of a 'regime'.

The Third Reich was certainly no static monolith, but nor was it just a simple political process. Alongside the monstrous dynamic of the Nazi *Weltanschauung* which pushed it towards its radical realization was a display of étatist power. There was a phase of consolidated rule with real and potential developments, influences and contemporaneous experiences, and these cannot be obscured just because, in political-historical terms, they remained largely episodes.

From the viewpoint of domestic politics the years between 1935 and 1938 can most obviously be designated as a period of consolidated Nazi rule. Basically there were only these four years in which the regime could develop its domestic policy with relatively few constraints. Beforehand, political factors relating to the coalition, and afterwards those relating to the war, forced it into numerous and varied compromises.

The middle years of the Nazi period entered the consciousness of the majority of German people as the 'good years' before the war. But even after the outbreak of war there remained a great deal of apparent normality. The horror of war reached most Germans with the Allies' bombs from 1942–3 onwards. Conversely, in the perception of some, the material situation could have appeared to be already somewhat improved before 1935. None the less, the 'normal times' remained only a brief interlude when measured against the one thousand years that the Nazi Reich was promised to last. But the recollections of contemporaries demonstrate that this was a period which was experienced with great intensity.

'Giddiness' is the word often used in this context to describe the way in which people experienced the breakneck speed of Germany's economic and foreign policy 'recovery' (*Wiederaufstieg* was the term the Nazis used). Many identified astonishingly quickly with the social 'will for reconstruction' of a 'national community', which kept all reflection and criticism at arm's length, and wished to hear no more about the achievements of the German-Jewish intelligentsia. People allowed themselves to be bewitched by the aesthetic of the Reich Party rallies in Nuremberg and cheered the victory of German athletes at the Olympic Games in Berlin. Hitler's successes in foreign policy evoked storms of enthusiasm. The apparent absence of political contradictions between interest groups and the ending of conflict between political parties were met with great satisfaction. In the brief amount of free time that was left after work and the demands of the overgrown jungle of Nazi organizations, people enjoyed modest prosperity and private happiness.

The Nazi economic miracle

At the beginning of the 1930s John Maynard Keynes was still developing his theory of 'deficit spending' and it was not yet part of the basic wisdom of economics to combat recession with state investment programmes and political psychology. But with precisely this remedy the Nazi regime produced an upswing that was soon acknowledged, at home and abroad, as an 'economic miracle'.

By 1936, while high unemployment continued to hold sway in other important industrial countries (in the USA it stood at almost 24 per cent), it was considered that in Germany full employment had been restored. It is true that the statistics still excluded an annual average of 1.6 million unemployed, yet that was only about 200,000 more than in the glittering year of 1928 – and the number was still falling (see table 2).[1] In individual sectors there was already even a shortage of skilled labour.

It is indisputable that, at the beginning, the Nazis benefited from being able to fall back on the investment plans of preceding governments, and even more from a change in economic trends which had become apparent since 1932, and which made the prospects of state intervention

Table 2 Unemployment in the German Reich 1928–1940

Year	Employees[a] (1000s)	Unemployed[d] (1000s)	Unemployment As % of trade union members	As % of employees
1928	21,995	1,391	8.4	6.3
1929	22,418	1,899	13.1	8.5
1930	21,916	3,076	22.2	14.0
1931	20,616	4,520	33.7	21.9
1932	18,711	5,603	43.7	29.9
1933	18,540	4,804	(46.3)[e]	25.9
1934	20,090	2,718		13.5
1935[b]	20,886	2,151		10.3
1936	21,507	1,593		7.4
1937	22,347	912		4.1
1938	23,222	429		1.9
1939	24,372	119		0.5
1940	28,592[c]	52		0.2

[a] Based on the figures of all members of statutory, miners' and seafarers' sickness insurance schemes.
[b] Including the Saar Region but without Saar mining workforce.
[c] Excluding (annexed) eastern territories.
[d] Unofficially calculated figures of the wholly unemployed for 1928 based partly on estimates of benefit payments. From 1929 official figures of the Reich Office.
[e] Calculated from the first half-yearly figures.

Source: Dietmar Petzina et al. (eds), *Sozialgeschichtliches Arbeitsbuch*. vol. 31, *Materialien zur Statistik des Deutschen Reiches 1914–1945* (Munich, 1987), pp. 119ff.

particularly promising. Thus the success of Nazi economic policy, which found expression – to the tune of 1.5 billion Reichsmarks – in the so-called Reinhardt Programme and a hastily enacted second Law for the Reduction of Unemployment, did not rest alone on the size of the injections of capital. But there was something extra in the therapy which differed fundamentally from what had come before: the populist manner in which it was presented. State funds were not simply given out; great care was taken to ensure that this was given due recognition. Instead of simply hoping that the monies would have an effect, they were accompanied by a campaign to influence opinion. Henceforth, propaganda formed a genuine component of economic and social policy. What could be better suited to a political movement which was intent on conquering people's consciousness, their very 'hearts'?

The legendary example of this was the building of the *Reichsautobahn* which began with great public ado in the late summer of 1933, having been prepared by semi-private enterprises since the mid-1920s. The pictures of Hitler turning the first sod and columns of workers with their spades marching to the job conveyed the optimistic and suggestive image of a forward-looking 'Führer', who was prepared to knuckle down and who was 'taking the unemployed off the streets' in order to have them build a mighty network of wide motorways without which a modern Germany could not survive. The 'Battle for Jobs' (*Arbeitsschlacht*) raged not just along the stretches of motorway being built under the supervision of Fritz Todt, the new 'Inspector-General for the German Road System', later to be manager of the creation of the western defence wall (the 'Siegfried Line'), but also in the illustrated magazines and weekly newsreels. On the building sites of the first Nazi projects, for example for the 'House of German Art' in Munich, symbolism and media-sensitive preparation were at least as effective as the project itself.

The so-called *Ehestandsdarlehen* (government loans to young married couples), introduced within the framework of the Reinhardt Programme, also possessed enormous propaganda value. Over half a million young couples applied for this interest-free subsidy towards the furnishing of a new home (a maximum of 1,000 Reichsmarks) in the first two years; in 1933 alone, there were 200,000 more marriages than in the previous year, and more than half of all newly-wed couples drew the allowance. What was on offer had the main aim of removing women from the labour market; it was therefore linked to a obligation on the woman to abandon her career. A secondary aim which justified the continuation of the programme even during the period of full employment, although now without the requirement of leaving one's profession, was the promotion of the birth rate: the debt could be 'babied-off'; with each newborn child the married couple was relieved of a quarter of the loan.

The introduction of general compulsory military service and a six-month compulsory labour service contributed to the aim of defeating unemployment even more than the Nazi economic programme, which demanded labour-intensive manual work instead of the use of machines. But it also contributed to ideological-political aims which were themselves contradictory: motorway construction (done, like swamp drainage, by pick and shovel), in any case hard to reconcile ideologically with romantic agrarian notions, offered temporary improvements in employment opportunities, but was no genuine alternative for an industrial society whose productive capacity was to be massively strengthened in the coming years. The Nazi model of the happily fecund mother at the domestic hearth could also only be given priority so long as the primacy of rearmament did not demand the exhaustion of all reserves of labour power.

After the 'Gleichschaltung' and the stabilization of the economy at the very latest, 'making Germany fit to fight' and preparation for war had absolute economic priority. Where general reactionary-utopian remnants of Nazi ideology still remained an economic barrier to its unique racist-imperialist plans, they were swept aside.

Since 1934–5 a rapidly growing proportion of state expenditure had flowed into rearmament. Each year, arms and the armed forces swallowed up more while other sectors registered only limited increases. The building of social housing, for example, which was the subject of such emphatic propaganda, even experienced a drastic decrease in comparison with the good years of the Weimar Republic. In 1934 the Wehrmacht laid claim to 18 per cent of all expenditure in the public budget; by 1938 this had already increased to 58 per cent (more than a fifth of national income).[2] The massive expenditure was financed mainly by the *Mefo*-bill, invented by the Reichsbank president, Hjalmar Schacht. To this end, Krupp, Siemens, Rheinmetall and the Gutehoffnungshütte steel company founded a 'Metallurgical Research Society' (Metallurgische Forschungsgemeinschaft – *Mefo*), whose bills of exchange were discounted by the Reichsbank. The state discreetly borrowed approximately 12 billion Reichsmarks before Treasury regulations and tax certificates replaced the bill in 1938. Meanwhile Schacht, though without success, was opposing the economic course, which had long ceased really to support the economy but was instead bound for inflation or a war of conquest. In this respect the financial director of rearmament was experiencing nothing different in his field than most of the 'conservative specialists' in the cabinet. In November 1937 Schacht resigned as Reich Economics Minister; just over a year later he also relinquished his post as Reichsbank president, though he remained a member of the government until 1943.

The point of potential conflict in the alliance between business and the Nazi leadership was, from the beginning, the primacy of ideology and politics, on which the regime tolerated no restrictions. Because of its function as a locomotive for the economy, the policy of rearmament met with almost unanimous approval in business circles. However, for the no less ideologically and politically motivated and consistently pursued policy of autarky which accompanied it, this was only partially true. Although the Economics Minister had succeeded, in autumn 1934, in erecting comprehensive controls on foreign trade (the 'New Plan') in order to overcome the acute foreign exchange problem, a year later the situation only worsened again. Not just bad harvests and rising world market prices, but also the ineffective market regulation policies of the Reich Food Estate, contributed to the difficulties in supplying food, a problem which Schacht repeatedly brought into the conflict with Darré. The beneficiary of the 'fats crisis' was Goering, whom Hitler appointed 'Commissioner for all Questions Concerning Foreign Exchange and Raw Materials', in April 1936.[3]

It was becoming ever more clear that the politically demanded and energetically pursued simultaneity of full-scale rearmament and autarky was leading to economic problems which could hardly be solved by the methods of private capitalism. In the period of full employment private consumer needs grew, but productive capacity was fully burdened with the production of ordnance goods. Despite considerable successes, the results of the 'battle for production' on the agricultural front could not keep pace with rising consumer demand. Projects which were unprofitable but central to the policy of autarky – amongst them ore extraction and steel production in the Hermann Goering Works in Salzgitter and, following the 'benzine contract' concluded with IG Farben at the end of 1933, the development of synthetic fuel – made total economic resources even scarcer without releasing sufficient foreign exchange for other purposes.

In the midst of this crisis, Hitler announced the Four-Year Plan at the 'Party Congress of Honour' held in Nuremberg on 9 September 1936. The chosen course was to be secured at any price. For, as the 'Führer' had himself written in a secret memo, in four years the economy had to be 'ready for war' and the Wehrmacht 'ready for action'. What developed in the following years as a result of these premises was a state command economy with private participation in the decision-making process. Private ownership was not affected and the Plan impacted on employers' power of disposal in sectors important for the policies of autarky and rearmament only to a limited extent, for it was the managers of industry who occupied the state management offices.[4]

Through strengthened planning and direction the Four-Year Plan was supposed to overcome the crisis and, at the same time, accelerate the production of synthetic substitutes and raw materials more decisively than before. This was in clear contradiction to Schacht's concept of a supra-national economy which would dominate south-east Europe but still be market-oriented, and went far beyond the control of foreign trade. The traditional economic bureaucracy had neither the organization nor the personnel for such tasks. Hitler reacted in typical fashion. He appointed

Goering as his 'Commissioner for the Four-Year Plan', and the latter first of all established new special offices, so called 'business groups', for raw materials, foreign exchange, deployment of labour, agricultural production and price control. Besides this there appeared a General Council of the Four-Year Plan. With additional general plenipotentiaries for the individual areas of production – who, in future, could be absorbed into the management system as required – any remaining illusions about a proper demarcation between the state administration and private business were finally dispelled. The aim was the closest possible alignment between the regime and big business. This was particularly clearly expressed by the increasing number of industrial managers who, without being removed from the payrolls of their companies, occupied important posts in the Four-Year Plan Organization alongside Wehrmacht officers.

The most blatant example of the increasing interlacing of politics and the economy was the appointment, in 1938, of Carl Krauch as 'General Plenipotentiary for Chemicals'. Krauch was not only the scientific expert for petrol and *Buna* synthetic rubber – the twin pillars of chemical synthetics production – but also a member of the board of IG Farben. This chemist had already proved his organizational qualities as an adviser in Goering's Aviation Ministry during the conclusion of the 'benzine contract'. Now he saw to it that the Four-Year Plan was effectively turned into an IG Plan. From 1940, Krauch even combined the most important tasks of state direction of the chemical industry with his position as chair of the board of directors of IG Farben. Thanks to a quasi-monopoly in central areas of production and Krauch's own energy, the company succeeded in extensively 'privatizing' a good part of the economic policy of the Third Reich. This trend was certainly less unique than it might appear in relation to the specifically Nazi policies of autarky and rearmament: the strengthened direct cooperation between big business and the state was also a result of the collapse of the liberal world economic order at the end of the 1920s and the worldwide rise of the trusts.

Despite remarkable results in some sectors, the lofty aims of the Four-Year Plan were not achieved. The announcement of a 'New Production Plan for the Defence Economy', which further narrowed the production pallet in favour of ordnance goods, made that clear. Less obvious were the distortions in the wider economy and the social costs of the arms economy, which the regime – with considerable success – vigorously endeavoured to conceal.

Agricultural policy was an example of this. Through its 'blood and soil' propaganda the regime had increased the ideological value of the peasants and via the Reich Food Estate[5] it had bound them to the 'national community'. It is true that the peasant population was not pleased with the accompanying bureaucratization, but the fact that, for the first time, they now experienced the permanent attention of the political system led to a change in their social (self-)esteem. But the rigid state pricing policy did nothing to reduce the unsatisfactory burdens, particularly on smaller and middle-sized farms.[6] And basically it was the peasants who were the first to feel the downside of the Nazi 'economic miracle', because from year to year the 'battle for production' had to be fought with less labour power. Up until the beginning of the war agriculture lost approximately 1.4 million people who took up better-paid jobs in industry, especially in the arms sector. The notorious lack of agricultural labour, which the regime sought to counter with the introduction of young people (Hitler Youth Land Service, Harvest Help, the Land Year) instead of with decisive mechanization, rationalization and land reform, was a source of discontent for years and only began to abate when prisoners of war and foreign forced labour could finally be brought in.

As in many sectors, National Socialism also seemed to effect in the countryside the exact opposite of what had been its original ideological intentions, and seems to have followed an international trend to a policy of regulating the market far more than is often believed.[7] The end result of Nazi agricultural policy was not the self-confident and independent 'free peasant farmer' who served the good of the 'national community', as artists faithful to the regime were wont to portray on canvas, but an agricultural producer caught in a web of regulations concerning cultivation, prices and guaranteed sales. Instead of the establishment of new farms there was a massive flight from the land. Peasant Teutons, supposedly so true to the soil, were rushing into the metropolitan conurbations.

The workers and the 'national community'

During the pre-war boom, established socio-economic and demographic trends continued in defiance of the rhetoric of the Nazi *Weltanschauung* and, to an extent, became even stronger. This was precisely the case for the largest group amongst the population – the working class. During the period of full employment, an unclear mixture of the deprivation of their civil rights, retention of substantial benefits from the Weimar welfare state and the new activism of the DAF on questions of social policy produced noteworthy changes in the worker as a social type. It seems that there was an acceleration in the trends towards socio-cultural levelling, which were also recognizable in other western industrial nations and which were moving in the direction of a consumption-oriented mass society.

The specifically Nazi impetus for this development had been supplied by the destruction of the political organizations of the labour movement, which also entailed a weakening of its social milieu. But it was only the onset of the economic upswing which provided the material basis for the ideological counter-pressure of the 'national community'. The disintegration of traditional structures of solidarity now advanced apace. Even steadfast old Social Democrats who saw through the rearmament policy and voiced their criticisms in the company of trusted comrades were less and less able to avoid the general enthusiasm for the speed and thoroughness with which the regime was reducing unemployment. The regaining of secure existence soon weighed more heavily than the preceding loss of political rights, even if further intrusions were to follow – for example, the introduction in 1935 of the 'work book', which restricted the freedom to choose a job and made possible the state control of the 'deployment of labour'.

Many were aware that the economic miracle was not being accompanied by widespread prosperity but rather by a slow readjustment to the standard of living of the period before the great crash. But there were only isolated stirrings of protest. The Germans were used to spreading their rye bread with margarine and four-fruit jam rather than with butter and sausage. In comparison with the English, French and Americans they ate more simply, even in the 'good' years of the pre-war period, but always as much as they wanted. Nobody had to go hungry any more. On the other hand, luxury articles or even things which just made life a little more comfortable remained scarce. Not that the Germans lacked purchasing power; it was simply that too few consumer goods were being produced. The regime was saving (or more precisely, investing) for war and was keeping the people short. It is true that from 1936 real hourly wages began to rise and two years later had reached the 1929 level (see table 3).[8] On the other hand it was not until 1941–2 that real net weekly earnings reached the 1929 level, and this took account not only of longer working hours but also of the increasing 'voluntary' deductions from gross wages for the DAF, Winter Aid and, during the war, for the compulsory saving scheme *Eisernes Sparen*. From then on they began to fall again. And if, at the beginning of the 1930s, business had complained about an excessive wage ratio, now it could be content: wages as a proportion of the national income fell continually from 1934–5 onwards.

Of course, the abolition of free collective bargaining and decentralized wage-fixing by the Trustees of Labour could not prevent wage increases during a boom. When, in 1939, the pace of rearmament was consequently in serious danger of slowing, the regime imposed a general wage-freeze. Yet even after this wages continued to rise, if not universally then via

Table 3 Gross earnings in the German Reich 1928–1944[a]

Annual average	Gross earnings				Cost of living
	Nominal		Real		
	hourly	weekly	hourly	weekly	
1928	122.9	124.5	100.9	102.2	121.8
1929	129.5	128.2	104.7	103.6	123.7
1930	125.8	118.1	105.7	99.2	119
1931	116.3	103.9	106.4	95.1	109.3
1932	97.3	85.8	100.7	88.5	96.9
1933	94.6	87.7	99.8	92.5	94.8
1934	97.0	94.1	99.7	96.7	97.3
1935	98.4	96.4	99.6	97.6	98.8
1936	100	100	100	100	100
1937	102.1	103.5	101.6	103.0	100.5
1938	105.6	108.5	104.7	107.5	100.9
1939	108.6	112.6	107.2	111.1	101.4
1940	111.2	116.0	106.4	111.0	104.5
1941	116.4	123.6	109.2	115.5	107.0
1942	118.2	124.3	108.6	113.3	109.7
1943	119.1	124.9	107.0	112.2	111.2
1944	118.9	123.4	104.7	108.6	113.6

[a] Based on the results of the official survey of wages and the official information on the cost of living, 1936 = 100; from 1938 including Austria, from 1942 also the Sudetenland and the incorporated eastern territories.

Source: Tilla Siegel, 'Lohnpolitik im nationalsozialistischen Deutschland,' in Carola Sachse et al., *Angst, Belohnung, Zucht und Ordnung. Herrschaftsmechanismen im Nationalsozialismus* (Opladen, 1982), p. 104.

productivity bonuses, which were paid especially in those sectors which were of military importance.[9]

There was method in what seemed, at first glance, only a means of avoiding the official wage-freeze: piece-work bonuses and such-like served to increase productivity and made it possible to differentiate more acutely both between individual workers and between specific groups according to their qualifications and importance. A finer gradation of wage groups and an ingenious system of assessing the value of individual jobs kept the total wages bill low and at the same time created effective incentives to higher productivity. Even with limited additional recruitment of labour a company could thus achieve considerable increases in productivity – and strengthen the conviction amongst the workforce that hard work was always rewarded. While the universal wage-freeze appeared to bear out the egalitarian propaganda of the 'national community', the failure to observe it in individual cases which were justified by reference to performance seemed to prove that society was open to upward social mobility. Certainly the Nazi slogan 'labour ennobles' was only rarely met with the response 'we'll remain commoners, thanks very much'. It was precisely young workers, who were less tied into the structures of paternalistic-proletarian solidarity, who took the sparingly offered chances of advancement seriously, as a possibility to break away from predetermined, class-related routes through life and work.

'Make way for the hard-working' was the corresponding, apparently quite non-political motto, and this was suitably concretized by the 'Reich Vocational Contest' (1.8 million participants in 1937)[10] run by the Reich Youth Leadership. Such early signs of a more strongly individualist orientation to performance led to a weakening of solidarity across a broad front which was to become more or less typical for West Germany's postwar society.[11]

Nazi glorification of the performance ethos corresponded to the requirements of a war economy – already begun in peacetime – just as much as to the unswervingly propagated ideas of Social Darwinism. By undermining solidarity it served to keep the workforce politically quiet and at the same time to transform Germany into a vast workshop. If, seen as a whole, this succeeded, then it was also because the Nazis understood how to remove from many people's minds the link between material circumstances and social consciousness emphasized by the old labour movement. Of course there was slackness and carelessness at work and absenteeism on the pretext of pretended sickness,[12] but to what extent this was an expression of political discontent and not primarily a result of the enormous pressure to perform is hard to say. In any case, taken overall, collective protest remained the exception. The Third Reich could thank not only the permanent threat embodied by the Gestapo, but also its own systematic efforts to uncouple wages from status, for the fact that on the whole a surprising tranquillity reigned on the social front.[13] In a manner that was deeply frustrating to its opponents, the regime demonstrated that people did not live by bread alone and that loyalty could be won by other means than a timely increase in basic wages.

The social policy of the consolidated Nazi regime was neither simply reactionary nor purely rhetorical and it was also more than just a carefully calculated means of totalitarian manipulation. Even if the early activism of the DAF on social policy issues had been motivated by considerations of power politics,[14] this developed into a social policy which was substantial and, in parts, even progressive.

Not all the terminology aimed at awakening a psychological association with a (false) idyll was hollow propaganda. The DAF bureau 'Beauty of Labour' (*Schönheit der Arbeit*), did indeed concern itself with the almost proverbial geraniums on the factory window-sill, but the Labour Front was also involved in the increased application of modern methods and knowledge of labour science already being practised by large companies. No doubt, industrial safety and industrial medicine indirectly served the interests of industry, which sought, during the period of full employment, to gild the cage of corporatism in which its workforce was held. But of course facilitation of work processes and improvements in industrial hygiene, often originating in suggestions by members of the company staff, also benefited the workers. And this was quite obviously the case for newly installed recreation rooms, canteens and sports facilities owned by the company. Precisely because almost nothing could be done about wages, non-pecuniary benefits were of particular importance. Leave entitlements, which rose during the Nazi period from an average of three to between six and twelve days, were an achievement even in international terms.

The social-political activism of the DAF was also peculiar in so far as it sprang from several, sometimes conflicting, motives. Even the annual 'Production Contest of German Firms', in which the supreme macro-economic goal of increasing production seemed to be the central issue, served at least two further purposes: it furnished the DAF with internal information about companies, and thus with possibilities for exerting influence; and its presentation in the style of a sports event fostered a team spirit within the companies themselves. Socio-psychological, and in the broadest sense social-medical considerations, informed the concrete policies of the Labour Front at least as much as its political and ideological aims and its intention to contribute to the optimizing of economic performance. A combination of all of these was symbolized, in a fairly successful way, by 'Strength through Joy' (Kraft durch Freude – KdF), the leisure organization of the DAF.

The KdF entered the consciousness of the *Volksgenossen* above all as an unbeatably cheap travel agency.[15] From 1934 onwards its ocean liners cruised between Madeira and the Norwegian fjords and on deck the German worker basked in the sun – at least, according to the propaganda. In reality it was overwhelmingly the middle classes who were on board, while average working-class families went for a week to the Bavarian forest or to the North Sea coast, which were somewhat more moderately priced. None the less, by 1939 over seven million Germans had been on holiday with the KdF (and there were an additional 35 million day-trippers); they could not all be 'Party big-wigs', as malicious gossips and depressed Social Democrats were claiming.

The regime was not in the least inhibited about exploiting its popularity as a travel entrepreneur. The popular success encouraged the Labour Front continually to develop new attractions to keep the *Volksgenossen* in good spirits. Those activities pointedly aimed at shaking class privilege: tennis and riding courses, theatre evenings, dances, adult education programmes, company sports festivals and workforce parties may have seemed parochial and frowsty to the critical outside observer. However, accompanied by permanent 'national community' propaganda they were not without effect. A commentator from the SPD in exile in Prague stated self-critically: 'The experience of the last few years has unfortunately taught us that the narrow-minded and philistine tendencies of a section of the workers are greater than we previously wished to accept.'[16] By this juncture in September 1937, the mammoth DAF/KdF organization had long offered almost all-embracing possibilities for leisure activities in which, in purely statistical terms, every adult German participated once a year.

Of course, most of the aspirations awakened at this time were only satisfied by the economic miracle of the post-Second World War period. But the mass tourism which erupted in the 1950s was first practised to some degree in the 1930s; though the 'KdF-car', to whose construction Hitler had personally given some thought, did not roll off the production line until after the war – as the Volkswagen 'Beetle'. But the anticipation of a cheap people's motor car induced 336,000 people to pay weekly instalments in advance to the DAF, which used the money to build from scratch the production plant (and town) of Wolfsburg, though only jeeps for the Wehrmacht were then built there. Using the population to finance popular projects was a basic idea of the hullabaloo of Nazi social policy: it was not to cost a penny – at least, not to the state, which had long been pumping all resources that could be cobbled together into rearmament.

One of the most noteworthy successes of Nazi social and societal policy was the spread of a sense of social equality. Where the erosion of differences of rank and status were consistently and consciously pursued, even modest signs of 'mass consumption' could qualify as indicators of a rosy future. In an atmosphere such as this, the hopes of building society investors and aspiring car-owners could, like the image of steamer trips to Salazar's Portugal, be multiplied by means of propaganda.

During the last of the pre-war years everything undoubtedly went better economically than before the 'seizure of power', but the official virtues praised by government still remained those of thrift and forgoing consumer goods. It was all the easier to comply when 'hard workers' could now and then 'afford a little something'. If directors and workers ate their pea soup together on 'one-pot Sundays' and Goebbels turned this into a celebrity spectacle in Berlin, then it was a showpiece of Nazi 'education of the people'. The messages that these events carried were that the 'national community' existed and everyone was taking part; that class distinctions were less important than 'good will'; and that material modesty bore witness to 'national solidarity'.

Perhaps these regular simple meals also conserved economic resources a little, but far more important for the regime was their socio-psychological effect. They suggested a collective readiness for sacrifice which found expression not least in the slogans of the National Socialist People's Welfare Organization (Nationalsozialistische Volkswohlfahrt – NSV) and the Winter Aid Scheme (Winterhilfswerk – WHW).[17] 'A people helping itself' was the defiantly determined motto of one of the first of countless collection drives. The 2.5 billion Reichsmarks begged up to 1939 was certainly a tidy sum, and one which made the NSV into an important factor in the economy and a major employer, above all in the realm of health care (with its 'NSV nurses'). But even more important in socio-political terms were its millions of voluntary helpers and approximately 16 million members (1942). Even if the interminable door to door collections and deductions from wages – and refusing to contribute could result in thoroughly unpleasant consequences – may have caused annoyance and 'donation fatigue', the mass participation and the enormous sums collected from donations could be interpreted as proof of the reality of the 'national community'. Certainly it required ceaseless mobilization, but where this succeeded the 'national community' was more than just a myth.

It was in the nature of the system of rule that the idea of the 'national community', like the 'Führer'-nimbus, was sustained by its constant actualization. Symbolic declarations of loyalty had to be constantly demanded and delivered. This was the function of the official 'Heil Hitler', but also of the frequent public events with which the Party continuously forced the 'national comrades' to recognize and acknowledge anew that they belonged to the *Volksgemeinschaft*.

Ideological mobilization

A marked tendency to stage itself as if Germany were a vast theatre lent the Third Reich certain theocratic traits. Marches, colour-parades and torch-light processions, in which brown shirts and swastikas formed the unmistakeable distinguishing surface characteristics, had already given the 'movement' a unique identity during the Weimar period. The stylized image corresponded to a particular consciousness which distinguished the Nazis – and not only in their own minds – from the 'normal' political parties: they wanted to be a community bound by a common ideology and by struggle much more than a political interest group. This pretension explains the later attempts at quasi-religious presentation.

The regime developed what was nothing short of its own liturgy.[18] The first date in the Nazi calendar was 30 January. Every year, on the evening of the 'seizure of power', thousands of Stormtroopers marched through the Brandenburg Gate in Berlin. At the end of February there followed the 'Party Festival in Remembrance of the Announcement of the 25 Point Programme of the NSDAP', in March 'Heroes' Remembrance Day' and the entry, stylized as the 'commitment of youth' of fourteen-year-olds into the Hitler Youth (Hitler-Jugend – HJ) and the League of German Maidens (Bund Deutscher Mädel – BDM). The birthday of the 'Führer', celebrated in imperial tradition on 20 April, was followed by the newly work-free May Day holiday and the ideologically revalued Mothers' Day. The summer and winter solstices in June and December were expressions of the Teutonic cult, although there was certainly never any success outside the SS 'Order' in replacing Christmas with 'Yuletide'. The greatest organizational and choreographic efforts were, without doubt, dedicated to the Reich Party congresses which took place in September in the vast space created in Nuremberg by Albert Speer. The harvest festival at the beginning of October on the Bückeberg in Westphalia was a mass spectacle specifically aimed at agrarian Germany. The conclusion and, in the opinion of the Party, the climax of the festival year was 9 November, on which Hitler and the cream of the NSDAP remembered the 'fallen' of the failed Munich beer-hall putsch of 1923. The lurid and eerie climax of this cult of the dead was the 'Führer's' lonely walk to one of the open temples and his pause before the sarcophagi of the sixteen 'martyrs of the movement'.

The great number of such staged events were aimed at more than just an outward *mise en scène* of public life. Apart from demonstrating the political and structural union of Party and state (the 'becoming one' or *Ineinswerdung*), they were also aimed at binding ideologically both individuals and whole groups of the population and thus, in the final analysis, at cultural hegemony. If the regular festivals of remembrance already seemed more like cult activities than political events, there were also occasions which were intentionally conceived as substitutes for religion. But they did not develop into a serious competition to the

Christian Churches. The 'life' and 'morning festivals' commended to 'believing' Nazis as alternatives respectively to Church baptisms, weddings and funerals, and devotions and Sunday services, remained a peripheral phenomenon – just like their persistent propagandist, the uninfluential 'chief ideologue' and 'Führer's Commissioner for the Supervision of the General Spiritual and Ideological Education and Training of the NSDAP', Alfred Rosenberg.[19] The attempts, supported by Himmler's SS, to form a link with supposed 'old Teutonic' traditions were criticized by both Churches as 'new heathenism'. Outside fanatical circles they were met with widespread indifference and – depending on people's courage – with mild to biting derision.

This cannot be claimed for the regime's endeavours in indoctrination in general. Youth in particular was able to offer little resistance to Nazi demands and impositions. In April 1933, with the forceful takeover of the Reich Committee of German Youth Associations, the Nazi Youth Leader Baldur von Schirach had already created the preconditions for the building of a state youth organization and Hitler rewarded him with the title of 'Reich Youth Leader'. This did not yet mean a Nazi monopoly over the organization of youth, but the Hitler Youth became increasingly attractive.[20] Above all in rural areas in which hitherto youth had been poorly organized (if at all), and wherever the binding power of Church youth associations had weakened, the state-supported HJ registered a rapid increase in membership. In spring 1934, the Protestant youth organizations joined it, and when in December 1936 the HJ was legally declared the state youth organization there existed alongside it only remnants of the Catholic youth groups (which were coming under increasing attack depite the Concordat and were soon to be banned altogether) and the Jewish youth groups. From 1936 onwards, the pressure on youngsters who refused to join the HJ greatly increased, but it was not until March 1939 that implementation orders relating to the Law on the Hitler Youth made 'youth service duty' obligatory. By this time the HJ had already lost a large part of its original attraction.

At first, the Nazi youth organization had tended to latch on to the – ideologically related – models of such youth associations as the Bündische Jugend and the Wandervogel and seemed to 'adopt' their idealism and spontaneity, whilst simultaneously placing the youth movement on a broader social basis. But out of it had grown an instrument of totalitarian imposition and indoctrination. Whereas, at first, mottos such as 'youth leads youth' and 'the younger generation awakens' had stirred hopes of emancipation, in a period of increasing paramilitary drills and consistent application of the principle of leader and followers disillusion spread. Instead of holiday camps and the romanticism of the Boy Scouts, the list of duties included 'martial sports', ideological training, Winter Aid and scrap material collections and, in summer, work on the harvest.

Young people reacted in differing ways to the demands and regimentation. While the activism of the Hitler Youth was seen – particularly in the provinces and above all by girls – as a chance to escape from sheltered boredom and parental control, many children in the big cities regarded their duties in the state youth organization to be a restriction of their right to spend their afternoons as they wished. Whether the HJ was seen as free space or as a penance also depended a great deal on the age of the young people, their class background and their previous socialization. Someone who had experienced the enmity of the Hitler Youth as a member of a Catholic youth association or of the socialist Workers' Youth (Arbeiterjugend) reacted on average differently from the ten-year-old from a nationalist, Protestant, petit-bourgeois family who had performed his duty until he was fourteen as a *'Pimpf'* in the *Jungvolk*, then in the Hitler Youth, entered the Labour Service at eighteen and finally went into the Wehrmacht. It was hardly to be expected that the latter would one day find himself in one of those youth cliques which arose towards the end of the 1930s, above all in the metropolitan conurbations, as an expression both of protest against cultural tutelage and of political opposition. What linked the bourgeois 'Swing kids', encountered primarily in Hamburg, with the Leipzig 'Hounds' who were at home in the proletarian milieu, the Munich 'Crew' and the 'Edelweiss Pirates' of the Ruhr region, was their refusal to surrender the modest remnants of youthful nonconformity and to join the ranks of the Hitler Youth, which disregarded every need for self-determination and individuality.[21]

However, the totalitarian demands of the Hitler Youth also, ironically, produced new free space. This was especially true in the educational sphere. The competition between school and the HJ became increasingly acute as it became clearer that the incursion of the Hitler Youth into the school system was not succeeding. This occasionally opened up the possibility of playing off one institution against the other. With a degree of skill it was possible to avoid disagreeable obligations at school by refering to duties in the HJ – and vice versa. In the burgeoning labyrinth of compulsory duties, meetings and 'official business', secret paths and bypasses were uncovered and whosoever trod them trained him- or herself to scrape through in a pragmatic and self-protective fashion.

While drill and obeying orders probably represented the central experience of the HJ for the majority of youth, the extensive organization offered a plethora of posts, both major and minor, and with them chances for individual self-assertion. In the Hitler Youth even youngsters from average or underprivileged homes could 'become something' and thereby develop a self-confidence that had hitherto been denied them. The brazen-faced tone and loud-mouthed behaviour of a whole generation of pupils, about which teachers complained increasingly often, was the price to be paid for the ideological, propagandistic glorification of youth.

The extraordinary respect enjoyed (for obvious reasons) by a discipline such as sport (which was, if anything, rather peripheral in the humanist education system), the encouragement of a new, anti-intellectual awareness of the body, the glorification of combative 'bearing' and the mentality of 'straightforward decisions' – all these had at least as much effect in altering the atmosphere in the schools as the more or less consistent ideological revision of textbooks and syllabuses,[22] which, despite some spectacular exceptions, remained within the framework of the overall attempt at indoctrination. More symptomatic of Nazi education policy than the teachings on race and eugenic hygiene in the guise of arithmetical exercises was, in the final analysis, the fact that although the grammar schools were not abolished, new value-concepts which demanded an equalization of the general education system and the establishment of the elite ideology schools were pitted against Humboldtian educational traditions.

Such a levelling was the aim of the abolition of the religious *Volksschulen* (the combined primary and secondary schools) and the ecclesiastical teacher training institutions, which began in 1935–6 against stubborn resistance, especially from the Catholic Church. At the same time the purpose of the closures was to roll back the influence of the Churches, and this intention did not meet with complete rejection in every quarter; a least part of the teaching body also saw it as a struggle for their social emancipation from clerical tutelage.[23] And the endeavours to unify the school system, just like the greater encouragement of technical knowledge, undoubtedly had the argument of modernity on their side.

The Nazi claim of a 'revolution in education' was represented – even more than by the thirty-five 'Nationalist Political Educational Institutes' (Nationalpolitische Erziehungsanstalten – *Napolas*), which operated in the form of state boarding schools – by the 'Adolf-Hitler Schools', which eventually numbered twelve. Schirach's Reich Youth Leadership laid claim to the supervision of these institutions, which were directed by Hitler Youth leaders, but without being able to enforce a compulsory curriculum and methodology; there was clarity about little other than the specific encouragement of athletic performance and 'endurance tests'. The inability ever to define the content of 'ideological training' was an expression both of the power struggles within the Party and of the inconsistency of Nazi ideology. Just like the three 'Castles of the Order' (*Ordensburgen*) which were established to educate young Party functionaries (and funded just as they were by the DAF), the claim of the 'Adolf-Hitler Schools' to be systematically 'sifting out leaders' was unjustified. The SS went even further than the rival Party bodies in its attempt to create the Nazi 'new man'. In Himmler's elite order the educational demands were, of course, more clearly linked with racial selection, at the end of which stood the 'weeding out' and selective breeding of human beings.

In the second half of the 1930s the omnipresence of the Party in the form of its mass organizations undoubtedly informed the political climate in society to a greater extent than the lunatic, anti-human vision of a *völkische* new order promoted in the elitist circles of the SS. Despite many endeavours to follow the establishment of political power with a corresponding ideological nazification, the success of training for this purpose – which extended far beyond youth alone – was limited. Apart from Party functionaries, and to a lesser extent ordinary members, only specific professional groups were affected with any intensity, amongst them teachers, aspirant university lecturers and (in Prussia) lawyers between their first and higher examinations, who had to attend 'ideology camps'. The development of the power of indoctrination remained modest in comparison with the mighty organizational potential of the NSDAP and its subsidiary organizations. All the activism of the proliferating Party apparatus, the Party organizations (SA, SS, HJ, Nazi Women's League, Nazi Students and Nazi Lecturers Leagues, Nazi Drivers' Corps) and the connected associations (DAF, NSV, Nazi Leagues of Physicians, Teachers, Lawyers and Civil Servants, the Nazi League of German Technology and the Nazi War Victims' Welfare) could do nothing to alter this.

The fact that, as the years passed, it was almost impossible for a German *Volksgenosse* not to be caught in some organizational way by the Nazi Party juggernaut did, however, bring about tangible changes in the composition of society. By purposely extending the Party's institutional network into the traditionally 'pre-political arena', it succeeded in mobilizing people to a hitherto unknown degree. The Nazis constantly emphasized the need to establish their rule firmly in people's minds. Viewed from this standpoint it was, in the first instance, rather immaterial whether the mobilization took place as a result of collective reception of one of the 'Führer's' speeches on the radio, or via active membership in subsidiary organizations – which accommodated apolitical interests – like the Nazi Drivers' Corps and the Nazi Community of Culture or via loyal activity as a residential block-leader of the NSDAP. The aim of demonstrating the omnipresence of the Party and of underpinning its claim to total power was served by every form of participation.

But the organizational extension and enlargement which resulted could not, in the long term, leave the Nazi Party unaltered. Signs of embourgeoisement were growing in the once dynamic and virulent protest movement. In the last years of the Weimar Republic a concen trated fighting force had already become a tendentially bureaucratic mass organization. The transformation into the sole political party had reinforced this trend. In 1935, working for the Party leadership in Munich alone, there were approximately 1,600 administrative employees in no fewer than 44 buildings, and altogether 25,000 people were receiving a good salary from the NSDAP.[24]

The still unclarified relationship between Party and state was perceived amongst functionaries as an encouragement to personal unions, accu- mulation of official posts and personal enrichment. But neither a solid political leadership cadre nor even a Nazi *politburo* developed; both the ideological preconditions and those relating to the structure of power were lacking. The inconsistency of the Nazi *Weltanschauung* made it impossible to refer to 'pure doctrine' and hindered the emergence of dogmatic authority. But what was decisive was the inviolability of the Führer-principle, which was valid even at the very lowest level of the Party Organization (PO). This form of organization, which had defeated scorned democracy but not the possibility of self-assertion through polit- ical activity and the exercise of power, was of enormous importance for the functioning of the vast network of command: on countless thousands of honorary officials fell a drop of the Führer's' power, a tiny shaft of light from his glory.

By 1937 the Party hierarchy – from the Reichsleiter via the leaders of the regions, districts, local groups and cells down to the block leaders – numbered some 700,000 persons, not including the officials of the sub- sidiary organizations. The war saw no fewer than two million 'little Hitlers' in the German Reich.[25]

The consequent intermeshing of personnel in the Party and the state was not the same at all levels. By no means all the *Parteigenossen* at the head of ministries also held correspondingly high-ranking positions within the Party. Goebbels, who combined his ministerial responsibility for propaganda with the position of Reich Propaganda Leader of the NSDAP, was, in this respect, a special case; not even the Reich Minister for Aviation and Prussian Minister President, Goering, although he was already chasing after the insignia of office as he was later to chase after art treasures in the occupied territories, could (or wanted to) come up with anything comparable. On the contrary, a whole string of important and influential Party figures had to manage without an commensurate office of state, amongst them many Gauleiter.

The interlacing of Party and state was strongest at local authority level, where district and local group leaders (Kreisleiter and Ortsgruppenleiter) increasingly often also occupied the mayoral posts. After two years of Nazi rule, about half of all local authority posts were occupied with *Alt-Pgs* ('Old Party Comrades' – *Alt-Parteigenossen*), that is, those who had joined the Party before 30 January 1933. It was not much different in the state sector: in 1937, 86 per cent of Prussian civil servants belonged to the NSDAP, in the rest of Germany 63 per cent; though the figure of 'Old Party Comrades' was, at 11 per cent, appreciably lower in the rest of the Reich than in Prussia, where it stood at 48 per cent.

The continuous emergence of new, special bureaucracies in the sphere of Party dominance was no less important for the ongoing alteration of the structures of power than the nazification of the civil service, which often remained superficial. The growing influence of administrative departments 'directly responsible to the Führer' (*führerunmittelbar*) which were active either alongside, or in competition with, state authorities, led to an insidious decline and deformation of traditional government. The struggles between various competencies, so characteristic of the 'Führer State' – and which were by no means always in Hitler's interest – were not least the consequence of a rampant organizational jungle which originated in the sphere of employment and economic policy (Inspector-General for the German Road System, Commissioner for the Four-Year Plan), but which then spread into the area of foreign, social and racial policy.

Of course, such shifts in institutional power usually remained hidden from the population. In everyday life the omnipresence of the Party showed itself in other ways: not only in the claim to political and social control excercised by local 'head officials' (*Amtswalter*) as more or less popular watchdogs and in the overflowing system of confidential personal files, but also in the new social welfare centres ('mothers' advice centres') and in the activism of the DAF in the sphere of social and cultural policy. Despite its omnipresence, the concrete power of the Party remained as limited as the overall balance of constantly reattempted ideological mobilization. Even the 'Führer' could do nothing to change this. It was true that, during the years of continuing (foreign-)political successes, Hitler, with his great public appearances and speeches, was able to engender, again and again, spontaneous enthusiasm and confidence, but this was not associated with a lasting consolidation of his party's prestige. On the contrary, the widespread discontent with the NSDAP and its unpopular 'big-shots' became particularly clear when seen alongside the image of the enthusiastically acclaimed 'Führer'. The reaction to unremitting attempts at indoctrination and ceaseless political demands soon showed itself as more and more people retreated into their private lives in their free time or sought diversion in traditional cultural activity, which had remained largely unaffected.

Culture and everyday life

The mistaken but still widely held belief that German cultural life and contemporaneous trends of popular culture were the subject of radical restructuring in the Third Reich is probably an indication of the stubborn and continuing impact of Nazi self-stylization. Contrary to the impression which a widely established bureaucracy of control and direction tried to create, the regime developed only relatively limited influence in the cultural arena. All the major trends already developing in mass culture either continued during the Nazi period or became even stronger – including those which are commonly held to have amounted to a democratization of access to culture. At the same time, despite the exodus of its Jewish and leftist representatives and the consequent enormous loss of creativity, there was a continuity of development in intellectual-artistic production in many areas. Neither in literature nor music nor in the fine arts did 1933 mark a complete developmental break. Although political circumstances forced many and various interruptions of individual and institutional continuity and to that extent this 'discontinuity' also signified the end of an epoch, it does not coincide with a corresponding division of periods in the history of art.

The limits of the regimentation of cultural activity were at once an expression of calculation, necessity and the unalterable. Goebbels' oft-repeated warnings of the ineffectiveness of excessively obtrusive propaganda and primitive indoctrination bore witness to the functional necessity of ensuring the continuation of a limited range of intellectual-cultural activity and of relatively unchanged fora in publishing. Precisely because of the otherwise very far-reaching uniformity imposed on the mass media, such periodicals and books fulfilled the function of intellectual safety valves or buffer zones. But by no means all of the non-Nazi periodicals and literary works which were able to survive owed their continued appearance to rational calculation on the part of the Nazis. There were also involuntary limits to power, resulting from the poverty of Nazi cultural production, the ambivalence of the Nazi *Weltanschauung* and from antagonisms within the cultural bureaucracy itself. And there was a practical lack of room for manoeuvre: a regime which pursued an all-embracing mobilization of society had to give sufficient consideration to cultural traditions and assets if it did not want to endanger the precondition of its success – the (as ever) graduated loyalty of the great majority of Germans. To this extent the avoidance of a completely consistent penetration and direction of cultural activity was functionally necessary and did not rest with the regime.

There is much to indicate that the Nazis had a sense of the limits of what they could demand of the people and there can be no doubt that the consideration of those limits decisively informed the reality of life and culture during the period.

The non-political free evening was certainly not one of the particular achievements of the Nazi years, but nor, despite propaganda to the contrary, was it abolished. Robert Ley's bumptious assertion that in Germany only sleep remained a private matter[26] perhaps described the intention, but not the reality, of the Third Reich. Even if it was often obscured by ideological rhetoric, there was a sphere that was free of politics, and it was precisely here that the epochal trends continued.

Amongst those aspects of modern mass culture which continued to develop during the Nazi period, and which in comparison to the 1920s were to a certain extent strengthened, was above all the cinema. Even after the great leap in the number of visits to the cinema during the economic crisis at the beginning of the decade, the number of cinema-goers continued to grow uninterrupted throughout the 1930s; in 1942 a billion cinema tickets were sold, four times as many as in 1933.[27] Statistically speaking, during the war every German went to a picture-palace once a month. Certainly, this was partly an expression of a need for entertainment and diversion from the pressing problems of every-day life, but the cinema boom signalled more than just a mass exodus into world of fantasy: the stagnating opportunities for material con-sumption produced a growing demand for leisure-time entertainment, and certain socio-cultural habits were obviously changing. The enthusiasm for the cinema attested not least to the attractiveness of the films on offer. This rested less on the effect than on the omission of specifically Nazi interference.

For the average production of the German film industry 1933 had not represented a turning point. Most of the feature films made in the early years of the Third Reich were no different in ideological and socio-political terms from the nationalist UfA (Universum-Film AG) produc-tions of the Weimar period. In the first wave of exuberance, propaganda films such as *Hitlerjunge Quex*, *SA-Mann Brand* or *Hans Westmar*, a failed homage to Horst Wessel in Goebbels' opinion, were unsuccessful, and Leni Riefenstahl's coldly aestheticized films of the Reich Party Congress of 1934 (*Triumph of the Will*) and the Olympic Games of 1936 (*Festival of the Peoples* and *Festival of Beauty*) were even then already in a cate-gory of their own. Reasonably entertaining analogous historical biopics like *The Old and the Young King* with Emil Jannings (1935), or Wolfgang Liebeneiner's *Bismarck* made in 1940, were more likely to awaken the desired associations in the minds of the audience. The indoctrinators miscalculated with anti-Semitic concoctions like *Jew Süss* and *The Eternal Jew* (a 'documentary' delivered by the 'Reichsfilmintendant' Fritz Hippler); and a film like *I Accuse* (1941), which advocated 'mercy killing', was hardly the correct prescription against unrest amongst the population, considering the news which was leaking out about the killing of the mentally ill.[28] Far better suited to strengthen the will to carry on during the second half of the war than heroics in the style of *Kolberg* (1945) were light, entertaining old films. Film fanatics like Goebbels – and Hitler – seemed to understand this. In any case, blatant propaganda films always represented only a fraction of the annual production of approximately 100 films.

It was not only during the war that entertainment dominated the screen. Just as before, romances and adventure stories, comedies, crime thrillers and musicals dominated the programme of the big film companies, nationalized by Goebbels after 1936–7. For the audience the most noticeable change in 1933 and during the following years was in the casting: some stars turned their backs on Germany, amongst them Elisabeth Bergner, Peter Lorre and Oskar Homolka. But in contrast to the directors – amongst whom top-ranking figures such as Fritz Lang, G.W. Pabst, Otto Preminger and Billy Wilder, and many of their promising would-be successors, left for Hollywood – 'politically and racially impeccable' actors and actresses of quality stayed behind in adequate numbers. 'Plain German fare' replaced 'Jewish' (film) culture. If sometimes this was not so easy to digest, it was probably because too many worthy cooks – the censors appointed in Goebbels' ministry – were spoiling the broth, feeling themselves obliged to stir additional and ersatz ingredients into the film scripts which had to be laid before them.

None the less, box-office hits succeeded time after time, especially if audience favourites like Heidemarie Hatheyer, Marika Rökk, the impish Ilse Werner or Zarah Leander, the almost obligatory representative of dark, Nordic passion, were in the cast. Willy Birgel and Willi Fritsch, Emil Jannings and Heinrich George were among the favourite leading men, but so too were comics like Theo Lingen and Hans Moser, as well as, interestingly, a figure such as Heinz Rühmann, so lacking in martial attributes. In 1943 Hans Albers was still playing the noble, daredevil strong man of undying optimism in the brilliantly staged *Münchhausen*, produced for the UfA jubilee and based on a script written under a penname by Erich Kästner. Such perfect vehicles of entertainment fulfilled singularly political functions, particularly in the circumstances of 'total war', precisely because they forwent political content. These films still breathe the spirit of the times, however: they demonstrate like little else of the Nazi cultural legacy not only the anti-intellectual, vigorous and –

in fighting against traditional class arrogance – partly emancipatory climate of those years, but also an ingenuous nostalgia and Arcadianism to which the *Heimatfilm* of the 1950s could attach itself uninterrupted.

The period after the Second World War was, of course, not the first time that the Germans had been exposed to other artistic influences. The 'Americanization' linked in current popular consciousness almost exclusively with the post-Nazi era had already begun in the Weimar Republic and had not simply come to a halt on 30 January 1933. Certainly, the importation of films from the USA was now restricted because of the chronic shortage of foreign exchange and decline in the export of German films, but right into the war years cinemas in the big cities kept current Hollywood productions in their programmes. As a result, the German public were still able to see Marlene Dietrich at least until 1936, and Gary Cooper, Clark Gable, Joan Crawford and Greta Garbo for even longer.[29]

Nor did the Nazi cultural bureaucracy in any way reverse the openness towards contemporary American literature. Rowohlt and S. Fischer could continue to publish authors such as William Faulkner, Thornton Wilder, Thomas Wolfe and, at first, even Sinclair Lewis; and Margaret Mitchell's *Gone with the Wind* was only one of a whole series of American bestsellers. Similarly, a large proportion of English and French literature was available. And there were also the works of German writers like Eich, Fallada, Koeppen, Bergengruen, Kasack, Langgässer and Kaschnitz, who could neither be counted as part of the Nazi literature of the period nor took refuge in writing undemanding traditionalism or regional literature.

A similar pattern could be observed on the music scene: swing and jazz, though unwelcome as the crystallization of youth nonconformity and derided as 'nigger music', remained present throughout the whole of the Nazi period. This was linked not least to the fact that Europe's largest record factories were in Germany and were busy producing for the export market in the occupied countries, from whence soldiers on home leave were re-importing the 'hot music' into the 'Old Reich'. But even the German big bands, disguised behind loyal German names, allowed themselves to be carried away by the 'hot sounds' in the style of Benny Goodman, and groups like Teddy Staufer with his 'Original Teddies' were swinging unabashed in the cafés of the big cities. At the same time, to the cost of classical music, the German 'hit' was on the advance. Modern light music, effectively made possible only by the massive spread of ownership of radio sets, became popular across all social classes, and after the outbreak of war was used in Sunday request concerts specifically to cheer up the 'national community'.

As in the field of literature, in which the *auto-da-fé* of May 1933 had 'only' affected public libraries and in which some of those authors who had emigrated (for example Thomas Mann), were at first quite able to continue to be published, there was a considerable difference between what music could be enjoyed in private and what was officially welcomed. In the space of a few years, this dichotomy cut through the whole of cultural life. There was no contradiction between this fact and the unprecedented ability of the Hitler regime to mobilize people – indeed, it was a consequence of that ability, and in the long term probably its precondition. Parallel to the increasing pressure to produce and to conform, niches of particular cultural consciousness developed, in which a growing number of, above all, younger people sought to quench that intellectual thirst which the censored press and propagandistic mass events offered nothing to satisfy.

Meanwhile, the German bourgeoisie held on to the traditional values of German culture. In comparison to the manifestations of modern mass culture, opera, theater and operetta had little to fear. The experiments with Teutonized *Thingspiele* – dramas mixing Nazi propaganda with ritualized dance, chorus and music, half-heartedly supported by Goebbels for a while and performed on open-air stages built expressly for the purpose – soon foundered on the lack of suitable pieces and public interest. But the attempts too to enrich the established theatres with Nazi heroic dramas seemed to miss the mark. Hanns Johst's *Schlageter* (1933) was both a showpiece and an alibi. Apart from concessions on Nazi holidays, the repertoire remained reasonably free of Nazi influence. In provincial theatre above all, which had in any case been left untouched by the now proscribed socially critical avant-garde of the Weimar period, hardly anything changed.[30] Of course, one would now have searched in vain for Brecht, Hasenclever and Toller in the repertoire of the metropolitan theatres; the less artistic than politically committed 'problem plays' of the 'theatre of the times' of the leftist workers' stages had disappeared, and the Nazi Community of Culture had farces put on in their place. Yet the classical cultural heritage was left untouched, so long as it was not Lessing's *Nathan der Weise* or plays like Schiller's *The Robbers*, which invited the audience to draw suggestive analogies.[31]

Sometimes the audience had changed. It was not just that princes of the Party had taken over personal patronage of specific theatres (as did, for example, Goering over the Prussian State Theatre under Gustav Gründgens) and occasionally held court there as the Kaiser had previously done; 'Strength through Joy' steered the 'ordinary *Volksgenossen*' into the bourgeois temples of moral edification with almost missionary zeal. In outlying districts, which were too distant to bring people to the theatre, the 'Strength through Joy' theatre truck (*KdF-Theaterwagen*) brought high culture into the village. Theatre and concert performances which carried the rider 'KdF' were cheap – and the object of alarm amongst the 'elevated audience'.

The rebellion against bourgeois cultural exclusivity which was reflected in such actions and which, in the eyes of those well-disposed towards National Socialism, conferred upon the latter a measure of honesty and authenticity, was one aspect of the comprehensive mobilization of society pursued in the Third Reich. It was not just an expression of resentment, but also of the populist demand for participation apparently denied by abstract and expressionist art which was difficult to understand. The mobilization against modernist painting, which, by 1937, rose to a level of brutality as in no other area of the arts, also has its roots there, and not just in anti-Semitism and 'blood and soil' ideology. Significantly enough, instead of 'degenerate' art, there was also talk of art that was 'alien to the race'. This, and the fact that, overall, what was at issue was a philistine 'democratization' – in the sense of accessibility through reification – of the arts, as much as one of ideological realignment, give some indication of the average output of the era. Heroic realism and genre painting borrowed from the nineteenth century dominated the 'Great German Art Exhibition' held in Munich in 1937. Simultaneously, only a few steps from the 'House of German Art' the 'degenerates' (Beckmann, Nolde, Kirchner, Klee, Kandinsky, Kokoschka, Dix, Grosz and many others) were on show. Apart from the American and English tourists, among the two million visitors there were obviously many who were using the opportunity for a last look at the proscribed modernists; the official 'German art' aroused far less interest.

During that same summer the 'capital of the movement' experienced a spectacle entitled '2000 Years of German Culture', which staged the Nazi Teutonic cult in the style of a popular festival. Consumers enthusiastic for enjoyment were susceptible to ideological abstrusities diluted in this fashion and enjoyed them just as they did the great sporting events of the time – the regime naturally doing its best to bask in the reflected glory of the heroes involved (Max Schmeling, Bernd Rosemeyer, Rudolf Caracciola). What made it increasingly difficult for people to get their bearings was the confusing simultaneity and often intertwining of an expanding, politically non-specific popular culture with ideological set-pieces which could themselves be extremely contradictory – as when man-sized architectural models were carried through the streets in a procession of shield-brandishing 'Teutons'.

Although only a few of the monumental Party and state buildings, planned mainly for Berlin and Munich, were ever realized, they have been the main basis upon which the architecture of the Nazi period has been judged. The supra-temporal megalomania of the projects, appropriate to the Nazi leadership's ideological and political self-image, and not least the intensive propaganda which sprang from them, were closely linked to Hitler's personal intervention in the planning. Yet, in observing what was actually built during the Third Reich, it is difficult to detect a specifically Nazi style: functional, modern civil engineering projects were not, it is true, built next to medieval-style 'Castles of the Order' but they were built at the same time. To a great extent, public buildings followed an architectural traditionalism represented, for example, by the Stuttgart school around Paul Bonatz, whose name is above all synonymous with motorway bridges fitted so harmoniously into the landscape. After the death of Paul Ludwig Troost, it was Hermann Giesler and Albert Speer, the General Building Inspector of the Reich Capital, who were mainly responsible for Hitler's overblown classicism. However, in Speer's Berlin office there were young technocrats, obsessed with performance and efficiency, who viewed the 'New Building' and Russian Constructivism as a challenge and who, in the 'Task Force for the Reconstruction of Towns Destroyed by Bombing' during the war, developed plans for the green belt of post-war towns from demands for improved protection against air-raids.[32]

The regime's attitude towards the natural and social sciences was also characterized by a pragmatic, utilitarian approach, barely inhibited by ideological reservations, and this determined the prevailing climate in the universities. Almost everything provided by contemporary research in terms of knowledge and skills was used. With the Third Reich, ideology and politics had undoubtedly broken into a world of learning, which, though generally conservative, liked to think of itself as apolitical. The dismissal of what finally amounted to a third of university lecturers and the brain drain entailed in the emigration of around 2,000 academics certainly damaged the quality of research and teaching. But during the process of the general consolidation the enthusiasm for the 'revolution in higher education' propagated by the Nazi Student League had already waned.[33] Positivist and painstaking research and study – in any event long the order of the day in many subjects and in the everyday university life which was now being resumed – also spread to disciplines which had previously tended towards social critique. Attempts to define a Nazi programme for science were torpedoed by contradictory opinions, and the higher education policy pursued by the Reich Ministry for Science, Education and Adult Education, newly created in 1934 under the weak Bernhard Rust, barely got beyond the direct political binding of the university vice-chancellors as 'Führers of the universities'.

In the humanities, especially amongst philosophers, historians and educationalists, academic work distorted by ideology was able to hold out longest: here the Nazis possessed not only (sooner or later) disappointed sympathizers, but also die-hard fanatics such as Ernst Krieck and Walter Frank. If their pseudo-scientific activism confused students and played havoc in the intellectual-cultural arena, at least it made no difference to the economy. Therein lay an important difference with research in the natural sciences, in which an industrial nation of Germany's calibre could on no account permit itself to be restricted by ideological hostility.[34] This was demonstrated particularly clearly by the wretched defeat of 'German physics', represented by Philipp Lenhard and Johannes Stark, in the struggle against the 'Jewish' theory of relativity – 'Jewish' because it had been developed by Albert Einstein. The acknowledgement of theoretical physics in an outright academic dispute in November 1940 (a dispute which had already loomed four years earlier when, as head of IG Farben, Carl Bosch rather than Stark was pronounced successor to Max Planck as president of the Kaiser Wilhelm Society for the Advancement of Science), sent a negative signal to the already peripheral proponents of 'German mathematics' and 'German chemistry'. Serious scientific research had powerful protectors in big business and in the Wehrmacht, but in the long run, of course, it hardly needed them, because the regime's plans for autarky and war meant it could not tolerate a general enmity towards science.

Political interest in the best possible utilization of modern research findings was also important in securing possibilities for work in the social sciences, which, given the ideological suspicion already voiced by Nazi activists during the Weimar period, had hardly been expected. Psychology, still a young academic discipline, experienced its professionalization precisely during the Nazi period despite the expulsion of its leading exponents; even psychoanalysis, easily branded as a 'Jewish invention' from the Nazi perspective, was not prohibited. Sociology as a practical science was highly regarded. While the question of further theoretical development in the social sciences in the Third Reich remains open, it does appear certain that, on the whole, empirical social research as the mother of modern social technology expanded.[35]

Reactionary vision and a belief in technocratic advance had become inextricably linked in the Third Reich without completely supplanting the traditional, the modern and the normal. The Nazis had clearly decisively cut certain traditional lines, others they had either bent just a little, emphasized or simply ignored. Rarely were the issues in the field of science and culture and in the reality of everyday life so clear as in the immediate political situation. How much normality in the life of each individual and how much change each experienced depended on personal circumstances, abilities, convictions, interests – and also on fate.

What had ceased to exist was a normality that could be the subject of reasoned calculation, and to this extent only its semblance remained. Because of the policies of the regime, life had become unpredictable in a way that Europe had not seen since the end of the Enlightenment. Collective and – so long as they were restricted to those within the 'Führer's' sphere of power – even private aversions and preferences of all sorts could be declared questions of policy and decided on the basis of the claim to absolute legal validity. The division between state, society and the individual had been abolished; the intervention of the Leviathan into the private life of the individual could happen at any time. This threat was embodied by the SS and the Gestapo.

The systemization of terror and the rise of the SS

During the early period of the Third Reich even apolitical people could not fail to notice that the situation of many minority groups was defined by political repression and social exclusion, yet after a few years this truth had slipped from most people's view. Nothing had changed in the power principle of enlisting the support of some while using force against others; however, the open terror directed against political dissidents, against groups and individuals who either partially or on principle refused to conform, and against Jews, had receded during the course of the consolidation of power. But the methods had also been refined. In consequence, a 'national community' which had become half reality while remaining half propaganda revealed itself as increasingly incapable of recognizing the dual reality of consent and coercion.

> Terror in its all-embracing form, in its totally inhuman brutality, remains concealed not only from those abroad; even in Germany itself there are certain circles of the population who have no inkling of what is occurring. It is not uncommon for a 'citizen' who has absolutely no enthusiasm for the system but has little interest in politics, who crosses the road to avoid a swastika flag which he would be expected to salute, to put the following question with an undertone of accusation: 'Do you personally know of anyone who is still in a concentration camp from then?' [By 'then' is meant the take-over in 1933.][36]

These observations, made by the SPD in exile in January 1936, were a bitter indication of the increasing hopelessness of underground political activity inside Germany, which – while the efficiency of the apparatus of repression was increasing – was also confronted with an ever-growing loyalty to and enthusiasm for the 'Führer'. In such a situation it was often possible 'only' to maintain mutual solidarity by concealed meetings and to prevent contact between people from being broken. And it was in itself a considerable achievement that those who remained active amongst the circa 5,000 emigré Social Democrats succeeded until April 1940, first from Prague and later from Paris, in maintaining the cleverly devised secret reporting system of border secretaries and agents in factories and communities.

The KPD's temporary attempts to seek an agreement with Social Democracy foundered because it simultaneously clung to its claim to leadership and to the aim of the dictatorship of the proletariat. But in the early years of the Third Reich approximately half of its 300,000 members (its membership in 1932) took part in some way or another in illegal activity. Apart from the maintenance of the banned organization itself, the main activities were the production and distribution of leaflets calling for the overthrow of the Hitler regime. The Communist Party, which had always had a strict, hierarchical form of organization, proved itself to be particularly efficient at this. For example, every ten days for a period during 1934, an illegal printing press in Solingen produced more than 10,000 copies of *Rote Fahne* (*Red Flag*), the central organ of the KPD, as well as a grand total of 300,000 pamphlets. But this form of resistance, based on the solidarity of many individuals and on the prospect of the rapid overthrow of the regime, was also extremely risky and claimed many victims. By the end of 1933 an estimated 60,000 to 100,000 Communists were detained in prisons or concentration camps and by the mid-1930s, following several waves of arrests, the Gestapo had almost completely destroyed the basis of the Communist resistance. The development of the Nazi system of terror and surveillance was completed with stealth and silence during these years. While the majority of 'national comrades' believed they were experiencing a transition to more peaceful times – the development of a 'normal dictatorship' (for which there was no lack of indicators) – within Heinrich Himmler's sphere of power the foundations of totalitarian ideological rule were being laid.

This small, almost fragile-seeming man, who sought to hide his obsessions and inhibitions behind thick spectacles and an indeterminate grin, had emerged empty-handed when power had been shared out in Berlin in the spring of 1933. Although as 'Reichsführer SS' already master of an elite troop of 56,000 'racially valuable' Party soldiers, Himmler had to be satisfied with the less impressive post of Acting Chief Commissioner of Police in Munich. The strategically more important police of the Reich capital and Prussia were under Goering's command. If, at first, the development of the political police system in the Third Reich ran a rather complicated course, then this was because of its dual beginning, which brought to the fore both conceptual contradictions and power rivalries. While Goering strove for a political police that would indeed be separate but still organized within the state administration – and to this extent proved himself to be a traditionalist – the ideologue Himmler's aim from the outset was the radical removal of all competence concerning the political police from the aegis of state power in favour of the SS. Political surveillance and terror were to be institutionalized by the ideological elite troops of National Socialism.

Himmler, supported by Reinhard Heydrich, the Chief of the Security Service (Sicherheitsdienst – SD), won an important intermediate victory in the spring of 1934. From his position, created twelve months earlier, as 'Political Police Commandant for Bavaria', the Reichsführer SS, during the winter of 1933/4, had taken over the command of the newly independent political police forces in all the *Länder* except Prussia and Schaumburg-Lippe. Subsequently, on 20 April 1934, Goering appointed him Inspector of the Prussian Secret State Police – the Gestapo.[37] Goering did indeed remain nominal Chief of the Gestapo, but henceforth Himmler was the *de facto* master of the entire Political Police of the German Reich. Heydrich, the new Head of the Secret State Police Office in Berlin (*Geheimes Staatspolizeiamt* or *Gestapa*), ensured its effective centralization and the filling of top positions with SS Führers. The 'detection and investigation of dissidents' pursued by the Security Service of the SS was now increasingly merged with the 'struggle against dissidents' by the (state) Political Police. The path to the 'SS State' (Eugen Kogon) was thus already largely cleared.

Until the SA was eliminated as a political force, the Reichsführer SS had been subordinate to the Chief of the SA, Ernst Röhm. As a consequence of its elimination in the summer of 1934, Himmler's power grew further. Henceforth the SS was an independent Party organization, with Himmler more bound in duty to the 'Führer', who on 30 June had transferred to him sole responsibility for all the concentration camps. This offered the opportunity to unify the extra-state system of terror, which the Reichsführer SS immediately exploited: Theodor Eicke, until then camp commandant in Dachau, became 'Inspector of the Concentration Camps and Führer of the SS Guard Units'. By 1937, in the place of numerous small prisons and prison camps still maintained by the SA, Eicke had organized two further large concentration camps near Berlin (Sachsenhausen) and Weimar (Buchenwald) based on the 'model of Dachau'. The SS Death's Head Units, which at that time numbered just 5,000 men, were responsible for the guarding and running of the concentration camps.

Apart from the Political Police and the concentration camps, the armed brigades of the SS formed the third springboard from which Himmler was able to extend his power. As early as summer 1933 a separate 'Adolf Hitler Bodyguard Regiment' (*Leibstandarte Adolf Hitler*) had been formed from the ranks of the SS and sworn to the 'Führer'. After the coup against the SA, Himmler did indeed succeed in a limited extension of the so-called SS special duty troop (*SS Verfügungstruppe*) (financed from Reich funds), but the creation of a proper SS army foundered, for the time being, on the opposition of the Wehrmacht. None the less, even before they were strengthened during 1938–9, the Blackshirt units had already become an example of that special force typical of Nazism which formed part of a 'Führer'-executive separate from the Party and the state.

In the summer of 1936, the Reichsführer was finally granted the institutional competence still required for the SS to consolidate its position as an independent nexus of power. A decree by Hitler on 17 June charged Himmler with the 'unified integration of police functions in the Reich'. It was therefore in this way, rather than in the context of a never-realized reform of the Reich, that the centralization of the entire German police was initiated and the – *de facto* already existing – central Reich organization of the Political Police was legally reconstructed. Himmler's new official title of 'Reichsführer SS and Chief of the German Police in the Reich Ministry of the Interior' (*Reichsführer SS und Chef der Deutschen Polizei im Reichsministerium des Innern*) signalled that this was not simply a matter of a personal union of posts but moreover of a firm organizational link between the SS and the police. As a secretary of state, the Chief of the German Police ranked nominally below the Reich Minister of the Interior, but in reality a decisive shift of power had occurred which meant that Frick was deprived of power at the centre. This was demonstrated not just by Himmler's demand, soon raised, that he should generally act in place of the Minister of the Interior, but also by his previous endeavours to open his own Ministry of Police.

Basically, the decree opened the way for the 'denationalization' of the police, and exposed the entire police system of the Third Reich to take-over by the SS. There immediately followed the establishment of separate 'head offices' of the regular constabulary and the Security Police under SS-Obergruppenführer Kurt Daluege and SS-Gruppenführer Heydrich respectively. While the amalgamation of the regular urban and rural constabulary with the SS was instituted only slowly, and often went no further than declared intent, Heydrich, as 'Chief of the Security Police and the Security Service', succeeded in making relatively quicker inroads in the criminal police sphere; after all, he could fall back on relevant experience gained in the alignment of the political police forces of the *Länder*.

The integration of state *and* criminal police with the security service of the SS became all the more significant for future developments when Heydrich, in opposition to Daluege (and above all with Hitler's approval), unambiguously claimed sole competence for the Security Police in handling all tasks that were political in the broadest sense of the word:

> As far as I am concerned, within the parameters of the Nazi view of things, the market police, census office and system of registration are things which are in my gift. . . . It is certain that the total, permanent registration of all the people of the Reich and the associated possibility of a permanent overview of the situation of individual persons belongs in the hands of that part of the police which has as its duty not only the securing of law-enforcement, but also ideological security and that relating to everday life.[38]

What Himmler and Heydrich were working towards went far beyond a political police occupied with surveillance and opinions. It was the totalitarian utopia of an ideologically racist supra-institution of ceaseless social reconstruction and social hygiene, the vision of a 'state in the sun' ('*Sonnenstaat*' – as in the political philosophy of Thomas Campanella) wrapped in the technocratic guise of the modern. Issues were no longer considered according to traditional police thinking, but rather formulated as if by an epidemiologist. Werner Best, Heydrich's representative in the Secret State Police, had already commented, in relation to the Gestapo Law of spring 1936, that the Political Police was 'an institution which carefully supervises the political health of the German body politic, which is quick to recognize all symptoms of disease and germs of destruction – be they the result of disintegration from within or purposeful poisoning from without – and to remove them by every suitable means'.[39]

Where the seat of disease was to be found according to the SS perspective was shown in the plan of work of the head office of the Security Police with its three sections: Administration and Justice (where responsibility lay, *inter alia*, for the passport and identity card system); Criminal Police; and Political Police. The last of these had the following departments:

> Communism and other Marxist groups; churches, sects, emigrants, Jews, lodges; reaction, opposition, Austrian affairs; protective custody, concentration camps; economic, agricultural and social policy affairs; clubs, societies and associations; control of broadcasting; affairs of the Party, its organizations and associated groups; foreign political police; situation reports; press; battle against homosexuality and abortion; counter-intelligence police.[40]

Within the sphere of duties of the criminal police now fell not just the solving of classic crimes, but also the struggle against 'elements harmful to the people' (*Volksschädlinge*). Parallel to this fundamental change in, and extension of, police activity, a significant change was taking place in the concentration camps.

While it was still mainly political prisoners who were being held in the 'model camp' at Dachau, the new Reich concentration camps Sachsenhausen and Buchenwald were increasingly being filled with so-called 'asocials': habitual criminals, homosexuals and Jehovah's Witnesses (then known as Bible Students or *Bibelforscher*) – that is, with people who could not be convicted by normal courts because they had broken no valid law but who were considered socially undesirable. More strongly than before, the concentration camps therefore took over a corrective function with regard to the judiciary. Since the assumption of power, the Gestapo had taken prisoners – especially political prisoners – into protective custody as soon as they had finished serving their sentences, and defendants after they had been acquitted or after stays of proceedings, often in the courtroom itself, and had then sent them to a concentration camp for an unspecified period. Now this practice was perfected with respect to 'elements harmful to the people'.

At the beginning of 1937, Himmler, as Chief of the German Police, ordered that, on the basis of lists drawn up shortly beforehand by criminal police stations throughout the territory of the Reich, 'around 2,000 professional and habitual criminals or dangerous sex-offenders' should be arrested and put in concentration camps. The operation of 9 March was to be carried out 'suddenly and without warning' and came exactly one year after a wave of arrests against the 'work-shy', announced at the time as 'unique, comprehensive and to be unexpected', and in which the labour exchanges had been required to provide legal assistance in the decision as to whom to select. In the middle of June 1938, after a now annexed Austria had also become the venue for a 'crime prevention campaign', the next operation took place in the 'Old Reich': from the area of each criminal police head office 'at least 200 male persons capable of work (asocials) and, in addition, all male Jews with a previous prison record' were to be sent to the Buchenwald concentration camp. Regarded as 'asocials' were: tramps; beggars, whether or not of no fixed abode; 'Gypsies and persons travelling about in the manner of Gypsies, if they have shown no willingness for regular work or have rendered themselves liable to legal penalty'; pimps; and 'such persons as have numerous previous convictions for resistance, bodily harm, brawling, disturbance of domestic peace or similar and have thereby shown that they do not wish to adapt themselves to the order of the national community.'[41]

In the justification of the so-called 'asocials operation' the argument of economic exploitability emerged for the first time – an argument which, linked with the concept of 'weeding out' supposedly inferior and un-productive life, was to gain explosively fatal influence in the years to come: 'the strict implementation of the Four-Year Plan requires the de-ployment of all labour power capable of work, and cannot permit asocial people to evade work and thereby sabotage the Four-Year Plan.' Mean-while, in fact, the key issue had become the recruitment of forced labour for the first SS-owned enterprises. Besides brickworks (Deutsche Erd- und Steinwerk GmbH), these also included granite quarries at Flossenbürg in the Upper Palatinate and at Mauthausen in Lower Austria – important for the 'Führer's construction projects' – where new concentration camps were being established (and later also at Gross-Rosen in Lower Silesia and Natzweiler in Alsace).

Himmler's motives for these mass arrests – which at the same time served as rehearsals for the 'mopping up operations' which were to take place later in the occupied territories – were not, however, simply eco-nomic and ideological/political. Questions of power were also at issue. The filling of the concentration camps, in which the number of prisoners had fallen to below 10,000 during the winter of 1936–7, was on the one hand intended to underline the institutional weight of the SS, and on the other to check the attempts of the administration in the Interior Ministry and the judiciary to define the devices of protective custody and 'police preventive custody' from a single viewpoint and to keep their application subject to control. Even though Himmler, in his dual role as Reichsführer SS and Chief of the German Police, was the direct representative of the 'Führer's' power, he was at this point still concerned to maintain the semblance of legality. So, for lack of a suitable justification for the opera-tion against 'habitual criminals', for example, he cited the Reichstag Fire Decree, which had hitherto only been wielded against political dis-sidents, while deliberately ignoring the law on the preventive detention of recidivists, which had been enacted in a 'normal' fashion in the autumn of 1933, but which did not match his purposes. And although the campaign against the 'work-shy' was clearly not directed at political dissidents, Himmler nevertheless entrusted the Gestapo rather than the criminal police with its execution because, as a result of the Gestapo Law of February 1936, they could order protective custody without the possibil-ity of a case being examined by the adminstrative courts.

A new 'Basic Decree' of the Reich Ministry of the Interior did indeed, at the beginning of 1938, restrict the authority to impose protective custody to the *Gestapa*, but at the same time it formally extended its application, hitherto limited to political dissidents, to persons 'who by their existence endanger the security of the people and the state'. A short while later, the Reich Office of the Criminal Police, in its guidelines on the Interior Ministry's 'Basic Decree' 'concerning the police's crime prevention campaign' of December 1937, expressly assigned to the SS's concentration camps the function of 'state correction and labour camps'. Thus the social reconstruction of the 'German body' (*Volkskörper*) was now recognized as the task of the now independent SS complex.

In line with its own self-image the SS could not, of course, restrict itself to particular areas of activity. As the instrument for the realization of the 'will of the Führer' its claim to power and action was unlimited in principle, and in all areas. Characteristically, for example, despite its orders, the Security Service of the SS (established as early as 1931) did not even balk at spying inside the Party. It is true that Heydrich's intelligence organization had lost its significance in terms of power politics since the Gestapo had been taken over by the SS, but in the collation and evaluation of reports about the prevailing situation and mood of the population it had soon found a long-term task and a justification for its existence. From 1936–7, the SD increasingly assumed the character of a secret institute of public opinion research, providing the Nazi leadership with regular 'Reports from the Reich' (the *Meldungen aus dem Reich*). Everyone who belonged to the approximately 30,000 honorary (that is, unpaid) contributors and secret agents known as *V-Leute* – civil servants, managers, doctors, teachers, journalists, priests, artists and scientists – was obliged

> everywhere in his family, in the circle of his friends and acquaintances, and above all in his workplace, to take every opportunity to find out, through conversations of a discreet nature, the real effect on opinion of all important foreign and domestic political events and measures. Furthermore, the conversations of national comrades in trains (workers' trains), trams, shops, hairdressers, at newspaper stands, in administrative offices (food and clothing coupon offices, labour exchanges, town halls etc.), at weekly markets, in pubs, factories and canteens, offer a great wealth of valuable leads, which are often not paid sufficient attention.[42]

Despite all the secrecy, after a few years of Nazi rule there was a widespread sense of being under surveillance. Certainly, only a few knew the details of the surveillance system; on the whole the differences between the SD, SS, Criminal Police, regular constabulary and Political Police remained unclear to the average citizen; but, if anything, this strengthened the widespread feeling of uncertainty and menace. The sight of dark leather coats and black uniforms made people afraid, and the word 'Gestapo' was linked with fear. The power of the Secret

Police was not only felt by those who were physically exposed to its terror.

And yet it would be a mistake to view the mid-1930s as being characterized primarily by political violence and repression. Loyalty to the regime and enthusiasm for the 'Führer', not opposition and resistance, determined the domestic situation at this time. After spectacular successes by the Gestapo, which brought hundreds of dissidents before the People's Court of Law (*Volksgerichtshof*),[43] but also faced with a constituency which was steadily losing its political resilience, the underground activity of Communists and Social Democrats had been brought to an almost complete halt. Even the popular opposition which frequently sprang from non-specific, often apolitical motives had tended to decrease. The latter could be divined from the stagnating number of people convicted by the 'Special Courts' (*Sondergerichte*) of 'malicious criticism' and 'continuous grumbling' – amongst whom, incidentally, peripheral social groups were disproportionately over-represented and, in the manner of the old class justice, more severely punished.[44]

Only a few considered it a bad omen that despite the calm which had supervened in domestic politics, there were no recognizable signs of a return to the constitutional state – violated in so many respects since 1933 – as some in the leading conservative elites were still hoping. The majority of Germans were entranced by the suggestive power of the concept of the 'national community' and by a 'Führer' myth underpinned by foreign policy successes. Under the spell of the general consolidation of the regime the concomitant continuing extension of the SS complex went unnoticed. In the years of consolidation, not least on the personal level, many of the preconditions of the later radicalization were created. During this period, especially in a comparatively flexible organization like the SD – far more dependent on intellect and organizational skills than on ideological fanaticism – that type of performance-oriented SS Führer could develop, for whom each new task presented nothing more than a personal challenge to be overcome. Here ripened the SS mentality, so highly valued by Himmler, which deemed nothing to be 'impossible' and in the final analysis accepted 'special duties', no matter how arduous, up to and including the leadership of the *Einsatzgruppen* and the murder of millions.

With the amalgamation of the SS and the police, the disposal of negative ideological elements by bureaucratic police methods could begin. Yet it was not only the ideological rhetoric about the enemy which was henceforth transformed into an active anti-dissident campaign: the police and internal administration themselves changed – and became instruments for prosecuting the war on the home front. So it was only logical to compare the 'National Socialist police' with the Wehrmacht, and specifically to postulate its 'right' to act outside the bounds of legal norms, as Heinrich Himmler did in a Festschrift on the occasion of his 'superior' Frick's sixtieth birthday: 'Like the Wehrmacht, the police can only act in accordance with the orders of the leadership and not with the law. As with the Wehrmacht, the constraints on police action will be determined by the orders of the leadership and by its own discipline.' With the outbreak of war these constraints were further reduced.

3

Radicalization, 1938–1945

The anti-Jewish pogrom which took place over several days in November 1938 demonstrated even more clearly than the developments in domestic and foreign policy during the preceding months that the Third Reich had reached a turning-point. Murders and beatings, burning synagogues, smashed shops and wrecked homes bore witness to the determination of the Nazi leadership to solve, in the immediate future, the 'Jewish question' which it had itself created. Two-fifths of the 562,000 people categorized as 'non-Aryans' by the Nuremberg Laws had already left Germany because of growing legal and economic discrimination. But the declared aim of the race ideologues was a 'Jew-free' Reich. The 'Crystal Night' (*Reichskristallnacht*) of 9–10 November – so-called because of the broken glass which littered the streets – made clear just how virulent this ideological axiom had remained within the inner circle of the Nazi movement. But it also left no doubt that the majority of the population rejected radical anti-Semitism and was thus decisive in the future strategy adopted on anti-Jewish policy – up to and including the consistent secrecy surrounding the eventual 'Final Solution' of the Holocaust.

Just as in its anti-Jewish policy, elements of the Nazi *Weltanschauung* now also clearly came to light in the regime's conduct of foreign affairs; the importance of the alliance with the old elites declined further. In the preceding years the racist components of the Nazis' programme of *Lebensraum* (literally 'living space') could only be vaguely discerned behind the widely supported demand for a revision of the Versailles Treaty. Hitler's strategic view eastwards, in particular, seemed to place the regime within the Wilhelmine tradition of aspirations to world power, to which the foreign policy establishment of the Weimar Republic had also clung. There were reservations within the *Wehrmacht* leadership about any radicalization of German foreign policy that would entail an early military solution to the 'problem of space' as demanded by Hitler (according to the Hossbach Memorandum of 5 November 1937), but these were diminished by the Blomberg-Fritsch crisis at the beginning of February 1938. At the same time as the reshuffle there were significant organizational changes: Hitler himself took over supreme command, and into the place of the Reich War Minister Blomberg, who was dismissed on a pretext, stepped the High Command (*Oberkommando*) of the Wehrmacht under General Wilhelm Keitel; General Walter von Brauchitsch became the new commander-in-chief of the army, replacing Fritsch, who, having been suspended on charges of homosexuality, resigned. Foreign Minister Neurath had to relinquish his office to the younger Hitler sycophant Joachim von Ribbentrop, but remained in the cabinet. A month later, German troops marched into Austria. Vienna gave the 'Führer' an enthusiastic welcome.

The Munich Agreement and the subsequent occupation of the Sudetenland at the end of September and beginning of October 1938 represented the climax and the conclusion of the pursuit of revisionist foreign policy. The 'pacifist record' (Hitler) had worn itself out; now the gramophone was playing battle songs. The secret preparations for 'finishing off the rest of Czechoslovakia', which were ordered shortly after the Sudeten operation, led in March 1939 to the establishment of the 'Reich Protectorate of Bohemia and Moravia' and a week later to the invasion of the Memel region. These continued the series of successes without actual war, but also provoked the end of Anglo-French appeasement. The eventful 'peaceful years' were over. The radicalization had begun.

If this radicalization of foreign policy became particularly clear particularly early, this was because the conquest of 'living space in the East' constituted a central point of the Nazi programme. For the same reason, what occurred during 1938–9 was, indeed, not a radicalization of the Nazi leadership but rather of the policy of the Third Reich. And in so far as Hitler, of his own accord, deliberately and resolutely steered this radicalization of its policies, the characteristic extensive structural inability of the regime to keep the dynamic driving force of the 'movement' under permanent control was of secondary importance.

Hand in hand with the tougher conduct of foreign policy and eventually with the beginning of the war went serious changes in domestic politics. The aggression directed abroad did not lead to any reduction of political pressure at home; on the contrary, there too it led to a radicalization involving a more determined realization of several of the ideological projects. Hence the war for 'living space', even if it was heralded by the *Blitzkrieg* campaigns fought on the wrong (that is, Western) Front, was not least the occasion for intensified eugenic/racist measures to 'cleanse' the German *Volkskörper*. According to the logic of the Nazi leadership, this was an integral part of the preparations necessary for the period which would follow 'final victory': indeed, the war of extermination, fought with relentless severity, was intended to produce the territorial basis for a greater German empire in the East, in which the Germans would occupy the role of a racially pure master race.

The Germans and the beginning of war

On his fiftieth birthday, 'General Unblutig' ('General Bloodless' – as in 'bloodless coup') enjoyed massive popularity:

> The population had certainly never decorated homes and shops with so much love and devotion as on this national holiday of the Greater German Reich. In town and country every street and square was resplendent with the richest decoration of flags and bunting. There was hardly a shop window to be seen without a display of the Führer's portrait and the victorious symbols of the new Reich. The numerous celebrations were very well attended; in the garrison towns the population was especially captivated by the military parades. Everywhere was a happy celebration of people, who were not in the slightest disturbed by the agitation incited in the nations which surround us, because they know their fate is safe in the Führer's hands.[1]

In the spring of 1939, similar reports flowed in from all corners of the Reich. The Germans knew, of course, that Hitler had been entertaining ever greater risks in order to achieve the foreign policy triumphs of the previous years. Many suspected that it could not continue like this for much longer – and yet clung to the hope that 'God's anointed' would continue to have 'providence' on his side. Combined with the stylization of the 'Führer' as the one who would fulfil Germany's historic destiny – an idea now no longer encountered simply amongst the nationalist Protestant bourgeoisie – was the unspoken fear of a war that would destroy everything that had been achieved. While popular opinion persisted, almost defiantly, in the belief that the maintenance of peace was possible, Hitler was ordering the planning of the attack on Poland.

The fundamental difference between the atmosphere in the summer of 1939 and that of twenty-five years earlier was the Germans' lack enthusiasm for war. For the regime this was cause for careful preparation. Bogus border incidents on the German-Polish frontier, which were supposed to convince the 'national comrades' of the need for a revenge attack in the days following the surprise signing of the Hitler-Stalin Pact, were part of the short-term propaganda measures. More important in the long term was the conciliation of two basic and objectively contradictory considerations which Hitler derived from the experience of the First World War: the material demands and fears of the population had to be taken into careful consideration, but at the same time it was necessary to achieve a comprehensive military and economic mobilization. The first gave rise to fears of a second November Revolution, the second to Hitler's determination not to make his strategic and political decisions dependent on the resources and productive capacity hitherto available in the arms industry.

Despite the policy of rearmament and autarky which had been pursued for several years, in economic terms the Third Reich was inadequately prepared for a protracted war. Resources were sufficient, however, for limited military campaigns and swift victories, especially as, each time, new reserves of raw materials and foodstuffs were to be found. In these circumstances it was possible to create the impression that the extraordinarily successful *Blitzkrieg* campaigns, which were used to full propaganda advantage, rested on a military strategy which had established a convincing parallel in the limited economic mobilization and which permitted far-reaching protection of the civilian population of Germany. Such an interpretation[2] seemed to be justified by the fact that German munitions production only reached its peak during the second half of the war. But this was more the consequence of previous mismanagement than an intentionally delayed take-off. There was no lack of will on the part of the political leadership to mobilize the economy totally. None the less, in the early part of the war, endeavours to that end seemed to have missed their mark.

This did not result, however, in any particular advantage for the consumer. Measured by indicators such as *per capita* consumer spending, the proportion of the workforce occupied in the arms industry, and military expenditure as a proportion of national income, by 1941 at the latest the Third Reich found itself in a state of mobilization which stood clearly above that of the United Kingdom.[3] Of course, an economy which had kept the people in spartan conditions even during peacetime was left with only limited possibilities for further reductions in the supply of consumer goods without risking unrest. A comparison with Great Britain, which began to make economies from the base of a markedly higher standard of living, shows that, in 1939–40, *per capita* consumer spending in both countries fell by approximately 10 per cent, but afterwards decreased significantly only in Germany, where in 1944 people had to be content with two-thirds of the 1938 supply of consumer goods – and this with a drastic reduction in quality and, as a matter of principle, preference in supply for the armed forces. In December 1939, butter already had to be mixed with margarine in order to increase the butter supply a little for the first Christmas of the war; at the same time the margarine ration was cut by a similar amount.

Although more than four-fifths of all foodstuffs now came from domestic agriculture, Germany was, as ever, reliant on imports, especially for fats and animal feed. In the closing days of August 1939, offices responsible for the economy and for nutrition therefore began the rationing of all vital and militarily important goods. Food ration cards, soon followed by a Reich clothing card and other special coupons, were what constituted the 'normal consumer'. The basic staples (bread, potatoes, pulses) were available in sufficient quantities, but there was only half a kilo of meat per head per week, 125 grammes of butter plus 100 grammes of margarine, 62.5 grammes of cheese and one egg.

Just as with food rationing, the financial burdens of the Decree on the War Economy were calculated so that although there was indeed some perceptible grumbling, there was rarely serious protest or anything as grave as a renunciation of loyalty. The new 'Ministerial Council for the Defence of the Reich' (Goering, Hess, Funk, Frick, Lammers and Keitel), was supposed to coordinate domestic policy measures instead of the cabinet, which had not met since 1938. In fact, the Council only functioned for a few weeks. Despite the original plan for a general reduction in wages, on 4 September 1939 it simply decided on a wage freeze. The simultaneous suspension of bonuses and leave was almost completely rescinded after only two months. What remained of direct financing for the war were supplementary taxes on alcohol, cigarettes, theatre tickets and travel, and a graded supplement on income tax. None the less, in comparison with the last year before the war, by 1942 the total tax burden had almost doubled to 34.7 billion Reichsmarks. Private savings rose even faster and higher, to 44.6 billion Reichsmarks, and quadrupled between 1938 and 1941. Without recourse to the ill-reputed methods of compulsory war loans, the regime, by cutting the production of consumer goods and by strict control of the economy in the grand style, diverted spending power into savings accounts. Thus, in an elegant fashion, it was precisely the 'little man' who was also enlisted in the financing of the war. The dream of home-ownership after the war, which was the subject of related propaganda, could not be shaken even by the Allied bombs: 'Save in the war – build later!' was the advertising slogan still being used successfully by Germany's 'largest and oldest building society', Wüstenrot, as late as 1943.

The recognizable endeavours to take the necessary war measures as quietly as possible were in no way a sign of indecisive leadership. They were rather a testimony to the (not unjustified) fear that, from the point of view of the population, it could make a difference whether they were to be burdened with a whole series of inconveniences for the purpose of national defence or for a war of aggression. This background also helps to explain why there was reticence in forcing women into 'labour duties'. It was not just ideological notions about the role of woman as a childbearing machine which moved the regime to grant soldiers' wives financial support which allowed many of them to give up their jobs. It is true that such a policy led – instead of to the planned increase in the number of working women, given the loss of male workers – to a re-duction which was not made good again until 1942 and was only just exceeded in the final phase of the war. None the less, there was no question of sheltering women. In comparison with England and the USA, at the beginning of the war the proportion of women in the *indigenous* workforce in Germany was, at 37.3 per cent, already more than 10 per cent higher. By mid-1944, 51 per cent of the total indigenous workforce in the Third Reich were women, in contrast with Great Britain where they comprised only 37.9 per cent and the USA at 35.7 per cent. Even if the increase in the percentage proportion had its main origins in the removal of men to military service, there was, none the less, eventually a marked shift of women's employment into munitions production. Moreover, particularly in agriculture and in the clearing of rubble created by air-raids, women were being saddled with ever greater workloads without it ever appearing in the statistics.

Contrary to what is suggested by much of the economic data from the early part of the war, even during the early campaigns of the *Blitzkrieg* the political signs pointed to total war. The loyal majority were indeed wooed, as ever, but even the ordinary citizen was not left unaffected by the increased use of fear as a means of repression. The regime now made unfettered use of the terrorist possibilities open to it against critics and ideologically undesirable minorities. The 'Decree on the Special Penal Law in the War and in Special Cases', published on 26 August 1939, created the punishable offence of 'demoralization of the armed forces': an imprudent critical word, if the Gestapo found out about it, could lead to the death sentence. On 3 September, the day Britain and France entered the war, Heydrich, in the secret 'principles of the internal protection of the State during the war' directed he Gestapo 'to ruthlessly suppress' every attempt 'to destroy the determination and fighting spirit of the

German people'. The Chief of the Security Police was to be informed of arrests, 'as, if need be, such elements will be brutally liquidated on instructions from above'.[4] Within the next 48 hours there followed strict decrees on the punishment of economic offences and crimes connected with the war (for example, punishable offences committed during the blackout). Listening to foreign radio broadcasts – for years, like the foreign press, only reluctantly tolerated and in any case impossible with the intentionally weak construction of the 'Volksempfänger' – was now prosecuted as 'spiritual self-mutilation'; in the second half of the war the Special Courts, whose number tripled to 74 between 1938 and 1942, even imposed the death sentence on several occasions on 'listeners to enemy broadcasts' (Feindhörer). The integration of the Security Police and the SD in the Reich Security Headquarters (Reichssicherheitshauptamt) at the end of September 1939 underlined the – de facto already long-existent – institutional and political amalgamation of the police and the SS which, with the establishment of the senior police and SS leaders in 1938, had also been carried out at regional level. With the introduction of a special SS and police jurisdiction at the end of October 1939, the ordinary prosecuting authorities lost all responsibility for conducting investigations if the SS or SD took 'Marxist saboteurs' or other dissidents away to concentration camps and executed them there. At the beginning of the war the instruments of surveillance and repression available within the SS's sphere of power served the intensified 'campaign against dissidents' and a population policy motivated by ideological racism both in the 'Old Reich' and in the new, yet-to-be-conquerered territories, even more than the contingency plans laid in case of a critical development of the war.

The triumphant 'Blitzkrieg campaigns' in which, by the summer of 1942, the German armed force subjugated successively Poland, Denmark and Norway, the Netherlands, Luxemburg and Belgium, France and finally Yugoslavia and Greece, ensured that, meanwhile, the changes to the internal structure of the regime went largely unnoticed. In 1940 and 1941, Hitler stood at the peak of his prestige. After initial scepticism, a war which produced nothing but rapid victories unleashed a level of enthusiasm for the 'Führer' from which almost no-one could escape. The last grousers fell silent, particularly when not only raw materials for the arms industries were ruthlessly procured from the occupied territories, but also the welcome supplementary ration of Danish butter for the normal consumer. Scruples about the force with which Germany had invaded Europe seemed to be obliterated, as was any trace of a sense of injustice. What worried people most in May 1940 was 'the Führer's life': the news of Hitler's 'personal involvement', according to the Meldungen *aus dem Reich*, had made a deep impression on the whole people and had 'strengthened the trust, throughout the land, in a successful outcome of the operations in the West'. But at the same time it was 'emphasized that, at this juncture, there could be only one fatal blow for Germany, namely the loss of the Führer'.[5]

In this situation there was no room for fundamental resistance to the regime. In its own way the loose group of military figures who were critical of Hitler was no less paralysed than the Communist resistance had been after the Hitler-Stalin Pact. By failing to act early in 1938, when its most senior officers were deprived of power, and also, in the final analysis, in the 'Sudeten crisis', the Wehrmacht had forfeited its chance, both politically and psychologically. At a time when Hitler's strategy had brought Germany into an unprecedented position of hegemony, a conspiracy had become hardly even thinkable. The intentions of oppositionist officers to arrest Hitler on the Western Front, which still existed even in the first weeks of the war, had, so it seemed, lost all justification. At the time of the 'Führer's' narrow escape from the bomb attack perpetrated, as an individual act, by the Swabian journeyman carpenter Johann Georg Elser, in the Munich Bürgerbräukeller on 8 November 1939, many Germans, as the SD recorded, had already expressed their indignation 'at the Englishmen and Jews who are basically considered to be the ones behind this attempted assasination'. Classes of schoolchildren had intoned hymns of thanksgiving and 'factory leaders' had thanked providence in the presence of their assembled workforces. 'Often – particularly amongst the workers – the opinion is expressed that in England "not a stone should be left standing".'[6]

Aggressive patriotism was not only a phenomenon of the second half of the war, when carpet-bombing by the Allies produced a defiantly hopeless determination to stick it out, rather than the expected rejection of the regime; under the command of the 'strategic genius Adolf Hitler' the unwanted war swiftly became a national duty which was recognized just as much in the widest circles of the working class as by the bourgeoisie. The majority of Germans identified with Hitler's war, the aims of which at first remained vague – intentionally, as Goebbels once admitted:

> National Socialism has never had a theory in the sense that it discussed details or problems. It wanted power . . . If today the question is asked, how do you envisage the new Europe, we must say we do not know. Of course we have an idea. But if we dress it up in words, that immediately brings us enemies and increases resistance . . . Today we say '*Lebensraum*'. Let each imagine what he will. When the time comes we will know what we want.[7]

The widely perceptible readiness to work for victory and to make certain sacrifices was not least an indication that the Nazis understood how to awaken a multitude of social and socio-political hopes on the 'Home Front' and to promise that they would be realized after the war had been won. Here it was less a matter of concrete promises to specific groups or to the population as a whole, much more of the ability to create in society a characteristic political atmosphere of departure towards an end and a mood of social expectation. Such desires for change found their proponents and propagandists in the – often competing – official elites of the Third Reich and, in particular, in the army of many thousands of political leaders. Of course, the emergence of this social-reformist atmosphere was, in part, a reflection of the regime's restricted room for manoeuvre, which existed even in the military and political phase of *Blitzkrieg*. To this extent it was, a least partially, a tactical concession. But at the same time it indicated a real and serious demand for social and political reorganization of society, in which the outlines of a post-war Nazi order could be discerned.

The latter was particularly true in the plan for a 'Social Security System for the German People' (Sozialwerk des Deutschen Volkes) which was presented to the public by the DAF leader Robert Ley in the autumn of 1940.[8] Ley interpreted his appointment, on 15 November, as Reich Commissioner for the – hitherto long neglected – building of social housing as a general go-ahead for his ambitious plans. It was the wish of the 'Führer', so Ley ordered his deputy to announce, 'that victory should bring every German a better life'.[9] That was why the Reichsorganisationsleiter (Ley's other title) 'had been entrusted with the five great tasks known under the following headings: 1. care of the elderly; 2. health care system [*Gesundheitswerk*] together with an Organization for Leisure and Recreation [*Freizeit- und Erholungswerk*]; 3. national regulation of wages; 4. professional training; 5. social housing building programme.'[10]

What Ley had the experts in the Institute of Labour Science of the DAF develop in the following months was an almost completely comprehensive social policy programme for the post-war period. Undoubtedly the power-conscious leader of the DAF was also concerned to extend his competency and to elevate the Labour Front to supreme and sole authority for the entire area of social policy. Yet at the same time there was a genuine need for action on social policy, which was, to an extent, regarded in a similar way in comparable industrial states. It hardly differed from the British 'Beveridge Plan' in terms of the delineation of those fields which were to be developed within the framework of an expanded state social policy; the difference arose, above all, from the (racist) ideological radicalism of the Nazi plans.

The plans of the Institute of Labour Science for a unified provision for the elderly and for health were already included in the form of a draft law in the autumn of 1940. According to Ley in a characteristic article for the *Angriff* (*Attack*) entitled 'State Socialism Advances', in the future all 'members of the Reich who are Germans or of related blood' were to draw a state pension regardless of 'stamps stuck in during the grey past'. Not only were the separation of workers' and salaried white-collar employees' pensions to end and guaranteed basic pensions to rise; in the further application of the laws already promulgated in 1937–8 there were plans to extend the social insurance system into a comprehensive insurance framework for the whole population. In the experts' opinion the future 'Pension Institute of the German People' (Versorgungswerk des Deutschen Volkes) could find its legitimation in the 'concepts of the national community' and in the principle of the contract between generations: 'if the working population hand over a part of their output to those national comrades who have expended their labours in the service of the community', then that was only just. This already hinted at what was being unequivocally formulated elsewhere: only those who had always fulfilled their 'duty to work' and had given their efforts 'unconditionally, for the good of the nation' could expect to receive a pension in old age – i.e. not the 'parasites on the people' nor 'asocial elements'. The basic principle of equal treatment and legal security in the pension system would thus have been destroyed, and the old age pension system perverted into an instrument of social discipline and the implementation of a brutal ideology of performance.

The DAF's draft reform of the health care system was also steeped in a biologistic concept of performance. 'Once this health care system starts to operate, we will become the healthiest and thus the most productive people on Earth', an exultant Ley told Party functionaries in December 1940. The broadening of access to sanatoria and spas within the framework of the 'Convalescence Organization', demanded in a telling comparison (and with an overtone of class conflict), had a clear purpose: 'We must succeed, every four or five years, in overhauling every German by means of the Convalescence Organization; just as one would periodically overhaul an engine, so must the human being also be periodically overhauled and thereby stay preventatively healthy.' The leader of the Labour Front was in agreement with the Reich Physicians' Leader, Dr Leonardo Conti, that there was a close connection between the 'management of health' and the 'deployment of labour'. The DAF's idea of a fixed system of family doctors ('German People's Protection' – Deutscher Volksschutz), in which the doctor should no longer be paid for his individual performance, but rather receive an inclusive sum for the health care and control of whole families, of course contradicted the interests of the medical profession.

If Ley's ambitions in the field of health policy met with altogether less success than his proposals for a reform of pension insurance, this was also because, in the person of Erich Hilgenfeldt, the Leader of the Nazi People's Welfare Organization, a further competitor claimed competence. With the 'Aid Organization Mother and Child' (Hilfswerk Mutter und Kind), Hilgenfeldt had, in 1934, already developed a social programme on population policy that was both important and successful in Hitler's eyes, and against which neither Ley nor Conti could do a thing. This meant that a temporary retreat was the only option, yet Ley knew 'the Führer's principle, that if an individual has had an idea and built on it, then he was to keep the work for himself and his organization.'

On the whole, the intense debate on social policy in the months after the French campaign brought virtually no concrete results. Neither the plans for old age and health care, nor the proposals for a comprehensive new arrangement of the wages system to make it more closely related to performance, nor Ley's plans for the building of social housing directed at population policy had an effect. Yet the direction which the development of social policy would eventually take had become clearer. And it had also become apparent that the German Labour Front would be allotted an important role in a post-war Nazi society in levelling out still existing social differences between classes within a racially defined national community.

If some elements of the social policy conceived within the DAF conformed to the general trends of the development of a welfare state, within the framework of the Nazi ideology of *Lebensraum* they gained a very specific and most deeply inhuman significance. According to the premises of the ideological *Weltanschauungskrieg* (the war based on the world view) conducted in the East, social policy as such could have no intrinsic value. In so far as it still fulfilled traditional purposes this did not contradict its sole aim of 'maintaining the productive capacity' of the *Volkskörper*. The reduction of a whole society as well as the individual human being to its productive capability was both the precondition and the consequence of the policy of *Lebensraum*: without a disciplined army of highly productive 'soldiers of labour' the 'reconstruction in the German East' would have foundered even before it had begun.

'Selection for performance' and the selective breeding of human beings thus became the counterpart in domestic policy to the racist-imperialist war of conquest in the East. It was no coincidence that Hitler backdated his supplementary authorization to liquidate the mentally ill to 1 September 1939. After the invasion of Poland, extermination was also introduced in principle in the 'Old Reich' wherever social policy could show no 'curative' results, nor any that would promote the productive capability of the individual.

Cure, exploit, exterminate

The simultaneous existence of the traditional activity of state administration and the dominance of special authorities with 'direct responsibility to the Führer' had long become unmistakeable. This often grotesque coexistence of a normative and a prerogative state undoubtedly helped Hitler and the inner circle of the Nazi leadership, at the beginning of the war, to push through their ideological policies. A significant example of this was the so-called 'euthanasia' programme, the secret preparation of which Hitler had entrusted, initially only orally, to the head of his private chancellery, Philipp Bouhler, and to his personal doctor, Karl Brandt. Only in October 1939 did Hitler sign a terse authorization which formed the basis for the mass murder carried out by 'Aktion T 4' (so named after a special office installed at number 4 Tiergartenstrasse).[11]

The gassing of around 70,000 of the mentally handicapped and mentally ill was systematically prepared with the cooperation of prominent medical opinion and actually put into action in six special death clinics by front organizations such as the 'Reich Association of Mental and Care Homes'. It formed merely the prelude to a socio-biological 'process of purification' which could indeed be introduced in peace time, with laws on sterilization and 'healthy marriage', but could only be carried out in its most radical form during the war.

Despite deceitful attempts to conceal the truth, and though it did take a few months after the onset of the programme of murder, rumours reached the public. By the beginning of 1941 practically everyone knew that dreadful things were happening in the psychiatric hospitals. 'Great agitation prevails in wide circles of the population', reported for instance, the president of the superior *Land* court in Bamberg,

and not only amongst those national comrades who count someone who is mentally ill within their family. Such conditions cannot be sustained in the long term, for they bear within them a series of most dangerous uncertainties . . . For example, it is already being said that in the course of the further development of things, in the final analysis, all life that is of no more use to the community as a whole, but rather – seen in purely material terms – is a burden upon it, would be declared, through administrative channels, to be no longer worthy of life and eliminated accordingly.[12]

Just how well-founded was this fear – especially prevalent amongst older people – was demonstrated by developments after the official halting of the 'euthanasia' programme. The action 'Special Treatment 14 f 13' which had meanwhile begun and in which thousands of concentration camp prisoners who were ill, unable to work, but also those who were politically or racially 'undesirable', were 'mustered out' and committed to the 'euthanasia' institutions to be killed, continued. So did the 'euthanasia' of children, which had begun in spring 1939 under the central management of the 'Reich Commission for the Scientific Registration of Hereditary and Constitutional Severe Disorders'. The police and social authorities extended the 'euthanasia' programme beyond the mentally ill to ever wider groups who were considered socially 'useless': eventually 'asocials', criminals, psychopaths, homosexuals, 'war-hysterics', exhausted foreign workers and the bed-ridden elderly were 'transferred'. The murders were now carried out in normal mental and care homes by the administration of drugs instead of in the gas chambers of 'Aktion T 4'.

Alongside the growing need for places for the evacuation of children to the countryside, the deteriorating food situation during the second half of the war served, right up to the spring of 1945, as an argument for the killing of 'unproductive consumers of food' by means of a carefully calculated 'starvation diet' (in Bavaria the Minister of the Interior issued a decree to this end). In total it is estimated that 150,000 people fell victim to this 'therapeutic killing'.[13]

In the majority of cases the political organizers and the technical personnel of 'Aktion T 4' recruited from the ranks of the SS were indeed ideologically committed Nazis; most of the advising doctors – and within the scope of scientific experiments even some of those actively engaged in the killings – saw their activity less as an ideological and political challenge than as a professionally justifiable, indeed necessary, task. In so far as we can tell, they were not, as a rule, at all motivated by a personal blood-lust, nor by vulgar Nazi biologism and patently unscientific concepts of racial hygiene as represented by Hitler and Himmler. If the scientific specialists none the less eagerly laboured to make such Nazi ideas normal within their profession, then they did so for the same basic reasons as other official elites – to maintain their group interests and out of professional ambition. And, of course, their efforts also took place against the specific background of a discussion on euthanasia which had been conducted with great intensity for decades, abroad as well as in Germany; an internationally growing respect for eugenic research; and fundamental changes in psychiatric therapy, which were, to an extent, closely connected with developments in the welfare state and the economy.[14]

The cuts in public expenditure during the world economic crisis had seriously affected what was specifically a newly established and reformist institutional psychiatry, and strengthened the tendency to differentiate between incurable patients and those who would respond to therapy. If, even before 1933, the notions of exterminating 'empty human shells' and 'deadweight life' had at least latent resonance amongst many proponents of the modern care of genetic illness ('prevention instead of treatment') and of a more intensive psychiatric medicine ('cure instead of care'), in the Third Reich activism in (occupational) therapy, advances in the knowledge of eugenics and a cold and extremist concept of performance and productivity combined to form a new and explosive basis for the conduct of psychiatry. In a self-accelerating process in which morality was progressively discarded, the scholars followed the direction of their ideas with fatal consequences: from the approximately 360,000 compulsory sterilizations which 'Eugenic Courts', dominated by physicians, ordered after 1934,[15] to the mass murders of an ever wider-reaching 'euthanasia' programme, behind which the monstrous contours of a 'Final Solution of the social question' were beginning to emerge.

Professor Ernst Rüdin, Director of the Kaiser Wilhelm Institute for Psychiatry in Munich, took interim stock in an article in *Archiv für Rassen-und Gesellschaftsbiologie* (The Archive of Racial and Social Biology) at the turn of 1942–3. Its inevitable pomposity on the tenth anniversary of the Nazi assumption of power could not disguise the sobering view of its context:

> The results of our science had earlier attracted much attention (both support and opposition) in national and international circles. Nevertheless, it will always remain the undying, historic achievement of Adolf Hitler and his followers that they dared to take the first trail-blazing and decisive steps towards such brilliant race-hygienic achievement in and for the German people. In so doing, they went beyond the boundaries of purely scientific knowledge. He and his followers were concerned with putting into practice the theories and advances of Nordic race-conceptions . . . the fight against parasitic alien races such as the Jews and the Gypsies . . . and preventing the breeding of those with hereditary diseases and those of inferior stock.[16]

The practice of 'weeding out' in the social hygiene sense was not a coincidental by-product of the policy of the Third Reich, but rather one of its most important fields. Its impact rested on the interlinking of scientific modernity, socio-technical rationality and a reactionary utopianism. Radicalized during the war – but already initiated beforehand – and designed for a post-war order freed of all racial and social 'inferiority', it indicated not least the destructive potential of modern social policy.

Despite many contradictions in the detail, the Nazi policy on race, population and health was the monstrous product of a comprehensive vision of 'renewal of the *Volk*'. Given the fanaticism with which its anti-Semitic components were carried out in the genocide against the Jews, there can be no doubt of the determination to have this vision turned into reality after the victorious conclusion of the war. Of course, as far as that part of the scheme directed 'internally' towards the 'Aryan' national community is concerned – and to a far, far greater extent than for the extermination of the Jews – the possibilities for action offered by modern techniques in the social sphere made a substantial contribution to defining the target. Population statisticians, labour scientists and nutritionists, anthropologists, human geneticists, physicians and the other experts of industrial civilization were far more than just agents of the policy: they specified what could be done at any particular stage.

This signified nothing less than a paradigmatic change for medicine and health care as a whole. The idea of medical services for the health of the individual and the simultaneous recognition of the right to control one's own body was removed politically by the concept of the health of the people. 'Your health does not belong to you!' ran the corresponding slogan, and within the framwork of a massively promoted medicine of performance, good health became a duty. Good health was no longer of value in itself, but rather the precondition for optimum capability in performance and productivity. Hence it was also to cost as little as possible. The attempt undertaken in the pre-war years, with particular support from Rudolf Hess, to institutionalize elements of the movement for naturopathy and a new way of life as a 'New German Science of Healing', fitted in with endeavours towards cheap medicine; the search for medicinal herbs and low-meat diets suited the autarkic economy, as did the collecting of recyclable scrap and the 'battle against spoilage'.

Right into the war years the real changes in the provision of health care took place in most respects, it is true, at a level at which they could be experienced in a thoroughly positive manner by the population. The new medical care and preventative measures for infants, in schools and in factories were an indisputable advance, although during the war company doctors were often recognized to be there for the purpose of driving performance and hence avoided. And the general view of the medical profession was mainly determined no doubt, as ever, by contact with family doctors, amongst whom both adherents and opponents of Nazi medicine could be found: both those who proposed their own patients for sterilization and those who urged the relatives of psychiatric patients to fetch them home from the clinic in order to protect them from 'euthanasia'.

Suddenly, alongside gestures of humanity and the real – as well as apparent – normality, there were signs of the departure into a future of complete madness. The social engineers of the DAF did not lose sight of their 'objective' aim: 'In the strongest sense a biological and therefore worthwhile aim for the management of health is . . . still the state of affairs when the moment of gradual loss of strength comes shortly before the occurrence of physiological death and coincides with the final marasmus.'[17]

Thinking along the same Social Darwinist lines were population planners, who – as a counterpart to sterilization and 'euthanasia' – pursued as an ideal the eugenically secured promotion of the birth rate by means of the 'complete family, free of heritary disease'. The value of human beings was determined from a racial viewpoint, right into the concentration camps. Leading experts talked, planned and thought as if the concept of human dignity had never existed.

From as early as spring 1940, at the same time as a law on 'euthanasia' intended to replace the secret 'Führer'-authorization was being considered, a 'Law on the Treatment of Community Aliens' was under discussion in the Reich Minstry of the Interior.[18] While the 'euthanasia' law had the lasting aim of integrating the practice of murder into the everyday life of mental hospitals, in which there would remain only 'the most active therapy and scientific work' but no patients in need of care, the aim of the community aliens law was an optimum combination of the various (and separately long existent) possibilities for combating socially deviant behaviour – effectively to regularize the area which preceded 'euthanasia' Any person who 'by his personality and way of life, in particular because of an abnormal deficiency of understanding or character, shows himself to be incapable of meeting the minimum requirements of the national community by himself' could as an alien to the community, be kept under police surveillance, sterilized, taken into custody in a camp and, if necessary, punished by death. The ultimate goal was a *Volkskörper* purged of every form of deviance. According to the estimates of two university doctors, the number of 'community aliens' ran to at least one million; the geneticists hoped to gain more exact information from the organization of a nationwide genetic card index, for which regional models were already in existence.

It was not just schemes like these which showed the 'euthanasia' programme to be part of a limitless plan – in both a literal and metaphorical sense – for 'weeding out' supposed social and racial inferiority. A telling indication of the connection between the campaign of extermination against the mentally ill and the race war in eastern Europe was the further use of personnel engaged in the 'euthanasia' killings in the gassing installations constructed on Polish territory. The genocide of the Jews and Gypsies was based, technically and organizationally, partly on the experience of the 'euthanasia' murders in the 'Old Reich'.

From the outset, the reality of Nazi occupation rule in Poland – and later in the Soviet Union – was determined by criteria of racial policy as well as from the viewpoint of the winning of '*Lebensraum*' and economic exploitation. Whereas the 'euthanasia' murders in the 'Old Reich' were organized under the greatest possible cloak of secrecy, the SS Action Groups (*Einsatzgruppen*) cleared Poland's psychiatric institutions at the beginning of 1940 with machine-gun fire. The conquered East became Himmler's parade ground of race-biological and population policies.[19] Unconstrained by laws and regulations, the Reichsführer SS acted as 'Reich Commissar for the Consolidation of German Nationhood' in the so-called 'incorporated territories' (Danzig-West Prussia, Upper Silesia, the Wartheland, South-east Prussia), and as Chief of the Senior Police and SS Leaders in the *Generalgouvernement* (the occupied rump of Poland under the governorship of Hans Frank).

Himmler's brutal policy of Germanization at first concentrated on the annexed territories of western Poland. Several thousand members of the leading strata of Polish society were simply liquidated. To the advantage of the 'settlement' of German Reich nationals (*Reichsdeutschen*) and ethnic Germans (*Volksdeutschen*) from the Baltic States, from Volhynia in the Ukraine, Bessarabia, Bukovina and other regions in the Soviet sphere of interest, by the spring of 1941, 365,000 Poles and Polish Jews were deported into the *Generalgouvernement*. With a total Polish population of over eight million a rapid 'Germanization' of the incorporated territories by methods such as these was obviously not to be expected. The resulting inclusion of Poles, especially in Upper Silesia and West Prussia, into Group 3 of the so-called 'German List of Peoples', by which German citizenship was linked to renunciation of other citizenship, seemed to indicate a partial return to the policy of assimilation pursued before the First World War. On the other hand, however, stood the radicalism, based on racial ideology, of the Nazi system of categories, which allotted the mass of Poles the status of 'Protectorate denizens' (*Schutzangehörigen*), deprived of rights and property, and which also led to a strict separation of German masters and Polish helots in everyday life.

Even before the attack on the Soviet Union a 'General Plan East' had been drafted on Himmler's direction under the central leadership of the Reich Security Head Office. In the light of this paper all previous Germanization measures proved to be simply a practice run for Hitler's *Lebensraum* fantasies, which were directed in particular towards the Baltic states and the Ukraine. Rosenberg's new, but otherwise rather uninfluential Ministry for the Occupied Eastern Territories and the Race Policy Office of the NSDAP were allowed to take part in the discussion of the plan, which henceforth envisaged the Germanization of the *General-gouvernement*; in addition, the 'borders of German Folkdom' were to be moved 500 kilometres further eastward. For the first quarter century after the end of the war the race strategists reckoned with the 'evacuation' to Siberia of 31 to 51 million 'members of alien races' from the future areas of German settlement. As with many other details, however, the experts were not agreed as to whether the survivors of these deportations were to be permitted to remain there in the long term. A further source of disagreement was how the 14 million 'racially valuable members of alien *Volk*', intended as slaves, above all Balts and Ukrainians, were to be separated from the 'undesirable tribes' in the Reich Commissariats of the 'East Land' (*Ostland*) and the Ukraine (a question in which the anthropologists of the Kaiser Wilhelm Institute also once again became involved).

After the French campaign, the rapid recognition by many experts of the difficulties of simply finding enough settlers of 'German blood' for the regions which were to be cleared of their indigenous population led to the decision that South Tyroleans intended for settlement in a future '*Gau* of Burgundy' were, after all, to be settled in the Ukraine. Despite this recognition, Himmler was not particularly satisfied with the final version of the General Plan East. What seemed to him to be inappropriate above all, was that instead of 'total Germanization', at first only German 'Marches' ('*Ingermanland*' around Leningrad, '*Gotengau*' (the 'Gau of the Goths') in the Crimea and the Memel-Narev Region) and a further thirty-six settlement support points' were envisaged. Himmler therefore demanded a new 'comprehensive settlement plan' which, alongside the earlier ideas for the incorporated eastern regions, was also to take into account 'in broad outline' the Reich Protectorate of Bohemia and Moravia, Alsace-Lorraine, Upper Carniola and southern Styria. Only when it had been established 'what we need in total in terms of people, workers, funds etc.' was it to be decided 'if something is really impossible, what can be deleted'.[20] The notion that the '*Volk* without space' could, in the end, lose itself in a 'greater Germanic' space without a *Volk* was alien to the chief ideologue of selective human breeding.

If the heads of the SS and the inner circle of the Nazi leadership did hold fast to their absurd eastern vision right up to the last months of the war, this was not just an indication of a gigantic refusal to accept reality. It was the consequence of the fact that, from the very first day, German occupation policy in eastern Europe had quite intentionally destroyed all possibility of even partial conciliation and had thus created a fundamentally different situation to all other parts of Europe – notwithstanding the many atrocities and war crimes which were also committed there. From the moment of the invasion of the Soviet Union, just as previously in Poland, there was only the path of ever further radicalization: a campaign determinedly conducted as a war of annihilation – including the 'liquidation' of all Communist functionaries who were encountered (the 'Commissar Order') and in which SS Action Groups murdered over a million 'undesirable elements' in the first year alone – continually begat new excesses of violence.

Hitler's and Himmler's ideological fixation made any revision of Nazi occupation policy impossible, even after it had become obvious that the tide of the war had turned. This was show particularly clearly in the *Generalgouvernement*, where the realization of the racist-imperialist ideas of dominance had become bogged down in the growing resistance of the Partisans' war. Even so, the principle of the oppression of the Polish population, which extended to all aspects of life – and clearly ran counter to the intention of maximum exploitation of the quasi-colony – was not abandoned. Intermittent, pragmatic endeavours by Governor-General Hans Frank at least to mollify the obvious contradiction, foundered on the immutability of the ideological theses. The 'leaderless worker race' of Himmler's cynical and primitive imagination was to be the object both of exploitation and of race policy. The result was a reign of terror dominated by the SS and maintained through fear alone, which deported approximately 1.2 million Poles to slave labour in the territory of the Reich, abducted hundreds of orphan children 'of good racial stock' to be Germanized through the Nazi People's Welfare Organization and the SS '*Lebensborn* Foundation', laid claim to Poland's agricultural and industrial production and, after establishing the ghettoes on Polish soil, eventually constructed the death factories to exterminate European Jewry.

The link between exploitation and extermination which characterized Nazi occupation policy in the East as much as the health policy directed against the German population became most clearly visible in Auschwitz.[21] There, from a transit camp set up in the summer of 1940 to receive Polish prisoners from the incorporated territories and the *Generalgouvernement*, the SS developed their largest concentration camp complex of all. On a site of 40 square kilometres, prisoners' labour was used to build an agricultural concern with experimental stations and SS-owned production plant, from spring 1941 the satellite camp Monowitz with a *Buna* plant belonging to IG Farben, from the autumn of the same year the Birkenau camp, and then, in its immediate vicinity, the installations for mass gassings. After the 'Final Solution of the Jewish Question' had begun, doctors selected the new arrivals at the railway station according to their ability to work. Those who were not immediately murdered were intended for 'extermination through work' or – like the Gypsies imprisoned since the beginning of 1943 in catastrophic conditions in a special camp[22] – for medical experiments and eugenic research.

With the deterioration of the military situation the exploitation of concentration camp prisoners for labour grew increasingly important. Around almost every camp there eventually stretched an often far-flung ring of outer and sub-command posts, which supplied the SS factories, armaments plants and other militarily important installations with cheap labour. For a time there existed almost a thousand of these auxiliary camps. During the war years, in many towns and parishes, columns of prisoners under SS guard marching to their workplaces were part of the daily street scene.

The deployment of prisoners was directed by the Economic Administration Head Office of the SS, which charged industry between 3 and 6 Reichsmarks per prisoner per day – prices which some companies rejected as exorbitant because the productivity of prisoners was far below average. But the managements of the factories were not disturbed by the fact that the physical and psychological energy of prisoners, often drafted in to perform the heaviest labour in 11-hour shifts, rapidly diminished because of inadequate food, clothing and accommodation and that the number of those dying from exhaustion rose month by month. In the shadow of the 'Final Solution' the camp doctors, above all in Auschwitz, murdered by injection prisoners who had become ill and unable to work. In Auschwitz III approximately 25,000 labour camp prisoners were 'consumed' in the production of synthetic rubber at Monowitz. Altogether at least half a million human beings died in the concentration camps from exhaustion, hunger and disease, half of these in the chaos of the final weeks of the war.

The genocide of the Jews

The policy of racial reconstruction of the *Lebensraum* claimed by Germany in the East was, to a high degree, closely interlinked with the fate of the Jews who had lived there hitherto and those who had been deported there, first from the 'Old Reich' and finally from all over Europe. At the same time, however, the 'Final Solution of the Jewish Question' carried out on Polish and Soviet soil still surpassed even the most terrible aspects of German occupation policy. With the genocide, Nazi race policy entered an altogether new category. The murder of the European Jews was without parallel or reference point in history; it was, to use the extravagant terminology of the *Historikerstreit* (the recent 'historians' dispute'), unique.

Separate from this fact, the question has to be addressed of how, when and at what level of the regime the decision to commit this crime was reached. It now seems to be generally accepted that the long searched-for, comprehensive, written order by Hitler himself to kill all the Jews within the German sphere of power never existed. There is a great deal to support the interpretation which conceives of the genocide as an event which resulted from successive individual initiatives and actions, not all of which necessarily emanated from Hitler. This does not, of course, mean that the 'Führer' is exonerated.

The fact that international research into the form and the course of the 'creation of the decision' continues to be the subject of controversial debate[23] cannot simply be blamed on the comparatively meagre and contradictory source material on which the interpretations have been based. One aspect of the controversy results from the differing opinions about the importance which Hitler and the Nazi inner leadership attached to anti-Semitism – and anti-Bolshevism. In reality this anti-Semitism was not just a fixed, unshakeable tenet of the Nazi *Weltanschauung*. Until well into the war, but especially in the pre-war years, it was also an instrument of ideological mobilization and negative integration, indeed of political rhetoric. Moreover, the policy of the Third Reich towards the Jews after 1933 in no way presents a completely cogent picture. The concrete measures were not, in any sense, consistent and unilinear.[24] In the final analysis the fact is that, at the beginning, the Holocaust was set in train in a rather impromptu manner. All this contradicts the view – admittedly rarely propounded so directly any longer – that once the war had begun the issue was solely one of realizing the decisive final phase of the long and firmly established 'grand design' of Nazi anti-Jewish policy. Despite the threats of extermination, which Hitler had already issued early on and had repeated publicly most recently on 30 January 1939, the diabolical reality was more complicated.

From the April boycott of 1933 to the systematic mass murder in the death-factories in the East was a long and, as historical research has shown, also a winding path. This was expressed in a confusing manner in the reality of everyday Jewish life in the Third Reich.[25] Alongside growing discrimination and exclusion from the 'Aryan' *Volksgemeinschaft* there were small areas and 'niches' of something almost resembling normal existence. The fatal consequences of these simultaneous but desperately misleading contradictions only proved themselves seemingly obvious from the 'post-Auschwitz' perspective. For a long time, despite everything, the situation appeared not to be completely hopeless, not only to the victims but also to many contemporaries who remained personally unaffected.

The tempo, direction and level of the discrimination was often subject to change, indeed sometimes it even appeared to be ceasing altogether. As a result, in 1934–5, after the first wave of anti-Jewish measures which followed the Law for the Restoration of the Professional Civil Service, not a few Jewish Germans returned from their emigration, especially from neighbouring France. But at about the same time the first 'Aryanizations' of firms owned by the Jewish middle class were under way; as early as 1933–4, under massive pressure, politically important concerns such as the renowned publishing houses of Ullstein and Mosse had already been transferred to Nazi Party holding companies. The anti-Semitic excesses and harassment otherwise extensively left to locally powerful figures in the Party were followed, from the early summer of 1935, by renewed and intensified boycott propaganda.

The 'Reich Party Congress of Freedom' dealt the severest legislative blow of all against German Jewry: on 15 September 1935, before the Reichstag which had been called to Nuremberg, Hermann Goering proclaimed the 'Reich Citizenship Law'. It made a distinction between 'Reich citizens of German or ethnically similar blood' as bearers of 'full political rights' and simple 'state citizens' who were, in future, to be without rights – the Jews. In addition a 'Law for the Protection of German Blood and Honour' prohibited marriages and sexual relations between Jews and non-Jews. Although these laws (both, of course, adopted unanimously) were first set down in detail by civil servants who had been summoned to the Congress, they had been preceded by much prior deliberation and announcements on the subject. Nevertheless they could not be said to have been particularly well thought through, as the ensuing two months of inter-ministerial disagreements about the implementation orders showed. Only in these was the decisive question 'resolved' as to who would be counted as a Jew under the terms of the Reich Citizenship Law. Here the concept of race legislation 'based on blood' also demonstrated its absurd logic: definitions such as 'Aryan', 'full Jew', 'first grade half-breed' and 'second grade half-breed' were based on the criterion of the religious affiliation of ancestors, but after the third generation the question of whether or not they were converts was left unexamined.

Particularly because Hitler announced the new laws to be the final regulation of the 'Jewish Question', the Jewish organizations even reacted, in parts, with restrained relief; those who had been pilloried by Nazi propaganda, especially by Streicher's *Stürmer*, as international conspirators against Germany, were attached to their homeland and in many cases preferred to accept restrictions in their familiar surroundings rather than risk the gamble of emigration. With the Nuremberg Laws the 'wild' or 'unauthorized' discrimination, which had already been occurring at the local level, was confirmed in terms of a specific and concerted exclusion of the Jews from society. The removal of their right to vote and their expulsion from public office was followed, in the same year, by a ban on professional practice for those Jewish lawyers and doctors receiving a salary from the state, for teachers and professors and soon, *de facto*, for pharmacists also.

Then, in 1936, as the Olympic Games focused international attention on Hitler's Germany, the anti-Jewish laws and statutory regulations were 'restricted' to peripheral areas. Of the Third Reich's approximately 2,000 anti-Jewish measures, 'only' about 150 materialized in 1936 and 1937. Hjalmar Schacht shared big business's disapproval of economically damaging 'racial criteria'. Only after he had relinquished the office of Minister of Economics, from early 1938, did an intensification of policy become discernible, and this was also expressed in the number of statutory regulations: around 300. These were now aimed at forcing the Jews out of the economy, but this was only advanced in a piecemeal fashion because, even under the now unfettered overall control of Goering's Four-year Plan authorities, it obviously clashed with the interests of the economy.

Divergent interests and competencies meanwhile led Nazi Jewish policy into deadlock. The assassination attempt on 7 November 1938 on Ernst vom Rath, a counsellor at the German Embassy in Paris, by the seventeen-year-old Herschel Grynszpan (whose parents were amongst the 17,000 Polish Jews who had been deported from the Reich shortly before), offered the Nazi leadership an ideal opportunity to give it a new and unambiguous direction. The central character of what was to be the most brutal attack on the Jews so far was, as in the April boycott of 1933, Joseph Goebbels. What was to enter the chronicles under the euphemistic title of 'Crystal Night' was an engineered pogrom of ghastly proportions, which lasted in some places for more than three days. Ninety-one people were murdered, more than a few in the open street. While the first local outrages on 8 November had been fomented by inflammatory newspaper reports, the mass pogrom of 9–10 November had its origin in the wild diatribe that Goebbels, as Reich Propaganda Leader of the NSDAP, had delivered directly after the arrival of the news of the counsellor's death to the Party's 'Old Guard', who were meeting in Munich. Its content was immediately passed on to Party branches as an instruction to strike. Where more circumspect District and Local Group Leaders remained inactive, provocateurs from outside saw to it that, even in the smallest rural communities, synagogues burned, shops were looted, entire families were maltreated and that altogether 30,000 Jews were detained in concentration camps. This was not a genuine expression of 'spontaneous anger on the part of the people' either; none the less, here and there, non-Party members did exploit the opportunity to settle scores with Jewish neighbours; in Berlin above all, a semi-criminal mob took part in the violent outrages and looting organized by SA and 'Party comrades' in civilian dress. More common, of course, even now, was the tendency for people consciously to turn their heads the other way. Only a few found the courage to help Jewish victims of their acquaintance. Sometimes, however, the police authorities did also register indignant protest.

'Crystal Night' heralded a new phase in Nazi policy towards the Jews. With it began the systematic economic exploitation of the Jews and their exclusion from the world of commerce. Whereas, since April 1938, they had had to register all property worth over 5,000 Reichsmarks, now a 'fine' was imposed upon them and, up to 1940, 1.12 billion Reichsmarks were collected in the form of a property tax. A ministerial conference held directly after the pogrom established the guidelines of the future 'Aryanization' and liquidation of Jewish businesses, which, for the moment, were being granted to 'Aryan' trustees. In this discussion between Goebbels, Goering and the Head of the SD, Heydrich, hardly a single utterance was too primitive or perfidious to serve as a law or decree introducing new and unbridled torments during the following months. Whilst Jews had already been locally prohibited from using cinemas, parks and swimming pools for several years, a 'ban on Jews' further restricted their freedom of movement. Railway sleeping cars and certain hotels could no longer be used and all jewellery was to be handed over.

In July 1939, the 'Reich Association of Jews in Germany', known until the Nuremberg Laws as the 'Reich Representative Body of the German Jews', was forced to change its name for the fourth time. As the 'Reich Union of Jews in Germany' (Reichsvereinigung der Juden in Deutschland), this amalgamation of Jewish organizations and congregations became a compulsory organization for all 'Jews by faith or race' (*Glaubens- und Rassejuden*). The interest group had been established under the leadership of Leo Baeck as a reaction to the Nazi assumption of power and had above all taken over responsibilities in the area of welfare care, cultural life and the coordination of emigration. It was now burdened with obligations imposed by the state. Ever since Jewish children had been barred completely from attending 'German' schools, the Reichsvereinigung had borne responsibility for the entire Jewish school system (which was tolerated until 1942), as well as for the welfare support for impoverished and unemployed Jews (partly financed through donations from abroad). The Jewish Cultural League, which was supposed to continue its work after the November pogrom on the express orders of the Propaganda Minister, also belonged to the Reichsvereinigung. Since the mid-1930s, a consequence of the exclusion of Jewish citizens from all social life had been the grotesque blossoming of a specifically Jewish, middle-class, intellectual culture. The special consciousness which Hitler had forced upon the assimilated Jews gave rise to expressions of social and cultural segregation which, only a few years before, nobody would have believed possible.

The 'Reich Central Office for Jewish Emigration' (Reichszentrale für jüdische Auswanderung), established on Heydrich's initiative in the Reich Ministry of the Interior by the beginning of 1939, converted the Reichsvereinigung, as a compulsory organization for Jews, into an administrative instrument for the policy of forced emigration, or more aptly put, expulsion. After 9 November 1938, the Haavara Treaty, on the basis of which around 30,000 Jews had emigrated to Palestine, especially in 1934–5, was denounced; a 'Palestine Trust Company' established by the Reich Ministry of the Interior for the export of German industrial goods had cooperated in this with the Zionist 'Jewish Agency for Palestine'. The new methods which were now to extend their grip into the 'Old Reich' – on the basis of the model already practised in Vienna by Adolf Eichmann – pursued even more strongly the aim of economic plunder. Wealthy Jews who wanted to leave Germany had to pay an 'emigration tax', which was collected via the Reichsvereinigung. According to the census in May 1939, there were still 233,646 people in the Reich (excluding Austria and the Sudeten region) who were Jews under the Nazi definition. By the outbreak of war their number had further fallen by almost 50,000; some 10,000 children had found temporary refuge, mainly in England, Belgium and Holland, before most of them were taken on to the USA or Palestine.

If the method of the expulsion of the Jews from Germany was already dominated by uncertainty in 'peacetime' – there was simply agreement that it should take place, but not how – then after the beginning of the war the situation soon became nothing short of chaotic. On the one hand, western European Jews could still emigrate, if with increasing difficulty, until the definitive ban on emigration imposed on 23 October 1941; but on the other, after the Polish campaign the first deportations of Jews from the 'Protectorate of Bohemia and Moravia' and from Austria began. Then, in the winter of 1939–40, huge numbers of Jews, but also Poles too, fell victim to more or less unplanned deportations from the '*Reichsgau* Wartheland' into the *Generalgouvernement*. The Jews of Stettin formed the first transport from the 'Old Reich'.

In the summer of 1940, the idea – occasionally discussed in pre-war

Poland – of deporting all European Jews to the French island colony of Madagascar was taken up by the German Foreign Office and the Reich Security Head Office. Even before the course of the war had put paid to the abstruse Madagascar plan, both it and the previous idea considered in spring 1940 of concentrating the Jews in West Galicia (Lublin) had been superseded by events. For the SS Actions Groups were present from the beginning of the war against the Soviet Union, having already wreaked havoc 'behind the Front' in Poland, not least against the Jews. After only a short time, the operations against Communist functionaries, 'Jews in Party and state positions' and 'other radical elements' were extended further and further and transformed into mass executions. The anti-Bolshevism which Hitler had aroused in his commanders in the East by referring to the defeat of the 'Jewish-Bolshevik intelligentsia' acted as a catalyst here; 'justified' in these terms, the acts of mass murder also became acceptable to the Wehrmacht. The massacre in the ravine of Babi Yar near Kiev, in which, according to the report of the *Sonderkommando* 4a of Action Group C, a total of 33,771 Jews – amongst them particularly large numbers of women and children – were shot on 29 and 30 September 1941, stood out only in respect of the number of people killed in a single operation, not in the manner of its execution.[26]

On 20 January 1942, state secretaries and senior Party officials met under Heydrich's chairmanship in a villa on Berlin's Wannsee to co-ordinate the 'Final Solution of the Jewish Question'. By this time some experts in killing from the now closed 'euthanasia' 'Aktion T 4' – amongst others – had already been engaged for a short while in making preparations for the gassing of the Jews in the *Generalgouvernement*, who had become the victims of extensive ghettoization. Since December 1941, specially prepared gas-vans had been deployed at the newly established death-camp at Chelmno, in which the people who had been crammed inside slowly suffocated from the exhaust fumes pumped into the van after the journey had begun. In Auschwitz, where the first experimental gassings using the fumigant Zyklon B had already taken place in early September, a first gas chamber was ready for use (in Auschwitz-Birkenau) from January 1942. From mid-March, as part of what was later to be known as 'Aktion Reinhard', the gas chambers of the death camp at Belzec were in operation; from April, those at Sobibor; from July, those at Treblinka. The gassing installations at the Maidanek concentration camp were in use for approximately one year, beginning in the autumn of 1942.

While the machinery of murder was gathering pace in the East, the exclusion of the Jews inside Germany was assuming a still harsher character. From 1 September 1941, the yellow star, which Jews in the

Generalgouvernement had already been obliged to wear for two years, also made Jews within the Reich immediately identifiable. Those who wore the star were now forbidden to do virtually anything. If they dared to go out into the street during the strictly limited time allowed (in Berlin between 4 and 5 p.m.) to buy the few things for which food coupons were still allocated, this often meant running the gauntlet. For it took great courage to exchange even a single word with someone bearing such an insignia, someone who was being denounced as sub-human by an ever-increasing propaganda of hatred. While some did indeed help Jews who had gone underground – in Berlin some 1,400 survived the war as a result – the Jews in Germany, long before they were deported, were in fact only present in the consciousness of many in the manner required by the official demonology: as the earthly incarnation of evil itself, and no longer as fellow citizens.

First of all, even before the end of 1941, those Jews designated for deportation, and then later, on 30 April 1943, German Jews in general, were stripped of their nationality. All the still remaining property of those delivered over to police tyranny fell to the state. Old and prominent Jews, who since January 1942 had been 'resettled' in the 'model ghetto' of Theresienstadt, were swindled out of their property by the Reich Security Head Office with special 'home purchase contracts'. For tens of thousands, the 'privileged camp' in northern Bohemia was nothing more than a transit station on the way to one of the places of extermination. While elsewhere the crematoria were smoking and the machine guns were firing, a commission of the International Red Cross was shown Theresienstadt as proof of the 'humanity' of Nazi Jewish policy, and it served not least to reassure those Jews still living in Germany who were receiving harmless sounding letters from their relatives there. Naturally the regime also exploited this sham idyll, in which thousands were dying from infectious diseases and malnutrition, for its domestic propaganda. For however openly the persecution and exclusion of the Jews had been pursued up to this point, the final act took place in the greatest possible secrecy: Hitler, Himmler and Heydrich knew, but so too did those who drew up the plans and those who carried them out, that for this, the assent of the majority of the population could not be maintained.

Even so, the knowledge that something monstrous was happening 'in the East' was more widespread than German society later wanted to accept. The genocidal character of the persecution of the Jews which extended throughout occupied Europe and the systematic nature of their extermination may have been hard to recognize. But more than a few knew how mercilessly Jews within the German sphere of power were being deported – and also the extent of the deployment of resources vital to the war effort involved – even if they had only observed how their own neighbours had been 'picked up'. Soldiers on leave from the Front brought information about the mass executions and also, if less often, about the extermination camps. In so doing they probably contributed to the creation of the legend according to which the Wehrmacht played no part at all in these crimes. For in order to avoid incriminating their comrades-in-arms, or even indeed themselves, they steered all the disgust and repugnance towards the SS and its Action Groups. In fact, however, there were not only isolated critics of the SS and the Action Groups to be found amongst the military commanders; there were also those who were privy and sympathetic to what was happening, and even willing accomplices.

The connection between war and and the crime of genocide involved not only primarily the military, but also most of the other elite groups of German officialdom, to a far greater degree than a glance at the immediate actors – which included a considerable number of non-German collaborators – suggests. At the same time, the initiators of the mass murder benefited from the division of labour and responsibility in modern industrial society: even, for example, those German civil servants, engineers, technicians or railway workers who were occupied with or heard about a component part – in itself often seemingly quite harmless – of the 'most dreadful task' (Himmler) were able psychologically to repress their knowledge of the genocide of the Jews.

Furthermore, there was the inconceivable nature of the events, which were veiled in secrecy. The – in the truest sense of the word – unbelievable process of the coldly initiated, conveyor-belt murder of at least 5.29 million human beings on the sole 'grounds' of their supposed otherness 'in terms of blood and race' made world opinion doubtful too, even of the reports of eye-witnesses who had escaped from the death camps. Studies of the information available to the Allies and their reaction show that a crime of such monstrosity seemed to be beyond the desire to know, as well as the ability to believe, of entire nations and their political leaders.[27]

Total war and the disintegration of Nazi rule

Twice, in February 1943 and in July 1944, the regime declared 'total war'. Yet the prospect of a rapid 'final victory' had already been shattered in the first winter on the Eastern Front. A year later, after the destruction of the Sixth Army at Stalingrad, it had become obvious to all that the tide of war had turned. For a long time there had no longer been any question of the 'total victory' which Goebbels, in his speech at the Berlin Sportpalast in February 1943, had promised as the reward for yet further increased efforts. Those who did not know at least suspected this to be the case. None the less, many Germans wanted to believe the 'little Doctor' – because the truth seemed so unbearable. And thus the Propaganda Minister's hour had come. For years he had sailed in the lee of political development and at times had almost sunk as a result of private affairs – but now he was needed; the more so as the 'Führer' began to avoid his *Volk*.

The 'front bench' to which Goebbels returned in the second half of the war had changed considerably. After the flight to Scotland of the Deputy 'Führer' Hess, who had always lacked influence, Martin Bormann pushed himself into Hess' place and out of a nominally subordinate position built up a unique direct relationship with Hitler. Hermann Goering, designated at the beginning of the war as the 'Führer's' official successor, had meanwhile lost influence over policy for the arms industry: this trend had already found expression in the establishment, in the spring of 1940, of a Reich Ministry for Armament and Munitions under Fritz Todt. Albert Speer, chosen as Armaments Minister after Todt's plane crash in February 1942, shifted the balance further to Goering's disadvantage. The prestige of the 'Reich Marshal' sank inexorably, determined above all by the failures of his Luftwaffe. In the sphere of domestic politics, which was now ever increasingly reduced to terror and violence, there was no doubt about Himmler's pre-eminence, even long before his appointment as Minister of the Interior as successor to Wilhelm Frick, who had been 'reshuffled' into the 'Reich Protectorate of Bohemia and Moravia'.

Himmler, Speer, Bormann and Goebbels, plus the Head of the Reich Chancellery, Hans Heinrich Lammers, as the mediating channel for the rest of the ministries and state authorities: the composition of the top leadership of the regime during the second half of the war symbolized the advancing decay of rational and orderly structures of government and decision-making. Certainly, the Third Reich had never been the strictly and thoroughly organized 'Führer State' which Hitler had always professed he would create; but now substantial complexes of power could clearly be seen to be diverging. While the 'Führer' became engrossed in the details of the conduct of the war, the power of the many – mutually competing – chancelleries and special commissars grew. It was as though the Nazis were returning to their roots: the propagandist activism, the unpre-dictability of permanent 'movement' and institutional restructuring, and in addition the furiously destructive aggressiveness of their designation of friend and foe – all this came clearly to the fore once again, but with other consequences than in the 'period of struggle'.

Goebbels gave a particularly impressive example of such regression. His appearance at the Sportpalast had indeed taken place before a hand-picked audience, but unlike Hitler he did not shy away from contact with people. On the contrary, in front of an audience he visibly shed the mantle of Reich Minister and liked to resurrect the semi-proletarian role of Gauleiter of Berlin. The war socialism which the 'stick it out' propagandist now preached awakened memories of his origins on the left wing of the NSDAP. His demands, laced with a quasi-religious flavour, for sacrifice, the fulfilment of duty and solidarity reached a peak when he lauded the air-raid damage as a basically desirable liberation from the 'ballast of civilization'.[28] Goebbels' diagnosis was that, in the bombing war, the last class barriers were finally disappearing.

He was right in so far as the war and its consequences – to a far greater extent than the preceding years of Nazi rule – had levelled a whole range of social, cultural and regional differences. But it was also true that the suffering and burdens of the war were by no means evenly distributed throughout the population. The allied air-raids were aimed primarily at the big cities, whereas, by contrast, rural areas in the interior of the Reich remained almost untouched right up to the final weeks of the war. Munitions workers were subjected to a far greater pressure to perform than office and administrative employees. Soldiers were killed more quickly on the Eastern Front than in the West. Despite a duty on the part of the peasants to deliver produce, which involved the threat of severe penalties and enormous organizational efforts in the distribution of food, industrial workers and their families in the conurbations were affected to a completely different extent from people in small towns and villages by the cuts in rations already being introduced during the spring of 1942. The people who suffered most of all were those who stood outside the 'national community' and for this very reason could be mercilessly exploited for Hitler's war: concentration camp prisoners, prisoners of war, and above all the so-called 'foreign workers'. It is precisely the policy of 'deployment of labour' practised with respect to these groups which demonstrates that little importance can be attached to the distinction, emphasized in the propaganda of the time, between the *Blitzkrieg* period and the subsequent total mobilization of forces in areas other than those of militarily strategic importance.

The drafting in of 'members of alien races' for the German war economy had begun immediately after the first military successes in Poland and then France.[29] In the summer of 1941 there were already almost three million foreigners working in Germany and an end to the deployment of forced labour was not envisaged even in the event of the war coming to a rapid end. The longer the war lasted and the heavier the losses, the more heavily dependent on foreign workers the German economy became. But, significantly, more effective recruitment began almost a year before Goebbels' proclamation of 'total war'. To this end the new 'Plenipotentiary for the Deployment of Labour', the Gauleiter Fritz Sauckel, at first had to suppress the reservations, based on race ideology, which existed within the Party and within Himmler's sphere of power, against the increased drafting in of Soviet labour. In order to achieve this Sauckel involved his fellow Gauleiter who, in their capacity as Commissars for the Defence of the Reich, were in any case enjoying a continual growth in their power (formally at least) in 'labour deployment' policy. At the same time, Sauckel gave Himmler's bureaucracy, which controlled the so-called 'labour education camps', a free hand to mete out draconian punishment for the slightest deviation from the rules, particularly to 'eastern workers' who were kept as slave-workers without rights. Hundreds of thousands of Soviet prisoners of war had been allowed to starve to death during the first months of the Russian campaign.[30] But as a result of pressure from big business, supported in this instance by the leadership of the Wehrmacht and the Reich Ministry of Labour, there began in mid-1942 the systematic 'recruitment' of increasingly large numbers of 'eastern workers' in the notorious 'Sauckel campaigns'.

In the summer of 1944, the German war economy was kept going by around 7.6 million foreign workers: almost 2.8 million Soviet Russians, 1.7 million Poles, 1.3 million French, 590,000 Italians, 280,000 Czechs, 270,000 Dutch and a quarter of a million Belgians. In agriculture almost half of all workers were foreigners; in the arms industry about one-third. On average there was one foreign worker for every three from the indigenous population. Just under two million of the foreigners were prisoners of war; all the others were so-called civilian workers. Yet as far as their lot was concerned, this distinction was less significant than their nationality. While the 'western workers' – some of whom were genuinely recruited and not conscripted – were, as a rule, hardly any worse nourished than their German colleagues and also received bearable treatment, the living conditions of the 'eastern workers' who were forcibly transported into the Reich were, for the most part, catastrophic. Ideological racism even penetrated into economic exploitation: on the lowest rung of the Nazi scale of value stood the Soviet forced labourers, both men and women, and the prisoners of war who were kept in the most primitive camps, given starvation rations, paid almost nothing and, like the Poles, constantly threatened with excessive punishments. If some of the camps in which 'eastern workers' were held improved slightly during the course of the war, then this was only because economic efficiency and the requirements of the arms industry demanded it.

Table 4 Industrial production in the German Reich 1928–1944 (Index)

Year	Total	Consumer goods (total)	Producer goods Total[a]	Mining[b]
1928	100	100	100	100
1929	100	97	102	108
1930	87	91	84	94
1931	70	82	62	79
1932	58	74	47	70
1933	66	80	56	74
1934	83	93	81	83
1935	96	91	99	96
1936	107	98	114	107
1937	117	103	130	124
1938	125	108	144	126
1939	132	108	148	135
1940	128	102	144	165
1941	131	104	149	169
1942	132	93	157	177
1943	149	98	180	185
1944	146	93	178	163

[a] From 1938 comprising raw materials, ordnance equipment, construction, other investments.
[b] 1933–4 coalmining only.
(All data relates to the respective territory of the Reich in each year.)

Source: Dietmar Petzina et al. (eds), *Sozialgeschichtliches Arbeitsbuch.*
vol. 31, *Materialien zur Statistik des Deutschen Reiches 1914–1945*
(Munich, 1978), p. 61.

The demands of an altered military situation – which could not be contested even by the SS ideologues in the Reich Security Head Office – explain the pragmatism with which the new Minister for Armaments and Munitions, already installed by Hitler shortly before Sauckel's appointment, pushed arms production to record levels. Albert Speer, not yet 37 years old and having repeatedly come to the fore as an organizational genius, not only enjoyed the 'Führer's' favour, but also rapidly gained the respect of industrial managers. Speer made the coordination of private industry and the state, which had begun with the Four-year Plan Organization, more effective by taking more responsibility for big business within the sphere of armaments policy while simultaneously allowing it extensive autonomy. The 'Principal Commissions' for the direction of arms production, already set up by Todt and run by employers, were complemented by a ring system for the sub-contracting firms. With the sole aim of maximum output, the Munitions Minister sought out the most efficient manufacturing plants for each of the individual products: production was then to be concentrated in the so-called 'best factories'. But Speer's most important instrument of direction was 'Central Planning'. There, every fortnight, with him in the chair, the distribution of all raw materials was laid down and the planning of demand for people and materials coordinated. Long before he also gained responsibility for civil production in early September 1943 (and the title of Reich Minister for Armaments and War Production), Speer had used 'Central Planning' to bring the most important aspects of the war economy under his control.

The success seemed to prove this almost silent organizer – but for that no less brutal than Sauckel in the procurement of labour power – right: under Speer's management, armaments production multiplied several times over. The building of heavy battle tanks, for example, increased six-fold between 1941 and 1944, that of aeroplanes three-and-a-half fold. Not until July 1944, at the same time as the climax of the Allies' aerial bombing war, did war production reach its peak. Because of the now ever greater superior strength and determination of Germany's adversaries, these almost unbelievable results could do nothing other than lengthen the war and make it even more brutal. Yet they seemed precisely to predestine Speer for the role of architect of post-war planning – the subject of deliberation in various parts of the regime right into the spring of 1945. In the intervening period however, opposition had developed to the 'Führer's' master builder, who had become all too powerful and seemed all too lacking in Nazi ideology.

Particularly in Himmler's sphere of power, the pragmatism with which Speer had recognized big business as the decisive factor in the mobilization of the war economy and had taken its interests into account encountered fundamental reservations. Total war had indeed given additional momentum to the concentration of enterprises, which had already been encouraged by the Four-Year Plan Organization, and big companies had continued to grow at the expense of small businesses and industries. Since the beginning of 1943, the 'mopping up' of personnel which released new forces for the Front or for deployment in armaments factories, and factory closures which saved raw materials in sectors of production unimportant for the war effort, had mainly affected commerce, artisans, and smaller industrial plants. Figures such as Dr Otto Ohlendorf, formerly Director of Research at the Institute of World Economy in Kiel, head of the SD in the Reich Security Head Office since 1939 and, from 1943, Deputy Secretary of State in the Reich Ministry of Industry, wished to reverse this development after the war by a concerted policy favouring the *Mittelstand* and a decartelization of the combines. In the opinion of the ideologues there had been too great a deviation from Nazi economic ideals.

If Ohlendorf, as the SS's economic specialist, became Speer's opponent in the final months of the war, then this was because of considerations of power politics and ideology directed towards the future rather than the politics of the moment. In their open attitude towards technology and modern expert opinion the two men, who were of almost the same age, were actually quite similar; both were part of the new technocratic elite which was working towards a more efficient and, at the same time, scientifically and technically controlled post-war regime. But what did distinguish Speer from people like Ohlendorf and what he lacked in the eyes of the SS were those basic ideological convictions which Ohlendorf had so unambiguously confirmed in the first year of the Russian campaign as head of Action Group D. With his involvement in the crimes committed in the East, Ohlendorf had proved himself to be a dyed-in-the-wool Nazi, 'worthy' of a high-ranking position in a post-war system controlled by the SS, the object of which would be to maintain the ideals of the movement in a reality permeated with ideology.[31]

Obviously, after about the middle of 1944, the vision of a German '*Lebensraum* in the East' no longer played a role in the plans for a Nazi peacetime order. Large concerns like Siemens began to adapt their organizational structures to the Allies' intended division of Germany into three occupation zones. Anticipating defeat, but without speaking openly about it, the experts oriented themselves towards the West; it was possible to discern the provisional, schematic outlines of an economic region which would, perhaps, still be dominated by Germany to the exclusion of a future Soviet-controlled south-east Europe. After Stalingrad, these ideas, which had long been quietly circulating, were taken up by Goebbels in an intensified 'Occident' propaganda, as part of his attempt to awaken a sort of European solidarity in a 'defensive struggle' against 'Bolshevism'. But the reality of Nazi occupation in the previous few years had destroyed any basis for such ideas. And that this was – at least on the part of the Nazi leadership – simply an implausible search for a way out of the war on two fronts was made clear by the ensuing speculation about a separate peace with Stalin and Hitler's Ardennes offensive (the 'Battle of the Bulge') at the turn of 1944–5 – speculation which Himmler, in this turn, superseded at the very last moment by trying to sound out the western Allies. If the European ideas of the early 1940s had to remain an illusion – simply because they wished to impose on the Europeans both unaltered German supremacy and the exclusion of the USA from the continent – they none the less already contained within them elements of later European integration, though one no longer, of course, to be dominated by Germany.

In leading industrial circles and in the political opposition, deliberations about Germany's future continued to the very end. The majority of the people, on the other hand, had other worries. Their attention was increasingly reduced simply to securing their sheer survival. Just how much the psychological mood had changed with the deterioration of the 'aerial situation' was shown by Goebbels' attempts to use the Allied demand for unconditional surrender as a bogey to fire the population's will to endure. Fanaticism had been exhausted by the everyday experience of the aerial bombing war; reality left increasingly little room for the promises of propaganda. None the less, right into the very last weeks of the war, many Germans clung on to the Propaganda Minister's promise of the effectiveness of the 'miracle weapon' with which the regime would avenge the destruction of Germany's cities and would still, even now, alter the course of the war. It was a mood fed by fear, anger, defiance and political self-deception, which moved people, against their better judgement, to continue to cling to the belief in a 'final victory'.

In the final analysis, this collective feeling simply reflected the high degree of political integration which had taken place in German society in the preceding years. This was closely connected with the fact that, even now, all thoughts of resistance to Hitler's regime would, in principle, have had to be pursued against the wishes of the population. The longer Hitler's rule lasted, the more 'socially isolated' the German opposition to Hitler found itself; those considering an assassination attempt were 'outsiders'.[32]

This was also the reason for the conspicuous indecisiveness and weakness of the small group of military opponents to the regime – and not just the fact that the aims and interests of the Wehrmacht as a whole were far too closely aligned with those of the political leadership for a broad and fundamental opposition to be able to develop within its ranks. It is true that, in the summer of 1938, consideration had already been given within the Wehrmacht to a coup d'etat. But as the threat of war seemed, at first, to have been averted by the Munich Agreement, the plans effectively collapsed. After the war had begun, plans and dates were repeatedly postponed; an assassination attempt in March 1943 was unsuccessful.

Apart from the military opposition and the group of primarily elderly, conservative-nationalist notables around Carl Goerdeler, at the end of 1938 younger opponents of the regime from various political backgrounds and mainly working in the civil service had come together around Count Peter Yorck von Wartenburg. The Kreisau Circle, which grew out of this, gathered several times for large meetings on Count Helmuth James von Moltke's estate in Lower Silesia. There, committed representatives of the generation of thirty- to forty-year-olds (amongst them former socialist politicians and trade unionists, professors, diplomats and priests from both denominations) discussed a political, social and societal new order for Germany for the period after Hitler. Assassination or coup were not the central issues here; Moltke himself believed tyrannicide to be incompatible with his Christian conscience.

From 1942–3 there were signs of growing opposition, though these continued to come from small, politically or religiously motivated groups and from individuals. But the terror and the resourcefulness of the persecutors were also increasing. At the end of August 1942 counter-intelligence and the Gestapo had uncovered, in Berlin, the largest espionage and resistance organization of the Second World War, in which a group of leftist intellectuals, writers and artists around Harro Schulze-Boysen and Arvid Harnack were working with Leopold Trepper, a Soviet agent operating out of Paris. Some 100 members of the 'Red Orchestra' were arrested and tortured, and the majority of them executed as 'Bolshevik traitors'.

From the summer of 1942 a group of students in Munich had been trying to end the situation in which 'everyone is waiting for someone else to make the first move', and under the name of the 'White Rose' had issued a call for sabotage and passive resistance. On 18 February 1943, the brother and sister Hans and Sophie Scholl were caught by a caretaker as they scattered leaflets on the staircase of the university; the Volksgerichtshof (People's Court of Law) under Freisler condemned both them and four further members of the group to death. The deeds of these young anti-Nazis continued to live particularly strongly in the consciousness of post-war German society; however it was the attempt on the 'Führer's' life on 20 July 1944 which became the embodiment of the German resistance against Hitler.

The smashing of the Kreisau Circle in January 1944, the removal from office of their collaborator, the Head of Counter-Intelligence, Wilhelm Canaris, and the developments of the immediately preceding days in which the 'Kreisau' Social Democrats Julius Leber and Adolf Reichwein had been arrested and the public hunt for Carl Goerdeler begun, had led those conspirators who were waiting for an opportunity to the decision that 'Operation Valkyrie' could no longer be put off. The time-bomb, which Colonel Count Claus Schenk von Stauffenberg planted during a meeting at the 'Führer's' headquarters near Rastenburg in East Prussia to discuss the current situation, did explode, but Hitler was only slightly injured. In the belief that he had killed the 'Führer', Stauffenberg flew back to Berlin where the further steps in the operation were progressing only hes-itantly. When the news of Hitler's survival was broadcast on the radio, the coup collapsed. Stauffenberg and several other officers were sum-marily shot the same night. Some 200 death sentences imposed by the Volksgerichtshof and 7,000 arrests were the dreadful outcome during the following weeks.

The moral and political significance of this late action by the conservative-nationalist resistance remains unaffected by its failure: the conspirators had given a sign of the continuing existence of 'another Germany'. That this Germany was not one of parliamentary democracy, but at best of an authoritarian constitutional state, did not detract from the human value of this 'uprising of conscience', but it did later limit the possibility of referring to it in terms of a continuity of democratic traditions.

The majority of the population reacted to the attempted coup with a hostility fed by the same moral and political blindness with which the barbaric treatment of foreign workers was usually accepted as unfeel-ingly as the deportation of Jewish neighbours. The news of the bomb attack caused widespread indignation. Many believed the 'Führer', who spoke on the radio of a plot by a 'tiny clique of stupid officers who were at once ambitious, unscrupulous and criminal'.[33] Certainly, there was also sympathy for the conspirators and pity for their families, to whom the regime also extended its draconian treatment; but in the first instance this was outweighed by relief at Hitler's escape. This attested not only to the fear of a civil war, but above all to the belief that no-one other than Hitler could bring the war to an end. It was not only convinced Nazis and officials, who had to fear the personal consequences of defeat, who thought this; for many it was simply not yet possible to bid farewell to the 'Führer' as the object of their long-standing, mythical adoration. Certainly, after the first excitement about the officers' opposition group had subsided, the reports on the mood of the population increasingly contained sober judgements: the chance that the war might be shortened – of a 'calamitous end' (rather than an endless calamity) – had been lost.[34]

The coming months did indeed become an endless horror, the closing phase of the war cost hundreds of thousands of lives. The militarily sense-less bombing of German towns and cities continued with ever bigger payloads; in the final year of the war American and British planes dropped more than a million tonnes of high explosives, only some of them on stra-tegic targets. In the air-raids which hit the densely populated Rhine-Ruhr region, the metropolitan conurbations, and towns and cities like Freiburg, Würzburg, Kassel, Magdeburg, Prenzlau and Emden, and in February 1945 visited particular devastation on Dresden, approximately half a million people died; hundreds of thousands were injured, millions lost their homes. The pendulum of violence now swung back with full force against the Germans.

Five days after the assassination attempt in the 'Führer's' headquarters, Hitler appointed his Propaganda Minister as 'Plenipotentiary-General for the Total War Effort'. The scant regard which the regime had still paid to the population hitherto had become null and void. In association, but not coordination, with Speer and Himmler, to whom Hitler had additionally transferred the supreme command of the reserve army, Goebbels ordered the mobilization of the last reserves. Men were 'combed out' of the administration and industry in order either to die on the Front or, now unemployed, simply to remain without useful work. In October 1944, the regime called up all men between the ages of 16 and 60 who were capable of bearing arms to the 'German Volkssturm'; four months later women and girls were called upon to provide it with auxiliary help. The 'measures' undertaken by the three despots in their own particular spheres proved to be the final stage of a regime that had run amok. As it experienced its final convulsion it released monstrous destructive forces.

After Hitler there was to be nothing. The notion that the 'Thousand Year Reich' could be followed by a state order which would rely on the political personnel swept aside in 1933 and in the years after seemed intolerable to the 'Führer'. This explained 'Operation Thunderstorm' (Aktion Gewitter) of August 1944, in which several thousand politicians and civil servants from the Weimar period were arrested (fear of a continuing opposition movement also played a role here). Similar motives resulted, in March 1945, in Hitler's 'scorched earth' policy. The 'Führer' not only accepted Germany's downfall, if necessary he was even prepared to bring it about himself. In defeat the nation was to exit from the world stage with him: 'If the war is lost, the Volk will also be lost. This fate is inevitable.' For this reason, Hitler told his Armaments Minister, it was 'not necessary to bother about the basic requirements which the German Volk needs to ensure even its most primitive survival.' On the contrary, in the worst instance it was even better to destroy everything, for 'the Volk had proven itself to be the weaker, and the future thus belonged exclusively to the stronger eastern Volk.'[35]

Speer, the Wehrmacht, but also most of the Gauleiter and the Reich Defence Commissars, opposed Hitler's 'Nero Order'. Its senselessness and egocentricity was too obvious, the people's 'will to survive', so often evoked by the 'Führer', too strong. Hitler's demand that the substance of Germany's technology and civilization should be destroyed – hard to reconcile with the posthumous claims in his political testament to have defined Germany's future – no longer affected the Germans, if they knew of it at all in the utter confusion of a disintegrating regime. Not yet released from the decaying 'national community', none the less each was now left to his own devices. In a painful process of disillusionment people began to remember their own interests.

In the East, the rapid collapse of the German Front forced millions, from January, into headlong flight before the advancing Red Army. Because of the official policy of holding out to the last, the evacuation of the civilian population had hardly been prepared at all – and turned into a catastrophe. Thousands died in the columns of refugees who tried, for example, to escape from East Prussia to the West over the ice of the Frische Haff in the Baltic Sea; others were overrun by enemy troops, victims of murders, rapes, deportations and internment for years in Poland, Yugoslavia and the Soviet Union. Those like Himmler, who at the beginning of November 1944 gave the order to conceal the gas chambers and mass graves of the murdered, would have had to reckon with new orgies of revenge and violence which the crimes committed in the East by Germans, and in the name of the Germans, now provoked.

In the process of the disintegration of Nazi rule, insanity, baseness and terror reached their final stage. In the growing chaos of destroyed towns and cities, collapsing supplies, flaring resistance activity and despairing self-preservation of people bombed out of their homes, of refugees, deserters and liberated foreign workers, it was – besides the SS and local Party leaders – above all the judiciary which offered itself as the merciless servant of the regime. Even during the very last days of Nazi rule not only the 'People's Court of Law' and Special Courts but also the normal criminal courts in the *Länder* passed death sentences for alleged treason and high treason or 'demoralization of the troops'; 'flying' courts-martial completed the military judiciary's wave of execution terror against deserters and 'mutineers'. In the final analysis, the beginning of the deployment of the *Werwolf*, announced in a radio broadcast by Goebbels on Easter Sunday 1945, had less effect on the Allied troops (who, because of the announcement, were advancing with unnecessary violence in the expectation of encountering strong groups of partisans) than on the indigenous population, who wished to avoid blood-letting and destruction in the final hour by surrendering their towns and villages without a fight. In a number of these, fanatical commandos of SA and SS men loyal to Hitler were still 'executing' courageous citizens when the Party notables had long removed themselves to safety.

Most of the top figures of the regime, foremost amongst them Goering,

Speer and Ribbentrop, left Berlin on the evening of Hitler's fifty-sixth birthday. On that day, 20 April 1945, they had met once more in the 'Führer bunker' fifteen metres under the bombed-out Reich Chancellery. Three days later, Goering, who had meanwhile fled to the 'Alpine Fortress' at Obersalzberg, enquired how things stood with regard to the succession to the 'Führer' and whether or not he now had freedom of action. Hitler's entourage experienced an outburst of uncontrollable rage, repeated on 28 April, when Himmler's attempts to make contact with the western Allies became known. The dictator, dug in, expelled the Reichsführer SS from the Party and designated Goebbels, who remained at his master's side until the very last, as Reich Chancellor. Admiral Dönitz was to be Reich President and Bormann 'Party Minister'. Before he left the stage, Hitler destroyed the very link between state and Party positions that had made the Third Reich into a 'Führer State'.

On 30 April 1945, in the bunker, twelve years and three months after he had moved into the Reich Chancellery, the 'Führer of the German Reich and the German *Volk*' put an end to the agony. But his suicide was nothing more than the consummation of the death suffered by his 'myth' in the preceding, long drawn-out weeks. The Germans were finished with Hitler. Even before the Third Reich had ceased to exist, its 'Führer's' nimbus had sunk into the nothing from whence it had come. Nothing remained of the political hubris which had kept Germany, and later the entire world, in fear and suspense – except misery, destruction and the suffering of millions. National Socialism was dead.

4

The 'Führer State':
Impact and Consequences

The rise and fall of the Third Reich raise a thousand questions in German history, and it is not only historians who will long be occupied by them. But it is precisely the monstrous final chapter of Hitler's rule which also provides answers, or at least some clues. The final blow of unconditional surrender on 8 May 1945, struck militarily and in terms of international law from outside Germany, is far less illuminating than the departure of German society from the Nazi era which occurred in the preceding days and weeks. The contrast between the visible chaos of destruction and defeat and the silent collective withdrawal from the Nazi 'national community', which took place almost exclusively in people's minds, could not have been greater. The situation was not characterized by an uprising of the discontented, the maltreated, the politically oppressed, by a general revolt based on the desire finally to put an end to the hopeless war, not even by acts of revenge, but rather by a waiting defined by resignation, emptiness and overwhelming exhaustion.

Yet this subdued *dénouement* also expressed a hidden sense of complicity. Had not the Germans cooperated enthusiastically and all too long, had they not cheered the 'Führer'? *'Ein Volk, ein Reich, ein Führer'* – had not the slogan also become a reality? Suddenly released from twelve years of ideological and political servitude, suddenly 'Führer'-less, many began to remember the personal opportunism, the compromises entered into with a greater or lesser degree of bad conscience, and noticed that they had not come through the 'great era' unscathed. The silence was not solely an expression of limitless disappointment and bitterness; it was sometimes also a sign of shame.

During the phase of the Third Reich's disintegration, Hitler's overwhelming importance as the charismatic bearer of political binding power was confirmed yet again. The 'Führer', as myth and medium – not in the human inadequacy of his personality – was to the very end the central reference point for the Nazi system of rule. Everything seemed to have its origins in him: the rise of the 'movement', the successes in domestic policy, the triumphs in foreign affairs, but above all – and linked with these – a hitherto unknown ability to integrate the masses. This ability was enduring and went far beyond the sphere of profane politics. Like a religion, this 'Hitler-faith' required constant reaffirmation and renewal in rituals and plebiscites, but it also required, at not too great intervals, a concrete political basis. From 1942, after the necessary successes ceased, the 'Führer' myth became exhausted. Goebbels, with his own desperate personal need to be able to believe in his 'Führer', may have been able to slow down the process of decay with fervent propaganda, but he could not stop it. In the second half of the war, as the demands on productive capability and the ability to suffer became ever greater and the grounds for political confidence became ever scarcer, the denazification of the Germans began.

The regime reacted to the decline of its military success – and hence its growing inability to convince the population – with intensified political repression. But even while the excesses of brutality and extermination were taking place (wherever possible in secret) in the theatres of this ideological war and in the occupation policy in the East, the terror directed against Germany's own population was kept within bounds. Now, as ever, the Nazi leadership gambled more on agreement than on coercion and remained susceptible and sensitive to fluctuations in the so very carefully observed 'mood of the people'. The disregard for all forms of restraint inside Germany was a phenomenon only of the final months of the war.

From this assessment flow consequences for a measured historical examination of the Nazi period. It must be remembered, for example, that the evidently violent character of the final phase of the Third Reich was preceded by a much more complicated history personally experienced by those who lived through this period, and if serious account is not taken of this, its history can be neither explained nor understood. Developments from 1933 to 1945 may well have been reasonably consistent, but they were less inevitable than might be suggested by an interpretation which starts from, or is determined solely by, the final orgy of violence and destruction. Such a moral-political, often 'well-meaning' attempt at representing the history of the period not only leads to simplification – and thus has an inevitably depoliticizing effect; it also involves a particular risk of self-righteousness. Of course, there are good grounds for starting from the high degree of evident determination to realize the

Nazi programme and to assign little importance to the freedom of action enjoyed by those other than the 'Führer'; but the mere thought that Hitler could have been the victim of assassination in 1938[1] necessitates the view that actual developments were not at all inevitable.

All this gives rise to the need to take a differentiated view of the political history and the history of the society of the Nazi period and not to evaluate it simply from the yardstick of the criminality of its ideology and the crimes which derived therefrom. Everyday life in the Third Reich was determined by the permanent simultaneity, rather than the alternatives, of enticement and coercion, seduction and crime, offers of integration and threats of terror. People behaved in a correspondingly multi-layered and non-uniform manner: agreement with the policy of the regime and active support for its measures, for example in the economic sphere, could coexist with open rejection of specific postulates of its *Weltanschauung* – and vice versa. In many locations in society there was much readiness to conform, and in others predominantly to resist. Under certain circumstances, from what was in the first instance non-political, traditional inertia could grow political resistance. What was regarded as an imposition and what as self-evident depended on mentality, religious conviction and socio-economic background. If and when someone became an opponent of the regime was often decided, not by basic issues of ideology, but rather by questions of practical politics and whether or not he or she was affected by concrete measures. The careful empirical examination of the political behaviour of the population contradicts the concept, inspired by the theory of totalitarianism, of the individual robbed of all social and spiritual links, 'atomized' and thus totally exposed to the power of indoctrination. To a certain extent even the partially existing *Volksgemeinschaft* speaks against such an idea.

While little doubt can exist about the totalitarian character of the Nazi *Weltanschauung* and the primacy of monopolized politics – in the final analysis also with respect to the economy – it is all the more clear that the implementation of totalitarian power encountered limits in many areas of society. In order to give a realistic description of the historical reality of life it is therefore insufficient simply to portray the totalitarian intentions of the regime – provable at every turn because they were so loudly proclaimed by Nazi propaganda. The decisive question is in which areas, at which juncture and how extensively these demands could be met. This perspective opens up a picture of niches, free space and private preserves which National Socialism was either unable to fill or could do so only to a very limited degree: above all in the spheres of mass culture, the arts and religion, but also in many areas of technical civilization and everyday life.

If the origins of this fragmentary nature of Nazi rule can be found largely in its chaotic internal structure – which stood in such conspicuous contrast to the monolithic façade of the 'Führer State' (and the contrast was already recognized by its contemporaries) – then this was in many respects not just functional, but also perhaps even structurally imminent. For it was precisely the ability of the regime, either in particular areas or at particular times, to tolerate effective limits to its power, which guaranteed – in conjunction with the 'Führer' myth and the political successes – its extraordinary integrative power. Measured against a theoretical ideal of totalitarian rule, the regime operated less perfectly, and Hitler could in fact almost appear a 'weak dictator';[2] but, measured against its practical efficiency and the effectiveness with which it developed its power, the opposite is true.

If the rise of the NSDAP to become a mass movement cannot be traced back only to the attractiveness of its propaganda and its coincidence with the world economic crisis, then neither certainly can the rapid development and wide acceptance of Nazi rule be attributed simply to the virtuoso use of the techniques of totalitarian manipulation. The latter undoubtedly played a special role; but what was decisive was that the regime, like the 'movement' before it, succeeded in convincingly addressing the needs and aspirations of broad strata of society, declaring them to be its concern and, at least to some extent, satisfying them. Herein lay the modernity of the Hitler State, and the explanation for its enduring ability to mobilize the masses and to maintain their loyalty.

Peasants, industrial workers, white-collar employees – for the first time, in the years after 1933, hundreds of thousands developed the feeling that they were being taken seriously politically and being understood. When before in German history had the people been the object of so much loud, demonstrative attention and social care? When had the state ever defined the sphere of the political and thus its responsibility for the individual more comprehensively? When before had so many comprehensible symbols of identification been offered at the same time as so many opportunities to participate? And finally: did it not seem that Germany was *en route* to a modern mass society in which achievement counted for more than social origin, but also one in which the frightening, almost incomprehensible complexity of industrial civilization would be removed by firm order, clear images of the enemy and simple value judgements?

The populist appeal of the Nazi movement, the simplicity of its message and the charisma of its 'Führer' also informed, in a broader and more intensified manner, the psychological reality of the Third Reich. The widespread hunger for social integration was answered with permanent, class-transcending mobilization and the explicit renunciation of political normality. The result was a society in a constant state of emergency. The loosening of ties of traditional social mores which this favoured released enormous social energy. This benefited the process of social and economic modernization as much as the ideological deed.

An indissoluble link between technological modernity and reactionary vision was central to the reality of the Third Reich. Unhindered by the retrogressive nature of many of its ideological postulates, National Socialism made use of all the methods of modern technology and promoted its implementation. In the 1930s, in sectors such as mass communications, motorization and the organization of leisure, but also in the education system, family structures and health care, the regime initiated developments which, in terms of neutral values, can be understood as nothing other than modernization. Many of these measures were ideologically motivated, yet their effects could be neither definitely predicted nor restricted to the desired, limited goal. This was even more true in the war years, during which the further pushes for modernization – as in the Wehrmacht – began and in which the general equalization of society was accelerated. Finally, what cannot be overlooked are elements of structural modernization which took place with the military defeat and to this extent were caused, though of course not striven for, by National Socialism: the end of junkerdom and the agrarian, pre-democratic social structure of the lands east of the Elbe; the levelling of regional and national characteristics as a result of the flight and expulsion of refugees; the 'rejuvenation' of industrial plant and of the cities as a result of the Allied air-raids.

Of course, National Socialism did not effect an earth-shattering and comprehensive change in the economy and society; for this too much was already embodied in the trends of the period, Germany was already too 'modern' in 1933, and a period of rule of twelve years was also too short. But just as certainly, the Third Reich did not leave behind merely a fundamentally geographically altered Germany. No, a revolution had not taken place, class structures had remained the same. Yet the Nazis had reduced the socio-psychological significance of class differences in a multitude of ways. Through their propaganda of the *Volksgemeinschaft*, their activism in social policy and the greater value placed upon the 'German skilled worker', and, as a complement to this, by drafting in 'racially inferior' foreign workers, they had altered the sense of status of a large section of the working class as well as the consciousness of German society as a whole.

At the beginning, the intention of the traditional political and economic elites had been to eliminate the labour movement with the help of the

NSDAP; to stabilize the authoritarian regime; and to shift the balance of power between labour and capital in favour of the latter. At the end there was a secularized, politically disillusioned society, averse to everything to do with nationalism and – as was soon to be shown – de-ideologized to a high degree; a society with far better structural preconditions for democratic reconstruction than in 1918. Whilst, with the end of the regime, the ideological core of Nazi politics had been rejected by all but isolated peripheral groups, 'attitudes' and opinions practised in the Nazi period remained present and proved their use once again in the new economic beginning; efficiency and emphasis on productivity, a readiness to take risks, pragmatism, an ability to improvize, material modesty and a turning away from snobbery and impractical class consciousness.

The Third Reich's enormous achievements in the arms economy and on the military front would have been almost inconceivable without the systematic promotion of that technocratic, 'string-pulling' mentality grounded in such 'youthful' virtues of industrial society as these. But just as inconceivable would have been the historically unprecedented crimes of mass murder which ideological determination alone was insufficient to realize. The regime was also expert at translating the social energies which were being released into moral disinhibition; and the continuous competition for power and influence initiated at all levels in the structure of the system strengthened the political radicalization. Thus there was no sudden descent into barbarism; the wartime acts of mass murder were much rather a continuation of the destruction of civilized society – a process accelerated by technocrats, scientists and ideologues, and the effects of which did not remain restricted to the immediate actors.

Amongst all the radicalism of the Nazi *Weltanschauung* it seems necessary to emphasize that, in the final analysis, the origins and possibilities of the successive destruction of humanitarian morality were – and remain – anchored in modern industrial civilization itself. It was indeed no coincidence that in the Nazi ideology components of Social-Darwinist and racist theories played a central role. The readiness of this eclectic *Weltanschauung* to take on board the findings of the outer fringes of contemporaneous research in the natural sciences such as eugenics and social biology is well known, and so too is the political use to which a science based on the perceived differences between races was put. But against the backdrop of the monstrous perversion of this perception into the planned extermination of millions of the 'racially inferior', what has become less significant are the far-reaching – and in their own way thoroughly 'realistic' – intentions of Nazi social planning.

The planning even continued in the shadow of the 'Final Solution', as a first generation of Nazi experts stopped following in the footsteps of the 'Old Fighters'. What the young technocrats envisaged was a post-war order, informed by the Nazi *Weltanschauung* but founded on science, which was supposed to be much more 'rational' and efficient than the Hitler State of its quasi-revolutionary beginnings. And, not least with the help of sophisticated technicians of power and government, the system was to be newly consolidated on a higher level. The period in which private obsessions and half-baked ideas, born at the regulars' table of the local public house, could determine Hitler's or Himmler's politics and *Weltanschauung* was to be overcome. In the areas of social and economic policy the outlines of these plans were clear; the seriousness of the intention to drive a genuine, National Socialist, 'German path' between capitalism and communism is unmistakeable.

From this perspective – which admittedly moves into the realm of historical speculation – the question arises, once again, of the structural capabilities of National Socialism as a system and the modernity of the 'Führer State': the many 'modern' elements of Nazi rule then appear, not simply as unintended or even disfunctional side effects of a basically reactionary, atavistic political philosophy, but rather as the harbingers of an attempt to complete the project of the modern in the particular variant of a racial order. Technical rationality and efficiency were the absolute values in this dead, technocratic world. Barbarism wore the clothes of modernity.

Documents

1 Observations of a senior lecturer. On the sociology of the
National Socialist Revolution

Rudolf Heberle, the author of the following notes which date from the first half
of 1934, was senior lecturer at the Institute for World Economics at the University
of Kiel from 1929 to 1938, and then Professor of Sociology at Louisiana State
University in Baton Rouge, USA. As early as 1934, Heberle compiled what today
still counts as an exemplary study of 'The Rural Population and National Socialism. A Sociological Examination of the Development of Political Objectives in
Schleswig-Holstein 1918–1932', but it was not possible for it to appear in print
until 1963. Heberle's observations on the changes which were taking place, above
all in the universities, stand out from other – in total not very numerous –
contemporaneous writings because of their studied 'sociological viewpoint'. In
his short preface to the first published edition of the document Heberle wrote:
'The manner of expression is obviously cautious, in some places ambiguous. It
was clear to the author that, were they to be found by the Gestapo, notes such
as these could be dangerous. But, for the benefit of today's reader, it must be said
that a few months later one would not have committed such thoughts to paper
at all. For every analysis considered to be objective aroused the suspicion of
animosity towards the Party and the state.'
Quoted from *Vierteljahrshefte für Zeitgeschichte*, 13 (1965), pp. 438–45.

It would be most interesting to write a sociology and social-psychology
of the 'German' revolution – above all about the process of conformity
and conversion amongst former opponents of National Socialism. Some
who honestly, but without clarity of thought, quite consciously sacrificed
intellect and, disavowing their former standpoint, resolutely declared their
loyalty to the new regime, are actively cooperating wherever they can
and are trying to make the spirit of National Socialism their own. A
second category is composed of those who, in spring 1932, still considered Hitler to be the devil himself, but since 5 March or 1 May have been
claiming that, deep down, they had really always been national socialist
but had just failed to recognize the movement, and that it was exactly
what they had always wanted. With some of them this is downright self-
deception, with others lies, yet with others still it is really so: this last group
had seen in Hitler the leader of a plebeian, semi-Bolshevik revolution,

which they feared would be the ruin of bourgeois society, and now they have recognized all of a sudden that Hitler means precisely maintenance of this bourgeois society, that the National Socialists have 'learned better' and that there is no way that they will wreck everything. These are the bourgeois types who were particularly enthusiastic when the end of the revolutionary period and the beginning of evolution were officially declared: Democrats, Centrists, supporters and members of the People's Party.

Genuine opportunists, who openly declare that one must simply swim with the tide and not invent some ideology of self-justification, are rare. More common, however, are the silent dissidents who avoid all public events and only give vent to their feelings in private. Amongst them are many German Nationalists and conservatives.

As these are forced into inactivity, their opposition remains fruitless. Furthermore, their basic sympathy with the new regime is so far-reaching that their criticisms are restricted to details and secondary phenomena: they 'bleat' ['*meckern*']. They complain in particular about the poor quality of the *homines novi*, about the egalitarian trends, about the suppression of free speech and any other bourgeois-liberal arguments you can think of.

Genuine will to resist, even if only in the form of passive resistance, only seems to have appeared in the working class. Thanks to the immediate establishment of absolute economic dependence of each and every individual on those with political power, the threat of hunger forced anyone who still had anything to lose to acquiesce.

Most eager to affirm their Nazi convictions were the politically handicapped 'March fallen'; *Old* Party Comrades [*Alt-Pgs, Parteigenossen*] were much more critical of many new phenomena and measures and their behavior towards those who had not changed sides was more tactful and decorous.

The lively sense of symbolism which characterizes the National Socialists made possible an extensive control of opinion. For example, the Hitler salute – I only began to use it when it was made compulsory for all civil and public servants and have often observed that old Nazi students greeted me in the Institute with a nod or a bow, while Nazis still wet behind the ears saluted me with 'Heil Hitler'. For people with any backbone, conforming to all these new conventions means a continuous series of humiliations.

In addition to this came the coordination of the most diverse organizations – from bodies representing various interests to gymnastics associations – which often took place in such a way that it entailed considerable humiliation for the defeated party. Almost everywhere it was particularly the long-serving and often very experienced and deserving incumbents of official positions who were replaced, not by the 'next' generation, who were bypassed, but by very young, inexperienced people whose only qualification was the fact of their Party membership.

In many cases the proverb 'skill comes with office' proved true for these young people, who often belonged to the post-war generation (those born in 1900 or after). (But that does not compensate for the injustice and injury caused to those who were dismissed or overlooked – yet here one can say 'c'est la guerre'.)

With certain political instinct the National Socialists have recognized that politics is struggle and that in the revolution there is no mercy for opponents. Acts of violence, ill-treatment, the concentration camp and simple intimidation have therefore been used to break any resistance. The National Socialists have had no need to worry about the fact that they have often accepted people of dubious loyalty into their ranks, for they have a perfect system of control over every Pg and SA-man, so that precisely these elements could entertain no risks.

On the other hand, they were in a position to reward their stalwarts with official posts: in the police; in the permanent service of the SA and SS; through preferential treatment of Pgs in the allocation of jobs in private enterprises and the purging of factories of 'Marxists' who were replaced by Nazis. The sense of insecurity of life which dominated and paralysed the dissidents at the beginning gave way, with the easing of physical terror, to a sense of powerlessness, of being constantly under surveillance, in which the mistrust of one's nearest and dearest played a major role. Critical remarks which were meant to be completely con-structive were often concluded with the remark: 'You won't report me, will you', or, 'Actually, one isn't allowed to say such things.'

A wealth of jokes soon gave vent to the discontent: a few about Hitler, many about Goebbels, but especially about Goering, whose love of pomp gave popular opinion a target for many good jokes.

The economic crisis was not only an essential condition for the emer-gence of the National Socialist movement but also for its success. If everyone had not been afraid of losing their jobs there would have been a great deal more resistance – as was the case in the resistance of the Protestant Church against the 'German Christians', albeit under the partial protection of the German Nationalists.

But this factor would not have benefited the National Socialists if they had not sent their agents into every factory, organization and public authority, and if the intimate involvement of each individual in the over-all structure of the modern economy had not made it impossible for even the otherwise so very independent peasants and small business people to buck the system.

None the less, in many instances, personal courage and energetic adherence to one's own individual rights proved effective against 'encroachments' from minor authorities. But that does not alter the substance of the matter. In any event, the dictatorship of the NSDAP was completed by the end of the summer with the subordination of the Stahlhelm to the supreme leadership of the SA. For in many places the Stahlhelm had become a reservoir for *all* opponents of National Socialism, from the German Nationalists to the SPD. Only former members of the KPD clearly preferred to join the SA and also found it easier to gain acceptance in its ranks – as was shown, for example, by the Brunswick conflict between the St(ahlhelm) and the SA.

The NSDAP was, of course, in danger of becoming diluted. This was the reason for the frequent moratoria on new admissions to membership and the introduction of a long probationary period for new members, and finally, towards the end of 1933, the separation of the PO (Political Organization) and the auxiliary organizations. This enabled the NSDAP to maintain the character of a political order without having to forgo the cooperation of experienced people from other camps working in the specialist economic and cultural organizations.

An example of the intimidation of political opponents: before the plebiscite in November 1933, the understandable rumour had spread that voting would be checked, i.e. voting would not only be compulsory but would afterwards be scrutinized to see who had had voted against the government. Of course, this was denied by the government, and in reality there was no attempt to infringe the secrecy of the ballot. This was attested to by the number of 'no' – votes, which was very high in places, and by the differences between the plebiscite and the Reichstag elections. But the fear that it might occur led some of my own personal acquaintances, confirmed opponents of National Socialism, to vote 'yes' and also to vote for Hitler in the Reichstag elections.

The restriction of the freedom of the press has led to an increased subtlety of style which requires the reader to read between the lines. Indeed, this skill has become highly developed, for the most important measures have been announced without comment, often disguised in the secret language of an apparently harmless decree. So anyone who wishes to keep abreast of things has to know how to distinguish the real from the apparent meaning of an official directive or from the text of Party orders, in order to deduce the actual situation they are supposed to regulate.

The monopolization of public opinion by the NSDAP and the government has given rise to the emergence of graffiti slogans on lavatory walls, the growth of verbal agitation amongst the proletarians, the turning of the educated towards foreign newspapers and foreign radio stations; but because of language difficulties and the costs in time and money this can be of little quantitative importance. None the less, one sees Swiss, English, Scandinavian and French, indeed even American newspapers on the newspaper stands in the town, whereas before they were only available at the station. Quantitively more significant is the fall in sales of the major daily papers and the advertizing gazettes.

The combination of press comment in *Blick in die Zeit* (View of the Times) sought to satisfy the need for information. *Deutsche Zukunft* (German Future), published by Fr[itz] Klein, allowed itself a cautious, immanent critique. It should really have been called 'German Past', for it essentially campaigned for what was valuable and enduring about liberalism.

One very effective means of mass suggestion on the part of National Socialism is its presentation of measures taken by the new government as completely new, as the original ideas of Nazism, even when it concerns questions for which there were already plans in the filing cabinets of the Brüning government and which had only become ripe for implementation in the summer of '33: for example the regulation of the River Eider, or measures which had already been implemented earlier in a similar fashion, as, for example, Winter Aid.

Or aims were announced as specifically Nazi, which other nations had long since accomplished under liberal ideology: e.g. that educational effect of the SA which leads to a far-reaching elimination of snobbery based on class or status and to an active spirit of comradeship – what causes this other than the respect for every man regardless of his social standing, self-evident amongst the Americans (even reaching limits of a plutocratic nature which could not be transcended here), and the 'team-spirit' of American 'college boys' [*sic*] or office workers?

Without diminishing the achievements of National Socialism, one can still state that this trick has the important counter-revolutionary function of diverting the attention of the masses away from everything which is aimed at the stabilization of the hegemony of big money.

In many cases symbolism too serves as a diversion from the essence of what is taking place. For example, if the 'radical opposition' in the Hitler Youth is angered by the system of decorations, then this is indeed a symptom of a specific anti-bourgeois – or at least anti-philistine – position, but at the same time diverts energy away from the struggle against the slavery of debt, from the energetic implementation of the programme to establish settlements in the East and other aims which convinced revolutionary National Socialists have in mind.

Indeed, anti-Semitism also has such a function. Incidentally, partly as a result of serious mistakes on the Jewish side, this is so widespread that it is almost unimaginable that a change of direction will take place in this regard. Even people who condemn the way in which it has been attempted to solve this question reveal themselves to be really deeply emotional anti-Semites, and if, on the other hand, one has observed the behaviour of the Jews in the revolution, one can understand why. Few have been as courageous as young Sp[iegel], who appeared at the ballot box the day after his father's murder.

During the period of the struggle for power, the ideology of National Socialism had been largely developed on an *ad hoc* basis and the creators of this ideology were, to an extent, only linked by the counter-revolutionary front. For these reasons, discrepancies between ideology and actions were bound to emerge after the seizure of power, alongside the discrepancies between the various directions of will within the movement and, of course, differences of opinion about the meaning of certain of its ideological maxims.

The ideology has also been realized most consistently in legislation on agrarian matters – but it was soon clear that the peasants had not taken this ideology very seriously at all and, to a certain extent, found its realization most uncomfortable. This ideological vagueness is, of course, an advantage in terms of *Realpolitik* and lends the system a great degree of flexibility.

For the top leadership, in addition to this freedom from the bonds of dogma comes the freedom from any controlling authority, the possession of absolute state power. This makes possible speed and consistency of governmental activity – no more compromises with the opposition and the coalition partners – and allows the speedy correction of defects and unforeseen side effects (e.g. the double income question!)

In times of crisis, the abolition of the separation of legislature and executive proves itself an advantage which outweighs the disadvantages: lack of openness, insufficiently thought through measures.

On the other hand it is quite obvious that conflicts of interest that were previously fought out in public are now being pursued behind the scenes, which makes the intimate links between 'objective' contradictions and personal rivalries much more difficult to uncover.

Due to the fact that everywhere, from the Hitler Youth upwards, a new class of professional politicians and professional functionaries has emerged, who are linked for better or worse with the posts which they occupy, it is obvious that objective contradictions are becoming matters of personal existence.

The charismatic following, which is how the immediate circle around Hitler in the Reich government must be seen, does not yet stretch into all provincial Party offices, nor will it ever do so.

That, on the other hand, the younger generation, in particular the Front generation, is to a large degree capable of forming a following and creating a comradely community, seems to be proved by experience, e.g. in the universities. There are very angry reactions, for example, against individualist behaviour.

Psychological side-effects: fear for one's economic existence, general recognition of the uncertainty of *all* social relations – hence partly a tendency to stare fate in the face manfully and stoically, and partly a desire by the propertied classes for security *à tout prix* (very dangerous for the further course of the revolution), partly favoured by the will for reconstruction and the fear of the alternative of anarchy and Bolshevism.

Human beings are extraordinarily inventive when it comes to allaying their fears: whoever believed before March that, like a magician, Hitler would alleviate all economic distress at a stroke, soothes his *disappointment* with the actually quite correct truth that 'Hitler can't be in two places at once';* or the French armaments industry is blamed for hindering reconciliation and disarmament, but the presence at home of similar forces is not recognized.

It is known for certain that, as with all the cultural assets of liberalism, radical, thoroughgoing National Socialism also negates academic freedom. But people delude themselves that academic freedom will be protected by 'reasonable National Socialists' (and I shall leave open the question of whether or not, in the long run, National Socialism also *needs* academic freedom – this includes freedom in the social sciences), except when academic *theory* impinges on the national interest – without considering at all that the *primary* decision about whether this is the case is specifically not left to academics; indeed, that a whole system of filtration is devised which makes it possible to exclude particular people with undesirable ways of thinking from academic activity altogether.

It is said that this has always been the case – but it is forgotten that previously dissidents who were excluded from academic activity in the civil and public service always still had the possibility of *private* research and writing, which is no longer the case today.

I am not criticizing the position taken by the National Socialist government, but rather the fact that the consequences which ensue from the regime of a political order are not admitted, even though Russia and Italy offer sufficient empirical evidence. Psychologically speaking, for many of its supporters, as for example with L.L., National Socialism is not just a substitute for religion, which is demonstrated, *inter alia*, in the frequent

---

* Statement of a lavatory attendant, decorated with Party medals, in Laboe in summer 1933, when asked whether everything was really better now [note by Heberle].

use of biblical phraseology in Nazi speeches – but rather, in the sphere of public opinion the NSDAP lays claim to exactly the same position that the Roman Church occupies in the sphere of religious faith. It cannot therefore tolerate academic research if it leads to results which stand in absolute contradiction to the dogmas of National Socialism.

A certain freedom results from the fact that, as yet, not many of these dogmas are 'theologically' fixed.

While it was inevitable for the Catholic Church to come into conflict above all with the natural sciences, these (apart from the theories on genetics and race) are not being restricted by National Socialist dogmatics, but rather it is only the social sciences, including social philosophy, which are threatened – ethics too is somewhat affected, and history.

Most threatened is the philosophy of law, political science and sociology. The last of these becomes especially 'dangerous', where it is required to analyse and unmask ideologies.

2 Potatoes instead of pork: Rudolf Hess on the 'fats crisis' of 1936

The 'Führer's Deputy' did not count amongst the Nazis' star speakers, nor did he shine with intellectual rigour. Moreover, Hess' solo public appearances were totally lacking in sparkle because, for the most part, the 'second man' in the Party only had 'secondary questions' to address. However, the difficulties with the provision of foodstuffs in the autumn of 1936 were anything but secondary: poor harvests, the Reich Food Estate's unsuccessful policies of market control, and higher prices on the world market at a time of a shortage of foreign exchange almost led to the introduction of a *Fettkarte* – a ration card for fats. The Four-Year Plan announced at the Reich Party Congress in Nuremberg was supposed to circumvent the problems of foreign trade and, at the same time, to secure the course of autarky and rearmament. As a practising apostle of healthy living, Hitler's deputy was predestined for the dialogue with the German housewife on policies concerning nutrition. Hess spoke in Hof in Upper Franconia on the occasion of the dedication of the new Adolf Hitler Hall there, and the *Völkischer Beobachter*, the Party organ, printed his speech, beginning on the front page.

Quoted from *Völkischer Beobachter* (Berlin edition), 13 October 1936.

How tremendous indeed are the achievements of the new Reich in the economic sphere alone! . . . How significant it was to take over a state which, in January 1933, stood on the brink of collapse, with an economy which should, realistically, have long since declared itself bankrupt, and then within the shortest space of time, by means of this state and this economy, to bring about the recovery, to bring millions back into work and bread, to build up a modern army and at the same time as these mighty efforts to secure bread for our people! This securing of bread for the German people had to take place through increased domestic food production.

We have succeeded in being able to supply the German people with 100 per cent of bread and flour, potatoes, sugar and milk, and that is completely from German production.

We need to supply a small percentage of the total requirement of fruit and vegetables, a somewhat larger proportion of eggs and dairy products and a still relatively high percentage of the requirement of fats through foreign imports. The fluctuations in provision and price policy are the result of this situation. But the fact that we have already achieved such a high degree of independence and feed ourselves completely in important areas, that alone is a tremendous achievement, for which we owe thanks to the Reich Food Estate, for which we owe thanks to the devoted labours of the German farmer.

Whatever is none the less still lacking must be imported. However, not only foodstuffs need to be imported, but also, as you know, a great number of raw materials which are needed to keep our industry going, to secure the jobs of millions, to complete rearmament . . .

We are prepared – in the future too – if need be, to consume a little less fat now and then, a little less pork, a few less eggs, because we know that this small sacrifice signifies a sacrifice on the altar of the freedom of our *Volk*. We know that the foreign exchange that we save by so doing goes to benefit rearmament. The slogan 'guns instead of butter!' still holds true today. The Führer is not one to do things by halves. Because a world under arms has forced us to rearm, we are rearming fully: each new piece of artillery, each new tank, each new aeroplane means increased certainty for the German mother that her children will not be murdered in an unholy war – nor tortured by Bolshevik bands. We are taking care that the desire to attack us will vanish once and for all!

We also know something else: during the course of the Führer's government food consumption has not decreased, but has increased substantially. We must be proud that the demand of the German people for foodstuffs has risen, because this presupposes that the German people and in particular the German workers as a whole can once again buy more, sometimes better and previously unaffordable foodstuffs. Millions and millions are now able to buy more food for themselves and their families than before, and furthermore they are also able to buy the type of groceries that they were previously unable to afford.

Today, there are approximately $6\frac{1}{2}$ million people who can say that, under Adolf Hitler, not only have they once again found work, but also that, on average, they are able to spend some 85 RM more each month than before the seizure of power, that is when they were unemployed and receiving benefits . . .

Is anyone suprised therefore that occasionally there are a few small difficulties?! I know that our *Volk* will happily undertake, from time to time, to consume a little less fat, pork or suchlike in the knowledge that, in return, millions of national comrades are currently being a little better nourished than before when they were unemployed . . .

Every good housewife knows how to keep her family in good spirits, and particularly those who personally – regardless of the overall situation – have ever had to endure more serious economic times know how to prepare a good meal with simple ingredients precisely by housewifely skills, even if, now and then, it contains either no meat or no butter or no eggs. The hardworking and efficient German housewives know what they have to do in the service of this great German family – the German people – if it has to overcome temporary small shortages. They simply do their shopping in accordance with the interest of the great German family! They do not attempt to buy expressly that which is in short supply at the time, but instead buy those things which are available in abundance and prepare them in such a way that they look really good and taste really good to their husbands and children. No good housewife particularly mourns the quarter-pound of pork which, from time to time, she now fails to get.

Every good German housewife is, for her own part, a mother of the German *Volk*. In many cases she has similar and higher duties to fulfil than the men of this *Volk*, who will respect and honour her composure. German women, show what you are capable of! . . .

If, in Germany, Führer and followers discuss a problem with one another and together come to an agreement as to how it is to be alleviated, foreign opinion hastily concludes: 'Thank God, the Germans are beginning to starve under the Hitlerian leadership and the German economy is collapsing.' Foreign opinion may rest assured. We Germans have nothing to hide from one another. It would be foolish if the German government were to unburden every trouble on the people, just as it would be foolish not to tell the *Volk* in what circumstance it finds itself and what is to be done for the common good.

We are an honest community of fate! And regardless of what others outside believe or say, we will, whether as leaders or as the led, always place this common fate openly before one another. What then, in the final analysis, is the motive of those outside who so fervently hope for hunger here in Germany? Yes, of course, it is just the last straw to which they cling in their longing that in the great conflict – on the one side Jewish Bolshevism, on the other German National Socialism – National Socialism might finally lose a position or a battle, so that there could still be hope that Jews and Bolsheviks will once again be victorious in Germany! To these foreigners we must say, their hopes are in vain.

But we should be happy that at the very worst, here and there for a few days each year we might have to go without butter for our bread, rather than without bread itself for a whole month, as in the celebrated land of the happiness and welfare of the masses, in Soviet Russia. The world knows, just as does each of us who has ever been able to have a first-hand look at other countries, that Germany is the most social country on earth.

3 Joseph Goebbels: 'The Führer is very happy'

The first and most defenceless victim of the Propaganda Minister's persuasive skills was Joseph Goebbels himself. Both of the the following extracts from his diary, from 1936 and 1937, show Goebbels not only in full possession of power and influence in Hitler's court, but also as the target of his own incessant tirade. They give the impression of the restless activity and wide-ranging interests of a man who, through long years of self-training, had taught himself to stop making a distinction between policy and propaganda, reality and wishful thinking. Goebbels drew extraordinary energy and receptiveness from this trait, but it also cost him his strength. Hardly an entry in the diary ends without the reference to his having had 'little sleep' or being 'dead tired'.

Quoted from Elke Fröhlich (ed.), *Die Tagebücher von Joseph Goebbels. Sämtliche Fragmente. Teil 1: Aufzeichnungen 1924 bis 1941* (Munich, 1987), vol. 2, pp. 703f.; vol. 3, pp. 109–12.

22 October 1936. (Thurs.)
Yesterday: in the morning on rising: outside everything covered in snow. A glorious sight!

Chatted downstairs. Worked with Hanke. All sorts of things to do. The Führer is working with Meissner. Funk reports from Berlin. Everything turns on Italy. Goering is keeping the press roaring.

Fully occupied until midday. In Spain the Nationalists are making brilliant progress. Their victory is only a question of a short time.

Führer downstairs with Meissner and Wagner. Ciano visit discussed and finalized. And massive arrangements, almost too big. But all the same. Meissner is very amusing.

Upstairs with the Führer discussion about 9 November. In traditional style. In this respect nothing can be altered. The Führer wants to bring the Party up to 7 million members. 10 per cent of the population. That is quite right. New blood in the organization. Otherwise it will turn senile. Dr Dietrich has tried to engage in intrigue with Goering against me. But he's a shit-stirrer.

Alone with the Führer my remaining questions: I should support Degrelle. He's coming along. Führer wants film and press to be more National Socialist. I've been searching for the people for ages. Where are they to be found? The Führer wants to make 70 million [RM] available for the construction of new radio stations. Seems to me to be a most opportune order. We want to build the greatest stations in the world. Let Moscow tremble. Well then, let's get on with it!

The Führer is also in agreement with Amann's law on the press. He thinks very highly of Amann. But Dr Dietrich doesn't rate any more. 'Frankfurter Zeitung' must go. This trash-sheet is no longer of any use at all. I've placed a few shrewd propagandists at the DNB [Deutsches Nachrichten Büro – German News Agency]. They must sift and correct all the news. And now I'm concentrating on the anti-Bolshevik cinema.

I'm the sole authority as far as theatre policy is concerned. Mutschmann will have to comply. Rosenberg too. Speer is assuming competency in construction matters in Berlin. Dr Lippert can then get his Berlin law through and become chief burgomaster.

Went for a walk in the snow. The Führer is touching. Places all his trust in me. Complains about Hess, who is turning the Party bourgeois. No inspiration. The Gauleiter parliaments must go. Give more direction, pay less heed to the grumbling. And either without representation or proper, decent, generous and elegant. Hess has no feeling for such things. The Führer intends to pay more attention to the Gauleiter.

He wants to admit all the Reich ministers into the Party on 30 January and award them all the gold medal of honour. That should then become the highest German order. Quite right.

The Führer expresses [himself] most content with Bormann. He has energy and discretion.

We arrive back *again* tired and determined. Still the problem of criticism. In the long run it must be completely eliminated. Then there may only be reports. Just as in politics. The stupid may not criticize the clever. If someone has ability he should not work off his talents in criticism but in performance.

Time to go. Very warm and intimate departure from the Führer. He likes Magda and me very much. He comes right the way downstairs to the car and waves to us for a long while as we drive off.

Leave for Berlin with Frau Dr Brandt. The Berlin press is completely full of the Ciano visit. They've done it well. I work with Hanke, evaluate the result of my visit, read, write, dictate. An excessive amount of work is piling up.

On the way, Amann joins the train to discuss the press law with me. I still have a few details which will stabilize the power of the Ministry. Otherwise we are in agreement. I hope the law will be perfect by December. I am selling Amann my diaries. To be published 20 years after my death. 250,000 Marks straight away and each year a further 100,000 Marks. That is very generous. Magda and I are happy. Amann has made a good investment . . .

13 April 1937. (Tues.)
Yesterday: a day filled with annoyance, bother and work.

The foreign press is babbling on about a leaflet from an ominous 'Freedom Party'. It's all happening as if by command. I.e. a proper Jewish trick. No one anywhere knows of the leaflet.

The Führer has not yet decided whether or not Ludendorff is to be allowed to put up posters. It seems to be making him somewhat uncomfortable. I would forbid it outright.

I choose a few smart journalists for the next coverage in Coblenz. The sky pilots will be surprised. The Rossaint trial is uncovering the entire collaboration between the papists and the commies. *Par nobile fratrum.*

I am having the Comics' Cabaret kept under surveillance. They are cracking jokes there against the state. That cannot be tolerated. These snobs should make jokes about themselves. They have enough reason. One cannot be generous in such matters. That is sentimentality. Unfortunately, as recently as this very Sunday Magda went to this cabaret with Helldorff. Words failed me. I'm bursting with rage. Left to her own devices Magda just does stupid things.

Film and personnel questions with Funk. Now I'll soon install a new board of directors at the *Ufa*. Hanke too is continually placing film questions before me. High time that the position of Reichsfilmdramaturg had a new occupant. Nierentz is a wash-out.

Dictated a speech for the Führer's birthday. It has, I believe, turned out very well . . .

Goering is letting loose on Rosenberg most sharply. He's a stubborn theoretician and mucking up the whole plan for us. If he had his way there would be no more German theatre, just cult, *Thing*, myth and similar bunk.

Hess has given Blomberg a picture of Blücher as a gift. Now it turns out that it portrays Blucher in a freemasons' state, and that the picture was confiscated from a lodge. Embarrassing affair!

Goering wants to travel to Italy to inaugurate cooperation for the 4 Year Plan. The Plan is causing him a lot of work and worry. We all have too much to do. We are almost at our wits' end. I get along with Goering very well now.

Read and proof-read at home. According to what Darré tells me, Walter Granzow has been plotting against him. That will probably cost him his neck. Good old decent Walter! Women are our misfortune!

With difficulty to the Bogensee. Everything goes wrong. Finally end up here. The weather is glorious. Outside they're building the jetty and the terrace. It will be lovely. It will just take a while.

Loads of work. And a little time for reading and music. Führer still in Godesberg. Stayed outside. Early to bed. A heavy working day today.

Our Ministry is now taking the Congress business in hand. Herr Knothe is moving lock, stock and barrel to Paris for the duration of the Paris World Exhibition to defend our position.

Great speculation: who will win the Book Prize on 1 May. If I don't find anything better, then Möller for the *Game of Dice at Frankenburg*.

Funk has a load of odds and ends. We're now buying a couple of beautiful pictures, a Defregger and a Spitzweg. I can make good use of them.

Discussion about Demandowski. He makes a good impression. Is to become Nierentz's successor as Reichsfilmdramaturg. A good swap, I think.

Prof. Ziegler is worried about the House of German Art. He must get on with it and prevail. I strengthen his backbone a bit. In Munich above all you need push.

Frau v. Kalckreuth has finished my bust. It's turned out excellently. She is pleased beyond measure.

Glasmeier and Kriegler outline the work they are doing in tidying up broadcasting. Hadamovsky has made a right pigsty out of it. But Glasmeier is setting to work with gusto and I believe he will manage it. In any case, he is proceeding ruthlessly and that's the main thing. Broadcasting had become a real institute of nepotism. That will now stop.

Schmeling describes his difficulties in America. Braddock is a coward and is always searching for new excuses. I advise Schmeling to challenge him publicly in an open letter, which will have to be written very skilfully. That will probably do the trick.

Randolph outlines the situation in England. Totally against us. Ribbentrop does not always proceed in the most psychologically skilful manner. He needs to have more of a go at Germany's enemies. And speak less, but instead act all the more. Randolph has developed a good relationship with him. In my opinion he will try to influence him.

Carried on working quickly at home. Although the warm spring sun entices one to go for walks and laze around. Dictated speech for the 4 Year Exhibition. It's turning out very well.

Played mummy and visits in the garden with the children. They both have a really blossoming imagination. Helga especially is inexhaustible in her invention of ideas and fantasies.

Worked, proof-read. The Führer is back from the Rhineland. I go to him for dinner. He is very kind and full of plans and impressions. I tell him the latest. Then we set out the 1 May in detail. Watch a bad American film.

Still lengthy debates on the Church question. We are now killing the sky pilots with trials and economic pressure. I have had all the printworks which printed the Pope's letter expropriated. And if the Coblenz trials liven it up yet again, well here's to it!

Czechoslovakia too has backed down in the face of pressure from our press. We are now a great power again and are able to defend ourselves. That creates a wonderful feeling. The Führer is very happy about it.

Worked at home until deep into the night again.

Today another heavy day.

4 The 'Führer' on the 'Führer State':
'The best type of democracy'

On 29 April 1937, on the first anniversary of the dedication of the Party training institutes established by the DAF at Crössinsee, Vogelsang and Sonthofen, Hitler spoke at the 'Castle of the Order' at Vogelsang in East Pomerania to an audience of 800 District Leaders of the NSDAP. Taking as his starting point the 'crisis of democracy' which, he said, could be observed throughout Europe, the 'Führer' attempted a definition of the 'Führer State' of the National Socialist type and an explanation of the obvious contentedness of the German people. He found these in his 'firm leadership', but also in the leadership qualities of his subordinate leaders and the openness of the system to young political talent.

The extraordinary triviality and lack of rhetorical lustre of the written speech give no indication of what succeeded in captivating Hitler's audience for almost two hours; however, the reactions of the audience are noted. The following extracts comprise just less than one-eighth of the speech.
Quoted from Hildegard von Kotze and Helmut Krausnick (eds) *'Es spricht der Führer'. 7 exemplarische Hitler-Reden* (Gütersloh, 1966), pp. 123–77.

We National Socialists have found a very specific definition for the state, that is, we say the state cannot be all things to all men, rather, it only has meaning if its final mission is yet again the preservation of a living Folkdom [*Volkstum*]. It must not just preserve the life of a *Volk*, but in so doing it must also be the guardian of the substance, the guardian of the blood of a *Volk*. Otherwise, in the final analysis, the state has no meaning. To create an organization simply for the sake of the organization is senseless . . . The state itself has the task of securing the Folkdom as such, maintaining the Folkdom as such and thereby guaranteeing it for the future. Therefore we recognize not a state with an indeterminate sense of purpose but one with a clearly defined sense of purpose. We also know that all achievements are only conceivable under the precondition of the existence of this state, i.e. therefore only through the combination of all forces in this organization is it possible to bring about really great, powerful and collective achievements.

For us, then, there is also no possibility of a discussion about the question of, let's say, primacy within the state; that means, therefore, to take a concrete example: we will never tolerate, in a *völkisch* state, that anything should place itself above the authority of this *völkisch* state. No matter what it is, and that includes the Church! [*Thunderous applause*]. Here too the inviolable principle applies: the authority of the state, that is, of this living national community, stands above everything. Everything must submit itself to this authority. If anyone attempts to take a position against this authority, he will be made to yield to this authority, whatever it takes! [*Bravo*] Only one authority is conceivable, and that can only be that of the state, again with the proviso that this state itself recognizes as it highest purpose only the maintenance, securing and continuation of a particular Folkdom. Such a state is then the source of all achievements . . .

The Idea does not live amongst the broad masses. We must finally recognize this, and that is also quite clear. If every human advance represents a higher achievement than the given, already existing, then it is evident that someone must have led the way. And this one person who will have led the way, he is the bearer of the Idea, and not the broad masses who stand behind him. He is the pioneer, not those who follow. And it is also only too logical and evident that an organization is only sensible if, from the very beginning, it concentrates on seeking to promote the most capable minds from every sphere into a position of leading and decisive influence and then in turn follows them.

Of course, this may be very hard. For the individual person, and especially for the weakling, that I emphasize expressly, and most of all for asocials, it is terrible. It is always hard if someone says, 'only one person can command; one commands and the rest must obey'. Then he says, 'why, why, why do I have to obey?' – Why? Because only in this way is anything to be accomplished, and because we are men enough to appreciate that that which is necessary must also occur. And because therefore this is not a subject for discussion with the individual. It is completely pointless then to say to each individual, 'Of course, of course if you don't want to, then of course you don't need to follow.' No, that simply won't work! Reason has also a right and therefore a duty; it has the right to elevate itself to dictatorial power and the duty to force the rest to obey.

For this reason our state is in no way based on plebiscites, I want to emphasize that, but rather it is our endeavour to convince the *Volk* of the necessity of that which takes place . . .

I can tell those of you here today one example form the great historical developments which have taken place: last year, at the end of February, it became clear to me personally that it was now necessary to exploit the given historical situation immediately and to carry out at once the occupation of the previously demilitarized zone which had been intended for later – naturally a decision of tremendous importance which one could have considered in different ways. And naturally there were discussions concerning this decision with the competent authorities. And it was simply unthinkable that a totally unified opinion on such a decision could be reached. For its importance was tremendous, its consequences possibly unforeseeable. It was now clear that one's own opinion could still have been further informed by counter-arguments and objections. But it was necessary to act in one way or another in a relatively short space of time if action was not to be postponed altogether. According to the previous, democratic way of dealing with such matters, this question would eventually have been laid before parliament, discussed in parliament, then it would have gone to the National Assembly and been discussed by the National Assembly. In other words, on the most difficult question of the fate of the nation, on which the most senior leading men could not perhaps completely agree, the little people out there would have had to decide – these little people who are in no way in a position to judge the matter. It would have been put before the National Assembly; the press would have written about it, leader articles would have been written, as indeed happens in other countries. Now imagine what you burden such a little human worm with, who, every day, goes to work out there, whose whole education, whose whole understanding, whose knowledge can in no way be capable of somehow evaluating the importance of these problems! I am thereby now placing on him the burden of making a decision here!

Perhaps it will be said: 'Yes, but you also held a plebiscite.' But I acted first. Acted first, and then of course I just wanted to show the rest of the world that the German people stands behind me, that's what it was about. If I had been convinced that perhaps the German people could, in this case, not go along totally, I would have acted nevertheless, but I would not then have held a vote. (*Animated applause*) . . .

In a genuine Führer State, it is now, let's say, the honour of him who leads that he also assumes the responsibility. All the world's really big organizations are based to a degree on such considerations, on such principles. All of them. One person always has to bear the reponsibility for a particular decision. And he can't then organize votes. The complete absurdity of this parliamentary democracy always becomes clearest when you come to the simplest of procedures. Just imagine that parliamentary democracy, that is, this select bunch which results from a majority vote, that they then have to make decisions on the greatest of problems. Now let's look at the detail of everday life. Just for once, let the house that's being built down the road, yes, let it be built by majority voting, let the workers meet together and now let them vote on the plans. Which plan is the right one? Yes, you may laugh, you'll say, of course that's idiotic. Of course it's idiotic! Of course you can't let either the inhabitants or the workers vote on the plan of the house, we all know that. But apparently it is reasonable to let them vote on the construction of, let's say, a state, a Reich, because that's naturally 'much easier' to understand. Of course, it's 'much easier' to govern a people of 68 million souls . . .

Today, the people are happier in Germany than anywhere else in the world. They only become uncertain if there is no leadership. The moment there is a firm leadership they are happy, for they themselves know very well: 'Yes, we don't understand this at all.' They are all of the same opinion: 'God, we can put our trust in our leadership, it will do things properly.' I saw the madness of the belief that the ordinary man does not want any leadership in the first place, I saw this never more starkly than during the war. If a company is faced with a critical situation, the company only has one wish, that it has a decent company commander, and then it will rely on him. And if he's a good chap, a real man, then he has his men behind him. They won't say: 'Well, why weren't we asked?' Nobody would think of it! On the contrary, they don't want to be asked at all, they want a commander who gives them instructions and then they follow him. [*Shouts of 'Heil' and thunderous applause*] . . .

Believe me: this current crisis can only be alleviated by a genuine state of leadership and thus a Führer State. At the same time it is quite clear that the purpose of such leadership lies in trying to obtain, from all walks of life, by means of a natural selection, always from the people, those who are suited for such leadership. And that is also the best, and in my view the most Germanic [*germanischste* (*sic*)] democracy. For what can be better for a people than the knowledge: out of our ranks the most able can attain the highest position regardless of origin or birth or anything else. He only has to have the necessary abilities. We are striving to find able people. What they have been, what their parents were, what their mummies were, that is completely unimportant. If they are able, all doors are open to them. They then only have to be willing to accept responsibility as well, that means they must really have the stuff of leadership in them. Purely abstract intellectual ability counts for nothing. The person really has to be able to lead as well. If he is placed somewhere, no matter where, he must also have the courage to say: 'Yes, that's what must be done now. I can see that.' He must consult those of his men who are responsible with him for the implementation of the decision, but in the final analysis he must answer for his ideas and for his decision. He must make the decision.

That is the best type of democracy there is . . .

And the Führer State doesn't need to be afraid of genius, that is precisely how it differs from democracy. If, in a democracy, someone were to become a Gauleiter, he would have to be terribly afraid that perhaps a talent would emerge beneath him, about whom he would have to say: 'If this chap carries on, in a short while he'll have the people behind him and then he'll unseat me. Bang! Then I'll have my reward for all my work.' So, in democracy you have to be careful that no talent comes to light. If a talent does come to light somewhere then you must destroy it as quickly as possible. That is the instinct of self-preservation there. [*Laughter*] In the Führer State this is not the case at all, because he knows perfectly well someone can be still be very talented but, nevertheless, still can't remove him. On the contrary, if he makes efforts to remove him he sins against discipline and obedience and thus shows that he himself is incapable of leading. And with that he is finished.

That is why there exists a far greater probability in the Führer State that talent will be encouraged. It cannot pose a threat to any leader. On the contrary, in finding talent he is still supporting himself, he is creating for himself classic [*sic*], excellent colleagues and out of all those colleagues only he can hope to achieve something who is himself absolutely loyal and obedient. For he is only demonstrating that he alone is capable of really leading one day. For where we would end up, if he who does not practise loyalty and obedience himself at some later date wanted to demand loyalty and obedience of others? Because he will have to, for things simply cannot be otherwise. These are iron principles which must be maintained.

5 Heinrich Himmler: Smoking ban and 'special treatment'

SS honour and domestic oilfields, runological research and selective human breeding, medicinal herb gardens and extermination of the Jews – a great many subjects flowed together in the mind of the Reichsführer SS. The following small selection from his letters can only hint at the awfulness and the lunacy of Himmler's ideas. Beyond the sickened shaking of the head which reading Himmler may cause it should not be forgotten that most of his orders and several of his 'suggestions' became policy and murderous reality.

Quoted from Helmut Heiber (ed.), *Reichsführer!... Briefe an und von Himmler* (Stuttgart, 1968).

To: SS-Stabsführer *Prof. Dr Karl Gebhard,*   *14.1.1938*
Chief Physician of the Hohenlychen Sanatoria

Dear Karl,
I spoke to you once a long time ago about an old remedy for tuberculosis which has been handed down through several generations in a family known to me.
I enclose the remedy and would ask you to try it out sometime.

Heil Hitler!
Your HH

To: SS-Sturmbannführer *Prof. Dr Walther Wüst*   *28.3.1938*

Dear Professor Wüst,
Today I would like to return to the subject of calendar science, about which I wrote to you once before.
What needs to be clarified above all is whether there existed two types of calculation regarding the division of the year, i.e. 13 months according to the natural lunar months of 28 days and then later 12 months determined in an arbitrary fashion.
Since when have there been these different ways of calculating time? Here the world ice theory must be taken into account, for the lunar months of 28 days can only have existed since the moon has been orbiting the Earth.
In this connection a number of other questions will certainly emerge.

Heil Hitler!
Your HH

To: SS-Sturmbannführer *Count Adalbert Kottulinsky*   *16.9.1938*

Dear Kottulinsky,

You have been very ill and have had serious problems with your heart. In the interest of your health I am placing a complete ban on your smoking for a period of two years.

After these two years have elapsed you will send me a doctor's medical certificate; I will then decide if the smoking ban is to be lifted or to remain in force.

Heil Hitler!
Yours, signed H. Himmler

To: SS-Gruppenführer *Oswald Pohl,*   *29.11.1941*
Head of the SS Head Office Administration and Economy

Dear Pohl,

Enclosed, I am sending you a paper on biologically dynamic fertilization. I have made a few comments on it. I can imagine the reports from IG-Farben very well, because, now more than 19 years ago, similarly highly efficient reports were required of me as a young assistant in a nitrogen works. In these I was supposed to prove that a particularly large-scale use of lime nitrogen would be best for agriculture, which I obviously did not do.

Once again I reiterate that the genuinely precise and neutral scientific investigation of the type ordered by me on the same soil and in the same climate in Auschwitz will probably, for the first time, bring objective and untainted results. I am therefore requesting that SS-Sturmbannführer Vogel gives very serious personal attention to the questions of these experiments and, if necessary, deploys someone on his own staff expressly for this purpose.

Heil Hitler!
Yours, signed H. Himmler

To: SS-Obergruppenführer *August Heissmeyer,*   *30.6.1942*
Head of the SS Head Office, Department Heissmeyer

Dear Heissmeyer,

As I understand it, a large number of the pupils of the National Political Educational Institute in Putbus are going to confirmation classes. Were you aware of this? Who is the leader responsible in these matters?

Of course, at the beginning, the boys will belong to various denominations. In my opinion, however, in the course of only a few years, ideological education should bring the boys so far that they convince their parents to permit them to leave the Church.

Altogether what reasons do you have for not pursuing the exit from the various denominations more strongly? As an explanation I could imagine that you want to avoid frightening off the parents too soon for fear of otherwise hindering the flow of valuable blood into the Reich schools from families still committed to various denominations.

Please inform me of your view of the overall problem and give me a clear presentation of the situation of all the National Political Education Institutes in this regard.

Heil Hitler!
Yours truly HH

To: SS-Obergruppenführer *Arthur Greiser,*   *27.7.1942*
Gauleiter and Reich Governor in the Wartheland

Dear Party Comrade Greiser,
Unfortunately, it has only today been possible for me to give a definitive response to your letter of 1.5.1942.

I have no objections to protectorate subjects and those who are stateless and of Polish racial origin living in the region of the *Reichgau* Wartheland, who are in custody and have obvious tuberculosis, undergoing special treatment in the way you suggest, so long as their illness is officially medically certified as incurable. I would ask, however, that the individual measures are discussed in detail in advance with the security police so that they can be carried out as discreetly as possible.

Heil Hitler!
Yours, signed H. Himmler

To: SS-Obergruppenführer *Friedrich-Wilhelm Krüger,*   *27.8.1943*
Senior SS and Police Führer East (Krakow)

Dear Krüger,
I am very happy to authorize your convalescence leave. Better still, take 4 weeks instead. But don't exert yourself hunting in Norway too much. It's very wearing. Let me know who you are naming as your deputy.

Heil Hitler!
Best wishes, your H. Himmler

To: SS-Obergruppenführer *Richard Hildebrandt,*   *17.12.1943*
Head of the SS Race and Settlement Office

Dear Hildebrandt,
Due to the importance of the matter, I am also acknowledging in writing your letter of 1.12.43 re. the Jewish ancestry of the SS members Katzenstein, Julius and Rolf Sütterlin.

It is my decision in these three cases that all three may marry their brides on their own responsibility and I have directed that their files should be resubmitted after the war. I am already making it clear today that – whatever my final decision may be – there is no question of the acceptance of the children of these 3 families [*Sippen*] into the SS or the authorization of their marriage with an SS man and that these families are barred from the SS.

I can in no way accept the reference from Prof. Dr B.K. Schultz. In my view he is scientifically completely intolerable. For by the same justification with which he explains that by the third generation it is impossible to expect even a single chromosome of Jewish origin, one could maintain that the chromosomes of all other ancestors would also disappear. If this is the case I have to ask the question: where then does the human being get his genetic inheritance from if, after the third generation, nothing remains of the chromosomes of his ancestors? One thing is clear to me: Herr Prof. Dr Schultz is not suited to be Head of the Race Office.

I am unable now to decide about the overall question dealt with in your letter, but I will do so after the war. It has a tremendous amount both for and against it. On the whole I tend to the view that with new recruits or new marriages we should, at the least, maintain the principle of at first going back to 1750 and then, depending on the state of genealogical research, to 1700 and then to 1650, and of demanding complete purity there.

Heil Hitler!
Your HH

To: Chief of the Reich Security Head Office   *8.9.1943*

I confirm the receipt of your telegram of 26.8.1943 – No: 151671 –. On the question of sexual relations by and with labourers from the Baltic, I have the following comments:

1. I am in favour of lifting the ban on sexual relations for Estonians and Latvians as well as with Estonians and Latvians.

2. I wish the ban for all Lithuanian men and women to remain in force. The Lithuanians are a *Volk* which behaves so badly and possesses such a low racial value that a lifting of the ban is neither justified nor justifiable.

I am instructing the Reich Security Head Office to discuss these questions, via SS-Obergruppenführer Berger, with Reich Leader Rosenberg.

HH

To: SS-Obergruppenführer *Karl Wolff,*   *8.11.1943*
Supreme SS and Police Führer in Italy

Dear Wolfy,
I suggest that you carry out the method of posting a reward of 5 Engl. pounds or an equivalent number of lire in every Italian town for any English prisoners handed over. I believe that in this way we will get a large number of Britons who are today still on the loose.

Heil Hitler!
HH

To: SS-Oberführer *Prof. Dr Walter Wüst,*   *31.3.1944*
Curator of 'Foundation for the Heritage of our
Forefathers inc.' ['Ahnenerbe e.V.']

In the future meteorological research which we want to build up after the war through the organization of innumerable individual observers, I would ask you to direct your attention to the following:
    In different years the roots and the bulb respectively of the autumnal crocus are at different depths in the ground. The deeper they grow, the harder the winter; the nearer they are to the surface, the milder the winter.
    The Führer pointed out this fact to me.

signed H. Himmler

To: Director General Paul Pleiger,   *13.8.1944*
Chairman of the Board of Directors and
Head of the Hermann Goering Corporation

Have received your telegram of 11.8. I find it unbelievable that this oilfield has still not been drilled. I hold it to be your national duty to get down to drilling immediately, with your own energy, and to overcome all difficulties, and – should you have success – to develop these reserves.
    You are requested to return a weekly progress report by telegram.

Heil Hitler!
signed H. Himmler

6 Robert Ley:
The Reich Vocational Contest and tiredness as *passé*

It was hard to find a more full-blooded propagandist of the *Volksgemeinschaft* than the Reich Organization Leader of the NSDAP and Leader of the German Labour Front. Ley, who came from the Rhineland and had a doctorate in chemistry, did not like to play the anti-bourgeois only in front of meetings of workers; he really was almost a caricature of the loutish 'Old Fighter.' His speeches had the advantage of being particularly short and to the point and in many respects they were also remarkably open. In the following extract Ley explains the justification for the 'Reich Vocational Contest of all Working Germans of 1938'.
Quoted from: Robert Ley, *Soldaten der Arbeit* (Munich, 1938), pp. 209–11.

Germany is poor in material goods. We have never been rich. In the course of the millennia the German *Volk* has given much to the world, but in the course of these millennia it has won few material things for itself, not even enough land. We are a *Volk* without space! We are poor in mineral ores, to say nothing of gold and precious stones. Indeed, we are always being told that we are 'poor starvelings'. We take note of this. In answer we say, 'Even so, we are happy, for we have the most industrious *Volk* on Earth!'

There is no shame in being poor. We would prefer to be poor and young than rich and sclerotic. We are young! It is precisely this youth which characterizes this new Germany! We are young; we must protect, preserve and promote this capital, the only capital we have: our industriousness, our skills and our high racial quality. We simply cannot do enough to increase the German's skills. In Germany's struggle for existence we can deploy nothing other than the German's industriousness, powers and skills. We want to do this. There should no longer be any unskilled workers in Germany. Don't tell us that our social measures are a luxury. On the contrary, they make the greatest economic sense. An entrepreneur who does not grasp this fact is neither an economist nor a German. If he wants to manage his business successfully he must liberate and make full use of the strengths that lie within his retinue [*Gefolgschaft*].

We want the community! Maximum performance can only be achieved within the community. People's happiness can only come from the community. We see our highest aim as a community of people, as an organic, meritocratic whole. We don't just want a mass of people. We wish everyone to have their place. But if we want this ordered community, then we must also grant that the individual has rights in this community. If we impose duties on him we must also give him rights. The first and foremost right: to make way for efficiency. The young man from the last village on earth should be able to make his way upwards if he is capable. And here I am also thinking of my own path through life. How hard it once was! Almost impossible for a young lad who had to scrape a living in some God-forsaken village to get anywhere. The war and the revolution which we experienced have changed all that. We have cleared the way for individual people. The opportunity for development must be independent of wealth and social origin. The poor person should have the same chances as the rich.

Before we came to power, we could often hear the phrase, 'I'm so tired, I need a rest.' The loafers were the most tired.

Work doesn't make you tired, that's not true. A person who masters his trade doesn't get tired. The only person who gets tired is he who cannot master his task, who is without hope, who has no faith. This bourgeois tiredness from former times must disappear from our *Volk* once and for all.

7 The regime and 'community aliens'

From 1940, discussions took place under the auspices of the SS (Reich Criminal Police Office) to amalgamate and systemize into a 'Law on the Treatment of Community Aliens' the police and judicial powers – greatly extended in the preceding years – for action against those regarded as socially undesirable and as persons (and groups of persons) 'damaging to the *Volk*'. The intended law was delayed by clashes of competence, but above all by the comprehensive adjustments of the Reich Penal Code (*Reichsstrafgesetzbuch*) and the legal provisions concerning criminal proceedings which were then becoming necessary. In the spring of 1944, the participating authorities agreed on the wording of the law (it was to be signed by the 'Führer', the President of the Ministerial Council for the Defence of the Reich, the Reich Ministers of Justice, the Interior, Labour, and Finance, the Chief of the High Command of the Armed Forces, the Head of the Reich Chancellery and the Head of the Party Chancellery). A one-week further training course on the new regulations was planned for the beginning of August 1944; the Munich law professor Edmund Mezger, who informed the Ministry of Justice of his classification of criminals by postcard, was to give a two-hour introductory lecture on 'The Community Aliens Law in the light of criminal biology'.

However, the course of the war – the summer of 1944 saw the 20 July bomb plot and the climax of the Allied bombing – then prevented the law from being passed. Nevertheless the following justification for the law, printed in its final version in the prison printing plant at Tegel, constitutes, both in style and content, and explicit summary of the dominant theory of the time.

Quoted from Bundesarchiv Koblenz, R 22/944, fol. 228f.

Dr Edmund Mezger   *Munich, 25.3.44*
Professor of Law at the University   *Kaulbachstr. 89*

[Postcard]

Ministerial Under Secretary Grau
Reich Ministry of Justice
(1) Berlin
Wilhelmstrasse 65

Dear Ministerial Under Secretary,
Regarding the question we mentioned of the 'classification of criminals',
I have now definitely decided on the following:

I.   Criminals of circumstance [*Situationsverbrecher*]
  1. Those whose crimes stem from conflict with the community
     [*Konfliktsverbrecher*]
  2. Those whose criminality has developed over time [*Entwick-lungsverbrecher*]
  3. Opportunistic criminals [*Gelegenheitsverbrecher*]
II. Those with a criminal personality
  4. Criminals by inclination
  5. Predisposed criminals
  6. Congenital criminals

With friendly best wishes,
Heil Hitler!
Yours truly,
Dr Mezger

Justification

Decades of experience teaches us that the criminal fraternity continually
supplements itself from inferior stock. The individual members of such
families usually end up with members of similar families and the result
is that the inferiority is not only passed from generation to generation but
often also develops into criminality. These people have mostly neither
the will nor the ability to integrate themselves into the national community. They lead a life alien to the ideas of the community, have
no community feeling at all, are often unsuited to or even hostile to the
community, and are thus, in any case, alien to the community.

The authorities charged with public welfare have long demanded that
those community aliens (asocials) who, as a result of their inability to
adapt to the community, become a continual burden to the nation, should
be taken forcibly into custody. Hitherto, existing welfare legislation has
only recognized custody for those with proven need and who submit

voluntarily . . . The order of the community, however, requires a juridical basis which goes beyond the inadequate powers of welfare legislation in order to be able to take community aliens into custody forcibly and in sufficient numbers.

The governments of the Weimar period [*Systemzeit*] failed in their measures aimed at community aliens. They did not use the findings of genetic theory and criminal biology as a basis for a sound policy on welfare and crime. As a result of their liberal way of thinking, all they ever perceived were the 'rights' of the individual and they were more concerned with protecting these against manifestations of state power than with the good of the nation.

In National Socialism, where the community is at stake the individual counts for nothing.

The pre-emptive crime prevention measures introduced by the Reich Criminal Police after the assumption of power, on the basis of progressively developing National Socialist police legislation, were based on this principle. At the same time, it came to be recognized that the treatment of community aliens does not so much belong within the scope of duties of the welfare system as within that of the police. According to National Socialist thinking, welfare can only benefit those national comrades who not only need it, but are also worthy of it. For community aliens who only inflict harm on the national community it is not welfare but compulsion by the police which is necessary. This should have the goal of either winning them back, through appropriate measures, as useful members of the national community, or of preventing them from doing further damage. In these matters the protection of the community is the prime consideration.

The draft of a law on the treatment of community aliens is intended to fulfil these demands by taking over and redefining previous police measures; furthermore, it aims to create additional, new juridical bases for judicial decisions, in so far as community aliens become liable to prosecution, or for the sterilization of community aliens if it is to be anticipated that they will have progeny who will be undesirable for the national community.

In applying the findings of genetic theory and criminal biology, the law designates 3 groups of people as alien to the community:

1. Failures,
   People whose personality and way of life, especially as a result of abnormal defects of intellect or character, show that they are unable to meet the minimum requirements of the national community of their own accord.

2. The work-shy and the dissolute,
   People who, either as ne'er-do-wells or parasites, lead a useless, uneconomic or disordered life and thus burden or endanger others or the nation as a whole, or, as good-for-nothings, display a tendency to beg, become tramps, be idle at work, steal or commit fraud or other minor offences. Amongst this group can also be counted persons who repeatedly disturb the peace of others or of the whole community out of cantankerousness or eagerness to quarrel and whom the draft law therefore designates as *troublemakers*.

3. Criminals,
   People whose personality and way of life show that they are disposed towards committing criminal acts.

In order to be certain that these community aliens, who by their behaviour cause damage to the national community, are either won back for the community, or, if this is not possible, are prevented by means of state compulsion from causing further damage, the draft proposes, in the first instance, *police measures* for community aliens not liable to prosecution. Here police surveillance is primarily envisaged, which is to be understood as surveillance with particular conditions, requirements and prohibitions. If surveillance measures are insufficient, the draft creates the juridical basis for directing these community aliens into the reformatories of the *Land* welfare organizations. If this, more custodial, deprivation of liberty is also insufficient the community alien will be accommodated in camp run by the police. In this way the idea of custody developed in welfare law has also prevailed in the field of preventive protection of the community.

Particular significance is attributed to the struggle against those community aliens liable to legal penalties. Apart from police treatment of community aliens the law therefore also regulates the *treatment by the courts of community aliens liable to legal penalties*. The task of reuniting with the community, as useful members, those community aliens *liable to legal penalties*, is not incumbent upon the police but upon the judicial authorities. The same applies to rendering them harmless, in so far as the punishment and its implementation makes this possible.

The punishment of criminal community aliens should not have the exclusive purpose of retribution for their crimes but should primarily serve their resocialization and thus correspond to the special nature of criminal community aliens. As it cannot be foreseen in advance what period of time is required to have a lasting influence on the criminal community alien, which will depend on his genetic and constitutional-biological peculiarities, his punishment must be open-ended so that he represents neither a danger nor a burden for the national community.

Just as the draft, therefore, makes available open-ended imprisonment to the police, so it gives the courts the power of open-ended sentencing and thus, via the Law on Habitual Criminals of 24.11.1933, provides them with a weapon which has long been demanded by penology and criminal biology.

Open-ended punishment not only has the advantage over specified punishment in that it can be adapted to suit the moral and intellectual development of the convicted criminal during his imprisonment, but also because it has a far greater effect on the convicted criminal. It does not permit him to sit out the period of his punishment more or less personally uninvolved, but rather rouses him and forces him to work on himself in order to deserve his release from prison because of his inner transformation.

In particular, the draft distinguishes between criminals who, by their way of life and personality, display a strong predisposition to commit serious offences, and others who are motivated by a less pronounced inclination to commit all sorts of offences. For the former the law sets a minimum open-ended punishment of 5 years' imprisonment, and it threatens the latter, depending on the gravity of their crimes, with imprisonment or a gaol term of not less than a year.

The judge should single out inveterate criminals from the start and hand them over to the police, whose duty it is to protect the national community from these elements. They are thus declared to be people of inferior rights and because of their inferior genetic make-up are subjected to treatment focused essentially on detention. Furthermore, the draft envisages the transfer into the hands of the police of tramps, professional beggars and similar good-for-nothings who cause more nuisance than harm. This is because this group of community aliens is closely associated with the group of parasites, inasmuch as the basis of the behaviour of both groups is to be sought in idleness or dissoluteness; therefore, the same type of treatment is indicated for both groups. Those with a predisposition or tendency towards criminality, on the other hand, for whom improvement and inner transformation can be expected, should be subject to an attempt to resocialize them while in prison. If the attempt should fail, the draft subsequently empowers and requires the higher executive authority to hand over the convicted criminal to the police. This regulation of the treatment of community alien offenders signifies a considerable but urgently necessary modification of penal law, namely foregoing the dual approach of penal sentencing (imprisonment and additional preventive detention) in favour of an appropriately planned sentence of corrective training, while the straightforward matter of detention is recognized as the task of the police.

Finally, the draft also extends the existing legal provision for the castration of sex offenders to persons who abandon themselves to a tendency to illicit homosexual practices. Recent medical experience shows that castration is also an effective weapon against these persons.

As far as the education of *minors* is concerned, account must be taken of the fact that, in the first instance, the corrective training regulations of the public youth services – namely correctional education and probation – are available, as are the methods of youth detention for those who have committed punishable offences. The law's *police measures* should therefore only be permissible against minors if, according to the declaration of the educational authorities, there is no prospect of achieving integration into the national community via the means available to the youth services. *Young persons* should only be sentenced to open-ended *punishment* if those preconditions exist as laid down in the Statutory Regulation against Serious Young Offenders of 4.10.1939, RGBl. I S. 2000, or the Statutory Regulation on the Open-ended Sentencing of Young Persons of 10.9.1941, RGBl. I S. 567.

Community aliens, especially failures and good-for-nothings, very often belong to families which as a whole, or whose individual members, continually occupy the police or are a burden on the national community in other ways. The draft therefore makes it possible for community aliens *to be sterilized* if they can be expected to produce undesirable progeny. *Whether* a community alien is expected to produce undesirable progeny is to be decided by the eugenic courts.

The implementation of the details of the law will be regulated by implementation orders of the departmental ministers involved.

8   A euthanasia doctor writes to his wife: 'Work is going very smoothly'

At the outbreak of war, Dr Friedrich Mennecke was director of the *Land* psychiatric hospital at Eichberg in the Rheingau, and not yet 35 years old. He had already made a rapid ascent of the social ladder: his father, who died young after returning, shell-shocked and crippled, from the First World War, had been a stonemason and an active Social Democrat. In spring 1932, whilst a medical student in Göttingen, Friedrich Mennecke had joined the NSDAP and the SS. In 1937 he became District Commissioner of the Race Policy Office of the NSDAP and in 1939, Local Party Leader [*Ortsgruppenleiter*] in Erbach-Eichberg and SS-Obersturmführer. During the first months of the war, Mennecke was a medical officer on the 'Siegfried Line'. Then, in the summer of 1942, he was recruited as an 'adviser' on so-called 'euthanasia' by the 'Führer's' Chancellery. Until 1942 this ambitious physician repeatedly took part in 'selection trips' to psychiatric hospitals and concentration camps. With oppressively scrupulous accuracy and undying enthusiasm, Mennecke described to his wife, an assistant medical technician eight years younger than he, not only the most banal details of his daily routine but also his activities in 'ticking off the lists'. The following letters come from a collection originally totalling almost 8,000 pages, a third of which could be offered, in 1946, as evidence in the so-called Eichberg trial. At these proceedings Mennecke was sentenced to death for the murder of at least 2,500 people; he died in custody a short while after from long-standing tuberculosis. In the first of the letters partly reproduced below, Mennecke reports on his period of residence as an 'adviser' for 'Action 14 f 13' in Sachsenhausen concentration camp near Oranienburg; there then follow reports of his activities in the concentration camps at Ravensbrück near Fürstenberg and Buchenwald near Weimar, and of a meeting in the Reich Chancellery with the organizers of the various parts of the 'euthanasia' campaign.

Quoted from Peter Chroust (ed.), *Friedrich Mennecke. Innenansichten eines medizinischen Täters. Eine Edition seiner Briefe 1935–1947* (2 vols, Hamburg, 1987); emphases in the original text.

Director   *Oranienburg, 7.4.41*
Dr med. Fr. Mennecke   *23.40 hrs*
Specialist in Neurology and Psychiatry

My dearest Mummykins,
I am just beginning my last letter from this first concentration camp stint, which I shall, however, bring with me and not send. I have just now finished the statistical survey of the prisoners whom I have examined, so far 109 of them. Tomorrow there'll be a further 25–30 who will be the final task. I am placing particular value on these files for possible later scientific evaluation because they concern solely 'asocials' *par excellence*. So before I deliver my registration forms to the Tiergartenstrasse I am listing all the most important details. There are still 84 prisoners to be examined tomorrow. Because, from today, Dr Hebold (a houseman at Eberswalde) is working with us as a third member of the team, each of us only has to deal with about 26 prisoners. I hope that we will be finished early enough so that I might possibly be able to start my journey home tomorrow . . .

Now, purse your lips, please, for a good night kissy and offer me your b . . . m to spank – and then: sleep well!! Good, goodnight!! Sweet dreams!! In 48 hours I'll be with you!! – Good night!! Ahoy!!

Fürstenberg, 20.11.41

My dearest Mummy,
It's a quarter to six, I've completed my day's work and am back at the hotel. The end result of my work today is 95 forms. After a thorough exposition of my statistical analysis at a further meeting with the camp doctor, SS-Obersturmführer Dr Sonntag and the camp commandant, SS-Sturmbannführer Koegel, the number of those in question was further extended by some 60–70, so I shall be busy up to and including Monday. I spoke with Prof. Heyde on the telephone this morning at 8.15 and told him that I would manage here on my own. As a result no-one turned up today and Dr Schmalenbach doesn't need to come either. I have now agreed with Heyde that after I finish my work here I shall return to Berlin in order to discuss a stint in Buchenwald. I will probably travel to Berlin early on Tuesday morning and then carry on to Weimar the same day. – Work is going very smoothly, because the headings are always already typed and I only have to fill in the diagnosis and the chief symptoms etc. I would prefer not to write anything here in the letter about the make-up of the patients, I'll tell you more later. Dr Sonntag sits with me and gives me details about their behavior in the camp, a Scharführer brings the patients in to me – it's working out perfectly. I'm working at the camp itself; today for lunch in the canteen there was lentil soup with bacon and pancakes for dessert . . .

Weimar, [26.] 11. 1941
(Hotel Elephant)

. . . ten to eight. Home again my little mouse!! The first day of work in Buchenwald is over. We were out early, at 8.30 this morning. First of all I presented myself to the prominent leaders [*Führer*]. The acting camp commandant is *SS-Hauptsturmführer Florstedt*, camp doctor: *SS-Obersturmführer Dr Hofen*. First of all there were around 40 forms to finish filling in from a first batch of Aryans on which both the other colleagues had worked yesterday. Of these 40, I dealt with around 15. When we had completely finished working on this batch, Schmalenbach cleared off to travel to Dresden and won't be coming back again until our work here is finished. Afterwards we started 'examining' the patients, i.e. an interview with the individuals and a comparison with the entries taken from the files. We still weren't finished with this by midday, because both my colleagues only did theoretical work yesterday, so that I 're-examined' those whom Schmalenbach (and this morning I myself) had prepared, and Müller did his own. We didn't break for lunch until 12 o'clock and ate in the Führer-canteen (A1! Soup, boiled beef, red cabbage and boiled potatoes, stewed apple – for 1.50 Mk!), *no* coupons.

During the introductions to all the many SS-Führers I also came across the U-Sturmführer who was adjutant in Camp Hinzert in December 1940. He recognized me immediately too and asked after your health. – At half past one we started examining again, but soon Ribbentrop's speech began, which we listened to first. He said a lot of good things. Did you hear the speech too? Afterwards we carried on examining until about 4 p.m. which means I did 105 patients, Müller 78, so that in the end 183 forms were finished as a first instalment. As a second batch there then followed 1,200 Jews, who were not all 'examined' at first, but for whom it was sufficient to take the reasons for their arrest (often very extensive) from the file and transfer it to the forms. It is therefore a purely theoretical task which will occupy us up to and including Monday, perhaps even longer. Out of this second batch of Jews today I then did another 17, Müller 15. At 5 o'clock sharp we packed up and went for our evening meal: cold platter of cervelat sausage (9 big slices), butter, bread, a portion of coffee! Cost – 0.80 Mk without coupons!! . . .

Berlin, 14.1.42
Hotel Esplanade

My dearest Mummkyins,
What a typical wartime winter journey to here from Fürstenberg! – The passenger train, which was supposed to leave Fürstenberg at 7.47 a.m., didn't leave until 9.20, full to bursting and with no heating. In Oranienburg they suddenly announce 'all change for Berlin!' So out I get and the whole crowd of people too – I with my suitcase, the briefcase and the parcel of registration forms (850 of them) – downstairs, upstairs – into the suburban train to Berlin.

. . . At half past two I entered the Reich Chancellery and immediately began the meeting with Dr Hefelmann, who had various points to discuss. Everything went fine! As the planned big meeting had to be dropped, we are meeting tomorrow in a small group: Dr Hefelmann, Prof. Nitsche, Prof. Schneider, Dr Heinze, Dr Straub and your old man! I shall go to the Reich Chancellery again at 11.30. Under discussion will be the question of 'the promotion of youth psychiatry'. Schneider and Heinze are considered to be the leading scientists in this field in the Reich; I'll be there as well (with Straub) to represent practical experience . . . I am to work closely with Schneider, Heinze and Straub on my special children's department, which is to be extended still further. Those 'weeded out' from this new 'clinic of youth-psychiatry' will receive their final treatment from me. In this we already have *the* project of the future, which I always expected of the special children's department. Besides some very agreeable flattery of the flawless set-up of my special children's department as the best along with Heinze's, Dr Hefelmann expressed some very pleasing signs of recognition for me personally, which, he said, were not only his perception but also that gained by Herr Brack . . .

Around 5 p.m. I left Dr H., who asked me at the very end to buy some wine for him, which I shall do. He gave me his home address. Afterwards I went to the Tiergartenstrasse to talk with Prof. Nitsche. The 'completely new changes', which Frl. Schwab hinted about on the telephone to me, had already been explained to me at Dr H.'s: since the day before yesterday a large detail from our operation, under the leadership of Herr Brack, has been in the eastern theatre of war in order to help with the recovery of our wounded in the ice and snow. There are doctors, clerical assistants, male and female nurses from Hadamar and Sonnenstein, a whole detachment of 20–30 people! This is *top secret*! Only those who could not be spared from the performance of the most urgent work of our operation did not go with them . . . He spoke about me now having to go to all the other concentration camps and that, for the time being, I should simply consider dealing with the concentration camps as my special task. But tomorrow morning I will tell him that I would, at least, prefer to finish off at Gross Rosen first, especially as I am expected from the '16–19.1' and because I am here in the East anyway. Amongst the total workload of about 1,000 there not many registrations are necessary, so that I certainly won't be busy for more than 8 days. After Gross Rosen the work will stop for a while in order to register the remaining concentration camps in the spring. I'm sure you agree with me, don't you, Mummy? – I then went to the accounts department and took a 200.-Mk advance for travel costs. Herr Riedel thought I would present a fat bill for expenses this time, because I had been travelling for so long and hadn't presented any interim bills. It was around a quarter to six before I left the Tiergartenstrasse.

9 Adolf Eichmann: The Wannsee Conference

While, in elegant surroundings, fifteen senior gentlemen were discussing future measures, he was in a corner whispering key words to his minuting secretary: thus Adolf Eichmann described his role at the conference at Berlin's Wannsee on 20 January 1942. As head of the department which dealt with the 'Jewish Question' within the Reich Security Head Office he had made the bureaucratic preparations for the meeting. When the conference was over he sat for a while drinking cognac with Heydrich and the Gestapo chief Heinrich Müller. But as he claimed at his trial in Jerusalem, he only experienced 'a sort of Pilate-like satisfaction' – the 'popes' had issued their orders and his duty was simply to 'obey'. The following

exchange is an excerpt from a pre-trial interrogation, in which Eichmann interpreted his minutes for police captain Avner Less.

In December 1961, the 'desk-murderer', having been tracked down and kid-
napped in Argentina by the Israeli secret service, was sentenced to death for
crimes against the Jewish people. He was executed six months later.

Quoted from Norbert Frei, ' ". . . unsere Arbeiten auf anständige Art und
Weise bearbeitet . . ." Adolf Eichmann und die Wannsee-Konferenz',
Tribüne 21 (1982), pp. 43–59, here p. 53f.

L.   Here, on page 7, Heydrich then says: 'In pursuance of the final
solution, conscript Jews should now be used in an appropriate fashion,
and under appropriate leadership, for labour duties in the East. Jews
capable of work will be escorted in large labour columns, separated by
sex, on road-building duties in these areas, whereby, no doubt, a large
number will drop out as a result of natural decline.' What is to be understood here by 'natural decline'? . . .

E.   'Natural decline' was always understood amongst us – I also borrowed this word, I didn't coin it myself, 'natural decline' is well a, is a
– a – how shall I put it – a technical term, not invented by the Security
Police or anything like that, but rather a technical term for normal death.
In Theresienstadt, for example, I also – er – applied this term, if people
died normally and were treated by the Jewish doctors and the Jewish
doctors determined the cause of death and all those things, – that then
had been a natural decline.

L.   Good, I would just like to get that clear; I can imagine that when
a person has to perform heavy physical work, doesn't get enough to
eat, – he becomes weaker – he becomes so weak that he has a heart
attack!

E.   Of course, if that happened – that would certainly be registered as
'natural decline' by the competent authorities in the East and it would
naturally come under this heading – of natural decline – in the Reich
Security Head Office, because it would have been registered as such. . . .

L.   Here on page 8 in the first paragraph Heydrich then continues:
'Those who might possibly still remain, and they undoubtedly will be
the toughest amongst them, will have to be treated accordingly, because,
representing a natural selection, they would, if released, have to be
considered as the seed of a new Jewish reconstruction.' – What does this
mean here: 'will have to be treated accordingly'?

E.   That's – that's a – this thing originates from Himmler – 'natural
selection' – that's – that's his – that's his hobbyhorse – 'natural selection' –

L.   Yes, but what does this mean here?

E.   Killed, killed, certainly . . .

10   Land of the East, land of illusion:
Nazi melodies and songs to boost morale

If the rising Nazi movement's repertoire of marching songs was considerable, the growth in the variety of ideological melodies as a whole during the Third Reich was almost incalculable. Every military campaign was set to music, every type of weapon had its own songs. The examples reproduced here illustrate the pathos and the blinkered nature of Nazi *Lebensraum* ideology: the notion that 'in the East' there was a land to colonize, without history, culture or people.

By way of contrast and to complete the picture there follow the refrains of a series of popular hits from the war. Their function – to entertain, distract and boost morale – is obvious, even if they make no use of political vocabulary.

> Quoted from *Gemeinschaftslieder. Lieder für Frauengruppen*, published by the Reich Women's Leadership ('In the East . . .' [no place of publication given], 1940); all hit songs from Monika Sperr (ed.), *Schlager. Das Grosse Schlager-Buch. Deutscher Schlager 1800-Heute* (Munich, 1978).

In the East lies our tomorrow, lies Germany's years to come,
There waits danger, a people's troubles, and the beat of the victory
  drum.

There our brothers kept the faith, so the banner never sank,
For five hundred faithful years – thus they kept watch without thanks.

There good earth lies awaiting, that carried no seed until now,
There lie no farms or cattle, the land's crying out for the plough.

There we must win back the foreign soil, which once was German
  domain,
There, there must be new beginnings, Germans, arm yourselves, hear
  this refrain!

                                        (Words and music: Hans Baumann)

Even far off in this far place,
The stars of the homeland shine down from above.
What they are telling, I like to think,
Is the sweet answer to the riddle of love.
Wondrous evening hours,
When the sky's like a diamond shower,
A thousand stars in the heavens above,
Sent to me by my own true love,
Far away I dream, I dream of the homeland I love.
(Film music from *Quax, the Hard-luck Pilot*, 1942)

Everything passes,
Time passes by!
Every December
Is followed by May!

Everything passes,
Time passes too!
But two people in love,
Will always stay true!
(1942)

I know that a miracle will happen one day
And a thousand dreams will come true.
I know no love can pass so quickly away,
That's so great and so wonderful too.
We both share the self-same star
And your fate is mine forever.
Your are far from me and yet not far,
For our hearts are bound together.
And that's why a miracle will happen one day –
And I know that we'll meet again!
(Film music from *The Great Love*, 1942)

It won't cause the world to end,
Just 'cause it sometimes seems grey,
One day it will fill with colour again,
It'll be bright sky-blue one day.
But even if our heads are in a whirl,
If you're sometimes up and sometimes low,
That won't cause the end of the world,
Because it's still needed, you know.
(Film music from *The Great Love*, 1942)

With music everything's better,
With music it falls into place,
Whether you're playing the trumpet,
The fiddle or double-bass.
But only playing so softly,
No, that's not the right idea.

Here and there it's just as right
To play out loud and clear.
(Film music from *Sophielund*, 1943)

So buy yourself a bright balloon
And with a little fantasy
You can fly away to a make-believe land
And be happy as can be.

(1944)

11   Count Helmuth James von Moltke:
Re-establishing the picture of man

For many of those members of the German upper class involved in the resistance against Hitler, particularly for the Prussian nobility, ethical-religious arguments played almost as important a role as political and strategic-military considerations. For Count Helmuth James von Moltke, who, as host of the opposition Kreisau Circle, was arrested in January 1944 and executed one year later, they were central. Moltke was able to write the following letter (in English) in April 1942 whilst on an official visit to Turkey, to his English friend Lionel Curtis. It gives an insight into the motives of this man, an expert in international law, who at that time was only 35 years old.

Quoted from Helmuth James Graf von Moltke, *A German of the Resistance. The last letters of Count Helmuth James von Moltke* (2nd edn, Oxford, 1948), pp. 26–9. Cf. further also Moltke, *Briefe an Freya 1939–1945*, ed. Beate Ruhm von Oppen (Munich, 1988).

Things are worse and better than anybody outside Germany can believe them to be. They are worse, because the tyranny, the terror, the loss of values of all kinds, is greater than I could have believed a short time ago. The number of Germans killed by legal process in November was 25 a day through judgements of the civil courts and at least 75 a day by judgements of the courts martial, numbers running into hundreds are killed daily in concentration camps and by simple shooting without any pretence of a trial. The constant danger in which we live is formidable. At the same time the greater part of the population has been uprooted and been conscribed to forced labour of some kind and has been spread all over the continent, untying all bonds of nature and surrounding and thereby loosening the beast in man, which is reigning. The few really good people who try to stem the tide are isolated as far as they have to work in these unnatural surroundings, because they cannot trust their comrades, and they are in danger from the hatred of the oppressed people even when they succeed in saving some from the worst. Thou sands of those Germans who will survive will be dead mentally, will be useless for normal work.

But things are also better than you can believe, and that in many ways. The most important is the spiritual awakening, which is starting up, coupled as it is with a preparedness to be killed, if need be. The back-bone of this movement is to be found in both the christian confessions, protestant as well as catholic . . .

You know that I have fought the Nazis from the first day, but the amount of risk and readiness for sacrifice which is asked from us now, and that which may be asked from us tomorrow require more than right ethical principles, especially as we know that the success of our fight will probably mean a total collapse as a national unit. But we are ready to face this . . .

For us, Europe after the war is less a problem of frontiers and soldiers, of top-heavy organizations or grand plans, but Europe after the war is a question of how the picture of man can be re-established in the breasts of our fellow citizens. This is a question of religion, education, of ties to work and family, of the proper relationship between responsibility and rights. I must say, that under the incredible pressure under which we have to labour we have made some progress, which will be visible one day. Can you imagine what it means to work as a group if you cannot use the telephone, when you are unable to post letters, when you cannot tell the names of your closest friends to your other friends for fear that one of them might be caught and might divulge the names under pressure? . . .

The hardest bit of the way is still to come, but nothing is worse than to slack on the way. Please do not forget, that we trust that you will stand it through without flinching as we are prepared to do our bit, and don't forget that for us a very bitter end is in sight when you have seen matters through. We hope that you will realize that we are ready to help you to win war and peace.

Yours ever,
James

12   The end of the 'Führer State': The Germans give up

The last surviving report of the Security Service [SD] of the SS, from the end of March 1945, offers a discriminating, realistic and remarkably open analysis of the mood and state of the population. Much to the annoyance of Hitler's 'secretary' Martin Bormann, who was in the habit of berating messengers for bad news, the Ohlendorf office in the Reich Security Head Office made no attempts to gloss over the hopelessness of the situation. The document is more than a snapshot of the moment; it offers an intense description of the catastrophic conditions of everyday life which had become the norm throughout the Reich in the period directly before the occupation. What has not survived are the two final sections of the report listed in the table of contents: '5. For millions the Führer is the final rock and the last hope, but even the Führer is daily being included in the question of confidence and in criticism of the situation. 6. The doubt in the sense of continuing the struggle is eating away at readiness for action, at the trust of national comrades in themselves and in each other'; otherwise it is reproduced here unabridged.

Quoted from Heinz Boberach (ed.), *Meldungen aus dem Reich 1938–1945.*
Die geheimen Lageberichte des Sicherheitsdienstes der SS,
vol. 17 (Herrsching, 1984), pp. 6734–40.

The Volk and the Leadership

The development of the military situation since the breakthrough of the Soviets from the bridgehead at Baranow to the Oder has burdened our *Volk* increasingly from day to day. Since then each individual sees him- or herself confronted with the naked question of life and death. This situation gives rise to a series of questions, phenomena and patterns of behaviour which are testing the relationship of the *Volk* with the leadership and the *Volksgemeinschaft* to breaking point. In this respect there are hardly any differences between the armed forces and civilians, Party and non-Party, those who lead and those who are led, between the milieu of ordinary folk and the educated, between workers and bourgeois, between town and country, between the population in the East and the West, North and South, those who support National Socialism and those who reject it, between national comrades who belong to the Church and national comrades who are not confessionally committed.

The following basic facts stand out:

1. *No one wants to lose the war. Everyone's dearest wish has been that we should win.*

Since the invasion of the Soviets every national comrade knows that we stand before the greatest national disaster with the gravest consequences for every family and every individual. Without exception, the entire people is filled with an anxiety which becomes more oppressive with every passing day. With the evacuees and refugees from the East, the horror of the war has reached every town and village within the now narrower confines of the Reich. The air-raids have destroyed what had been a relatively normal routine of daily life to such an extent that no single individual has remained unaffected. The population is suffering a great deal from the terror bombing. Contact between people has been extensively broken.

Today, there are still tens of thousands of men at the Front who have no information about whether their relatives, their wives and children, are still alive and where they are. They do not know if they were slain long ago in the bombing or have been massacred by the Soviets. Hundreds of thousands of women remain without news of their husbands and sons, who are still somewhere out there. They are filled with a permanent sense of foreboding that they could no longer be amongst the living. There is a general trend that families and extended families are coming closer together; if the most extreme misfortune befalls Germany, people who belong together at least want to bear it together.

Here and there, no doubt, people desperately try to reassure themselves that perhaps, in the end, it will not be so bad. After all, a people of 80 million souls could not be wiped out to the last man, woman and child. The Soviets could not really turn against the workers and peasants, for they are needed in every state. In the West people listen attentively to everything which permeates through from the areas occupied by the English and the Americans. But behind all these so loudly expressed words of comfort lies a deep-seated fear and the wish that things should not go so far.

For the first time during this war the food question is becoming acutely noticeable. The hunger of the population is no longer assuaged by what they have. There are no longer adequate supplies of potatoes and bread. Women in the big cities are now having difficulty in getting food for their children. On top of all misfortune comes the spectre of hunger.

For days nobody has dared hope of a victory. For a long while now, everyone would have been more than happy just for us not to lose the war outright but to emerge from it to a certain extent intact.

Right up until the last few days the entire population of the homeland has still continued to provide an example of the fulfillment of daily duty and exemplary work discipline. In the towns hit by the terror bombing, tens of thousands make their way to work even though they have lost their homes, despite lack of sleep and all the obstacles which accompany everyday life in wartime, just so as not to shirk the task upon the fulfilment of which a less severe conclusion of the war might depend. The German *Volk*, and in particular the worker, who has slogged to the limits of his physical endurance in this war, have shown a loyalty, patience and readiness for sacrifice to a degree unknown to any other *Volk*.

2. *No one believes in victory any longer. The spark that has been preserved up to now is about to be extinguished.*
If defeatism is interpreted as superficially as has mostly been the case hitherto, since the Soviet offensive it has been a general phenomena

amongst the people. Nobody can imagine how we still can or want to win. Even before the enemy's penetration into the upper Rhine region, everybody was thinking that we could not maintain resistance for much longer without the Oder area, without the industrial region of Upper Silesia and without the Ruhr region. Everyone can see the chaotic mess that traffic is in. Everyone can sense that, under the blows of the enemy air force, total war is coming to naught. For hundreds of thousands who were brought into the labour process during the last few months, there are no longer any jobs in the factories and offices. Ever growing numbers of factories, where the retinue [*Gefolgschaft*] know that their work is essential for armaments, are subject to lay-offs. The mad search for every possible worker is being superseded by rapidly spreading unemployment. Hundreds of thousands of foreigners who provided us with valuable help are becoming unnecessary extra mouths to feed.

All the planning is beginning to fail. It looks as if all the ceaseless improving is no longer of any use. Even now, miracles of effort are still being performed in order to plug holes, but where one gap is closed two or three others spring open. If everything carries on as it has up to now, every national comrade will be able to work out on the fingers of one hand that it simply can't continue like this idefinitely. The fear is spreading that we are on our last legs, that basically we have already reached the end. People tolerated everything as long as only personal possessions were being lost, home, property, as long as administrative buildings and cultural monuments were being destroyed. However, with the loss of workplaces, with the damage to the most important parts of armaments production, all hope is disappearing of holding out militarily in the war, of bringing about a change for the better; and with it is disappearing the belief that there is any sense in any further effort and sacrifice.

In the last few years the German people have put up with everything. Now, for the first time, they are showing themselves to be tired and worn out. Everyone still refuses to accept that it is over. Right up until the last few days a belief in miracles has remained, resolutely nurtured since the middle of last year by skilful propaganda about the new weapons. Deep in people's hearts there is still hope that, so long as the Front holds to some degree, we can achieve a political solution to the war. No-one believes that we can still avoid catastrophe, given the weaponry and opportunities in the war which we have had until now. The last rays of hope are for salvation from abroad, for perfectly normal circumstances, for a secret weapon of terrible capability. Even these rays of hope are fading.

It is the broad masses of the ordinary population who have set themselves against the dreadful hopelessness for the longest period of time. The conviction that the war is lost was to be found earliest where the insight into the larger scheme of things was greatest. This should not be a cause to inveigh against the 'intellectuals'. The intelligensia has made no less of a contribution during this war than the munitions worker; the bourgeoisie has endured the terror of bombing in the same way as the ordinary man. Leading civil and public servants, factory leaders [*Betriebsführer*], officers, Party comrades in the highest positions and other persons of the leading strata – in the widest sense – can neither be prevented nor prohibited from reflecting on developments. The German *Volk* in particular has no talent for running around with blinkers on. All those who are no longer able to see any possibility of a good conclusion to the war unless there are drastic changes reject the accusation that they are defeatists. Pointing to their own contribution during this war and their still continuing, ceaseless efforts, they would consider it an insult to be put in the same bracket as those who undermined the German Home Front between 1914–18. They simply feel themselves unable to believe that black should be white and vice versa. They stick to what they see, what they themselves experience daily in their own sphere of life and in comparison with other areas. They will be not be dissuaded, even by force, from soberly – even if until now reluctantly and with a last hope that it might not be true in the end – drawing the bitter conclusions which follow. They can be ordered to keep quiet. But that does not stop them from believing any more or any less.

The most varied personal consequences are being draw from the general hopelessness. A majority of the people have accustomed themselves to living just for today. They take advantage of every pleasure available. Any trivial excuse leads to the last bottle being drunk, originally kept for the victory party, for the end of the black-out, for the return of the husband and son. Everywhere there is a great demand for poison, for pistols and other means of putting an end to one's life. Suicides from genuine despair at the inevitable catastrophe are the order of the day. Numerous conversations within the family with relatives, friends and acquaintances are dominated by plans for how one could survive even under enemy occupation. Emergency funds are set aside, places of refuge sought. Elderly people in particular are tormenting themselves day and night with terrible thoughts and are no longer able to sleep for worrying. Things which only a few weeks ago no one dared even to think are now the subject of open discussion on public transport and between complete strangers.

3.   If we lose the war there is a general conviction that we ourselves will
have been responsible, and not the little man, but the leadership.

Across the whole breadth of the population there exists no doubt that the
negative military developments up to and including the present situation
were not inevitable. The general opinion is that it was unnecessary for
things to have gone so far downhill for us that, without a last-minute
change, we will certainly lose the war. Amongst the broad masses numerous criticisms are being made of a more emotional, vague and certainly
largely unjust nature, directed against our conduct of the war, above all
with regard to the Luftwaffe, against our foreign policy and our policy in
the occupied territories. It is difficult, for example, to meet anyone who
is of the opinion that German policy in the occupied territories in the
East was correct. Everyone believes they can identify numerous mistakes
and failures.

It is certainly typically German that most of the population in the
homeland and at the Front want, in a self-tormenting fashion, only to
uncover mistakes and weaknesses, that they start from ideal premises
and reach their verdicts, which are one-sided and exaggerated, without a correct historical perspective. It is only with great difficulty that
national comrades can be moved to a realistic comparison with our
opponents, to the understanding that the opposition is also tired of war,
or, for example, that in Europe, the English, much praised for their
experience in dealing with different peoples, are now faced with many
unsolved political problems. The extent to which the expression of this
merciless self-criticism is justified or not is not crucial. Important alone is
the fact that the view that if we lose the war it will have been our own
fault has become so prevalent, and that it affects trust in the leadership.

In this regard it is also a general phenomenon that the broad strata of
the *Volk* deny any responsibility for the way the war developed. They
point to the fact that they have not been the ones responsible for policy
or for the conduct of the war. Rather they say that, since the beginning
of this war, they have done everything which the leadership has demanded of them.

The worker who in all these years has done nothing but slog his guts
out, the soldier who has put his life on the line a million times, the civil
servant who has been brought back into service from retirement, the
women who stand at the machines in the munitions factories – they have
all depended on the leadership. The leadership, they say, had repeatedly
declared that everything had been subject to thorough planning, that it
had anticipated all difficulties and that it was doing everything which
needed to be done. In matters of the conduct of war and major policy
it had been the people's task to place their trust in the leadership. This

had happened completely. Of course, since Stalingrad, there had been many doubts about whether the war was suffering from many half measures and whether above many measures – for example the total war effort – the words 'too late' should not have stood. The *Volk* had always allowed itself to be placated. Now the issue of responsibility and blame was being raised all the more sharply.

The profound disappointment amongst the national comrades in having had false confidence is resulting in a sense of mourning, dejection and bitterness and in an increasing anger, above all amongst those who have known nothing during this war but hard work and sacrifice. The perception that all that has occurred may have been to no purpose causes hundreds of thousands of German people almost physically tangible pain. Out of the feeling that we are powerless, that our enemies will do with us what they will, that our destruction is immanent, is developing, beyond the attitude towards the enemy, a dangerous attitude towards our own leadership, which is heralded by such expressions as: 'We did not deserve the present situation', or 'We did not deserve to be led into such a disaster' etc.

4.   *The Volk no longer has any trust in the leadership. It is expressing strong criticism of the Party, of specific figures in the leadership and of propaganda.*

During the last few days trust in the leadership has fallen away like an avalanche. Everywhere criticism of the Party, of specific figures in the leadership and of propaganda is rife. With a clean conscience for having done everything possible, the 'little man' in particular is assuming the right to speak his mind in the most open manner and with extreme frankness. People are not mincing their words. Up until now it has been said repeatedly that the Führer will make it, but first we want to win the war. But now the passionate, nervous, and in parts rancorous disappointment is breaking out, that National Socialist reality, in many respects, does not correspond with the idea, nor the development of the war with the official statements.

In contrast to the propaganda commentaries, the realization then slowly dawned that the offensive had run aground prematurely. From then on the feeling has been deepening that we can do no more and that there is nothing more to be done.

Since then there can be less and less talk of a unified formation of public opinion in terms of leadership and propaganda. Everyone develops their own views and opinions independently. A tangled web of reasons, reproaches and accusations is emerging about why the war could not have gone well. A mood is spreading in which the national comrades are

now hardly being reached and addressed by the propaganda media.
Apart from fear, even the revelation of the disgusting behaviour of the
Soviets in the German territory they occupy has caused only sullen indignation that our military leadership has exposed German people to the
Soviet terror. It was the leadership which had constantly, and right into
the last few weeks, portrayed our enemies in a fashion which underestimated them. Countless discussions in the air-raid shelters typify how
detached the individual is from the leadership, of how much he has
regarded himself only as an object and is now proceeding from a position of simply having to participate to one of criticism: 'What are "they"
thinking of?'

There can be no talk of a genuine hatred for our enemies. The population views the English and the Americans with critical contemplation.
The anger relates to *how* these swine *brutally* exploit their opportunities
and to the extent of the damage they have inflicted on the individual.
That they are seizing the opportunities is, in the final analysis, not disputed. War is war. This too is part of the general conviction that we
ourselves have been far too inconsistent and far too considerate. All the
talk in the press of heroic resistance, of the strength of the German heart,
of an uprising of the whole *Volk*, all the pomposity expended in empty
phraseology, especially that of the press, is cast aside with anger and
scorn. People are instinctively distancing themselves from slogans such
as 'Walls can break, but not our hearts', or 'They can destroy everything
we have, but not our faith in victory'. Even if they are true, the population has long ceased to want slogans written on walls and the façades
of burnt-out buildings. The population has become so circumspect that
it will no longer be possible to instigate a popular uprising. People are
hardly participating even superficially any more. The production management which previously aided the success of mass meetings at the
Sportpalast is no longer functioning, because what it was that once gave
those rallies content, life and movement, no longer exists.

Gradually, explanations are being demanded more openly. Disparag-
ing remarks like this from a farmer and Party comrade in Linz are typical:
'The big-shots who made the mistakes and who must answer for them
deserve a summary court-martial.' This applies especially in relation to
the Luftwaffe for, according to general opinion, the outcome of the entire
war depended on them. Harsh and bitter verdicts are pronounced on the
men who made the decisions concerning the Luftwaffe's strategy in both
attack and defence and who, as a result of the failures demonstrated
throughout the war and right up to the present, have brought so much
privation and misery to the German people. This does not occur without
unjustified generalizations, for example, when in relation to Fighter command [*die Jagdwaffe*] people talk about 'useless toy pilots' [*Puppenflieger*]

and 'line-shooters'. The Front feels that it has been left in the lurch by the Luftwaffe. Anybody coming from the West sadly shrugs their shoulders at the fact that, despite all the valour that has been shown a million times in this war, it is simply impossible to get the better of the carpet bombing, the fighter-bombers and the fighters. In the air-raid shelters of the towns and cities, the Reich Marshal is the object of violent invective and abuse. Of him, who with all his personal attributes once enjoyed the respect of the entire *Volk*, it is said: 'He sat in Karinhall and stuffed his brat with food, instead of keeping the Luftwaffe in the air' (armaments worker), or, 'He is to blame that everything that we possess now lies in ashes and ruins. If I get hold of the bastard, I'll kill him' (working-class woman).

On the surface, the population is still keeping very calm and although becoming daily more common, such criticism of the leadership and leading figures is only expressed here and there and by individual persons or groups of persons. But this fact should not obscure the real inner disposition of the national community in its attitude towards the leadership. The German *Volk* is patient like no other. Most people stand by the Idea and by the Führer. The German *Volk* is accustomed to discipline. Since 1933 it has felt itself watched over and supervised from all sides right up to the front door by the many branches of the Party apparatus, its organizations and associations. Traditional respect for the police is a further reason. People swallowed everything they did not like, or moaned and grumbled about this or that phenomenon or person, always good-humouredly, in private. Only the heavy air-raids caused the accumulated anger, since then often blunt and to an extent malicious, to burst out in utterances like: 'The pig-heads up there will fight to the last babe in arms.' Often it is women who do the talking, for example, in Vienna, in particularly rabble-rousing manner: 'Them up there won't stop of their own accord', or, 'If two million people are prepared to put up with it, then you can't do a thing', or, 'If only someone would have the courage to start.'

All observations lead to the conclusion that no-one intervenes, even if Party comrades in uniform, soldiers or civil servants are present. It would be difficult to say anything to the contrary. It would be understandable if one day people finally flew off the handle. Every individual who wears one of the many uniforms of our state drags the same questions, doubts and feelings around with him like every other national comrade. Even those who end up cursing, are, as a rule, people who do their duty, who have lost relatives or have fathers or sons at the Front, who no longer possess a home, who throughout the night have been fighting fires or working with the rescue squads. The – as in Dresden or Chemnitz – their dead . . .

Notes and References

Part I The Regime in Crisis, Spring 1934

1 *Deutschland-Berichte der Sopade* vol. 1: *1934*, p. 50;
2 Ibid., p. 49
3 Cf. Ludwig Eiber, *Arbeiter unter der NS-Herrschaft. Textil- und Porzellan-arbeiter im nordöstlichen Oberfranken 1933–1939* (Munich, 1979) pp. 95–8 and 219, n. 143; on the following as a whole, see *Deutschland-Berichte der Sopade, 1934*, pp. 33–48.
4 *Deutschland-Berichte der Sopade, 1934*, p. 107 (report from southern Bavaria).
5 Ibid., p. 232.
6 Ibid., p. 52.
7 Ibid., p. 230.
8 Minutes of discussion with ministers of 7 June 1934, in *Akten der Reichs-kanzlei. Regierung Hitler 1933–1938*, part I: *1933/34*, (2 vols, Boppard, 1983), here I/2, p. 1310.
9 *Akten der Regierung Hitler* I/2, pp. 1197–1200.
10 Cf. ibid., pp. 1345–51.
11 Ibid., pp. 1322–31.
12 Thus the headlines of the *Völkischer Beobachter* of 13 May 1934.
13 Ibid.
14 Ibid.
15 *Deutschland-Berichte der Sopade, 1934*, p. 101.
16 Ibid.
17 Cf. Mathilde Jamin, 'Zur Rolle der SA im nationalsozialistischen Herrschafts-system', in Gerhard Hirschfeld and Lothar Kettenacker (eds), *The Führer State: Myth and Reality. Studies on the Structure and Politics of the Third Reich* (London, 1981), p. 332 (article in German with English summary).
18 IfZ, Fa 88, Bormann's written communication to Hess of 5 Oct. 1932.

19 *Akten der Regierung Hitler* I/2, p. 1200.

20 IfZ, ED 1, Lieutenant-General Curt Liebmann's record of the discussions amongst commanders in Stuttgart and Kassel on 15 and 18 Jan. 1934.

21 Ibid.

22 Despite previous amnesties and quashing of cases, in May 1934 there were still 4,037 cases to be heard against members of the SA and SS; IfZ, MA 108.

23 IfZ, Fa 107/1, Röhm's circular of 31 July 1933.

24 *Akten der Regierung Hitler* I/1, p. 631.

25 *Völkischer Beobachter*, 10 Apr. 1933.

26 Ibid., 8 May 1933.

27 Ibid.

28 Ibid., 25 Sept. 1933.

29 Ibid., 27 Dec. 1933.

30 *Deutschland-Berichte der Sopade, 1934*, p. 188.

31 On the following see Karl-Martin Grass, 'Edgar Jung, Papenkreis und Röhm-krise 1933/34' (dissertation, University of Heidelberg, 1966), pp. 50ff.

32 Thus the title of an essay by Hermann Graml (ed.), in *Widerstand im Dritten Reich. Probleme, Ereignisse, Gestalten* (Frankfurt, 1984), pp. 172–83.

33 In his book *Sinndeutung der deutschen Revolution*, quoted by Grass, 'Edgar Jung,' pp. 79ff.

34 On this subject see Fritz Günther von Tschirsky, *Erinnerungen eines Hochverräters* (Stuttgart, 1972), pp. 164ff.; copy of the 'Marburg Speech' in Edmund Forschbach, *Edgar J. Jung. Ein konservativer Revolutionär. 30. Juni 1934* (Pfullingen, 1984), pp. 154–74.

35 Ibid., pp. 154–74.

36 See Ansgar Diller, Der Frankfurter Rundfunk 1923–1945 unter besonderer Berücksichtigung der Zeit des Nationalsozialismus (dissertation, University of Frankfurt, 1975), p. 252.

37 Forschbach, *Edgar J. Jung*, pp. 154–74.

38 Broadcast speech by Hess on 25 June 1934 in Cologne, in *Der Aufbau des deutschen Führerstaates. Das Jahr 1934*, 2nd edn (Berlin, 1937), pp. 12–22.

39 IfZ, ED 172/62.

40 Cf. Klaus-Jürgen Müller, *Das Heer und Hitler. Armee und national-sozialistisches Regime 1933–1940* (Stuttgart, 1969).

41 IfZ, ED 172/62.

42 Cf. Theodor Eschenburg, 'Zur Ermordung des General Schleicher', *VfZ*, 1 (1953), pp. 71–95.

43 Quoted from Heinz Höhne, *Mordsache Röhm. Hitlers Durchbruch zur Alleinherrschaft 1933–1934* (Reinbek, 1984), p. 273.

44 Hans Bernd Gisevius, *Adolf Hitler, Versuch einer Deutung* (Munich, 1963), p. 291.

45 RGBl, I (1934), p. 529.

46 *Akten der Regierung Hitler* I/2, pp. 1354–8; in detail on Gürtner's position, see Lothar Gruchmann, *Justiz im Dritten Reich 1933–1940. Verwaltung, Ausschaltung und Anpassung in der Ära Gürtner* (Munich, 1987), pp. 451ff.

47 *Rede des Reichkanzlers Adolf Hitler vor dem Reichstag am 13. Juli 1934*, (Berlin, n.d.), p. 26.

48 Quoted from Ian Kershaw, *Der Hitler-Mythos. Volksmeinung und Propaganda im Dritten Reich* (Stuttgart, 1980), p. 76f. Cf. also Kershaw, *'The Hitler Myth': Image and reality in the Third Reich* (Oxford, 1989), pp. 90–1.

49 See 'Erlebnisbericht Werner Pünders über die Ermordung Klauseners am 30. Juni 1934 und ihre Folgen', *VfZ* (1971), pp. 404–31.

50 IfZ, MA 198/2, wireless telegram from the President of the Government in Münster to the Reich Ministry of the Interior, 15 Aug. 1934.

51 IfZ, ED 1, Liebmann's record of a meeting of commanding officers on 5 July 1934.

52 Ibid.

53 IfZ, Party Chancellery 101 212 55.

54 IfZ, MA 311, Himmler's address in Breslau on 19 Jan. 1935.

55 *Neue Zürcher Zeitung*, 13 July 1934.

56 Carl Schmitt, 'Der Führer schützt das Recht. Zur Reichstagsrede Adolf Hitlers vom 13. Juli 1934', *Deutsche Juristen-Zeitung*, 39 (1934), pp. 945–50.

57 *Akten der Regierung Hitler* I/2, p. 1387.

58 *Deutschland-Berichte der Sopade, 1934*, p. 356f.

Part II

1 Regimentation and Coordination (1933–1934)

1 Elke Fröhlich (ed.), *Die Tagebücher von Joseph Goebbels, Sämtliche Fragmente, Teil I: Aufzeichnungen 1924 bis 1941* (Munich, 1987), vol. 2, p. 357.

2 *Akten der Reichskanzlei. Regierung Hitler 1933–1938, Teil I: 1933/34* (2 vols, Boppard, 1983), vol. 1, p. 6.

3 Cf. Rudolf Morsey, 'Die Deutsche Zentrumspartei', in Erich Matthias and Rudolf Morsey (eds), *Das Ende der Parteien 1933* (Düsseldorf, 1960), pp. 339ff.

4 *Akten der Regierung Hitler* I/1, p. 10.

5 Ibid., p. 9.

6 *Martin Broszat, The Hitler State. The Foundation and Development of the Internal Structure of the Third Reich*, trans. J.W. Hiden (Harlow, 1981), p. 58.

7 Cf. Hildegard Brenner, *Ende einer bürgerlichen Kunst-Institution. Die politische Formierung der Preußischen Akademie der Künste ab 1933* (Stuttgart, 1972).

8 Cf. Norbert Frei and Johannes Schmitz, *Journalismus im Dritten Reich* (Munich, 1989).

9 *Akten der Regierung Hitler* I/1, p. 9.

10 *Ministerial-Blatt für die preußische innere Verwaltung. Teil I, Ausgabe A, 94* (1933), p. 169.

11 Cf. Hans-Ulrich Thamer, *Verführung und Gewalt. Deutschland 1933–1945* (Berlin, 1986), p. 256.

12 *Akten der Regierung Hitler* I/1, p. 128; on the subject of the old controversy about the authorship of the Reichstag Fire, cf. Uwe Backes et al., *Reichstagsbrand. Aufklärung einer historischen Legende* (Munich 1986).

13 Ernst Fraenkel, *The Dual State. A Contribution to the Theory of Dictatorship*, trans. E.A. Shils (New York, 1969), p. 3.

14 For examples cf. Hartmut Mehringer, 'Die KPD in Bayern 1919–1945', in Martin Broszat et al. (eds), *Bayern in der NS-Zeit* (6 vols, Munich, 1977–83), cf. here vol. 5.

15 Quoted from Ian Kershaw, *'The Hitler Myth', Image and Reality in the Third Reich* (Oxford, 1989) (abbreviations removed and interpunction completed by the author), p. 52.

16 Details in Jürgen W. Falter, Thomas Lindenberger and Siegfried Schumann, *Wahlen und Abstimmungen in der Weimarer Republik* (Munich, 1986); also contains bibliography of more recent psephological research.

17 Broszat, *The Hitler State*, p. 75.

18 Hans Mommsen, 'Zur Verschränkung traditioneller und faschistischer Führungsgruppen in Deutschland beim Übergang von der Bewegungs- zur Systemphase', in Wolfgang Schieder (ed.), *Faschismus als soziale Bewegung. Deutschland und Italien im Vergleich* (Hamburg, 1976), pp. 157–81.

19 *Akten der Regierung Hitler* I/1, pp. 159f.

20 The following from Broszat, *The Hitler State*, pp. 96–104.

21 Details in Falk Wiesemann, *Die Vorgeschichte der nationalsozialistischen Machtergreifung in Bayern 1932/33* (Munich, 1975); Ortwin Domröse, *Der NS-Staat in Bayern von der Machtergreifung bis zum Röhm-Putsch* (Munich, 1974); Jochen Klenner, *Verhältnis von Partei und Staat 1933–1945. Dargestellt am Beispiel Bayerns* (Munich, 1974).

22 Broszat, *The Hitler State*, p. 77.

23 Cf. Günther Kimmel, 'Das Konzentrationslager Dachau. Eine Studie zu den nationalsozialistischen Gewaltverbrechen', in Broszat et al. (eds), *Bayern in der NS-Zeit*, vol. 2, pp. 349–413.

24 *Akten der Regierung Hitler* I/1, p. 208, n. 9.

25 Friedrich Meinecke, *Die deutsche Katastrophe. Betrachtungen und Erinnerungen* (Wiesbaden, 1946), p. 25.

26 For comprehensive details cf. Karl Dietrich Bracher, *Stufen der Machtergreifung* (Frankfurt, 1979), pp. 218–36; the widespread assumption that the agreement of the Centre had been necessary overlooks the preceding alteration to the standing orders; independently of this, Thamer's assertion in *Verführung und Gewalt*, p. 274, that the SPD could have thwarted the Enabling Law by absenting themselves is incorrect.

27 *Akten der Regierung Hitler* I/1, pp. 239 and 252 respectively.

28 Quoted from *Verhandlungen des Reichstags, Stenographische Berichte der 2. Sitzung vom 23.3.1933*, pp. 33f. and 37 respectively.

29 *Akten der Regierung Hitler* I/1, p. 239.

30 Cf. table 1, p. 46.
31 *Akten der Regierung Hitler* I/1, p. 251.
32 Quoted from *Schulthess' Europäischer Geschichtskalender. Neue Folge* 49 (1933), pp. 77f.
33 *Akten der Regierung Hitler* I/1, p. 271, n. 3.
34 Further cf. Hans Mommsen, *Beamtentum im Dritten Reich. Mit ausgewählten Quellen zur nationalsozialistischen Beamtenpolitik* (Stuttgart, 1966).
35 Uwe Dietrich Adam, *Judenpolitik im Dritten Reich* (Düsseldorf, 1972).
36 *Akten der Regierung Hitler* I/1, pp. 17ff.; emphasis in the original.
37 Ibid., p. 55.
38 Cf. Bracher, *Stufen der Machtergreifung*, pp. 112–15; Dirk Stegmann, 'Zum Verhältnis von Großindustrie und Nationalsozialismus 1930–1933. Ein Beitrag zur Geschichte der sog. Machtergreifung', *Archiv für Sozialgeschichte*, 13 (1973), pp. 399–482, here 440 and 477–80.
39 *Akten der Regierung Hitler* I/1, pp. 17ff.
40 Ibid., p. 280.
41 Ibid., p. 188; cf. Heinrich August Winkler, *Der Weg in die Katastrophe. Arbeiter und Arbeiterbewegung in der Weimarer Republik 1930 bis 1933* (Berlin / Bonn, 1987), *passim* and esp. pp. 867–949.
42 Quoted from Gotthard Jasper, *Die gescheiterte Zähmung. Wege zur Machtergreifung Hitlers 1930–1934* (Frankfurt, 1986), p. 166; cf. Bernd Martin, 'Die deutschen Gewerkschaften und die nationalsozialistische Machtübernahme', *Geschichte in Wissenschaft und Unterricht*, 36 (1985), pp. 605–31; Manfred Scharrer (ed.), *Kampflose Kapitulation. Arbeiterbewegung 1933* (Reinbek, 1984); Klaus Schönhoven, *Die deutschen Gewerkschaften* (Frankfurt, 1987), esp. pp. 179–83.
43 Quoted from *Schulthess'* (1933), pp. 110–17.
44 Ibid.
45 André François-Poncet, *Als Botschafter in Berlin 1931–1938* (Mainz, 1948), p. 116.
46 Cf. Martin Broszat, 'Die Ausbootung der NSBO-Führung im Sommer 1934', in Manfred Funke et al. (eds), *Demokratie und Diktatur* (Bonn, 1987), pp. 198–251; Volker Kratzenberg, *Arbeiter auf dem Weg zu Hitler? Die Nationalsozialistische Betriebszellen-Organisation. Ihre Entstehung, ihre Programmatik, ihr Scheitern 1924–1934* (Frankfurt, 1987).
47 Details in Broszat, *The Hitler State*, pp. 142f.
48 David Schoenbaum, *Hitler's Social Revolution. Class and Status in Nazi Germany 1933–1939* (New York, 1980), p. 85.
49 Quoted from Broszat, *The Hitler State*, p. 146; his emphasis deleted by me.
50 Cf. Reinhard Nebe, 'Die Industrie und der 30. Januar 1933', in Karl Dietrich Bracher, Manfred Funke and Hans-Adolf Jacobsen (eds), *Nationalsozialistische Diktatur 1933–1945. Eine Bilanz* (Düsseldorf, 1983), pp. 155–76.
51 Cf. Heinrich August Winkler, *Der entbehrliche Stand. Zur Mittelstandspolitik im 'Dritten Reich', Handwerker, Einzelhändler, Bauern* (Frankfurt/New York, 1979); cf. also the direct controversy between Winkler and von Saldern in *Geschichte und Gesellschaft*, 12 (1986), pp. 235–43 and 548–57 respectively.

52 Cf. Horst Gies, 'Die NS-Machtergreifung auf dem agrarischen Sektor', *Zeitschrift für Agrargeschichte und Agrarsoziologie*, 16 (1968), pp. 210–32, here 212.

53 Fundamental to the following is Matthias and Morsey (eds), *Das Ende der Parteien*.

54 *Neuer Vorwärts*, 25 June 1933.

55 Quoted from the minutes, probably written by Reich Governor Epp, in *Akten der Regierung Hitler* I/1, pp. 629–36.

56 Ibid.

57 Ibid.

57 Ibid., p. 658.

59 *Völkischer Beobachter*, 8 July 1933.

60 Ulrich Walberer (ed.), 10, *Mai 1933. Bücherverbrennung in Deutschland und die Folgen* (Frankfurt, 1983).

61 Cf. Norbert Frei, *Nationalsozialistische Eroberung der Provinzpresse. Gleichschaltung, Selbstanpassung und Resistenz in Bayern* (Stuttgart, 1980).

62 Cf. Volker Dahm, 'Anfänge und Ideologie der Reichskulturkammer. Die "Berufsgemeinschaft" als Instrument kulturpolitischer Steuerung und sozialer Reglementierung', in *VfZ*, 34 (1986), pp. 53–84.

63 On the following cf. *passim* Klaus Scholder, *The Churches and the Third Reich, vol. 1: Preliminary History and the Time of Illusions 1918–1934* (London, 1987); vol. 2 in German only: *Die Kirchen und das Dritte Reich, Band 2: Das Jahr der Ernüchterung 1934. Barmen und Rome* (Berlin, 1985).

64 Detailed analysis in Bracher, *Stufen der Machtergreifung*, pp. 485–98.

65 *Akten der Regierung Hitler* I/2, p. 938.

66 Ibid., pp. 939f.

2 Consolidation (1935–1938)

1 Cf. Table 2, p. 72.

2 Cf. Rolf Wagenführ, *Die deutsche Industrie im Kriege 1939–1945* (Berlin, 1955), p. 17.

3 For further information cf. Alfred Kube, *Pour le mérite und Hakenkreuz. Hermann Göring im Dritten Reich* (Munich, 1986), pp. 138–50.

4 The following is based primarily on Dieter Petzina, *Autarkiepolitik im Dritten Reich* (Stuttgart, 1986); cf. also Kube, *Pour le mérite*, pp. 185–201.

5 For further information cf. Horst Gies, 'Die Rolle des Reichsnährstands im nationalsozialistischen Herrschaftssystem', in Gerhard Hirschfeld and Lothar Kettenacker (eds), *The Führer State: Myth and Reality. Studies on the Structure and Politics of the Third Reich* (London, 1981), pp. 270–304 (article in German with English summary).

6 Cf. David Schoenbaum, *Hitler's Social Revolution: Class and Status in Nazi Germany 1933–1939* (New York, 1980), pp. 152–77; Horst Gies 'Aufgaben und Probleme der nationalsozialistischen Ernährungswirtschaft 1933–1939', *Vierteljahrsschrift für Sozial- und Wirtschaftsgeschichte*, 66 (1979), pp. 466–99.

7   Cf. Ludolf Herbst, *Der Totale Krieg und die Ordnung der Wirtschaft. Die Kriegswirtschaft im Spannungsfeld von Politik, Ideologie und Propaganda 1939 bis 1945* (Stuttgart, 1982), p. 29.
8   Cf. Table 3, p. 79.
9   On the following cf. Tilla Siegel, *Leistung und Lohn in der nationalsozialistischen 'Ordnung der Arbeit'* (Opladen, 1982).
10 Cf. Franz Neumann, *Behemoth: The Structure and Practice of National Socialism 1933–1944* (London, 1967), pp. 430–1.
11 Cf. Lutz Niethammer (ed.), *'Die Jahre weiss man nicht, wo man die heute hinsetzen soll.' Faschismuserfahrungem im Ruhrgebiet* (Berlin/Bonn, 1983); Detlev Peukert, *Inside Nazi Germany. Conformity, Opposition and Racism in Everyday Life* (London, 1987), p. 117.
12 Cf. Timothy W. Mason, *Sozialpolitik im Dritten Reich. Arbeiterklasse und Volksgemeinschaft* (Opladen, 1977), and by the same author, 'Die Bändigung der Arbeiterklasse im nationalsozialistischen Deutschland. Eine Einleitung', in Carola Sachse et al., *Angst, Belohnung, Zucht und Ordnung. Herrschaftsmechanismen im Nationalsozialismus* (Opladen, 1982), pp. 11–53.
13 Cf. Schoenbaum, *Hitler's Social Revolution*, pp. 73–112.
14 For further details and on the following, cf. Gunther Mai, ' "Warum steht der deutsche Arbeiter zu Hitler?" Zur Rolle der Deutschen Arbeitsfront im Herrschaftssystem des Dritten Reiches', *Geschichte und Gesellschaft*, 12 (1986), pp. 212–34.
15 On the following, cf. Hasso Spode, 'Arbeiterurlaub im Dritten Reich', in Sachse et al., *Angst, Belohnung*, pp. 275–328.
16 *Deutschland-Berichte der Sopade, 1937*, p. 1259.
17 For further details, cf. Herwart Vorländer, 'NS-Volkswohlfahrt und Winterhilfswerk des deutschen Volkes', *VfZ*, 34 (1986), pp. 341–80.
18 On the following, cf. Karlheinz Schmeer, *Die Regie des öffentlichen Lebens im Dritten Reich* (Munich, 1956); Hans Joachim Gamm, *Der braune Kult. Das Dritte Reich und seine Ersatzreligion* (Hamburg, 1962); Klaus Vondung, *Magie und Manipulation. Ideologischer Kult und politische Religion des Nationalsozialismus* (Munich, 1979).
19 Rosenberg's position in the Third Reich is the subject of the exemplary study by Reinhard Bollmus, *Das Amt Rosenberg und seine Gegner. Zum Machtkampf im nationalsozialistischen Herrschafssystem* (Stuttgart, 1970).
20 On the following cf. Arno Klönne, 'Jugendprotest und Jugendopposition. Von der HJ-Erziehung zum Cliquenwesen der Kriegszeit', in Martin Broszat et al. (eds), *Bayern in der NS-Zeit* (6 vols, Munich, 1977–83), vol. 4, pp. 527–620; by the same author, *Jugend im Dritten Reich. Die Hitler-Jugend und ihre Gegner*, (Düsseldorf, 1982).
21 A comprehesive survey can be found in Heinrich Muth, 'Jugendopposition im Dritten Reich', in *VfZ*, 30 (1982), pp. 369–417; cf. also Peukert, *Inside Nazi Germany*, pp. 145–74.
22 Cf. Kurt-Ingo Flessau, *Schule der Diktatur. Lehrpläne und Schulbücher des Nationalsozialismus* (Frankfurt, 1979); on the following, cf. Rolf Eilers, *Die nationalsozialistische Schulpolitik. Eine Studie zur Funktion der Erziehung*

im totalitären Staat (Cologne/Opladen, 1963); Manfred Heinemann (ed.), *Erziehung und Schulung im Dritten Reich* (2 vols, Stuttgart, 1980); also useful is Marcel Reich-Ranicki (ed.), *Meine Schulzeit im Dritten Reich. Erinnerungen deutscher Schriftsteller* (Munich, 1984).

23 Cf. Franz Sonnenberger, 'Der neue "Kulturkampf". Die Gemeinschaftsschule und ihre historischen Voraussetzungen', in Broszat et al. (eds), *Bayern in der NS-Zeit*, vol. 3, pp. 235–327.

24 Statistics from Karl Dietrich Bracher, *The German Dictatorship. The Origins, Structure and Consequences of National Socialism* (Harmondsworth, 1973), pp. 435f.

25 Ibid.

26 Ley to workers at the Leuna works on 2 July 1937; quoted from Robert Ley, *Soldaten der Arbeit* (Munich, 1938), p. 71.

27 A rich source of material for this whole section is Richard Grunberger's *A Social History of the Third Reich* (Harmondsworth, 1974), here pp. 273, 476; cf. also Gerd Albrecht, *Nationalsozialistische Filmpolitik. Eine soziologische Untersuchung über die Spielfilme des Dritten Reiches* (Stuttgart, 1969).

28 Concerning '*Jud Süss*', the SD reported 'that often, only that part of the population which is politically active have been to see the film, while the typical cinema audience is, to a certain extent, avoiding it and locally there is oral propaganda against the film and its starkly realistic portrayal of Jewry.' In Heinz Boberach (ed.), *Meldungen aus dem Reich 1938–1945. Die geheimen Lageberichte des Sicherheitsdienstes der SS* (17 vols, Herrsching, 1984), vol. 6, p. 1918; on the reception of the euthanasia film, ibid., vol. 9, pp. 3175–8.

29 Cf. Hans Dieter Schäfer, *Das gespaltene Bewusstsein. Über deutsche Kultur und Lebenswirklichkeit 1933–1945* (Munich/Vienna, 1981), pp. 131f.

30 Cf. the case study by Friederike Euler, 'Theater zwischen Anpassung und Widerstand. Die Münchner Kammerspiele im Dritten Reich', in Broszat et al. (eds), *Bayern in der NS-Zeit*, vol. 2, pp. 91–173; Konrad Dussel, 'Theatergeschichte der NS-Zeit unter sozialgeschichtlichem Aspekt. Ergebnisse und Perspektiven der Forschung', *Neue Politische Literatur*, 32 (1987).

31 Cf. Berhard Zeller (ed.), *Klassiker in finsteren Zeiten 1933–1945. Eine Ausstellung des Deutschen Literaturarchivs im Schiller-Nationalmuseum Marbach am Neckar* (2 vols, Stuttgart, 1983).

32 Cf. Barbara Miller Lane, *Architektur und Politik in Deutschland 1918 bis 1945* (Braunschweig/Wiesbaden, 1986); Werner Durth, *Deutsche Architekten. Biographische Verflechtungen 1900–1970* (Braunschweig Wiesbaden, 1986).

33 On the following, cf. Helmut Seier, 'Universität und Hochschulpolitik im nationalsozialistischen Staat', in Klaus Malettke (ed.), *Der Nationalsozialismus an der Macht. Aspekte nationalsozialistischer Politik und Herrschaft* (Göttingen, 1984), pp. 143–65; by the same author, 'Der Rektor als Führer. Zur Hochschulpolitik des Reichserziehungsministeriums 1934–1945', *VfZ*, 12 (1964), pp. 105–46.

34 For further details cf. Alan D. Beyerchen, *Scientists under Hitler: Politics and the Physics Community in the Third Reich* (London, 1977).

35   Cf. Ulfried Geuter, *Die Professionalisierung der deutschen Psychologie im Nationalsozialismus* (Frankfurt, 1984); Geoffrey Cocks, *Psychotherapy in the Third Reich: The Goering Institute* (New York, 1985); *Geschichte und Gesellschaft*, 12 (1986), Heft 3 (Wissenschaften im Nationalsozialismus, ed. Wolf Lepenies).

36   *Deutschland-Berichte der Sopade*, vol. 3: 1936, p. 9.

37   Fundamental to the following, cf. Hans Buchheim, 'Die SS – das Herrschaftsinstrument', in *Anatomie des SS-Staates*, (3rd edn, 2 vols, Munich, 1982), vol.1; also Heinz Höhne, *The Order of the Death's Head; The Story of Hitler's SS* (London, 1980); Shlomo Aronson, *Reinhard Heydrich und die Frühgeschichte von Gestapo und SD* (Stuttgart, 1971).

38   Quoted in Buchheim, *Anatomie des SS-Staates*, vol. 1, p. 100.

39   Quoted from Martin Broszat, 'The Concentration Camps 1933–45', in Martin Broszat and Hans Buchheim (eds), *Anatomy of the SS State* (London, 1970), p. 171. [This English edn only contains two of the essays which appear in the German edn cited in n. 37 above.]

40   Composition at the beginning of 1938; quoted from Buchheim, *Anatomie des SS-Staates*, vol. 1, p. 57.

41   'Vorbeugende Verbrechensbekämpfung', *Erlasssammlung* (Berlin, 1941).

42   In *Meldungen aus dem Reich*, vol. 1, p. 17.

43   Until the beginning of the war, the 'People's Court', with a reasonably constant number of accused, imposed approximately 100 death sentences a year. Later the numbers rose into the thousands; cf. Walter Wagner, *Der Volksgerichtshof im nationalsozialistischen Staat*, (Stuttgart, 1974), p. 876 and pp. 944f. respectively.

44   Cf. the case study by Peter Hüttenberger, 'Heimtückefälle vor dem Sondergericht München 1933–1939', in Broszat et al. (eds), *Bayern in der NS-Zeit*, vol. 4, pp. 435–526.

3 Radicalization (1938–1945)

1   Monthly report of the *Regierungspräsident* in Ansbach, Middle Franconia, of 6 May 1939, quoted from Marlies Steinert, *Hitlers Krieg und die Deutschen. Stimmung und Haltung der deutschen Bevölkerung im Zweiten Weltkrieg*, (Düsseldorf/Vienna, 1970), p. 81.

2   This interpretation is above all that of Alan S. Milward, *The German Economy at War* (Stuttgart, 1966); cf. most recently Ludolf Herbst, *Der Totale Krieg und die Ordnung der Wirtschaft. Die Kriegswirtschaft im Spannungsfeld von Politik, Ideologie und Propaganda 1939–1945* (Stuttgart 1982), pp. 103–26.

3   This and the following information from Richard J. Overy, '"Blitzkriegswirtschaft"? Finanzpolitik, Lebensstandard und Arbeitseinsatz in Deutschland 1939–1941', *VfZ*, 36 (1988), pp. 379–435. Cf. also, by the same author, 'Mobilization for total war in Germany 1939–1941', *English Historical Review*, 408 (1988), pp. 613–39.

4 Quoted from Martin Broszat, 'The Concentration Camps 1933–45', in Martin Broszat and Hans Buchheim (eds), *Anatomy of the SS State* (London, 1970), p. 209.

5 Heinz Boberach (ed.), *Meldungen aus dem Reich 1938–1945. Die geheimen Lageberichte des Sicherheitsdienstes der SS* (17 vols, Herrsching, 1984), vol. 4, p. 1128.

6 Ibid., vol. 2, pp. 441f.

7 Goebbels' secret declaration before representatives of the German press on 5 April 1940, quoted from Hildegard von Kotze and Helmut Krausnick (eds), *'Es spricht der Führer'. 7 exemplarische Hitler-Reden* (Gütersloh, 1966), p. 94, n. 20.

8 Translator's note: The term '*Werk*' is usually employed in German to denote both a charitable organization and its activities. Cf. Marie-Luise Recker, *Nationalsozialistische Sozialpolitik im Zweiten Weltkrieg* (Munich, 1985), pp. 82–154.

9 Ibid.

10 Ibid.

11 On the following, cf. Klaus Dörner, 'Nationalsozialismus und Lebensvernichtung', *VfZ*, 15 (1967), pp. 121–52; Ernst Klee, *'Euthanasie' im NS-Staat. Die 'Vernichtung lebensunwerten Lebens'* (Frankfurt, 1983); Ernst Klee (ed.), *Dokumente zur Euthanasie* (Frankfurt, 1986); Eugen Kogon et al. (eds), *Nationalsozialistische Massentötungen durch Giftgas. Eine Dokumentation* (Frankfurt, 1983), pp. 27–80; Götz Aly (ed.), *Aktion T 4 1934–1945. Die 'Euthanasie'-Zentrale in der Tiergartenstr. 4* (Berlin, 1987); Hans-Walter Schmuhl, *Rassenhygiene, Nationalsozialismus, Euthanasie. Von der Verhütung zur Vernichtung 'lebensunwerten Lebens' 1890–1945* (Göttingen, 1987).

12 Quoted from Steinert, *Hitlers Krieg*, p. 158.

13 Robert Jay Lifton, *The Nazi Doctors. Medical Killing and the Psychology of Genocide* (New York, 1986).

14 Cf. Hans Ludwig Siemen, *Menschen blieben auf der Strecke . . . Psychiatrie zwischen Reform und Nationalsozialismus* (Gütersloh, 1987).

15 Cf. Gisela Bock, *Zwangssterilisation im Nationalsozialismus. Studien zur Rassenpolitik und Frauenpolitik* (Opladen, 1986).

16 Quoted from Benno Müller-Hill, *Murderous Science. Elimination by Scientific Selection of Jews, Gypsies and Others, Germany 1933–1945* (Reinbek, 1984), p. 61.

17 Thus the 'Leader of the DAF Office for Popular Health', Dr Bockhacker, quoted from Sepp Graessner, 'Neue soziale Kontrolltechniken durch Arbeits- und Leistungsmedizin', in Gerhard Baader and Ulrich Schultz (eds), *Medizin und Nationalsozialismus. Tabuisierte Vergangenheit – ungebrochene Tradition?* (Berlin, 1980), p. 149; cf. also Angelika Ebbinghaus, Heidrun Kaupen-Haas and Karl Heinz Roth (eds), *Heilen und Vernichten im Mustergau Hamburg. Bevölkerungs- und Gesundheitspolitik im Dritten Reich* (Hamburg, 1984).

18 On this cf. also document 7; cf. Götz Aly, 'Der saubere und der schmutzige Fortschritt', in *Reform und Gewissen. 'Euthanasie' im Dienst des Fortschritts*

(Berlin, 1985), pp. 7–78, here p. 15; and Müller-Hill, *Murderous Science*, pp. 39f.

19 On the following, cf. Martin Broszat, *Nationalsozialistische Polenpolitik 1939 bis 1945* (Stuttgart, 1961); Czeslaw Madajczyk, *Die Okkupationspolitik Nazideutschlands in Polen 1939–1945* (East Berlin, 1987); cf. now also Götz Aly and Susanne Heim, *Vordenker der Vernichtung. Auschwitz und die deutschen Pläne für eine neue europäische Ordnung* (Hamburg, 1991).

20 Quoted from Helmut Heiber, 'Der Generalplan Ost', *VfZ*, 6 (1958), pp. 281–325, here p. 325.

21 On the following cf. Broszat, 'The Concentration Camps 1933–45', esp. pp. 227ff.

22 Cf. Michael Zimmermann, *Verfolgt, vertrieben, vernichtet. Die national-sozialistische Vernichtungspolitik gegen Sinti und Roma* (Essen, 1989).

23 A good overview of this subject is offered by the conference report by Eberhard Jäckel and Jürgen Rohwer (eds), *Der Mord an den Juden im Zweiten Weltkrieg. Entschlussbildung und Verwirklichung* (Stuttgart, 1985); since then especially Christopher R. Browning, *Fateful Months. Essays on the Emergence of the Final Solution* (New York, 1985); Hermann Graml, *Anti-Semitism in the Third Reich* (Blackwell, Oxford, 1992); Arno Mayer, *Why did the Heavens not Darken? The 'Final Solution' in History* (New York, 1988); Philippe Burrin, *Hitler et les Juifs* (Paris, 1989; English translation in preparation).

24 Cf. especially Uwe Dietrich Adam, *Judenpolitik im Dritten Reich* (Düsseldorf, 1972).

25 For a general summary on the following, cf. Wolfgang Benz (ed.), *Die Juden in Deutschland 1933–1945. Leben unter nationalsozialistischer Herrschaft* (Munich, 1988; English translation in preparation).

26 Cf. Helmut Krausnick and Hans-Heinrich Wilhelm, *Die Truppe des Weltanschauungskrieges. Die Einsatzgruppen der Sicherheitspolizei und des SD 1938–1942* (Stuttgart, 1981); on this subject cf. also the classic, repeatedly extended general history by Raul Hilberg, *The Destruction of the European Jews*, 1st edn (Chicago, 1961).

27 Cf. especially David S. Wyman, *The Abandonment of the Jews. America and the Holocaust, 1941–1945* (New York, 1984); Deborah E. Lipstadt, *Beyond Belief. The American Press and the Coming of the Holocaust 1933–1945* (New York/London, 1986). On the question of the total number of those murdered and the problem of ascertaining statistics, above all with regard to the eastern European victims, cf. now Wolfgang Benz (ed.), *Dimension des Völkermords. Die Zahl der jüdischen Opfer des Nationalsozialismus* (Munich, 1991).

28 Leader article by Goebbels, *Das Reich*, 30 June 1944.

29 Cf. Ulrich Herbert, *Fremdarbeiter. Politik und Praxis des 'Ausländer-Einsatzes' in der Kriegswirtschaft des Dritten Reiches* (Berlin/Bonn, 1985); for the following statistical data, cf. p. 271.

30 Of the 5.7 million Soviet prisoners of war, 3.3. million died in German captivity; cf. Christian Streit, *Keine Kameraden. Die Wehrmacht und die sowjetischen Kriegsgefangenen 1941–1945* (Stuttgart, 1978).

31   Cf. Herbst, *Der Totale Krieg*, pp. 341–452.

32   Hans Mommsen, 'Der Widerstand gegen Hitler und die deutsche Gesellschaft',
     in Jürgen Schmädecke and Peter Steinbach (eds), *Der Widerstand gegen den
     Nationalsozialismus. Die deutsche Gesellschaft und der Widerstand gegen
     Hitler* (Munich/Zürich, 1985), pp. 3–23; the conference report offers a cross-
     section of opinion on the following.

33   Quoted from Eberhard Zeller, *Geist der Freiheit. Der zwanzigste Juli*, 2nd
     edn (Munich, 1954), p. 282; cf. also Peter Hoffmann, *Widerstand – Staatsstreich
     – Attentat. Der Kampf der Opposition gegen Hitler*, 3rd edn (Munich, 1979).

34   Cf. Ian Kershaw, *The Hitler Myth. Image and Reality in the Third Reich*
     (Oxford, 1987), pp. 215ff.

35   Quoted from Percy Ernst Schramm (ed.). *Kriegstagebuch des Oberkom-
     mandos der Wehrmacht 1940–1945* (Frankfurt, 1961–9), vol. 4, pp. 1582f.

4   The 'Führer State': Impact and consequences

1   Cf. Joachim C. Fest, *Hitler. A Biography* (London, 1979), p. 9; and, in contrast,
    Sebastian Haffner, *The Meaning of Hitler* (London, 1979), pp. 40–3.

2   The opinion of Hans Mommsen, 'Nationalsozialismus', in *Sowjetsystem und
    demokratische Gesellschaft* (Freiburg, 1971), vol. 4, cols 695–713, here 702.

Sources, review of research and bibliography

Historical and political consideration of National Socialism is as old as Nazism itself, and books were being written about the Third Reich even before it existed. But a detailed examination is not an option here, for what has previously stood – necessarily – in small print above the conclusion of so many works on the subject is equally true for this volume: given the extent of the literature available, even a semi-representative overview would be far more extensive than is possible here. For the present I have therefore followed the tried and tested formula of mentioning the most important works, the parallel use of which should leave (almost) no desire for information unanswered. In the following, extremely brief, sketch of the progress of research it has not, however, been possible to refer to all titles which deserve mention.

For almost forty years, the *Bibliograpie zur Zeitgeschichte* (Bibliography of Contemporary History)[1] compiled by the Institut für Zeitgeschichte in Munich has documented new publications both in Germany and abroad, especially on German history since 1918. Particularly for those who are seeking older treatises it is indispensable. Apart from this, above all for the military history of the Second World War, the *Jahresbibliographie* (Annual Bibliography) of the Stuttgart Library of Contemporary History must be mentioned.[2] Single-volume bibliographies are, as always, very quickly overtaken by the broad flow of research; they are none the less useful as a first point of reference.[3]

The path through the original sources remains more complicated than that through the secondary literature. More recently, however, some source material has been published. Due to their overall significance for the Nazi period the following must be mentioned: the *Documents on German Foreign Policy*,[4] the *Kriegstagebuch* (war diary) of the OKW,[5] the documentation *Ursachen und Folgen* (Causes and Consequences)[6] and – with the obvious proviso that the collections concern material which was designed for use as evidence either for the prosecution or the defence – the editions of the documentation and proceedings of the

Nuremberg Trials.[7] In principle, the *Akten der Reichskanzlei* (Documents of the Reich Chancellery)[8] are of central importance for the internal development of the Third Reich. However, the volumes so far available, covering 1933–4, give an indication of the difficulties which the historian studying the later years of the 'Führer State' may face in overcoming, by normal methods of evaluating files, the diminished relevance of Reich Chancellery documents which resulted from the increasing disintegration in the political decision-making process. A just completed treasure-house of material, which the research community has not yet properly discovered, is the microfilm edition, compiled over the last two decades by Helmut Heiber with a team from the Institut für Zeitgeschichte, of the files of the Party Chancellery.[9] This has been reconstructed from the records of recipients, the original collection having been destroyed at the end of the war. Recently there has also been a reprint of the archival material of the Institute of Labour Science of the DAF.[10] Finally, the major editions of Catholic and Protestant church files edited by their Commissions for Contemporary History also deserve mention.[11]

The volumes by Jacobsen and Jochmann,[12] Ruge and Schumann[13] and Wolfgang Michalka[14] present collections of documents which are intended more for instruction and political education than for academic use. Their different foci implicitly demonstrate the movement in research. In addition, two more recent documentations of the first weeks and months of Hitler's government[15] provide good complementary material.

The historian wishing to gain some insight into public reaction to and the opinions of so-called ordinary people about either specific political measures or general developments can usually turn to newspapers and periodicals as a source. Given the censorship and prescriptive use of language in the Nazi period, using the contemporaneous press for this purpose is more difficult. Unvarnished reports – assuming that they can be identified as such – are a rarity, and commentaries or letters to the editor which are actually critical of the regime are almost never to be found. But, as for so many areas of life in the Third Reich, here too there is a 'substitute' which is both extremely valuable and now available in a published edition: from spring 1934 to April 1940 the SPD in Exile (*Sopade*) was able to maintain a network of informants throughout the Reich, who delivered information about the political and general situation in their own particular walk of life or area of work. At first in Prague and then later in Paris, these bulletins were processed, month by month, into the *Deutschland-Berichte* (Germany Reports), which contained an extraordinary wealth of information.[16] In 1938, with other motives and results, but out of the same need to penetrate beyond the façade of manipulated public opinion[17] to ascertain the genuine views and moods of the population, the Security Service (SD) of the SS organized the *Meldungen aus dem Reich* (Dispatches from the Reich).[18] Although the information content of both series of reports is enormous and, in principle, their authenticity is to be highly valued, the user has to school him- or herself in the criticism of historical sources and remain aware that both the *Sopade* and the SD were pursuing their own specific interests.

The edition of Goebbels' handwritten diaries from 1924–41,[19] which appeared in 1987, can lay claim to a special place in the category of published personal papers and memoirs. The propaganda Minister's diaries, the vast majority of which first came to light in the 1970s, are, in principle, the only major personal testimony from the inner circle of the Nazi leadership. The wretched attempt in 1983 to elevate the 'Führer' posthumously to the status of personal diarist not only revealed questionable socio-psychological fixations and a serious squalidness in certain parts of the journalistic profession, it was also a delayed reaction to the perplexing lack of personal, written testimony by Hitler of his own life, though that which covers the period until 1924, in all its paucity, had already been collated and published.[20] Apart from this, we have at our disposal his two books from the 'years of struggle', an older edition of his speeches and, covering a few months of the war, the records of the so-called 'table talk' (which were, in fact, bombastic nocturnal monologues).[21] Himmler's secret speeches and letters are available,[22] as are some fragments of Rosenberg's diaries[23] and Hans Frank's monstrous official diaries from Poland.[24] In addition, there are the contemporaneous personal testimonies of some leading military figures.[25] Otherwise, from the leading strata of the Third Reich there are only the subsequent, more or less apologetic self-justifications of that small group who had the opportunity to write them after the end of the war.[26] But these can already no longer be counted amongst the original sources which continue to concern us here.

What has survived of state and 'Party bureaucracy' sources from the Nazi period reflects, to a high degree, the political and material destruction wrought by the Second World War and its consequences. Immense quantities of historically valuable documentation were lost during the bombing and the confusion of the immediate post-war period, or were intentionally destroyed; a large proportion of the surviving files were confiscated by the Allies. If the seizure of documents at the end of the Third Reich turned out to be particularly rigorous, then this was because the victorious powers did not just need files for administrative purposes but were also seeking information in preparation for the Nuremberg Trials, for analysis of the German political and economic system, for de-Nazification and for the documentation of Nazi crimes. During the Berlin Blockade of 1948–9, the British and Americans carried off the most important parts of the captured documentation to England and some of it still further to various locations in the USA.[27] The Soviets too removed German files, but began to return them to the GDR as early as 1950. While the former Reichsarchiv in Potsdam provided the necessary accommodation and, under the title Deutsches Zentralarchiv, resumed work from 1946, in the Federal Republic the newly established Bundesarchiv in Koblenz did not open until 1952. The return of German archival material to the Federal Republic from the safe-keeping of the western Allies commenced in 1956 and was substantially completed by the beginning of the 1980s. In accordance with a condition laid down by the occupying powers, the files from the Nazi period have not been subject to the 30-year embargo formally introduced by the Law on the Federal Archive in 1988. Research into contemporary history in the Federal Republic has profited a great deal from this exemption from normal practice.

Since the reunification of Germany the archival landscape has also begun to change. For those seeking a preliminary overview of which groups of files of the highest Reich authorities, their subsidiary offices and the NSDAP have survived and where they are to be found, the Federal Archive's catalogue of holdings[28] is to be recommended for the area of the 'old' Federal Republic, especially as it also provides outline information about the material held in the former GDR and a list of addresses of many important archives in Germany and abroad. Of comparable fundamental value is the overview drawn up by Wolfgang Mommsen of individual bequests of personal papers in German archives.[29] The files of former *Länder* and annexed territories of the German Reich and the Nazi *Gaue* are to be found primarily in the relevant (main) state archives of the *Länder* of the Federal Republic, the Archive of Recent Files and the Archive of the Main Commission for the Investigation of Nazi Crimes in Warsaw, and in the voivodeship archives of the former German, now Polish territories. A complete, integrated index of the available files from the Nazi period is in the making.[30]

Similarly I can only draw general attention here to town and municipal archives, which often possess material which is helpful specifically for social history and the history of everyday life; the same is true of non-state and non-local authority archives, and above all of those of businesses and their self-governing bodies and of trade union and industry archives etc. Amongst the many specialist archives[31] particular mention must be made of the archive of the Institut für Zeitgeschichte in Munich, which because of its specialist collections and catalogues, is a stopping-off point for almost every researcher working on the Nazi period.[32]

German historical activity on the Third Reich in the immediate post-war period began under the influence of a singular culture of internalization – a combination of collective exhaustion, national self-pity and melancholy. The Germans reacted to being forced to look at last at what had happened, above all by the Americans with films about the liberation of the concentration camps, more with distress than anger. Friedrich Meinecke's book on the 'German Catastrophe',[33] which appeared as early as 1946, was the most prominent product of this mood. The metaphorical and distanced language of his work was soon to be overtaken by a plethora of works aimed at the demonization of Hitler and the Nazi period. None the less, Meinecke, who was already well into his eighties, certainly indicated not only the political helplessness of historicism when confronted with what was perceived above all as the tragedy of the German nation-state, but also the still almost complete lack of documentary sources necessary for solid historiography.

The situation began to change in the late 1940s, when the duplicated transcripts of the Nuremberg Trials, the so-called 'Nuremberg Documents', became available. Little by little it now became possible to reconstruct systematically the important train of events, actions and institutions of the 'Führer State', over which the veil of Third Reich propaganda had previously lain. A new generation of historians, who had experienced National Socialism as adolescents and young soldiers, devoted themselves to this task. Rather in the manner of detectives, they set to work with gusto to find out 'what had actually happened'. For their teachers the problem of continuity was of central importance. They were arguing about whether the Third Reich should be regarded as a radical break with Prusso-German history (Gerhard Ritter), or as the consequence of a lengthy special historical path (Ludwig Dehio and, to a lesser extent, Hans Rothfels). In contrast, the empirical approach to research taken by the young academics in newly established institutions such as the Institut für Zeitgeschichte in Munich, the Hamburg Research Centre for the History of National Socialism and at certain universities, was characterized by their concentration on facts and structures.

Amongst the older generation, Rothfels, Theodor Eschenburg, Ludwig Bergsträsser and Hans Herzfeld in particular gave emphatic support to the endeavours to establish research on the Nazi period as a new discipline of 'contemporary history'. Alongside intensive research of details, reflected above all in the *Vierteljahrshefte für Zeitgeschichte* and the testimonial evidence for courts and reparations authorities,[34] there also emerged in the 1950s the first comprehensive accounts by young historians such as Hermann Mau,[35] Hans Buchheim,[36] Helga Grebing,[37] Martin Broszat[38] and Helmut Heiber,[39] which today can themselves be read almost as 'original sources' on the history of research. At the Institute of Political Science of the Free University of Berlin, Gerhard Schulz and Wolfgang Sauer, in collaboration with the political scientist Karl Dietrich Bracher (who had already risen to prominence as a result of his pioneering examination of the disintegration of the Weimar Republic), began highly systematically structured studies of the Nazi seizure of power.[40] The proximity of the sources meant that all these works remained only relatively mildly influenced by the theory of totalitarianism, soon dominant in public debate. This theory, especially in the USA, had rapidly distanced itself from Hannah Arendt's great work[41] and transformed itself into an almost ahistorical model which postulated a direct comparability between the regimes of Hitler and Stalin, and to which an important political function was therefore attached during the Cold War. It was indicative of the general intellectual climate of these years that the critical studies already written during the war and published in American exile by Ernst Fraenkel and Franz Neumann, who had maintained a joint legal practice in Berlin during the 1920s, were only accepted after a considerable delay. Although both of them returned to Germany in the early 1950s, Fraenkel's trend-setting interpretation of the 'dual state'[42] did not appear in German until 1974, and Neumann's *Behemoth*,[43] an eminent analysis of the political, social economic structures of the Nazi system, not until three years later.

At about the same time as the Auschwitz Trial, which opened in Frankfurt/Main in 1963, a new phase of intensive research into National Socialism began.[44] The return of German files from the hands of the western Allies, which was by then under way, contributed to this; but it was also a reaction to strong tendencies within German society to declare the process of coming to terms with the Nazi past to be complete. Once the investigative endeavours of the judiciary had finally been centralized in 1958,[45] the generation of collaborators and accessories suddenly found themselves confronted with the German crimes in the East, and in them the generation of war-children caught sight of their own parents, silenced by their own suppressed feelings of personal guilt. Parallel to a new academic research interest in 'Fascism in its Epoch' – the original German title of Ernst Nolte's fundamental study[46] – there developed in the subsequent years a renaissance of leftist theories of fascism. However, these had little to do with the undoubtedly existing need of contemporary history to recover theoretical perspectives and, in the final analysis, their contribution to the furtherance of his torical understanding of the Nazi period remained slight.

The debate about the structure of the Nazi system proved itself altogether far more productive, informing the research of the 1970s, and emanating above all from Martin Broszat's pioneering interpretation of the Hitler State.[47] Growing differences of interpretation between representatives of a rather traditional political historiography and exponents of a newer social and societal history formed the background to this controversy, which developed partly into a bitter argument about the ability of the theories of totalitarianism and of fascism to aid academic understanding.[48] While the so-called 'intentionalists' interpret the Third Reich as a totalitarian dictatorship, determined essentially only by Hitler's unlimited position of power and his political 'programme', and which basically 'unravelled' in a predictable manner, the so-called 'structuralists', partly by referring to comparable phenomena in other fascist movements, emphasize the existence of competing power groups, chaotic internal structures and the resulting need for Hitler constantly to secure his rule through compromise and radicalization.[49] The dispute finally became engrossed in the question of whether the Third Reich was characterized by a monocratic or polycratic power structure.[50] At the outset, however, the discussion had taken place in the context of new detailed investigations and regional research which, sometimes using quantitive methods, drew from the structure-controversy part of the framework for its hypotheses. Scholars from abroad participated greatly in this research,[51] and its findings helped to refute the interpretation of the Third Reich as a monolithic 'Führer State' (though, in any event, this was a position barely still represented in academic circles).

In the 1980s, the history of everyday life became the dominant trend. The first large-scale attempt was the 'Bavaria Project'[52] of the Institut für Zeitgeschichte in the late 1970s – developing rather cautiously from regional and case studies which, in the final analysis, had remained bound to a central political perspective. Historians, educationalists and teachers who identify with and feel a sense of duty towards the younger generation's need for awareness and understanding, see in 'history from below' a fruitful way of imparting knowledge about the Nazi period, and the results of two competitions for school students, dedicated to daily life during the Nazi period, seem to have proved them right.[53] The everyday perspective cannot and should not replace the history of political structures, but it offers a great deal for the whole subject area of popular opinion in the Third Reich; for the more exact determination of the origins of resistance and conformity; and for the examination of the attractions and the defence against the demands of the system. The history of the foreign workers is an example of how some problematics were only recognized as such through this view 'from below'. In this particular case it was certainly also linked to the immediacy of the mass phenomenon of the time, initially remaining on the political agenda after the war in the form of displaced persons, but yet hardly touched upon as an aspect of the history of Nazism. As far as the question of financial compensation for those affected is concerned, it is still a topical issue.[54]

Following initial scepticism, the fruitfulness of the 'everyday approach' is now hardly disputed in specialist circles. But in the beginning there was no shortage of warnings against a grass-roots historiography which possesses neither intellectual rigour nor methodological interest in the central political and social processes of power. Yet the agitation which it caused amongst representatives of established social and structural history in particular, and which led to a sometimes all too polemical dispute,[55] has subsided. Both the fears of an epistemological decline in historical work and some of the expectations placed on the history of daily life have proved to be exaggerated. Indeed, the research of 'history workshops' and local initiative groups have led to a considerable extension (though often only the reinforcement) of knowledge about discrete historical structures, though without being able to fulfil the claim made by some of their protagonists to be rewriting history (and not just that of the Third Reich). Some of what is fêted, in the context of the history of daily life, as an addition to understanding simply shows how much of what had been known before has been forgotten.[56] Of course that should not give grounds for cultural pessimism, because for one thing history is not a property of society set in tablets of stone, but rather a permanent dialectical process of learning; and for another the changing conjunctures of themes and methods reflect, to a certain degree, the intellectual make-up of a society, the alteration of which also results in the postulation of different historical questions.

There is some indication that, in the 1980s, contemporary social problems and uncertainties were a substantial cause of the interest in the socio-political development and fate of minority groups during the Nazi period. The impetus for research into the more specialist areas of health policy and the development of medicine and psychiatry in the Third Reich, for example, have not come from the historical profession but mainly from doctors and psychologists who are tracing those dark chapters of they professional history for which their teachers' generation was responsible, and which they kept silent about after 1945.[57] And if our factual knowledge about the sterilization of the 'genetically diseased', the killing of the mentally handicapped, the persecution of Gypsies, the discrimination against homosexuals and other, then undesirable, groups has increased, then this is above all because, after decades of silence and shame, those affected, or their relatives, are coming forward and becoming involved in the political and moral recognition of their own history. The assimilation of experiences dammed up for so long is accompanied by a high degree of emotion, and the shocking nature of much of the information uncovered and taken up by a new generation does not make their appropriate historical and political integration any easier. And therein, of course, lies the special duty of professional history, which has to do more than simply 'expose' what has been hushed up and suppressed.

So, as the more recent research on the social policy of the Third Reich[58] continues during the coming years, the aim may well be to improve further the knowledge of the measures, planning and institutions of social policy and – by crossing, at the same time, the often only apparent boundaries presented by 1933 and 1945 – to link this with studies of their historical consequences. Thus it might also be possible to integrate the recent research on medical history and health policy – which has emphasized what were really, in many respects, exceptional aspects (sterilization, 'euthanasia', human experiments) – into what constituted normal medical practice, and to distinguish better between long-term develop mental tendencies of the welfare state and those specific to National Socialism.

We have to thank the recent research interest in the war years, long regarded primarily from a military and foreign policy viewpoint, for the illumination of sometimes little-known developments in domestic, social and economic policy, and above all of post-war planning.[59] It also diminishes the hitherto strongly emphasized distinction between the phases of *Blitzkrieg* and subsequently of 'total war'. At the same time, however, it appears to run counter to the opinion (possibly strengthened with apologetic intent after 1945) according to which the possibility of the reconsolidation of a post-war Nazi regime would have been absolutely unthinkable.

In many respects, the radical nature of the political break which did take place in 1945 is proving to be less significant in socio-historical terms. Recent studies on 'personal history and social culture'[60] and on the 'social history of upheaval in Germany',[61] partly based on oral history techniques, show that in the perception of the population, but often also from a structural-historical perspective, decisive moments and changes lay not in 1945, but at the time of the turning point of the war in 1942–3 and in the currency reform of 1948. Similar, at first surprising, findings were made in the field of intellectual life and mass culture in the Third Reich by the initial studies which were informed by an historical approach based on perceptions and outcomes.[62] Consistent research which concentrates on the concrete consequences of political programmes and measures will be able to make further progress in illuminating the reality of life during the Nazi era. With that, perhaps, the time approaches when the widespread desire for a comprehensive social history of the Third Reich can also be satisfied.

Efforts in this direction are also necessary because, with the growing distance in time, there is an increasing danger that, on the one hand, the history of the Third Reich is being degraded into a cheap, moralistic, didactic example of political pedagogy, and on the other, to a construct rendered almost devoid of morality and subjected to the growing demands of an increasingly diverse academic discipline for artificially dissected angles and hypotheses.[63] Such tendencies to dehistoricization are nothing new, but they are the exact opposite of that 'historicization' for which Martin Broszat pleaded in a highly regarded essay published even before the *Historikerstreit*.[64] For research, this means what Broszat drew attention to years ago[65] – taking the reality of National Socialism not just seriously but also rigorously; to evaluate it as it variously relates to long-term trends in the development of civilization and the economy and to integrate it into German history more precisely than before. This should not be confused with attempts to smooth over or relativize this unique chapter of German history. That would be as inappropriate as seeking to exclude it altogether, which was the aim of the old description of the Third Reich as an 'occupational accident in the course of German history'.

However unreasonable it may seem, given this background, the question of whether historical research on the Third Reich is now not slowly coming to an end has none the less been raised repeatedly for years. And this has not only been in pub-talk, by the gullible and by the – now small and naturally ever diminishing – group of those who feel themselves personally affected by, or under attack from, the study of the Nazi period; it has occasionally been heard even within historical circles.[66] Long before the so-called *Historikerstreit* erupted in 1986 and reached the review sections and eventually the political columns of daily and weekly newspapers,[67] it had become apparent that there was a need, not to draw a line under the decades of research into National Socialism, but rather to take stock. The outward occasion for this was offered above all by the fiftieth anniversary in 1983 of the Nazi assumption of power, which was accompanied by numerous public events, an international conference in the Berlin Reichstag[68] and a flood of publications of books both new and old. In this context the problem of the 'unique nature' of the Third Reich and, eventually, also its crimes, was touched upon – at least implicitly. And it is undoubtedly no coincidence that, in the 1980s, there were increased efforts to meet the justified demand of a wider public for comprehensive interpretations and reference works on the history of National Socialism.

Indeed, anyone with an interest in history will find a greater range of information available than ever before. Apart from anthologies clearly intended as reviews of research,[69] there is a handbook (combining a chronology with general accounts),[70] a two-volume chronology which is extraordinarily rich in facts,[71] more recent collections of short biographies,[72] and a very useful dictionary of terms.[73] In addition, in the last few years, there have been books which have aimed, sometimes in conjunction with a condensed review, to trace and evaluate the development of research in general[74] – over which an overview has become almost impossible – or of specific important fields.[75] Above all, the justification for broader, more comprehensive presentation and analysis, which had almost disappeared in the wake of growing specialization, seems to have been recognized once more. After a period of fifteen years in which Karl Dietrich Bracher's work on the 'German Dictatorship'[76] and Joachim Fest's biography of Hitler[77] had seemed to have been without competition in the publishing world, Hans-Ulrich Thamer's book offers a new, broadly constructed history of National Socialism and the Third Reich.[78]

Contrary to many people's fears (or hopes), there is no slackening of interest on the part of the Germans in German history between 1933 and 1945. It is, however, changing, and that should be no bad thing.

Notes

1 *Bibliographie zur Zeitgeschichte 1953–1980*, ed. Thilo Vogelsang and Hellmuth Auerbach with the assistance of Ursula von Laak for the Institut für Zeitgeschichte (3 vols, Munich, 1982–3), continuing publication as an annual supplement to the *Vierteljahrshefte für Zeitgeschichte*.

2 Bibliothek für Zeitgeschichte (ed.), *Jahresbibliographie* (Frankfurt, 1960–), (1953–9 under the title *Bücherschau der Weltkriegsbücherei Stuttgart*).

3 Peter Hüttenberger (ed.), *Bibliographie zum Nationalsozialismus* (Göttingen, 1980); Karl Dietrich Bracher, Hans-Adolf Jacobsen and Albrecht Tyrell (eds),

Bibliographie zur Politik in Theorie und Praxis (Düsseldorf, 1976, completely rev. edn 1982); Helen Kehr and Janet Langmaid (eds), *The Nazi Era 1919–1945. A Select Bibliography of Published Works from the Early Roots to 1980* (London, 1982); *The Third Reich, 1933–1939. A Historical Bibliography* (Santa Barbara, CA, 1984), comprises abstracts of almost 1,000 recent articles from academic journals.

4 *Akten zur deutschen Auswärtigen Politik 1918– 45*, Series C 1933–37, 6 vols; Series D 1937–41, 13 vols; Series E 1941–45, 8 vols (Bonn, 1950–81). An incomplete but none the less comprehensive selection in translation has been published under the title *Documents on German Foreign Policy, 1918– 1945*, Series C (1933–37), 6 vols; Series D (1937–45), vols 3–13 (London, 1954–67).

5 Percy Ernst Schramm (ed.), *Kriegstagebuch des Oberkommandos der Wehrmacht (Wehrmachtsführungsstab) 1940–1945* (Frankfurt, 1961–9; new edn in 8 vols, Herrsching, 1982).

6 Herbert Michaelis/Ernst Schraepler (eds), *Ursachen und Folgen. Vom deutschen Zusammenbruch 1918 und 1945 bis zur staatlichen Neuordnung Deutschlands in der Gegenwart. Eine Urkunden- und Dokumentensammlung zur Zeitgeschichte* (25 vols, Berlin, 1958–77).

7 *The Trial of the Major War Criminals before the International Military Tribunal, Nuremberg 14.11.1945–1.10.1946: Proceedings*, vols 1–23, (Nuremberg, 1947–9) *Documents in Evidence*, vols 24–42 (Nuremberg, 1947–9). Published as a documentation of the so-called successor trials: *Trials of War Criminals before the Nuremberg Military Tribunals under Control Council Law No. 10. Nuremberg 1946–April 1949* (15 vols, Washington, 1950–3).

8 *Akten der Reichskanzlei. Regierung Hitler 1933–1938* (thus far 2 vols [Part 1: 1933/34], Boppard, 1983).

9 *Akten der Partei-Kanzlei der NSDAP. Rekonstruktion eines verlorengegangenen Bestandes. Teil I: Regesten Band 1 und 2, Registerband.*, ed. Helmut Heiber; *Teil II: Regesten Band 3 und 4, Registerband*, ed. Peter Longerich (Munich etc., 1983, 1992); microfiche edition of the archival holdings, Parts 1 and 2 (Munich, 1983 and 1985).

10 *Sozialstrategien der Deutschen Arbeitsfront. Teil A: Jahrbücher des Arbeitswissenschaftlichen Instituts der Deutschen Arbeitsfront 1936–1940/41. Teil B: Periodika, Denkschriften, Gutachten und Veröffentlichungen des Arbeitswissenschaftlichen Instituts der Deutschen Arbeitsfront*, ed. Michael Hepp and Karl Heinz Roth (microfiche edition, Munich, 1986–92).

11 *Akten deutscher Bischöfe über die Lage der Kirche 1933–1945*, ed. Bernhard Stasiewski and Ludwig Volk (6 vols, Mainz, 1968–85); *Verantwortung für die Kirche. Stenographische Aufzeichnungen und Mitschriften von Landesbischof Hans Meiser 1933–1955*, vol. 1, ed. Hannelore Braun and Carsten Nicolaisen (Göttingen, 1985); *Inventar staatlicher Akten zum Verhältnis von Staat und Kirchen 1933–1945*, ed. Christian Abele et al. (3 vols, Kassel, 1987–8), offers a bibliographical overview of the editions of files and documents of both churches.

12 Hans-Adolf Jacobsen and Werner Jochmann (eds), *Ausgewählte Dokumente zur Geschichte des Nationalsozialismus 1933–1945* (10 instalments, Bielefeld, 1960–6).

13 Wolfgang Ruge and Wolfgang Schumann (eds), *Dokumente zur deutschen Geschichte 1933–1945* (4 vols, East Berlin, 1975–7).

14 Wolfgang Michalka (ed.), *Das Dritte Reich:* vol. 1, *'Volksgemeinschaft' und Grossmachtpolitik 1933–1939*; vol. 2, *Weltmachtanspruch und nationaler Zusammenbruch 1939–1945* (Munich, 1985).

15 Wieland Eschenhagen (ed.), *Die 'Machtergreifung'. Tagebuch einer Wende nach Presseberichten vom 1. Januar bis 6. März 1933* (Darmstadt, 1982); Josef and Ruth Becker (eds), *Hitlers Machtergreifung. Vom Machtantritt Hitlers 30. Januar 1933 bis zur Besiegelung des Einparteienstaates 14. Juli 1933* (Munich, 1983).

16 *Deutschland-Berichte der Sozialdemokratischen Partei Deutschlands (Sopade) 1934–1940* (7 vols, Salzhausen/Frankfurt, 1980).

17 *NS-Presseanweisungen der Vorkriegszeit. Edition und Dokumentation*, ed. Gabriele Toepser-Ziegert (thus far 3 vols [1933–35], Munich, 1984–7).

18 Heinz Boberach (ed.), *Meldungen aus dem Reich 1938–1945. Die geheimen Lageberichte des Sicherheitsdienstes der SS* (17 vols plus index, Herrsching, 1984).

19 Elke Fröhlich (ed.), *Die Tagebücher von Joseph Goebbels. Sämtliche Fragmente. Teil I: Aufzeichnungen 1924 bis 1941* (4 vols, Munich 1987); *Teil II: Die maschinenschriftlichen Aufzeichnungen*, in progress.

20 Eberhard Jäckel and Axel Kuhn (eds), *Hitler. Sämtliche Aufzeichnungen 1905–1924* (Stuttgart, 1980); by the same authors and Hermann Weiss, 'Neue Erkenntnisse zur Fälschung von Hitler-Dokumenten', *VfZ*, 32 (1984), pp. 163–9. The edition is being continued in a series intended to comprise 6 vols: *Hitler. Reden, Schriften, Anordnungen. Februar 1925 bis Januar 1933* (Institut für Zeitgeschichte, Munich, 1992ff.).

21 Adolf Hitler, *Mein Kampf. Vol. 1: A Reckoning. Vol. 2: The National Socialist Movement*, ed. D.C. Watt (London, 1969; originally published in Munich in 1925 and 1927); Gerhard L. Weinberg (ed.), *Hitlers Zweites Buch. Ein Dokument aus dem Jahre 1928* (Stuttgart, 1961); Max Domarus (ed.), *Hitler. Reden und Proklamationen 1932–1945* (2 vols, Munich, 1965); Werner Jochmann (ed.), *Adolf Hitler. Monologe im Führerhauptquartier 1941–1944. Die Aufzeichnungen Heinrich Heims* (Hamburg, 1980); Henry Picker, *Hitlers Tischgespräche im Führerhauptquartier* (enlarged new edn, Stuttgart, 1976); the best available edition in English remains Hugh Trevor-Roper (ed.), *Hitler's Table Talk* (London, 1953).

22 Bradley F. Smith and Agnes F. Peterson (eds), *Heinrich Himmler. Geheimreden 1933 bis 1945 und andere Ansprachen* (Frankfurt, 1974); also Helmut Heiber (ed.), *Reichsführer! . . . Briefe an und von Himmler* (Stuttgart, 1968).

23 Hans-Günther Seraphim (ed.), *Das politische Tagebuch Alfred Rosenbergs 1934/35 und 1939/40* (Göttingen, 1956; repr. Munich, 1964).

24 Werner Präg and Wolfgang Jacobmeyer (eds), *Das Diensttagebuch des deutschen Generalgouverneurs in Polen 1939–1945* (Stuttgart, 1975).

25 Franz Halder, Kriegstagebuch. Tägliche Aufzeichnungen des Chefs des Generalstabs des Heeres 1939–1942, ed. Hans-Adolf Jacobsen (3 vols, Stuttgart, 1962–4); Helmut Groscurth, Tagebücher eines Abwehroffiziers 1938–1940, with further documents on the military opposition to Hitler, ed. Helmut Krausnick and Harold C. Deutsch (Stuttgart, 1969); Hildegard von Kotze (ed.), Heeresadjutant bei Hitler 1938–1943. Aufzeichnungen des Majors Engel (Stuttgart, 1974).

26 Rudolf Diels, Lucifer ante portas. Zwischen Severing und Heydrich (Zürich 1949); Otto Meissner, Staatssekretär unter Ebert, Hindenburg und Hitler. Der Schicksalsweg des deutschen Volkes von 1918–1945, wie ich ihn erlebte (Hamburg, 1950); Lutz Graf Schwerin von Krosigk, Es geschah in Deutschland. Menschenbild unseres Jahrhunderts (Tübingen/Stuttgart, 1951); Franz von Papen, Der Wahrheit eine Gasse (Munich, 1952); Hans Frank, Im Angesicht des Galgens. Deutung Hitlers und seiner Zeit auf Grund eigener Erlebnisse und Erkenntnisse (Munich, 1953); Hjalmar Schacht, 76 Jahre meines Lebens (Bad Wörishofen, 1953); Joachim von Ribbentrop, Zwischen London und Moskau. Erinnerungen und letzte Aufzeichnungen, edited from the bequest by Anneliese von Ribbentrop (Leoni, 1953); Otto Dietrich, Zwölf Jahre mit Hitler (Munich, 1955); Walter Schellenberg, Memoiren (Cologne, 1956); Albert Speer, Inside the Third Reich (London, 1970) and Spandauer Tagebücher (Frankfurt, 1975).

27 On the following cf. Josef Henke, 'Das Schicksal deutscher zeitgeschichtlicher Quellen in Kriegs- und Nachkriegszeit. Beschlagnahme – Rückführung – Verbleib', VfZ, 30 (1982), pp. 557–620.

28 Das Bundesarchiv und seine Bestände (3rd edn, Boppard, 1977). A new edition is to be expected once the details of the amalgamation of the hitherto fragmented holdings in Potsdam and Koblenz has been decided.

29 Die Nachlässe in den deutschen Archiven (mit Ergänzung aus anderen Beständen), ed. Wolfgang A. Mommsen (in 2 parts, Boppard, 1971 and 1983); supplemented by Ludwig Denecke and Tilo Brandis, Die Nachlässe in den Bibliotheken der Bundesrepublik Deutschland (Boppard, 1981).

30 Inventar archivalischer Quellen des NS-Staates. Die überlieferung von Behörden und Einrichtungen des Reichs, der Länder und der NSDAP, ed. Heinz Boberach for the Institut für Zeitgeschichte in Munich. Teil 1: Reichszentralbehörden, regionale Behörden und wissenschaftliche Hochschulen für die zehn westdeutschen Länder sowie Berlin (Munich etc., 1991).

31 For information about such archives and their collections: Quellen zur Zeitgeschichte (= Deutsche Geschichte seit dem Ersten Weltkrieg, vol. 3), (Stuttgart, 1973).

32 Details in a brochure available on request from the Institut für Zeitgeschichte, Leonrodstr. 46b, D-8000 München 19.

33 Friedrich Meinecke, The German Catastrophe (London, 1950).

34 Gutachten des Instituts für Zeitgeschichte (2 vols, Munich, 1958 and Stuttgart, 1966).

35 Hermann Mau and Helmut Krausnick, German History 1933–1945: An Assessment by German Historians (New York, 1963).

36 Hans Buchheim, *Das Dritte Reich. Grundlagen und politische Entwicklung* (Munich, 1958).

37 Helga Grebing, *Der Nationalsozialismus. Ursprung und Wesen* (Munich, 1959).

38 Martin Broszat, *Der Nationalsozialismus. Weltanschauung, Programm und Wirklichkeit* (Stuttgart, 1960).

39 Helmut Heiber, *Adolf Hitler. A Short Biography* (London, 1961).

40 Karl Dietrich Bracher, *Die Auflösung der Weimarer Republik. Eine Studie zum Problem des Machtverfalls in der Demokratie* (Villingen, 1955); Karl Dietrich Bracher, Wolfgang Sauer and Gerhard Schulz, *Die nationalsozialistische Machtergreifung. Studien zur Errichtung des totalitären Herrschaftssystems in Deutschland 1933/34* (Cologne/Opladen, 1960).

41 Hannah Arendt, *The Origins of Totalitarianism* (New York, 1951).

42 Ernst Fraenkel, *The Dual State. A Contribution to the Theory of Dictatorship* (New York, 1969).

43 Franz Neumann, *Behemoth. The Structure and Practice of National Socialism 1933–1944* (London, 1967).

44 The expert studies which emerged in this context – by Hans Buchheim on the SS, Martin Broszat on the concentration camp system, Hans-Adolf Jacobsen on the *Kommissarbefehl* and the mass executions of Soviet prisoners of war, and Helmut Krausnisck on the persecution of the Jews, were published under the title *Anatomie des SS-Staates* (Olten/Freiburg 1965; 3rd edn in 2 vols, Munich, 1982); the contributions by Broszat and Krausnick were published in translation as *Anatomy of the SS State* (London, 1982); cf. also the early study by Eugen Kogon, *The Theory and Practice of Hell: The German Concentration Camps and the System Behind Them* (New York/London, 1950).

45 The 'Central Office of the Judicial Authorities of the *Länder* for the Prosecution of National Socialist Crimes of Violence' established in Ludwigsburg at this time performed valuable work during the following years which also advanced research; Adalbert Rückerl, *NS-Verbrechen vor Gericht. Versuch einer Vergangenheitsbewältigung* (Heidelberg, 1982).

46 Ernst Nolte, *Three Faces of Fascism. The* Action Française – *Italian Fascism – National Socialism* (London, 1965).

47 Martin Broszat, *The Hitler State. The foundation and development of the internal structure of the Third Reich* (Harlow, 1981).

48 For a documentation of the clash of the two positions, cf. *Totalitarismus und Faschismus. Eine wissenschaftliche und Begriffskontroverse* (Munich/Vienna, 1980); it also contains bibliographical information. Karl Dietrich Bracher, Eberhard Jäckel, Klaus Hildebrand and Andreas Hillgruber declared themselves on the side of the 'intentionalists', while principally Hans Mommsen and Martin Broszat and, with some reservations, Wolfgang Schieder, took the side of the 'structuralists'.

49 Cf. for example, Eberhard Jäckel, *Hitlers Herrschaft. Vollzug einer Weltanschauung* (Stuttgart, 1986); and, from the other viewpoint, Hans Mommsen, *Der Nationalsozialismus und die deutsche Gesellschaft. Ausgewählte Aufsätze* (Reinbek, 1991).

50 Gerhard Hirschfeld and Lothar Kettenacker (eds), *The Führer State: Myth and Reality. Studies on the Structure and Politics of the Third Reich* (London, 1981). Just how hollow the argument had become was summed up by Hans-Ulrich Thamer's assertion (see. n. 78 below) that 'the Third Reich possessed a strong monocratic elite and at the same time polycratic power structures. The one determined the other.' Cf., more recently, Dieter Rebentisch, *Führerstaat und Verwaltung im Zweiten Weltkrieg. Verfassungsentwicklung und Verwaltungspolitik 1939–1945* (Wiesbaden, 1989).

51 For example, Edward N. Peterson, *The Limits of Hitler's Power* (Princeton, NJ, 1969); Dietrich Orlow, *The History of the Nazi Party. 1919–1933, 1933 to 1945* (Pittsburgh, 1969, 1973). Even earlier, and hardly ever equalled in its vividness by later studies, William Sheridan Allen, *The Nazi Seizure of Power. The Experience of a Single German Town* (Chicago, 1965).

52 Martin Broszat et al. (eds), *Bayern in der NS-Zeit* (6 vols, Munich, 1977–83): as a partial summary, Martin Broszat and Elke Fröhlich, *Alltag und Widerstand. Bayern im Nationalsozialismus* (Munich/Zürich, 1987).

53 Cf. the yearbooks of the schools history competition for the prize awarded by the President of the Federal Republic of Germany: Dieter Galinski and Ulla Lachauer (eds), *Alltag im Nationalsozialismus 1933 bis 1939* (Hamburg, 1982); also Dieter Galinski, Ulla Lachauer and Wolf Schmidt (eds), *Die Kriegsjahre in Deutschland 1939 bis 1945* (Hamburg, 1985).

54 For a long time the only German work on the subject was the predominantly organizational history by Hans Pfahlmann, *Fremdarbeiter und Kriegsgefangene in der deutschen Kriegswirtschaft 1939–1945* (Darmstadt, 1968); more recently Ulrich Herbert, *A History of Foreign Labor in Germany 1880–1980. Seasonal Workers – Forced Laborers – Guest Workers*, ch. 4: 'Labor as Spoils of Conquest 1933–45' (Michigan, 1990); for a more detailed exposition of the subject during the war years cf. Ulrich Herbert, *Fremdarbeiter. Politik und Praxis des 'Ausländer-Einsatzes' in der Kriegswirtschaft des Dritten Reiches* (Bonn, 1985).

55 *Alltagsgeschichte der NS-Zeit. Neue Perspektive oder Trivialisierung?* (Munich, 1984); includes suggested further reading.

56 Martin Broszat drew attention to this in exemplary fashion in ' "Holocaust" und die Geschichtswissenschaft', *VfZ*, 27 (1979), pp. 285–98.

57 By way of an interim appraisal, Norbert Frei (ed.), *Medizin und Gesundheitspolitik in der NS-Zeit* (Munich, 1991).

58 E.g. Carola Sachse et al., *Angst, Belohnung, Zucht und Ordnung. Herrschaftsmechanismen im Nationalsozialismus* (Opladen, 1982); Marie-Luise Recker, *Nationalsozialistische Sozialpolitik im Zweiten Weltkrieg* (Munich, 1985); Wolfgang Zollitsch, *Arbeiter zwischen Weltwirtschaftskrise und Nationalsozialismus. Ein Beitrag zur Sozialpolitik der Jahre 1928 bis 1936* (Göttingen, 1990).

59 Ludolf Herbst, *Der Totale Krieg und die Ordnung der Wirtschaft. Die Kriegswirtschaft im Spannungsfeld von Politik, Ideologie und Propaganda 1939 bis 1945* (Stuttgart, 1982); Detlev Peukert, *Inside Nazi Germany. Conformity, Opposition and Racism in Everyday Life* (London, 1987).

60 Lutz Niethammer (ed.), 'Die Jahre weiss man nicht, wo man die heute hinsetzen soll.' Faschismuserfahrungen im Ruhrgebiet (Berlin/Bonn, 1983); and Niethammer (ed.), 'Hinterher merkt man, dass es richtig war, dass es schiefgegangen ist.' Nachkriegserfahrungen im Ruhrgebiet (Berlin/Bonn, 1983).

61 Martin Broszat, Klaus-Dietmar Henke and Hans Woller (eds), Von Stalingrad zur Währungsreform. Zur Sozialgeschichte des Umbruchs in Deutschland (Munich, 1988).

62 Hans Dieter Schäfer, Das gespaltene Bewusstsein. Über deutsche Kultur und Lebenswirklichkeit 1933–1945 (Munich/Vienna, 1981).

63 This is more or less true for the attempt – unsatisfactory also in terms of methodology and critical use of sources – to describe Hitler above all as an intentional 'modernizer', without taking sufficient account of the extreme racist foundation of this modernity; cf. Rainer Zitelmann, Hitler. Selbstverständnis eines Revolutionärs (Hamburg/Leamington Spa, 1987), provoking Jeffrey Herf, Reactionary Modernism. Technology, Culture and Politics in Weimar and the Third Reich (Cambridge, 1984).

64 Martin Broszat, 'Plädoyer für eine Historisierung des Nationalsozialismus' (1985), in Broszat, Nach Hitler. Der Schwierige Umgang mit unserer Geschichte (Munich, 1988), pp. 266–81.

65 Martin Broszat, 'Eine Insel in der Geschichte? Der Historiker in der Spannung zwischen Verstehen und Bewerten der Hitler-Zeit', (1983), in Broszat, Nach Hitler, pp. 208–15.

66 Thus the – rhetorical – common title of two lectures by Andreas Hillgruber: Endlich genug über Nationalsozialismus und Zweiten Weltkrieg? Forschungsstand und Literatur (Düsseldorf, 1982).

67 The academic results of the controversy were slim. The most important of many publications are: 'Historikerstreit'. Die Dokumentation der Kontroverse um die Einzigartigkeit der Judenvernichtung (Munich/Zürich, 1987); Ernst Nolte, Vergangenheit, die nicht vergehen will. Der sogenannte Historikerstreit. Darstellung, Auseinandersetzung, Dokumente (Berlin, 1987); Jürgen Habermas, 'Eine Art Schadensabwicklung', Kleine Politische Schriften VI (Frankfurt, 1987); Hans-Ulrich Wehler, Entsorgung der deutschen Vergangenheit? Ein polemischer Essay zum 'Historikerstreit', (Munich, 1988); Dan Diner (ed.), Ist der Nationalsozialismus Geschichte? Zu Historisierung und Historikerstreit (Frankfurt, 1987); Martin Broszat and Saul Friedländer, 'Um die "Historisierung des Nationalsozialismus". Ein Briefwechsel', VfZ, 36 (1988), pp. 339–72; Charles S. Maier, The Unmasterable Past. History, Holocaust and German National Identity (Cambridge, MA, 1988); Richard J. Evans, In Hitler's Shadow. West German Historians and the Attempt to Escape from the Nazi Past (New York/London, 1989).

68 Martin Broszat et al. (eds), Deutschlands Weg in die Diktatur. Internationale Konferenz zur nationalsozialistischen Machtübernahme im Reichstagsgebäude zu Berlin. Referate und Diskussionen. Ein Protokoll (Berlin, 1983).

69 Karl Dietrich Bracher, Manfred Funke and Hans-Adolf Jacobsen (eds), Nationalsozialistische Diktatur 1933–1945. Eine Bilanz (Düsseldorf, 1983);

Martin Broszat and Horst Möller (eds), *Das Dritte Reich. Herrschaftsstruktur und Geschichte* (Munich, 1983); Klaus Malettke (ed.), *Der Nationalsozialismus an der Macht. Aspekte nationalsozialistischer Politik und Herrschaft* (Göttingen, 1984).

70   Martin Broszat and Norbert Frei (eds), *Ploetz Das Dritte Reich. Ursprünge, Ereignisse, Wirkungen* (Freiburg/Würzburg, 1983); rev. paperback edn by the same authors, *Das Dritte Reich im Überblick. Chronik, Ereignisse, Zusammenhänge* (Munich, 1989).

71   Manfred Overesch and Friedrich Wilhelm Saal (eds), *Chronik deutscher Zeitgeschichte. Politik, Wirtschaft, Kultur. Das Dritte Reich. Band 2/I: 1933 bis 1939; Band 2/II: 1939–1945* (Düsseldorf, 1982, 1983).

72   Ronald Smelser and Rainer Zitelmann (eds), *Die braune Elite. 22 biographische Skizzen* (Darmstadt, 1989); Robert Wistrich, *Wer war wer im Dritten Reich. Anhänger, Mitläufer, Gegner aus Politik, Wirtschaft, Militär, Kunst und Wissenschaft* (Munich, 1983); cf. also Erich Stockhorst, *Fünftausend Köpfe. Wer war was im Dritten Reich* (Velbert/Kettwig, 1967).

73   Christian Zentner and Friedemann Bedürftig (eds), *Das Grosse Lexikon des Dritten Reiches* (Munich, 1985); by the same authors, *Das Grosse Lexikon des Zweiten Weltkriegs* (Munich, 1988); cf. also Louis L. Snyder, *Encyclopeadia of the Third Reich* (New York, 1976).

74   Klaus Hildebrand, *The Third Reich* (London, 1984); Ian Kershaw, *The Nazi Dictatorship. Problems and Perspectives of Interpretation* (London, 1985, 3rd revised edition 1992).

75   Gerhard Schreiber, *Hitler, Interpretationen 1923–1983. Ergebnisse, Methoden und Probleme der Forschung* (Darmstadt, 1984).

76   Karl Dietrich Bracher, *The German Dictatorship. The Origins, Structure and Consequences of National Socialism* (Harmondsworth, 1973).

77   Joachim C. Fest, *Hitler. A Biography* (London, 1979); too little notice was given, unjustly, to the essay, rich in ideas, by Josef Peter Stern, *Hitler. The Führer and the People* (Munich, 1978).

78   Hans-Ulrich Thamer, *Verführung und Gewalt. Deutschland 1933–1945* (Berlin, 1986). Now cf. also Heinz Höhne, *Die Zeit der Illusionen. Hitler und die Anfänge des Dritten Reiches 1933–1936* (Düsseldorf, 1991).

Appendix 1:   Chronology 1933–1945

1933

Jan. 30   Hitler becomes Reich Chancellor of a coalition government of the NSDAP, DNVP and Stahlhelm.

31   Negotiation with the Centre Party about their possible participation in the government.

Feb. 1   Reich presidential decree to dissolve the Reichstag.

4   Reich presidential decree 'For the Protection of the German People' permits infringement of the freedom of the press and assembly; the first legal grounds for the persecution of political opponents.

6   Reich presidential decree to dissolve the Prussian state legislature [*Landtag*].

17   'Shooting Decree' [*Schiesserlass*] issued by the Prussian Interior Minister Hermann Goering.

22   Recruitment of approximately 50,000 auxiliary police officers from the SA, SS and Stahlhelm in Prussia.

27   Reichstag Fire; arrest of the arsonist Marinus van der Lubbe.

28   Reich presidential decree 'For the Protection of the People and the State' (Reichstag Fire decree) suspends all basic civil rights, makes possible arbitrary, extra-judicial police 'protective custody' and establishes the basis for an extended state of emergency. *De facto* ban on the KPD and on the SPD press.

Mar. 5   Reichstag elections: despite Nazi terror and unconstitutional obstruction of the KPD, SPD and Centre, only 43.9% of votes cast are for the NSDAP, but there is a slim absolute majority for the government coalition. Beginning of the conquest of *Länder* ruled by non-Nazi governments (until 9 Mar.).

13   Joseph Goebbels head of the new Reich Ministry for Propaganda and Popular Enlightenment.

21   'Potsdam Day': opening of the new Reichstag with Hindenburg and Hitler. Decree on the prevention of malicious practices punishes even verbal criticism of the NSDAP and the government. Establishment of special courts.

22   Establishment of Dachau concentration camp.

23   Enabling Act adopted only against the votes of the SPD (KPD deputies already fled, in protective custody or underground); government can now decree laws, even those which entail changes to the constitution, without the Reichstag.

31   'Interim Law for the Coordination of the *Länder* with the Reich'.

Apr. 1   Boycott of Jewish shops. Reichsführer SS Heinrich Himmler becomes Political Police Commander of Bavaria.

7   'Law for the Restoration of the Professional Civil Service' makes possible the dismissal or compulsory retirement of politically 'unreliable elements' and, as per the 'Aryan paragraph', Jews. 'Second Law for the Coordination of the *Länder* with the Reich' installs Reich Governors.

11   Hermann Goering becomes Deputy Reich Governor and Prime Minister of Prussia.

21   Rudolf Hess becomes the 'Führer's Deputy'.

28   Goering becomes head of the new Reich Ministry of Aviation.

29   Bavarian *Landtag* agrees the *Länder* Enabling Law (Prussia 18 May, Saxony 23 May, Württemberg 8 June, Baden 9 June).

May 1   'Day of National Labour' as official public holiday with mass rallies. Moratorium on recruitment to the NSDAP.

2   Trade unions smashed: buildings, businesses and Arbeiterbank (Workers' Bank) occupied by the SA and the NSBO; leading officials in 'protective custody'.

3–4   Compulsory Nazi cartels ('Reich Estates' [*Reichsstände*]) for craft trades and commerce under Adrian von Renteln.

10   Book burnings in university cities. Foundation of the DAF; trade unions forced to disband and to incorporate into the DAF.

17   SPD parliamentary party votes in the Reichstag for Hitler's foreign policy declaration (the 'peace speech'); SPD party executive in exile in Prague under Otto Wels and Hans Vogel.

19   'Law on Trustees of Labour' abolishes free collective bargaining.

28   Richard Walter Darré, leader of the NSDAP's 'Agrarian Policy Unit' becomes 'Reich Peasants' Leader' [*Reichsbauernführer*] of the agricultural associations coordinated since March/April.

Jun. 1   Law to reduce unemployment (Reinhardt Programme). 'Adolf Hitler Donation of German Industry'.

17   Baldur von Schirach becomes 'Youth Leader [*Jugendführer*] of the German Reich'.

22   SPD banned. The other remaining parties dissolve themselves:

	DNVP (subsumed into the NSDAP parliamentary party) and DVP 27 June, DDP 28 June, BVP 4 July, Centre Party 5 July.
27	Resignation of Alfred Hugenberg, Reich Minister for Industry, Food and Agriculture.
Jul. 1–2	Stahlhelm under Franz von Seldte placed under the command of the SA.
14	'Law Against the Establishment of Political Parties' legalizes the NSDAP's monopoly of power and completes the *Gleichschaltung* of the parliaments. 'Law to Prevent Progeny with Hereditary Diseases'. 'Law on the Confiscation of Property Belonging to Enemies of the People and the State' retrospectively legalizes the expropriation of the SPD.
20	Conclusion of the Reich Concordat secures the existence and activity of the Catholic organizations; Vatican prohibits priests from all party-political activity.
Aug. 8	The radical Nazi League of Struggle for the Commercial Middle Class incorporated into the National Socialist Craft, Trade and Commerce Organization, 'NS-Hago'.
Aug. 31– 3 Sep.	NSDAP 'Party Congress of Victory' in Nuremberg.
Sep. 11	Protestant 'Church struggle' begins with the founding of the 'Pastors' Emergency League'.
13	Proclamation of the Winter Aid Organization. Law on the Reich Food Estate regulates agricultural markets and prices.
21	Reichstag Fire trial: death sentence for van der Lubbe; on 23 Dec. Ernst Torgler, Chair of the KPD parliamentary party, acquitted, along with Georgi Dimitrov, member of the Executive Committee of the Communist International and two further defendants.
22	Law to establish the Reich Chamber of Culture (president Joseph Goebbels, vice-president Walther Funk), with Reich Chamber of Literature (president Hans Friedrich Blunck), Reich Press Chamber (Max Amann), Reich Chamber of Broadcasting (Horst Dressler-Andress), Reich Theatre Chamber (Otto Laubinger), Reich Chamber of Music (Richard Strauss), and Reich Chamber of Fine Arts (Eugen Hönig); the Reich Film Chamber (Fritz Scheuermann) had already been in existence since 14 July.
29	'Reich Entailed Farm Law': farmers must be 'German citizens, of German or ethnically similar blood and honorable'; prohibition of division of inherited farms of between 7.5 and 125 hectares.
Oct. 4	'Law on Editors' regulates training for and entry into journalistic professions (with Aryan paragraph).
15	Hitler lays the foundation stone of the 'House of German Art' in Munich.
Nov. 12	Sham elections to the Reichstag: NSDAP unity list 92.2 per cent, invalid votes 7.8 per cent, turnout 95.2 per cent.

24	Law on preventive custody extends imprisonment to recidivists. 'Law for the Protection of Animals'.
Dec. 1	'Law to Secure the Unity of the Party and the State' seeks to limit the influence of the NSDAP in public administration.
14	'Benzine Agreement' between the Reich government and IG Farben.

1934

Jan. 20	'Law for the Regulation of National Labour' makes the Trustees [*Treuhänder*] Reich officials; 'works community' [*Betriebsgemeinschaft*] established, weighted in favour of the employer to the detriment of the DAF (19 sectoral Reich factory groups).
30	Law for the reconstruction of the Reich suspends the *Land* parliaments and jurisdiction of the *Länder*.
Mar./Apr.	In factory 'Council of Trust' elections approximately half the votes cast against the Nazi slate.
Apr. 20	Heinrich Himmler becomes Inspector of the Gestapo throughout the Reich; Reinhard Heydrich Leader of the *Gestapa* (22 Apr.).
24	Law to establish the People's Court of Law [*Volksgerichtshof*] for proceedings concerning treason against Germany [*Landesverrat*] and high treason [*Hochverrat*].
May. 1	Bernhard Rust becomes head of the new Reich Ministry for Science, Education and Adult Education.
11	Propaganda campaign 'against defeatists and fault-finders' also directed against the SA.
29–31	Barmen (first) Confessing Synod proclaims 'emergency regulations' against the Church leadership.
Jun. 17	Franz von Papen's Marburg speech (written by Edgar Jung) criticizes political circumstances from a right-wing conservative viewpoint.
Jun. 30–2 Jul.	SA leadership around Ernst Röhm murdered and deprived of political power, murder of conservative critics of the regime; Viktor Lutze new SA Chief of Staff. Hitler places all concentration camps under Himmler's control; SS becomes independent (20 July).
Jul. 3	Action against the SA leadership and conservatives legalized retrospectively as 'justified in the interests of state security'.
30	President of the Reichsbank, Hjalmar Schacht, also takes over the Ministry of Economics (from Kurt Schmitt).
Aug. 1	'Law on the Supreme Head of the German Reich' unites the office of Reich President and Reich Chancellor.
2	Death of Hindenburg. Hitler 'Führer and Reich Chancellor'; Reichswehr swears personal oath of allegiance to Hitler as new Commander in Chief.

10	Decree on allocation of labour restricts free choice of workplace.
Aug. 5–9 Sep.	Reich Party Congress 'Triumph of the Will' in Nuremberg. (Women's Congress 8 Sep.).
Sep. 24	Schacht presents the 'New Plan' to steer the economy by means of controls on foreign exchange and foreign trade.
30	Harvest festival on the Bückeberg: Hitler speaks to audience of 700,000 farmers and peasants.
Oct. 19–20	Dahlem (second) Synod of the Confessing Church protests against Reich Bishop Ludwig Müller (chosen by the National Synod of the 'German Christians' on 27 Sep.).
24	Hitler's decree on the 'Substance and Aims of the German Labour Front'.
Nov. 11–18	Second Reich Peasants' Congress in Goslar calls for a 'battle of production'.
27	Division of industry into six 'Reich Groups' of the 'Reich Chamber of Industry'.
30	Youth gymnastics and sports organizations [*Turn- und Sportjugend*] incorporated into the Hitler Youth.
Dec. 5	'Reich Law on Credit' makes the big banks subordinate to the President of the Reichsbank.

1935

Jan. 13	Saar plebiscite under the terms of the Treaty of Versailles: 90.9 per cent vote for reincorporation into the German Reich; emigration of anti-Nazis from the Saarland.
30	'Law Concerning the Reich Governors' and new local government regulations abolish municipal self-government and the sovereignty of the *Länder*.
Feb. 1	Henceforth powers of appointment and dismissal of Reich and *Land* officials from senior executive officer [*Regierungsrat*] level upwards reserved for Hitler.
15	Opening of the first annual Reich Vocational Contest.
26	Law on employees' record books to control the workforce and employment relationships.
Mar. 4–5	Synod of the Confessing Church agrees proclamation from the pulpit against Nazi race ideology and 'new heathenism'; 700 pastors arrested.
14	Hitler's edict makes Luftwaffe an independent branch of the Wehrmacht.
16	'Law on the Strengthening of the Armed Forces' heralds reintroduction of general conscription.
Apr. 1	*Land* judicial authorities taken over by Reich Ministry of Justice.
24	Official order by Reich Leader for the Press, Max Amann, makes concentration of the press possible.

25	Official order of the Reich Chamber of Literature concerning 'damaging and undesirable literature'.
25–30	International Film Congress in Berlin.
May 17–21	Wave of trials begins against members of monastic orders. Hitler's Reichstag speech on foreign policy emphasizes readiness for peace. New Defence Law. Secret 'Law for the Defence of the Reich' obliges industry to engage in armaments production; Schacht becomes 'Plenipotentiary-General for the Arms Industry'.
Jun. 26	Introduction of compulsory labour service in the Reich Labour Service under Konstantin Hierl.
Jul. 8	'Aryan Certificate' obligatory for students; for officers since 21 May, for soldiers from 25 July.
27	All Freikorps and war veterans' associations disbanded.
Aug. 17	Ban on all still existing Freemasons' lodges.
19	Catholic pastoral letter condemns state agitation against the Church and Christianity.
Sep. 10–16	NSDAP 'Reich Party Congress of Freedom': Reich Citizenship Law' and 'Law for the Protection of German Blood and Honour' (Nuremberg race laws).
24	Reich Church Minister Hanns Kerrl (since 16 July) assumes full legal powers over Protestant churches.
Oct. 6	Student Fraternity [Deutsche Burschenschaft] dissolved.
18	'Law to Protect the Genetic Health of the German Volk' and intensified propaganda against 'life unworthy of life'.
Nov. 3	Topping-out ceremony for Party buildings on the Königsplatz in Munich.
Dec. 13	Foundation of the SS Lebensborn to encourage 'suitable' women to bear large numbers of children.

1936

Feb. 6–16	IV Winter Olympics in Garmisch-Partenkirchen.
Mar. 7	Hitler denounces Locarno Pact, Wehrmacht occupies demilitarized Rhineland.
29	Reichstag 'election': plebiscite on Hitler's policies, 99 per cent yes vote.
Apr. 18	Volksgerichtshof becomes ordinary court and as the supreme penal court is made equal to the Reichsgericht.
24	'Castles of the Order' in Vogelsang, Crössinsee and Sonthofen formally opened for the training of Nazi cadres.
Jun. 17	Himmler's appointment as 'Reichsführer SS and Chief of the German Police in the Ministry of the Interior' unites Party and state office; head offices for the regular police [Ordnungspolizei] (Kurt Daluege) and Security Police (Heydrich).

Jul.	1	Child benefit for parents of moderate means but with many children.
Aug.		Sachsenhausen concentration camp established.
	1–16	XI Olympic Games in Berlin.
	24	Introduction of two-year military service.
Summer		'Fat crisis' as a result of foreign trade deficit and shortage of foreign exchange; since 4 Apr. 1936, Goering 'Commissioner for all Questions Concerning Foreign Exchange and Raw Materials', from 18 Oct. for the Four-Year Plan; rearmament.
Sep.	8–14	NSDAP 'Party Congress of Honour' proclaims the Four-Year Plan.
Oct.	29	'Law on the Four-Year Plan'; Goering demands wage freeze and industrial peace.
Nov.	23	Nobel Peace Prize for Carl von Ossietzky, imprisoned in concentration camp since 1933.
Dec.	1	Hitler Youth becomes the state youth organization.

1937

Jan.	15	Founding of the first 'Adolf Hitler Schools'.
	26	Law on the Civil Service requires special loyalty to the 'Führer' and the Reich.
	30	Reichstag extends Enabling Act for a further four years.
Feb.	10	Legislation to place the Reichsbank and the Reichsbahn (German Railways) under the control of the Reich government.
Mar.	9	Wave of arrests of 'habitual criminals' with previous convictions.
	14	Papal Encyclical 'With Burning Concern' condemns Nazi policy towards the Church; Gestapo seize copies from ecclesiastical printing works, priests arrested.
May	1	Provisional, and then on 1 May 1939 final, lifting of the ban on admission of new members to the NSDAP. Robert Ley proclaims the 'Production Contest of German Firms'.
Jun.	18	Dual membership of Hitler Youth and Catholic youth associations forbidden.
	26	Nazi Cultural Circle, the Office for 'Leisure Time' and the German Adult Education organization merge to form the Nazi leisure organization 'Strength through Joy' [*Kraft durch Freude*].
Jul.	15	Establishment of Buchenwald concentration camp (outside Weimar). Foundation of the 'Reich Works Hermann Goering' in Salzgitter (steel production).
	18	Festive procession and 'Great German Art Exhibition' in the new 'House of German Art' in Munich; 'Degenerate Art' exhibition.
Sep.	6–13	NSDAP 'Party Congress of Labour'.
Oct.	4	Legislative framework established for the reshaping of the cityscapes of Berlin, Munich, Stuttgart, Nuremberg and Hamburg.
Nov.	8	Goebbels opens 'The Eternal Jew' exhibition in Munich.

26 Schacht resigns (Walther Funk Reich Economics Minister from 4 Feb. 1938).

1938

Jan. 19	Establishment of the BDM organization 'Faith and Beauty' for girls and young women from 17 to 21 years of age.
Feb. 4	'Fritsch Crisis': dismissal of the War Minister Werner von Blomberg and the Commander-in-Chief of the Army Werner von Fritsch; Foreign Minister Konstantin von Neurath resigns (succeeded by Joachim von Ribbentrop); formation of the High Command of the Armed Forces [Oberkommando der Wehrmacht – OKW] under General Wilhelm Keitel; Commander-in-Chief of the Army General Walther von Brauchitsch.
15	Introduction of one-year compulsory Reich Labour Service for women.
Mar. 12–13	German troops march into Austria; Anschluss (annexation) law.
Apr. 10	Referendum and 'election' of the 'Greater German Reichstag' (over 99 per cent yes vote).
Apr.	Start of the systematic 'Aryanization' of Jewish businesses.
Apr. 30	Youth Protection Law, prohibition of child labour.
May 5	'Degenerate Music' exhibition in Düsseldorf.
31	Law for the confiscation without compensation of all 'degenerate art'.
May/Jun.	Establishment of concentration camps at Flossenbürg (Upper Palatinate) and Mauthausen (Lower Austria).
Jun.	Reich Labour Service and the 'Organisation Todt' commence construction of 630-kilometre long *Westwall* (Siegfried Line).
Jun. 13–18	Gestapo imprisons thousands of 'asocials' in concentration camps.
22	'Decree to Secure the Labour Required for Tasks of Special National Political Significance' makes possible the imposition of compulsory labour duties on every German as required.
Aug. 18	Chief of the Army General Staff Ludwig Beck submits his resignation (succeeded on 1 Nov. by General Franz Halder).
19	Pastoral letter of the Catholic Fulda Episcopal Conference against anti-Church agitation and trials of members of monastic orders.
Sep.	'Sudeten Crisis'. Senior officers around Beck plan Hitler's arrest.
Sep. 5–12	'Greater Germany Party Congress'.
29–30	Munich Conference agrees the transfer of the Sudeten region to Germany; German invasion of Czechoslovakia on 1 Oct.
Nov. 8–13	Mass pogroms ('Crystal Night' – *Reichskristallnacht*) against Jews.
Dec. 8	Himmler issues decree for the systematic registration and official identification of Gypsies.
16	'Cross of Honour of German Motherhood' awarded to mothers of more than seven children.

1939

Jan. 20	Reichsbank President Schacht dismissed.
Feb. 6	Gestapo dissolves Catholic Young Men's Association.
Mar. 14–16	German invasion of rest of Czechoslovakia, 'Reich Protectorate of Bohemia and Moravia'.
23	German invasion and reincorporation of the Memel Region.
25	All youths between 10 and 18 years obliged to serve in the Hitler Youth.
Apr. 3	Hitler orders preparation of a war of aggression against Poland.
May 15	Establishment of Ravensbrück concentration camp for women.
22	German-Italian Military Pact.
Aug. 23	German-Soviet Non-Aggression Pact.
26	'Party Congress of Peace' cancelled.
27	Rationing of food with coupons and later also of consumer goods.
Sep. 1	German attack on Poland without declaration of war; beginning of the Second World War.
3	Britain and France declare war on the German Reich. Secret decree by Heydrich on 'internal security during the war': Gestapo may execute dissidents and saboteurs without sentence of a court.
4–5	Strict punishments decreed for crimes against the war economy and criminality during wartime.
27	Unification of the Security Police (Gestapo and Criminal Police) with the Security Service (SD) of the SS makes the Reich Security Head Office the headquarters for all measures of repression and terror.
Oct.	Hitler gives written authorization (backdated to 1 Sep.) for the beginning of the 'euthanasia campaign'.
Oct. 8–12	Incorporation of the western regions of Poland into the Reich, establishment of the *Generalgouvernement* under Hans Frank.
14	Introduction of ration cards for clothing.
Nov. 8	Georg Elser fails in his attempt to assassinate Hitler in Munich.

1940

Feb. 11	German-Soviet Economic Treaty secures oil, precious metals and grain supplies for Germany.
Mar. 17	Fritz Todt becomes Reich Minister for Armaments and Munitions; development of a new armaments organization in close understanding with industry.
May 10	Beginning of the German western offensive.
Jun. 22	Franco-German armistice.
Autumn	Establishment of numerous Jewish ghettos in eastern Europe.

Dec. 18   Hitler's directive no. 21: preparation of the invasion of the Soviet
                   Union.

1941

Mar. 17–30.   Hitler speaks to senior officers: the impending Russian cam-
                   paign is to be fought as a 'war of annihilation'.

26   Foundation of the 'Institute for Research of the Jewish Question'
                   in Alfred Rosenberg's 'Higher School' in Frankfurt-am-Main.

Apr. 6   German invasion of Yugoslavia and Greece.

21   'Reich Coal Consortium' to coordinate mining and coal trade
                   because of bottlenecks in supply.

May 10   Rudolf Hess' flight to Scotland; Martin Bormann becomes 'Head
                   of the Party Chancellery'.

Spring   'General Plan East' developed to resettle indigenous population
                   and 'Germanize' the occupied territories, signed by Himmler on
                   12 June 1942.

Jun. 6   *Kommissarbefehl* ('Commissar Order') of the OKW: Soviet
                   functionaries are to be 'liquidated'.

22   German invasion of the Soviet Union. SS *Einsatzgruppen* (special
                   action groups) murder Communists, Jews and Gypsies.

Jul. 14   Shift of emphasis in arms production from the Army to the
                   Luftwaffe and Navy. Rosenberg 'Reich Minister for the Occupied
                   Eastern Territories'.

28   Bishop Clemens Graf von Galen protests in Munich against
                   euthanasia.

Sep. 1   Jews in Germany (from six years of age) must wear yellow star,
                   from 1 Oct. ban on emigration.

Oct. 2–   Battle of Moscow: Soviet counter-offensive reveals failure of
     5 Dec.   *Blitzkrieg* campaign.

14   Order to deport German Jews to ghettos in eastern Europe.

Dec. 11   Hitler declares war on the USA.

16   Hitler dismisses General von Brauchitsch and himself assumes
                   supreme command of the Army.

Dec./Jan.   Adjustments in the war economy to increase production.

1942

Jan. 20   Wannsee Conference to coordinate measures for the 'Final
                   Solution of the Jewish Question'.

Feb. 8   Albert Speer becomes Reich Minister for Armaments and
                   Munitions.

End of Mar.   First transportations of Jews from western Europe and the
                   territory of the Reich to Auschwitz.

Mar. 21	Fritz Sauckel Plenipotentiary-General for Deployment of Labour; by summer 1944 approximately 7.6 million 'foreign workers' in Germany.
Apr. 26	Hitler 'Supreme High Justice'.
May 17	'Law to Protect Mothers-to-be and Nursing Mothers'.
Jun.	Beginning of mass gassings of Jews in Auschwitz-Birkenau.
Aug. 20	Roland Freisler President of the Volksgerichtshof; his predecessor Otto Georg Thierack becomes Reich Minister of Justice.
Autumn	Gestapo smashes the 'Red Orchestra' resistance organization; approximately 100 executions.
Nov. 22	German Sixth Army surrounded at Stalingrad.

1943

Jan. 13	Secret decree by the 'Führer' on the comprehensive deployment of men and women in the defence of the Reich.
Jan. 31– 2 Feb.	Sixth Army surrenders in Stalingrad.
Jan./Feb.	Schoolchildren and women obliged to perform duties as 'Luftwaffe auxiliaries'.
Feb. 4	Closure of all businesses not vital to the war effort in the retail, craft and hotel and catering sectors.
18	Goebbels at the Berlin Sportpalast: 'Do you want total war?' White Rose student resistance group smashed.
Apr. 19	Warsaw Ghetto uprising; finally suppressed on 16 May.
25–26	'Munich (Catholic) Lay Letter' condemns the extermination of German Jewry.
Jun. 26	Speer controls all arms production (except the Luftwaffe).
Aug. 19	Pastoral letter of the Catholic Episcopate against the killing of innocent life ('euthanasia').
24	Himmler becomes Reich Minister of the Interior.
Sep. 2	Speer, now 'Reich Minister for Armaments and War Production', pursues the concentration of the war economy.
Oct. 16–17	Confessing Synod of the Protestant Church of the Old Prussian Union condemns the killing of people on grounds of age, illness or race.
Dec. 22	Nazi Operations Command formed in the OKW to strengthen the influence of the Party and ideological indoctrination.

1944

| Jun. 6 | Allied invasion of Normandy. |
| 22 | Soviet grand offensive against the German Central Army Group. |

Jul.		Communist resistance organizations in Berlin, Leipzig and Thuringia smashed.
Jul.	20	Attempt to assassinate Hitler by the resistance group around Claus Graf Schenk von Stauffenberg fails.
	24	Maidanek death camp liberated by the Soviet Army.
	25	Goebbels 'Reich Plenipotentiary for the Total War Effort'. Himmler Commander-in-Chief of the army reserve.
Aug.		Climax of the Allied aerial bombing campaign.
Aug.	24	Freeze on holidays and 60-hour week as measures of the total war effort.
Sep.		German V2 rockets launched against London and Antwerp.
Sep.	25	Call-up of all men between 16 and 60 years into the German 'Volkssturm' (Home Guard).
Oct.	21	Aachen the first large German city to be occupied by the Americans.
Nov.	1	Himmler orders the end of gassings in Auschwitz.
Dec.	16	German Ardennes offensive ('Battle of the Bulge').

1945

Jan.	27	Auschwitz liberated by Soviet troops.
	30	Hitler's last broadcast radio speech. Première of the 'hold out to the last' film *Kolberg* in Berlin and in the Atlantic stronghold of La Rochelle.
Feb.	15	Courts-martial in those 'parts of the Reich threatened by the enemy' are to use death sentences to ensure the will to fight.
Mar.	19	Hitler's 'Nero Order' (not carried out).
Apr.	13–16	Red Army in Vienna; major assault on Berlin.
Apr./May		Numerous local and regional resistance organizations against final defensive actions and destruction; often put down by the SS and the *Werwolf.*
Apr.	30	Hitler commits suicide. Grand Admiral Karl Dönitz succeeds him as Head of State.
May	7–9	Surrender of the German Wehrmacht in the American Head-quarters in Reims; repeated in the Soviet HQ in Berlin.
Jun.	5	Berlin Declaration of the four Allied military commanders; assumption of supreme governmental authority in Germany.

Appendix 2:   Organization and Leadership of the NSDAP (November 1936)

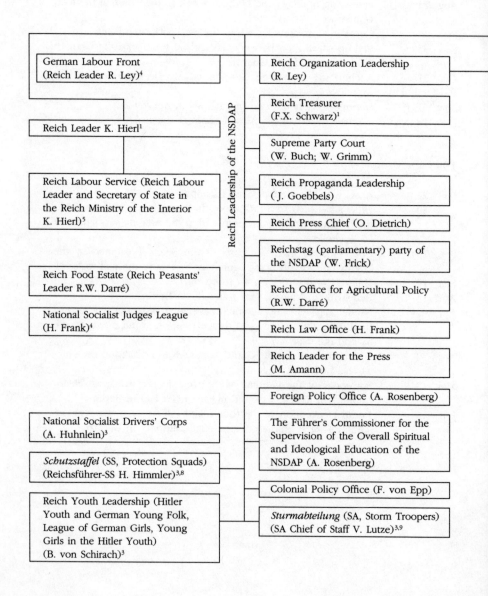

German Labour Front
(Reich Leader R. Ley)[4]

Reich Leader K. Hierl[1]

Reich Labour Service (Reich Labour
Leader and Secretary of State in
the Reich Ministry of the Interior
K. Hierl)[5]

Reich Food Estate (Reich Peasants'
Leader R.W. Darré)

National Socialist Judges League
(H. Frank)[4]

National Socialist Drivers' Corps
(A. Huhnlein)[3]

Schutzstaffel (SS, Protection Squads)
(Reichsführer-SS H. Himmler)[3,8]

Reich Youth Leadership (Hitler
Youth and German Young Folk,
League of German Girls, Young
Girls in the Hitler Youth)
(B. von Schirach)[3]

Reich Leadership of the NSDAP

Reich Organization Leadership
(R. Ley)

Reich Treasurer
(F.X. Schwarz)[1]

Supreme Party Court
(W. Buch; W. Grimm)

Reich Propaganda Leadership
(J. Goebbels)

Reich Press Chief (O. Dietrich)

Reichstag (parliamentary) party of
the NSDAP (W. Frick)

Reich Office for Agricultural Policy
(R.W. Darré)

Reich Law Office (H. Frank)

Reich Leader for the Press
(M. Amann)

Foreign Policy Office (A. Rosenberg)

The Führer's Commissioner for the
Supervision of the Overall Spiritual
and Ideological Education of the
NSDAP (A. Rosenberg)

Colonial Policy Office (F. von Epp)

Sturmabteilung (SA, Storm Troopers)
(SA Chief of Staff V. Lutze)[3,9]

Führer of the NSDAP,[6] and Supreme SA-Führer
(A. Hitler)[7]

Chancellery of the Führer
(Reich Leader P. Bouhler)

Organization Head Office

Personnel Head Office

Training Head Office

National Socialist Factory Cell

Organization Head Office

Head Office for Craft and Commerce

Head Office for Municipal Policy
(Reich Leader K. Fiehler)[1,9]

Head Office for Civil Servants (H. Neef)[9]

Head Office for Educators

Head Office for War Victims
(H. Oberlindober)[9]

Head Office for Public Health
(G. Wagner)[9]

Head Office for Public Welfare
(E. Hilgenfeldt)[9]

Office for Technology (F. Todt)[9]

National Socialist Women's League
(Head Office Leader E. Hilgenfeldt; Reich
Women's Leader G. Scholtz-Klink)[3,9]

National Socialist Students' League
(Reich Students' Leader G.A. Scheel)[3,9]

National Socialist Lecturers' League (Office
Leader W. Schultze)[3,9]

Deputy of the Führer
(R. Hess)[2]

Chief of Staff
(Reich Leader M. Bormann)[1]

Department of Party Affairs

Department of Affairs of State

German Municipal Congress
(Chair K. Fiehler)

Reich League of German Civil
Servants reg. assoc. (Leader H.
Neef)[4]

National Socialist Teachers' League
reg. assoc. (F. Waechtler)[4]

National Socialist War Victims
Support Organization reg. assoc.
(Reich War Victims Leader H.
Oberlindober)[4]

National Socialist German
Physicians' League (Reich
Physicians' Leader G. Wagner)[4]

National Socialist Public Welfare
Organization reg. assoc
(E. Hilgenfeldt)[4]

National Socialist German Technical
League (Inspector-General F. Todt)[4]

notes overleaf

Notes to Appendix 2

1 The so-called Reich Leadership (or Directorate) of the NSDAP was in no sense a collective body. It was comprised of individual Reich Leaders (the Corps Leader of the National Socialist Drivers' Corps did not bear this title), each of whom was directly and solely responsible to the 'Führer'. Due to the special status of their official positions, the Reich Leaders Bouhler, Hierl, Bormann and Fiehler were not, strictly speaking, members of the Reich Leadership.

2 The 'Führer's Deputy' was not counted as one of the Reich Leaders and had, effectively, a parallel position alongside them. This led to conflicts of competencies, especially with the Reich Organization Leader.

3 Subsidiary organizations of the NSDAP without their own legal corporate entity or property.

4 Associations of the NSDAP.

5 The Reich Labour Service did not belong to the NSDAP; it was under the control of the Reich Minister of the Interior, and the Reich Labour Leader exercised authority of command.

6 The NSDAP was divided vertically into 32 regions (*Gaue*), and then further in districts (*Kreise*), local branches (*Ortsgruppen*), cells and blocks. At the various levels the organization of the leadership corresponded largely to that of the Reich Leadership. They were subordinate in matters of policy and discipline to the Führer of the Party, and in technical matters to the departments of the Reich Leadership and the 'Führer's Deputy' respectively.

7 The SA was divided into 21 Groups as well as Brigades, *Standarten*, *Sturmbanne*, *Stürme*, *Trupps* and *Scharen*.

8 The SS was divided into 12 *Oberabschnitte*, 31 *Abschnitte*, as well as *Standarten*, *Sturmbanne*, *Stürme*, *Trupps* and *Scharen*. The first three of these subdivisions can be loosely translated as the equivalents of army corps, divisions and regiments, the *Sturmbann* was the equivalent of a battalion (so a *Sturmbannführer* was of similar rank to a major), the *Sturm* of an army company; a *Trupp* had approximately 40 men and a *Schar* about 12.

9 In 'matters of administration, technical personnel issues, organization and discipline' under the authority of the Reich Organization Leader, 'politically' under that of the 'Führer's Deputy'.

Source: Martin Broszat and Norbert Frei (eds), *Ploetz Das Dritte Reich. Ursprünge, Ereignisse, Wirkungen* (Freiburg/Würzburg, 1983), pp. 48f. (Designed by Albrecht Tyrell.)

Abbreviations and glossary of German terms and names used in the text, with translator's notes on terminology

ADGB	Allgemeiner Deutscher Gewerkschaftsbund (General Federation of German Trade Unions)
Ahnenerbe e.V.	'Foundation for the Heritage of our Forefathers' – the SS research foundation established in 1936
Aktion T4	Code name for the 'euthanasia' programme, derived from the address of an office at Tiergartenstrasse 4, Berlin
Alter Kämpfer	'Old Fighter' – a term used by the Nazis for those who had joined the Party or the SA before 30 January 1933, as opposed to those who joined after, who were often viewed as opportunists
Alt-Pgs	*Alt-Parteigenossen* (Old 'party Comrades'), the same meaning as *Alte Kämpfer*, 'Old Fighters'
Der Angriff	Goebbels' Nazi Party newspaper in Berlin, founded 1927
(Reichs)Arbeitsdienst	(Reich) Labour Service
BAK	Bundesarchiv Koblenz
BDM	Bund Deutscher Mädel (League of German Girls – Hitler Youth girls' organization)
Beamten	Civil and public servants (includes not only government officials but also, for example, teachers)
Betriebsführer	'Works (or factory) leader' of the *Betriebsgemeinschaft* (see below), i.e. the employer
Betriebsgemeinschaft	'Works (or factory) community' – Nazi concept of a corporatist, conflict-free workplace; in fact, the *Betriebsführer*, in accordance with the 'Führer principle', enjoyed even greater power over the workforce

Betriebsrat	Works council, replaced by the Nazis with the *Vertrauensrat* (see below)
Blut und Boden	'Blood and Soil' – a key tenet of Nazi ideology and propaganda
Bonzen	'Big-shots' or 'big-wigs' – a term of contempt for those with political and/or economic power, implying the corrupt nature of their rule
Buna	Synthetic rubber
BVP	Bayerische Volkspartei (Bavarian People's Party) – closely linked to the Centre Party (see below)
Centre Party	The main Catholic party outside Bavaria during the Weimar Republic
DAF	Deutsche Arbeitsfront (German Labour Front)
DDP	Deutsche Demokratische Partei (German Democratic Party)
Deutsches Zentralarchiv	German Central Archive, Potsdam, formerly the central state archive of the German Democratic Republic, now being amalgamated with the Bundesarchiv (see BAK above)
Deutschland-Berichte der Sopade	'Reports an Germany of the Sopade' (see below), 1934–1940 (7 vols, Frankfurt am Main, 1980), collated from clandestine reports furnished by Social Democrats throughout the Reich
DHI	Deutscher Industrie- und Handelstag (German Council of Industry and Commerce)
DNB	Deutsches Nachrichten-Büro (Nazi-controlled German News Agency)
DNVP	Deutschnationale Volkspartei (German National People's Party)
DSP	Deutsche Staatspartei (German State Party)
DVP	Deutsche Volkspartei (German People's Party)
(SS) *Einsatzgruppen*	'Action Groups' – mobile terror squads of the Security Police and the Security Service (SD), operating behind the lines and murdering Jews, Gypsies, the mentally ill and others considered 'undesirable'
Einsatzkommando	A special detachment of an *Einsatzgruppe*
Eisernes Sparen	Compulsory savings scheme during the war
Freikorps	Right-wing volunteer paramilitary units, formed after the November Revolution in 1918
'Führer'	Leader – Hitler's self-assumed title as head of the Nazi movement and later of the state ('Führer and Reich Chancellor'). [The author has invariably employed inverted commas when using the term; I have maintained this in the English translation.]
Gau	Administrative region of the Nazi Party organization
Gauleiter	Head(s) of Nazi Party regional administration

Gauleitung	Regional headquarters/leadership of the Nazi Party
Gefolgschaft	Literally the 'retinue' of the *Betriebsführer* (i.e. the workforce)
Gemeinschaftsempfang	'Collective (or communal) reception' of radio broadcasts by means of loudspeakers; often an obligatory part of working life and activity in the mass organizations
Generalgouvernement	The area of Poland not incorporated into the Reich, but under direct German rule
Gestapa	*Geheimes Staatspolizeiamt* (Head Office of the Secret State Police)
Gestapo	Geheime Staatspolizei (Secret State Police)
Gleichschaltung	Nazi term for 'coordination' or, more exactly, 'bringing into step' (i.e. nazification) of state and society after January 1933
Gruppenführer (SS)	Equivalent to major-general in the British Army
Hauptsturmführer (SS)	Equivalent to captain in the British Army
Heimatfilm	(Sentimental) film with a regional background
Historikerstreit	The recent and significant 'historians' dispute' about the uniqueness of the Holocaust and the place of Nazism in German history
HJ	Hitlerjugend (Hitler Youth)
Hochverrat	High treason against the political system (see also *Landesverrat*)
IfZ	Institut für Zeitgeschichte (Institute of Contemporary History, Munich)
IG Farben	Interessengemeinschaft der deutschen Farben-Industrie (Union of Interests of the German Dye Industry) – German chemical cartel
Jungvolk	Junior division of the Hitler Youth, for boys aged 10–14
Kampfzeit	The 'period of struggle' before the Nazis assumed power in 1933
KdF	Kraft durch Freude ('Strength through Joy'), leisure organization of the DAF)
Kommissarbefehl	'Commissar Order' – order to execute all Soviet functionaries captured during the invasion of the Soviet Union, rather than recognizing them as prisoners of war
KPD	Kommunistische Partei Deutschlands (German Communist Party)
Kreisleiter	NSDAP District Leader
Land (pl. *Länder*)	German province or state with its own government – there were 15 in the Weimar Reublic; after 1933 they were controlled by the central government through the Reich Governors

Landesverrat	Treason against the country (i.e. Germany)
Landtag	*Land* parliament
Lebensborn	Literally 'Fount of Life' – SS foundation to promote the breeding of 'valuable racial stock' by providing superior maternity care for 'suitable mothers'
Lebensraum	The key Nazi notion of 'living space', deemed necessary for Germany
Luftwaffe	The Air Force
Marxisten	Nazi term for Social Democrats as well as Communists
Meldungen aus dem Reich	'Reports from the Reich': monthly reports collated by the SD for the Nazi leadership
Mittelstand	Literally the 'middle estate', the (traditionally independent) lower middle class or *petite bourgeoisie*
Nationalsozialistische Kulturgemeinde	Nazi Community of Culture – mass organization with theatre, art, book and lecture rings; attached to KdF from 1937
Nazi	National Socialist
Neuer Vorwärts	The Sopade (see below) paper, first published in Prague in June 1933
November Republic	Denunciatory Nazi term for the Weimar Republic, established after the November Revolution of 1918, more usually described by them as the 'Republic of the November Criminals'
NSBO	Nationalsozialistische Betriebszellen-Organisation (National Socialist Factory Cell Organization)
NSDAP	Nationalsozialistische Deutsche Arbeiterpartei (National Socialist German Workers' Party – the Nazi Party)
NSF	Nationalsozialistische Frauenschaft (Nazi Women's League)
NS-Hago	Nationalsozialistische Handwerks-, Handels- und Gewerbeorganisation (National Socialist Craft, Trade and Commerce Organization)
NSV	Nationalsozialistische Volkswohlfahrt (Nazi People's Welfare Organization)
Oberabschnittsführer (SS)	The SS leader of an *Oberabschnitt* – the main territorial division of the SS which was similar to a *Wehrkreis* (see below)
Obergruppenführer (SS)	Equivalent to a lieutenant-general in the British Army
Obersturmführer (SS)	Equivalent to a first lieutenant in the British Army
OKW	Oberkommando der Wehrmacht (Armed Forces High Command)
Ordensburgen	'Castles of the Order' – institutions established to train Party functionaries
Organisation Todt	Semi-military organization under Fritz Todt, formed in 1938 as a 'joint venture' of private firms and the state

	to handle heavy construction projects, mostly for military purposes
Ortsgruppenleiter	NSDAP local (ward) leader
Pg	*Parteigenosse* (Nazi 'Party Comrade')
PO	Partei-Organisation (NSDAP Party Organization)
RDI	Reichsverband der Deutschen Industrie (Reich Confederation of German Industry)
Reichsbanner	Reichsbanner Schwarz-Rot-Gold – paramilitary organization established by the SPD, Centre and Democratic Parties in 1924 to defend the Weimar Republic
Reichsbauernführer	Reich Peasants' Leader (Richard Walter Darré)
Reichsbeauftragter	Reich Commissioner
Reichsdeutsche	German citizen of the Reich (see also *Volksdeutsche*)
Reichsführer-gemeinschaft	'Community of Reich Leaders'
Reichsführer-SS	Reich Leader of the SS; Himmler's title as head of the SS
Reichsgericht	State Supreme Court situated in Leipzig
Reichskristallnacht	'Reich Crystal Night' – the nationwide pogrom against the Jews of 9–10 November 1938
Reichsleiter	Reich Leader – official appointed for special duties in the Reichsleitung der NSDAP, directly and solely responsible to the 'Führer'
Reichsleitung der NSDAP	Reich Leadership (or Directorate) of the NSDAP
Reichsnährstand	Reich Food Estate
Reichsorganisationsleiter	Reich Organization Leader of the NSDAP
Reichsstand	'Reich Estate' – compulsory state cartels
Reichsstand der Deutschen Industrie	Reich Estate of German Industry
Reichsstatthalter	The Reich Governor of a German state
Reichstreuhänder der Arbeit	Reich 'Trustees of Labour'
Reichstag	German Parliament
Reichsvereinigung	Reichsvereinigung der Juden in Deutschland – Reich Union of Jews in Germany
Reichswehr	The armed forces under the Weimar Republic
RGBl	*Reichsgesetzblatt* (Reich Law Gazette)
RSHA	Reichssicherheitshauptamt (Reich Security Head Office)
SA	Sturmabteilung (Nazi Storm Troop, paramilitary organization, also known as Brownshirts)
Schiesserlass	'Shooting Decree' issued by Goering on 17 February 1933, in his capacity as Prussian Interior Minister; directed police 'if necessary' to use fire-arms against enemies of the state, without regard for the consequences

Schutzhaft	Literally 'protective custody' – in the Third Reich a euphemism for summary arrest and imprisonment, often in a concentration camp
SD	Sicherheitsdienst (Security Service)
Sondergericht(e)	'Special Courts(s)' – established by decree 21 March 1933, specifically to prosecute political crimes with simplified and 'streamlined' procedures
Sopade	Sozialdemokratische Partei Deutschlands (im Exil) – exiled SPD executive based in Prague from 1933–8, Paris 1938–9 and London from 1940
SPD	Sozialdemokratische Partei Deutschlands (German Social Democratic Party)
SS	Schutzstaffeln der NSDAP ('Protection Squads') – police and security organization headed by Himmler. Included the armed Waffen-SS and the general Allgemeine-SS, which provided the staff and guards of the concentration camps.
Stahlhelm	(Bund der Frontsoldaten) conservative-nationalist army veterans' organization (1918–35)
Stand	Estate (class), as in *Mittelstand* or *Reichsstand* (see above)
Standartenführer (SS)	Equivalent to a colonel in the British Army
Stürmer	Infamous, obscene and rabidly anti-Semitic paper published by Julius Streicher
Systempolitiker	Disparaging Nazi term for the politicians of the Weimar Republic
Systemzeit	Disparaging Nazi term for the Weimar Republic
Ufa	Universum-Film AG, pre-eminent German film company
Untersturmführer (SS)	Equivalent to second lieutenant in the British Army
Vertrauensräte	Literally 'Councils of Trust' – part of the Nazi strategy for industrial relations; replaced the 'works councils'
VfZ	*Vierteljahrshefte für Zeitgeschichte*
völkisch	Racist-nationalist
Völkischer Beobachter	The main official Nazi daily newspaper
Das Volk	Can be used in a relatively neutral sense to mean simply 'the people' or in the racist-nationalist sense as by the Nazis. Where the context implies the latter I have retained the German word.
Volksdeutsche	'Ethnic Germans' who were not citizens of the Reich, for example those in Romania or the Soviet Union
Volksempfänger	Literally 'People's Receiver' – cheap radio sets
Volksgemeinschaft	'National Community' – Nazi social concept implying a racially 'pure' society free of class conflict and division. There is no ideal English translation – 'Folk Community' and 'Racial Community' do not convey the purportedly

	harmonious and corporatist nature of class relations, while 'People's Community' omits the key racist-nationalist element
Volksgenosse	'National comrade' – a member of the 'national community', a Nazi term for ordinary citizens
Volksgerichtshof	'People's Court of Law' – established in 1934 to try cases of treason and high treason (*Landesverrat* and *Hochverrat*)
Volkskörper	Literally 'the body of the German *Volk'* – most commonly translated as 'body-politic', though admittedly this does not adequately convey the sense in which the Jews, for example, were deemed by the Nazis to be 'parasites' or 'vermin' damaging the said 'body'
Volkssturm	Home Guard, established towards the end of the war as Germany's last defence, mainly boys and old men
Vorwärts	The main SPD party newspaper
Wehrkreis	Defence District – the main military territorial division in Germany
Wehrmacht	German Armed Forces; the term replaced 'Reichswehr' in 1935
Werwolf	Guerilla force, established at the end of the war and intended as a resistance movement against Allied occupation
WHW	Winterhilfswerk (Winter Aid Scheme)
Zähmungskonzept	The notion of the German nationalist bourgeoisie that Hitler could be 'tamed' and kept under control

Index

academic freedom *see* universities

ADGB *see* General Federation of German Trade Unions

'Adolf Hitler Donation of German Industry', 55

'Adolf-Hitler Schools', 87–8

AEG, 50

Agricultural Policy Unit (of NSDAP), 56–7

agriculture: auxiliary labour scheme (*Landhilfe*), 5–6; 'battle for production', 74, 76, 77; bureaucratization of, 77; 'business group' for, 76; central purchasing points, 5; Christian farmers' unions, 57; food production, 164; foreign forced labour in, 77; labour shortage in, 77; Nazi policies, 5, 49, 77, 161; Political Police surveillance of, 103; pricing policy in, 77; youth labour in, 86

'Ahnenerbe e.V' *see* 'Foundation for the Heritage of our Forefathers inc.'

'Aid Organization Mother and Child', 119

'Aktion Reinhard', 134

Albers, Hans, 93

Allianz insurance co., 55

Allies: advance of, 147, 196–8, 200, 202; demand unconditional surrender, 143; disbelief in Holocaust, 136; Himmler attempts contact with western, 142; plans for post-war Germany, 142; *see also* bombing; Great Britain; Soviet Union; USA

Alter Kämpfer see 'Old Fighters'

Amann, Max, 64, 167, 168

Amtswalter, 90

Angestellte see white-collar employees

Angriff, 118

anti-Bolshevism, 129; as catalyst for mass murder, 134

anti-Semitism, 43; and boycotts, 46, 130; central to Nazi leadership, 109, 129; as diversion from other Nazi policy, 160; expressed by Hess, 166; in films 93, 211 n. 28; importance for Hitler, 129; limited role in Nazi rise to power, 48; in Nazi ideology, 129; and negative integration, 129; within NSDAP, 47, 129; popular, 49, 160–1; and aim of 'racial purity', 123; racist variety, 48; rejection of modernist art, 96; rejection of radical, 109; in science, 98; *see also* Jewish Question; Jews; Jews, genocide of

appeasement, 110; *see also* Munich Agreement

Arbeiterjugend, 86

Arbeitsschlacht see 'Battle for Jobs'

architecture, 95–6

Archiv für Rassen- und Gesellschaftsbiologie, 122

Argentina, 191

armaments and munitions, production of, 112, 141; and 'Central Planning', 141; and employers, 141; expenditure on,

112; foreign workers in, 139; Goering loses influence over, 137; lay-offs in, 198; Ministry of, 137; policy, 141; Speer becomes minister for, 137; Todt first minister of, 137; women in, 114; workers, 199, 200

Armed Forces, 32, 113, 196, 197, 199, 200, 203; Ministry of the, 32; see also Luftwaffe; Reichswehr; war; Wehrmacht

arts, fine, 62, 63, 64, 65, 91, 95; censorship of, 65; 'degenerate art' exhibition, 96; emigration of Jewish and leftist artists, 91; 'Great German Art Exhibition', 96; House of German Art, 96, 169; modernist painting, 96; remaining free space in, 151

'Aryan paragraphs', 48, 64, 66

'Aryanization' of Jewish businesses, 132

'asocials', 104, 118; 'euthanasia' of, 187; custody proposed for, 182; mass arrests of, 104–5

assumption of power, 132, 183; see also 'seizure of power'

Auschwitz death camp, 129; establishment of, 127; experiments in, 128, 176; 'extermination through work', 128; first gassings with Zyklon B, 134; Gypsies in, 128; murder of ill prisoners, 128; 'selection' on arrival, 128; synthetic rubber production, 128; see also Birkenau; Monowitz

Austria: Anschluss of, 104, 110; deportations from, 133; Political Police surveillance of, 103

autarky, 5, 7, 55, 74, 75, 76, 98, 112, 123, 163

Babi Yar, massacre at, 134

Backe, Herbert, 6,

Bad Godesberg, 20, 22, 169

Bad Wiessee, 19, 22

Baden, 40

Baeck, Leo, 132

Baltic states: occupation policy in, 125–6; foreign workers from, 178

Bamberg, 120

'Battle for Jobs', 5, 73

'Battle of the Bulge', 142

Baumann, Hans, 192

Bavaria, 38, 40–2; reports of Rural District Offices, 24

Bavarian Ministry of Interior, decree on 'euthanasia by starvation', 121

Bavarian People's Party (BVP), 40, 44, 60, 65, 68

Bavarian Political Police, 20, 60

Beamten, 48, see also civil and public servants

Beckmann, Max, 96

Belgium, 115, 133

Belzec death camp, 127; and 'Aktion Reinhard', 134

'benzine contract' (1933), 75, 76

Berchtesgaden, 24

Bergengruen, Werner, 94

Berger, Gottlob, 178

Bergner, Elisabeth, 93

Berlin, 18, 21, 22, 23, 35, 52, 62, 64, 71, 83, 84, 96, 97, 100, 101, 144, 145, 166, 167, 187, 189

Berufsverbote, 65; for Jews, 131

Best, Werner, 103

Bethel Institute, 66

'Betriebsführer' see 'factory leader'; see also 'works community'

Beveridge, William, 117

big business, 4, 32, 49–50, 56; and armaments, 141; disapproval of economically damaging 'racial criteria', 131; and Nazi economic policy, 74, 76; Nazi policy aims to stabilize hegemony of, 160; and 'Sauckel campaigns', 139; and scientific research, 98; and Speer, 140; and state administration, 76

'big-shot economy', 6

'big-shots', 'big-wigs', 9, 82, 90, 202; see also Bonzen

Birgel, Willy, 93

Birkenau death camp, 127; see also Auschwitz; Monowitz

Bismarck, Otto Prince von, 41, 58

Blick in die Zeit, 160

Blitzkrieg, 112, 114, 115, 117, 138

Blomberg, Werner von, 19, 24, 25, 32, 110, 168

'blood and soil' see 'Blut und Boden'

Blücher, Gebhard Leberecht Prince, 168

'*Blut und Boden*', 5, 56, 57, 76, 96
Bodelschwingh, Friedrich von, 66
Bogensee, 169
Bohemia, 135
Bohemia and Moravia, Reich Protectorate
　　of: deportations from, 133;
　　establishment of, 110; Frick
　　'reshuffled' to, 137; resettlement
　　policy in, 126
Bolsheviks; Bolshevism, 8, 142, 162, 164,
　　166
bombing, 71, 97, 113, 116, 138, 141, 142,
　　145, 147, 181, 196–7, 198, 199, 203;
　　post war consequences of, 153
Bonatz, Paul, 97
Bonzen, 5, 11; *see also* 'big shots'
book burnings, 62, 63
Border Secretaries (*Grenzsekretäre*) of the
　　Sopade, 100
Bormann, Martin, 7, 11, 67, 137, 148, 167,
　　195
Bosch, Carl, 98
Bose, Herbert von, 16, 21, 25
Bouhler, Philipp, 120
bourgeoisie, 16, 62; attacks on, 43;
　　attitudes towards Nazi assumption of
　　power, 37; attitudes towards regime,
　　8, 27, 34, 157, 162; and bombing,
　　199; cultural values of, 95; in defeat,
　　196; political parties of, 57; support
　　for Hitler, 32
Brack, Viktor, 190
Braddock, James, 169
Brandenburg, 5
Brandt, Karl, 120
Brauchitsch, Walther von, 110
Brecht, Bertolt, 95
Bredow, Ferdinand von, 21
Bremen, 40
Breslau, 26
broadcasting, 63, 64; Political Police
　　control of, 103; *see also* radio; media
Brüning, Heinrich, planned policies
　　implemented by Nazis, 160
Brunswick, 159
Buchenwald concentration camp, 101,
　　104, 187, 188
Bückeberg (Westphalia), 84
Buna, 76; production by IG Farben in
　　Monowitz, 127, 128

Bündische Jugend, 85
bureaucracy, 32, 35, 42, 48; and big
　　business, 76; disputes with Gestapo
　　and SS, 25; economic, 75
BVP *see* Bavarian People's Party

cabinet, 23–4, 31–2, 33, 35, 36, 46, 50,
　　51, 60, 68, 74, 113
Campanella, Thomas, 103
Canaris, Wilhelm, 144
Caracciola, Rudolf, 96
'Castles of the Order', 87–8, 97, 170
Catholic Action, 21
Catholic Church *see* Church
censorship, 34, 35, 69, 95, 159; of film
　　scripts, 93; *see also* press
'Central Planning', 141
Centre Party (Zentrum), 33, 34, 38, 57, 60,
　　65, 157; action against, 37, 59; and
　　Enabling Act, 44–6, 202 n. 26;
　　dissolution of, 68
Cham, 5
Chambers of Agriculture, 57
Chelmno death camp, 127
chemical industry, 76
Chemnitz, 203
children: abduction of, 127; 'euthanasia'
　　of, 190–1; Jewish refugees, 133; and
　　defeat, 197; murdered at Babi Yar,
　　134; *see also* education; Hitler Youth;
　　youth
Church, 45; attitudes towards Nazism, 8,
　　85; and coup against SA, 25; criticism
　　of 'new heathenism', 85; limited
　　influence of regime on, 151;
　　members in defeat, 196; and *Napolas*,
　　176–7; Nazi policy towards, 65, 171;
　　Political Police surveillance of, 103;
　　priests in resistance, 144; 'Struggle',
　　67; schools, 87; teacher training
　　institutions, 87; Catholic, 59: bishops,
　　65–6; Koblenz trials, 168, 170;
　　political Catholicism 60, 65;
　　prohibitions against Nazi movement
　　(pre-1933), 65; resistance, 195;
　　resistance to abolition of religious
　　schools, 87; social provision, 65; and
　　national community, 65; and natural
　　sciences, 163; NSDAP compared
　　with, 163; youth associations, 85,

86; Protestant (evangelical):
Gleichschaltung of, 67; Nazi policy
towards, 66; Protestant support for
Nazis, 66, 68; relationship with Nazi
regime, 67; resistance, 195; resistance
to 'German Christians', 158; youth
organizations, 85
Ciano, Count Galeazzo, 166, 168
cinema, the, 92–4, 211 n. 28
Citizenship Law, Reich, 130
civil and public service, 7, 48, 162;
nazification of, 35, 61, 90; in Prussia,
90
civil servants, 130; arrested after 20 July
1944, 146; in defeat, 199, 203; Hitler
salute compulsory for, 157; and Nazi
leadership, 200; in resistance, 144
Civil Service, Law for the Restoration of
the Professional, 48, 130
class, consciousness, 154; distinction, 138,
153, 160, 174; -transcending anxiety
in defeat, 196; -transcending
mobilization, 152–3; see also social
mobility
coalition government, 33, 50, 69; as
constraint on Nazi domestic policy,
70
collective bargaining, 50, 53; abolition of,
78
Comics' Cabaret, 168
'Commissar Order', 127
Communist Party (KPD): ban on
publications of, 35–6, 37, 64; election
results, 32, 38, 39, 41; Gestapo action
against, 100, 107; members join SA,
159; Political Police surveillance of,
103; press taken over by Nazis, 64;
reaction to Nazi assumption of
power, 37; resistance, 100, 116;
suppression of, 37, 39, 44, 58;
theory of Fascism, 34; violence
against, 35–6
'community aliens', 124, 182–6;
classification of, 183; 'criminal',
184–5; custody proposed for, 182,
184; proposed Law on the Treatment
of, 124, 181–6; proposed sterilization
of, 183, 186; surveillance of, 184; and
youth, 186
'Community of Reich Leaders', 57

concentration camps, 20, 23, 43, 58, 100,
104, 105; 'euthanasia' in, 187;
executions in, 115, 194; influx of
prisoners after 'Crystal Night', 132;
'natural decline' in, 191; prisoners'
labour exploited in, 128, 138; race
ideology in, 124; used to break
resistance, 158; SS control of, 101,
103; as 'state correction and labour
camps', 106, 139
Concordat, Reich, 85
Concordats, Länder, 65
'Confessing Church', 66–7
conformity, 151, 156–7
conservatives: in coalition, 36, 39;
opposition, 40, 157; see also
right-wing opposition
constitution, 45; see also Weimar Republic
construction industry, 73, 105
consumer, goods, shortage of, 78, 83, 113;
spending, 112
consumption, mass, 82; of food, 164
Conti, Leonardo, 118
Cooper, Gary, 94
'coordination' see Gleichschaltung
Coordination of the Länder, Second Law
for (1933), 42
Coordination of the Länder with the
Reich, Interim Law for (1933), 41
'Councils of Trust', 4; elections to, 54
counter-intelligence, 103
Crawford, Joan, 94
Criminal Police, 103, 106; and 'community
aliens', 183; persecution of
'Volksschädlinge', 104
criminals: classification of, 181, 182;
'criminal biology', 183; imprisonment
of, 185; Law on Habitual (1933),
185
Crössinsee, 170
'Crystal Night' (Reichskristallnacht), 109,
131–2
culture, 62–5; Americanization of, 94;
bourgeois, 95–6; complexity of,
151; limited influence of regime
on, 151; popular trends in, 91–6;
rebellion against bourgeois
exclusivity, 96
Curtis, Lionel, 194
Czechoslovakia, 110, 170

Dachau concentration camp, 20, 23, 43, 101, 104
DAF *see* German Labour Front
Daluege, Kurt, 35, 101, 103
Darré, Richard Walter, 6, 56, 169; as leader of Community of Reich Leaders, 57; as Reich Agriculture Minister, 57, 75; as Reich Peasants' Leader, 57
death camps: auxiliary camps of, 128; establishment of, 127; mass murders in, 134; 'natural decline' in, 191; witnesses to, 136
death sentence, 114, 115, 194, 212 n. 43
defeat of Germany, 196–203; chaos of, 196; and the elderly, 199; and everyday life, 196; families in, 197; popular opinion and, 197–203; suicides, 199
Defence Commissars, 146
'Defence Districts' (*Wehrkreise*), 12, 66; Commands, 19
Defence, Ministry of, 41
Defregger, Franz von, 169
Degrelle, Léon, 167
Demandowski, Ewald von, 169
democracy, Hitler on, 172–4
demographic trends, 77
denazification, 150
Denmark, 115
department stores, 49
Deutsche Erd-und Steinwerk, 105
Deutsche Zukunft, 160
diet, 78, 113, 163, 165
Dietrich, Marlene, 94
Dietrich, Otto, 167
Dietrich, Sepp, 20, 22
dissidents: exclusion from civil service, 162; execution of, 115; silent, 157; surveillance of, 158; terror against, 99, 105, 115, 158; *see also* opposition; resistance
District Leaders (Kreisleiter) of NSDAP, 64, 89–90, 170; and 'Crystal Night', 131
Dix, Otto, 96
DNVP *see* German National People's Party
Döblin, Alfred, 62
Dönitz, Karl, 148
domestic policy of Nazi regime, 70; radicalization of, 110; terror as

instrument of, 137, 150; *see also* separate policy areas
donations, 8; 'fatigue', 83
Dresden, 146, 188
'dual state', 43

East Prussia, 144, 147
Eberswalde, 187
economic crisis, 61, 163; and rise of Nazi movement 31, 39, 152, 158
economic policy, 71–3; populist presentation of, 72–3; primacy of rearmament, 74; privatization of, 76; struggle between various competencies about, 90, 142;
Economics, Reich Ministry of, 7, 55, 74, 75, 131
economy, 31, 49, 68; boom, 77; concentration of enterprises, 141; dependence on foreign workers, 139; Political Police surveillance of, 103; recovery, 71, 77–8, 163–4; state command, 75; state intervention in, 71–3; total mobilization of, 138; trends in, 77, 140; war, 138
Edelweiss Pirates, 86
Editors, Law on (1933), 64
education, 86–8; modernization of, 153; and racial selection, 88; *see also* Adolf-Hitler Schools; 'Castles of the Order'; Church; Hitler Youth; *Napolas*; schools; training; universities
Eich, Günter, 94
Eichberg 186; trial, 187
Eichmann, Adolf, 133, 190–1
Eicke, Theodor, 23, 101
Eider river regulation scheme, 160
Einsatzgruppen (SS), 107, 125, 127, 134, 136, 142
Einstein, Albert, 62, 98
Eisernes Sparen, 78
elderly, the, 199
elections, 50; November 1932, 32, 38; March 1933, 32–3, 35, 37–9, 41–2, 44, 49–50, 156; November 1933, 66, 67, 68; and *Länder* parliaments, 41; secrecy of ballot, 159; electoral violence, 68; voting patterns in, 39, 68, 159

elites, initial aims of, 153–4; resistance of, 194

Elser, Johann Georg, 116

Eltz von Rübenach, Baron Paul, 32

Emden, 146

emigration, 91, 97; Jewish, 109

emigrés, 46, 93, 100; Political Police surveillance of, 103

employment, full, 75, 77

employment offices, 51, 104, 106

employment policy, 50, 71–3; role of military and labour service in, 73; popular enthusiasm for, 78; struggle between various competencies about, 90; towards women, 73; work creation, 4, 165

'Enabling Act' (1933), 39, 44–6, 57, 58, 59, 207 n. 26

England see Great Britain

Epp, Franz Xaver Ritter von, 7, 22, 40, 41, 42

Erbach-Eichberg, 186

Essen, 19

Esser, Hermann, 41

Establishment of Political Parties, Law against (1933), 60, 67

Estonia, Estonians, 178

eugenics, 110, 119, 154; 'Eugenic Courts', 122, 186; and 'euthanasia', 121; and psychiatry, 122

European, idea, 142, 195; integration, 143

'euthanasia', 186–90; 'Aktion 14 f 13', 187; 'Aktion T4', 120, 121; of Aryans, 188; of 'asocials', foreign workers and elderly, 121; of children, 121, 189–90; in concentration camps, 121, 187–90; Führer's Chancellery and, 187; Himmler authorizes, 177; Hitler authorizes, 120; law on, 124; Mennecke's letters on, 186–90; of mentally ill, 119–20; officially halted, 121; of people with learning disabilities, 120; personnel used in genocide in Poland, 125, 134; physicians' role in, 121, 123, 186–90; and psychiatry, 122, 186, 187; representation in films, 93; scientists' role in, 123; by SS in Poland, 125; by starvation, 121; and vision of 'social and racial purity', 122, 124

evacuees, 196

everyday life, 151; and defeat, 196

'factory leader', 54, 116, 199

Fallada, Hans, 94

family, modernization of, 153; in defeat, 197

farmers' unions, Christian, 57

Fascism, 34; see also Nazism

'fats crisis', 6, 75, 163–6

Faulkner, William, 94

Fiehler, Karl, 244–5

film, 64, 65, 167, 168, 169, 170; anti-Semitic, 93, 211 n. 28; songs from, 192–4; see also cinema

'Final Solution' see Jewish Question; Jews, genocide of

Finance, Ministry of, 32, 49, 181

Fischer Verlag, 94

Florstedt, Hermann, 188

Flossenbürg concentration camp, 105

food supply, 6, 75, 113, 115, 121, 147, 163, 165, 197; see also agriculture; consumption; diet

forced labour, 105, 194; see also foreign workers

Foreign Affairs, Ministry of, 32, 46, 134

foreign exchange, 6–7, 75, 76, 95, 164

foreign opinion, 46, 47, 165; disbelief in genocide, 136

foreign policy, 11, 58, 68, 162; Hitler's success in, 27, 71, 90, 107, 111; popular criticism of, 200; radicalization of, 109–11; struggle between competencies about, 90; and Wehrmacht, 110; of Weimar Republic, 109–10

foreign trade, 75, 163

foreign workers, 138; in agriculture, 139; in arms industry, 139; dependence of war economy on, 139; 'eastern', as slaves, 139; at end of war, 147, 198; 'Sauckel campaigns', 139; sexual relations of, 178; Soviet, 139; and German workers, 153

'Foundation for the Heritage of our Forefathers inc', 179

Four-Year Exhibition, 170

Four-Year Plan, 75, 163; and big business, 76, 140; Goering and, 169; and

economic measures against Jews, 131;
  as justification for persecution of
  'asocials', 105; Organization, 140, 141
Fraenkel, Ernst, 37, 43
France, 114, 115, 138, 162
François-Poncet, André, 52
Frank, Hans, 22, 125, 127
Frank, Walter, 98
Frankfurt am Main, 18
Frankfurter Zeitung, 167
Frederick the Great, 44
Free Word', Congress of 'The, 34
freemasons, 168; Political Police
  surveillance of, 103
Freiburg, 146
Freisler, Roland, 144
Freud, Sigmund, 62
Frick, Wilhelm, 7, 31, 35, 36, 40, 58, 59,
  60, 61, 102, 108, 137
Fritsch, Baron Werner von, 19, 110,
Fritsch, Willi, 93
'Führer', 6, 9, 14–15, 17–18, 20, 22, 24,
  25, 26, 33, 52, 61, 62, 67, 84, 89, 99,
  101, 105, 110, 117, 137, 145, 148,
  149, 151, 164, 165, 166, 167, 168,
  169, 170, 179, 181, 196, 201, 203;
  'bunker', 148; Chancellery of, 187;
  charisma of, 152; see also Hitler,
  Adolf
'Führer myth', 1, 9, 24, 27, 69, 90, 107,
  111, 145, 148, 162; centrality of,
  149–50; end of, 150, 196, 203
'Führer-principle', 17, 89, 97; Hitler on,
  170–4 passim
Führer State, 1, 26, 27, 32; end of,
  195–203; historical impact of,
  149–55; Hitler on, 170–4 passim;
  Hitler destroys, 148; integrative
  power of, 152; modernity of, 152,
  155; overlapping competencies in,
  61, 90, 137, 152
Fürstenberg, 187, 188, 189
Funk, Walther, 7, 166, 168, 169

Gable, Clark, 94
Garbo, Greta, 94
Gauleiter, 40, 42, 64, 89, 167, 174, 177;
  oppose 'Nero Order', 146; as Reich
  Governors, 11, 42; and SA, 11; and
  'Sauckel campaigns', 139

Gebhard, Karl, 175
Gefolgschaft see 'retinue'
Gendarmerie (rural constabulary), 4, 6,
  102
General Federation of German Trade
  Unions (ADGB), 51–3
'General Plan East', 125
Generalgouvernement: 'Aktion T4' and
  gassing of Jews in, 134; deportations
  of Jews to, 125, 133; partisans'
  resistance in, 127; slave labour from,
  127; SS in, 127; see also Poland
genetic 'theory', 183
Geneva, 67
genocide see Jews, genocide of; Gypsies
George, Heinrich, 93
Gerade Weg, Der, 22
Gerlich, Fritz, 22
German Agricultural Council, 57
'German Christians', 66–7, 158
German Council of Industry and
  Commerce (DHI), 49, 50
German Democratic Party (DDP), 157
German Labour, Action Committee for the
  Protection of, 53
German Labour Front (DAF), 7, 53–5, 56,
  64, 88, 180; 'Beauty of Labour', 81;
  'Castles of the Order', 170; cultural
  policy, 90; deductions for, 78; health
  policy 117, 118, 124; housing policy;
  117, 119; Institute of Labour Science,
  117–18; leisure activities, 81–2, 117;
  pensions policy, 118; post-war
  aspirations, 117, 119; 'Production
  Contest of German Firms', 81; 'Social
  Institute of the German People', 117;
  118; social insurance policy, 118;
  social policy, 77, 81, 90, 117; see also
  Ley, Robert
German National Clerical Association, 53
German National People's Party (DNVP),
  23, 31, 33, 38, 39, 43, 57, 59, 68, 157,
  158, 159
German News Agency (DNB), 167
German People's Party (DVP), 59, 157
'German physics', 98
German State Party (DSP), 45, 59
German Students' Association, 62
Germanization policy, of abducted
  children, 127; in Poland, 126

'Germany Reports' see Sopade
Gestapa, 101, 105; Law (1936), 105;
Gestapo, 11, 16, 18, 21, 22, 80, 99, 106,
    156; and death sentence, 114;
    Himmler becomes Inspector of, 101;
    almost destroys KPD resistance, 100;
    Law, 103; object of fear, 106,
    persecution of 'Volksschädlinge',
    104–5; success against opposition,
    107; and SS, 25; and state
    bureaucracy, 25; uncovers 'Red
    Orchestra', 144; and Wannsee
    Conference, 190
Giesler, Hermann, 97
Glaeser, Ernst, 62
Glasmeier, Heinrich, 169
Gleichschaltung, 9–10, 37, 39–43, 54, 56,
    57, 61, 68, 69, 157; of Church, 67; in
    cultural sphere, 62–5
Goebbels, Helga, 170
Goebbels, Joseph, 18–21, 24, 31, 34; and
    anti-Jewish measures 131, 132, 133;
    and cinema, 167; diary extracts,
    166–70; as father, 170; film fanatic,
    94; as Gauleiter of Berlin, 138; and
    Goering, 167; and Hess, 167; and
    Hitler, 150, 167, 170; target of jokes,
    158; as Minister of Propaganda and
    Reich Propaganda Leader, 8–9, 44,
    47, 52, 59, 63, 64, 83, 89, 95, 131,
    150, 166–70; promises 'miracle
    weapon', 143; on Nazi theory, 116;
    'Occident' propaganda against
    Bolshevism, 142; Plenipotentiary-
    General for the Total War Effort',146;
    views on propaganda, 91, 92;
    designated Reich Chancellor, 148;
    promises 'total victory', 137, 138;
    proclaims 'total war', 139; and
    theatre, 167; preaches war socialism,
    138; deployment of Werwolf, 147
Goebbels, Magda, 167, 168
Goerdeler, Carl, 143, 144
Goering, Hermann, 7, 11, 16, 18–19, 21,
    22, 26, 31, 35, 36, 44, 46, 50, 166;
    and anti-Jewish measures, 130, 132;
    loses influence in arms industry, 137;
    as Commissioner for Foreign
    Exchange and Raw Materials, 75; as
    Commissioner for Four-Year Plan, 76,

131, 169; and failures of Luftwaffe,
    137, 203; flees Berlin, 148; and
    Goebbels, 167; hopes to succeed
    Hitler, 148; target of jokes, 158; as
    Minister for Aviation 12, 31, 89; as
    Minister-President of Prussia, 42, 47,
    89; patronage of theatre, 95; popular
    anger towards, 203; in charge of
    Prussian police, 100–1; and
    Rosenberg, 168
Görlitz, 3
Göttingen, 186
Goodman, Benny, 94
Graf, Oskar Maria, 62
Granzow, Walter, 169
Grau, Fritz, 182
Great Britain, 112, 114, 133, 169, 197, 200,
    202
Greece, 115
Greiser, Arthur, 177
Gross Rosen concentration camp, 105, 190
Grosz, George, 96
Gründgens, Gustaf, 95
Grynszpan, Herschel, 131
Gürtner, Franz, 23, 31, 60
Gutehoffnungshütte, 74
Gypsies, 104; genocide of, 125; Nazi
    racism towards, 122; experiments in
    Auschwitz on, 128

Haavara Treaty, 133
'habitual criminals', 104, 105
Hadamar, 190
Hadamovsky, Eugen, 169
Hamburg, 35, 40, 68, 86
Hanke, Karl, 166, 168
Harnack, Arvid, 144
Hasenclever, Walter, 95
Hatheyer, Heidemarie, 93
Hayn, Hans, 22
Head of State of the German Reich, Law
    concerning the (1934), 27
health care: and biologistic concept of
    performance, 118, 123; company
    doctors, 123; DAF policy, 117–19,
    124; family doctors, 123; 'German
    People's Protection', 118; medical
    profession, 118–19; modernization of,
    153; and NSV, 83; positive changes
    in, 123

health and safety at work, 81
Heberle, Rudolf, 156
Hebold, Otto, 187
Hefelmann, Hans, 189–90
Heine, Heinrich, 63
Heines, Edmund, 21, 22, 23
Heinze, Hans, 189–90
Heissmeyer, August, 176
Held, Heinrich, 40, 41
Helldorf, Count Wolf Heinrich von, 168
hereditary disease, 124
Hermann Goering Corporation, 75, 179
Hermes, Andreas, 57
Hess, Rudolf, 7, 14, 18–19, 21, 22, 26, 66,
    168; flight to Scotland, 137; Hitler
    complains about, 167; and 'New
    German Science of Healing', 123; on
    'fats crisis', 163–6
Hessen, 40
Heyde, Werner, 188
Heydebreck, Peter von, 21, 22
Heydrich, Reinhard: and anti-Jewish
    measures, 132, 133; and genocide of
    Jews, 135; as Head of Gestapa, 101;
    ideological aims, 103; on 'natural
    decline', 191; on 'natural selection',
    191; orders execution for
    demoralization of Volk, 114–15; as
    Chief of SD, 18, 21, 22, 26, 106; as
    Chief of Security Police and SD, 102,
    103, 115, 178; and Wannsee
    Conference, 134, 190–1
Hildebrandt, Richard, 198
Hilgenfeldt, Erich, 119
Himmler, Heinrich, 18, 20–2, 41, 43, 107;
    action against 'asocials', 105; on
    'calendar science', 175; as
    Commandant of Bavarian Political
    Police, 101; concentration camps,
    sole responsibility for, 101;
    convalescence leave authorized by,
    177; on English PoWs; 179; expelled
    from NSDAP, 148; on fertilizer, 176;
    on genealogy, 178; and 'General Plan
    East', 125, 126; and genocide of Jews,
    135, 136, 147; and Germanization
    policy, 125–6; and Hitler, 179; as
    Inspector of Gestapo, 101; ideological
    aims, 103; becomes Interior Minister,
    137; letters, 175–9; lunacy of ideas,

175; on marriage, 178; on
meteorology, 179; as Chief of Munich
Police 60, 100; on Napolas and
religion, 176; on oil production, 179;
compares police to Wehrmacht, 108;
'racial hygiene', concept of 121,
126, 177–88; racist ideology, 127,
139, 177–8; as Reichsführer SS, 26,
100–1; as Reichsführer SS and
Chief of German Police in Reich
Min. of Interior, 102, 104; as Chief
of Senior Police and SS Leaders in
Generalgouvernement, 125; on sex
and Baltic workers, 178; on smoking,
176; and Speer's policies, 141; aims
SS control of political police, 101;
SS State, lays foundations of, 100;
assumes supreme command of
reserve, 146; on tuberculosis, 175,
177; and western Allies, 142, 148;
on 'world ice theory', 175
Hindenburg, Paul von, 17–18, 27, 31, 33,
    35, 40, 44, 48, 51
Hippler, Fritz, 93
Hirsch-Duncker Trade Union Ring, 53
Hirschfeld, Magnus, 62
Historikerstreit, 129
Hitler, Adolf, 9, 15, 18, 34, 49, 75, 138,
    142, 156; and anti-Bolshevism, 129,
    134; and anti-Semitism, 47, 129;
    appointment as Reich Chancellor, 1,
    31, 37; architecture, interest in, 97;
    and Army, 14–15, 110; attempts on
    life of, 116, 143, 145; attitudes
    towards, 4, 9, 15, 32, 156–7; and big
    business, 50, 55; and Bormann, 137,
    167; bourgeois society, maintains,
    157; centrality of, 150; charisma of,
    149, 161; and Churches, 45, 66, 67;
    and cinema, 93, 167, 170; and draft
    'Community Aliens Law', 181; on
    democracy, 172–4; as dictator, 61,
    152; disregard for basic needs of
    Volk, 146; economy, opinions on, 7,
    43, 49; and elections, 35, 39, 49, 156,
    159; and 'Enabling Act', 45–6; end of
    revolution and beginning of evolution
    declared by, 157; and 'euthanasia'
    programme, 120; '-faith', 150; and
    foreign policy, 58, 67, 71, 90, 110,

111; as Führer 17, 19, 20, 54, 57, 58, 60, 73, 84; and 'Führer myth', 69, 90, 111; on 'Führer principle', 170–4 *passim*; destroys Führer State, 148; on Führer State', 170–4 *passim*; and Gauleiter, 42, 167; and genocide of Jews, 129, 135, 150; and 'German Christians' 66; as Head of the German Reich, 27; and Goebbels, 167, 170; and Hess, 167; and Himmler, 148, 179; target of jokes, 158; and labour policy, 52; learns lessons from First World War, 112; *Lebensraum* fantasies, 125; on meritocracy, 174; and *Mittelstand*, 56; and 'national community', 52, 171; and Nazi festivals, 84; on Nazi state, 171; 'Nero Order' 146–7; on Nuremberg Laws, 130; on Party membership, 167; on plebiscites, 172–3; popular opinion towards, 38, 51, 90, 100, 111, 115, 162, 196, 201, 203; on press, 167; and primacy of politics, 49, 50; 'racial hygiene', concept of, 121, 122; racist ideology, 127; and radicalization of policies, 110; on radio, 167; and rearmament, 164; regards March 1933 elections as a revolution, 39; as Reich Chancellor, 4, 7, 26, 27, 32, 33, 39, 41, 42, 44, 45, 47, 49, 52, 55, 61, 67, 68, 146; as Reich Governor of Prussia, 41; and Reich Governors, 60, 61; and Reichstag Fire, 36; right-wing support for, 31–33, 39, 44; and Röhm, 13, 20, 23; and SA, 14–15, 18, 21–4, 35; and SS, 103; and state administration, 43; suicide, 148; as Supreme Commander, 110; testament, 147; totalitarian efficiency, concept of, 17; engrossed in war, 137; *see also* Führer; resistance; *Zähmungskonzept*
'Hitler Greeting', 61, 83, 157
Hitler-Stalin Pact, 112, 116
Hitler State *see* Führer State
Hitler Youth (HJ), 84–8; 'Adolf-Hitler Schools', 87; attitudes towards, 86; and behaviour, 87; Law on, 85; 'radical opposition' in, 160; and schools, 86; and social mobility,

86–7, 161; *see also Jungvolk*; League of German Girls
Hof, 163
Hohenlychen Sanatoria, 175
Holland, 133,
Homolka, Oskar, 93
homosexuals, 11, 21, 22, 23; persecution of, 104; Political Police surveillance of, 103; proposed sterilization of, 186
Hossbach, Friedrich, 110
housing, 74, 113; DAF policy, 117, 119; homelessness, 203
Hühnlein, Adolf
Hugenberg, Alfred, 31, 33, 49, 55, 56, 57, 59
hunger, 197

ideological mobilization, 1, 54, 83–90 *passim*,
ideological education and training, 88, 176
IG Farben, 50, 75, 76, 98, 176; *Buna* production at Monowitz, 127
industrial commissioners (of NSDAP), 54
industry, 7, 32, 55, 74–6; hire of concentration camp labour, 128; production, 140
Industry, Food and Agriculture, Reich Ministry of, 31, 54, 142
intelligentsia, 34, 63, 199
Interior, Reich Ministry of, 31, 40, 41; 'Basic Decree', 105; and draft 'Community Aliens Law', 124, 181; Himmler in, 102; attempts to define 'protective custody' etc, 105; purge of, 35; 'Reich Central Office for Jewish Emigration' in, 133
International Red Cross, 135
internment of Germans, post-war, 147
Israel, 191
Italy, 32, 162, 166, 169, 179

Jannings, Emil, 92, 93
Jehovah's Witnesses (*Bibelforscher*), 104
Jerusalem, 190
Jewish Question, 109; and Eichmann, 190–1; 'Final Solution' of, 109, 127–8; Nuremberg Laws and, 130; Wannsee Conference, 134, 190–1; *see also* Jews, genocide of

Jews, 104; actions against Jewish
    businesses, 43, 46, 49, 56; actions
    against doctors and civil servants, 46;
    in arts, 91; 'Aryanization' of firms,
    130, 132; ban on emigration, 133;
    Berufsverbot on, 131; big business
    disapproves of economically
    damaging racial criteria, 131; boycotts
    against, 47–8; children barred from
    German schools, 132; Community in
    Berlin, 47; 'Crystal Night' as turning
    point, 132; depersonalization of, 135;
    deportations of, 125, 128, 131, 133,
    135; discrimination against, 55, 69,
    130, 131, 132; 'euthanasia' of, 189;
    forced labour of, 191; forced out of
    economy, 131; economic plunder of,
    133, 135; emigration of, 91, 109, 130,
    131, 132, 133; emigration becomes
    expulsion, 133; everyday life in Third
    Reich, 129; first measures against,
    48–9; ghettoization, 134; Goebbels
    on 8, 168; intelligentsia, 63, 71, 91;
    Heberle's views on conduct of,
    160–1; Hess on, 166; Jewish Cultural
    League, 132–3; Nazi racism against,
    122; Nuremberg Laws, reactions to
    130–1; open terror against recedes,
    99; organizations, 132; Political Police
    surveillance of, 103; refugee children,
    133; Reich Citizenship Law defines,
    130; Reich Representatives of Jews in
    Germany, 47; *Reichsvereinigung*, 132,
    133; resistance help for, 135; sexual
    relations with non-Jews forbidden,
    130; stripped of German nationality,
    135; in Theresienstadt concentration
    camp, 191; unemployed, 132;
    violence against, 47; war veterans, 8;
    yellow star introduced for, 134; youth
    groups, 85; *see also* anti-Semitism';
    'Crystal Night'; Jewish Question; Jews,
    genocide of; Nuremberg Laws
Jews, genocide of, 125, 128–36, 191;
    based on 'euthanasia' experience,
    125; as continuation of destruction
    of civilization, 154; elite groups'
    role in, 136; knowledge of, 135–6;
    non-German collaborators' role in,
    136; origins of, 129; secrecy of, 135,

150; SS and *Einsatzgruppen* and, 136;
    unparalleled, 129; and war, 136;
    Wehrmacht's role in, 136; world
    opinion, disbelief of, 136; *see also*
    Jewish Question
Johst, Hanns, 95
judiciary: attempts to define 'protective'
    custody etc, 105; and draft
    'Community Aliens Law', 184–5;
    death sentences imposed by, 147,
    194; legalization of coup against SA,
    23; wave of terror of military, 147
Jung, Edgar Julius, 16–18
Jungvolk, 86
Justice, Reich Ministry of, 31, 60; and draft
    'Community Aliens Law', 181, 182

Kaas, Ludwig, 33, 45, 59
Kästner, Erich, 62, 93
Kageneck, Count Hans Reinhard von, 16
Kahr, Gustav von, 22
Kaiser Wilhelm Society for the
    Advancement of Science, 98; and
    racist ideology 122, 126
Kalckreuth, Barbara von, 169
Kampffront Schwarz-Weiss-Rot, 38, 44
Kampfzeit see 'period of struggle'
Kandinsky, Wassily, 96
Karinhall, 203
Kasack, Hermann, 94
Kaschnitz, Marie Luise, 94
Kassel, 146
Kaufering, 20
Keitel, Wilhelm, 110
Kempten, 24
Keppler, Wilhelm, 55
Ketteler, Baron Wilhelm von, 16
Keynes, John Maynard, 71
Kiel, 14
Kirchner, Ernst Ludwig, 96
Kirdorf, Emil, 55
Klausener, Erich, 21, 25
Klee, Paul, 96
Klein, Fritz, 160
Koblenz, 168, 170
Koeppen, Wolfgang, 94
Kogon, Eugen, 101
Kokoschka, Oskar, 96
Kollwitz, Käthe, 34
Kottulinsky, Count Adalbert, 176

KPD *see* Communist Party
Kraft durch Freude (KdF) *see* Strength through Joy
Krakow, 177
Krauch, Carl, 76
Kreisau Circle, 143–4, 194–5
Kreisleiter *see* District Leaders
Kreigler, Hans, 169
Krieck, Ernst, 98
Krüger, Friedrich-Wilhelm, 177
Krupp von Bohlen und Halbach, Gustav, 50, 54, 55, 74
Kurhessen, 68

labour, deployment of, 76, 105, 114; concentration camp, 128; and 'management of health', 118; and 'Sauckel campaigns', 139; slave, 127; women's, during war, 114; 'work book', 78; *see also* employment; forced labour; foreign workers; unemployment
Labour, Ministry of, 32, 54; and draft 'Community Aliens Law', 181; and 'Sauckel campaigns', 139
labour movement: destruction of, 7, 33, 34, 42, 43, 50–3, 78, 154; disunity within, 34; and opposition to regime, 45; weakening of social milieu, 78; *see also* Communist Party; General Federation of German Trade Unions; Social Democratic Party; *Sopade*; trade unions
labour, Nazi policy, 52–4
Labour Service, Reich, 5, 20, 50, 73, 86
labour shortages, in industry, 71; in agriculture, 77
Lammers, Hans Heinrich, 137
Länder, 37; *Gleichschaltung* of, 39–42, 69; parliaments, 59; political police in, 101, 102
Landhilfe see agriculture
landowners, 16, 32, 56, 57
Lang, Fritz, 93
Langgässer, Elisabeth, 94
Latvians, 178
lawyers, 88
League of German Girls (BDM), 84, 86
'League of Struggle for German Culture', 65

'League of Struggle for the Commercial Middle Class', 56
Leander, Zarah, 93
'*Lebensborn* Foundation', 127
Lebensraum: Hitler's statements on, 110; inhuman significance for social policy, 119; in Nazi ideology, 109–10, 116, 160; racial reconstruction in, 128; and Second World War, 125, 142
legality, formal in Third Reich, 43
Leipart, Theodor, 51
Leipzig, 86
leisure, 81–2, 92; DAF policy, 117; modernization of, 153; *see also* cinema; 'Strength through Joy'
Lenhard, Philipp, 98
Less, Avner, 191
Lessing, Gottfried Ephraim, 95
Lewis, Sinclair, 94
Ley, Robert, 7, 53, 54, 92; on Reich Vocational Contest (1938), 180–1; social policy proposals, 118–19; *see also* German Labour Front
Lichterfelde, 23
Liebeneiner, Wolfgang, 92
Lingen, Theo, 93
Linz, 202
Lippert, Julius, 167
literature, 64, 91, 94, 169
Lithuanians, 178
living standards, 78, 164–5
local government, 42, 43, 59, 89–90
Local Party Leaders, 186; and 'Crystal Night', 131–2
London World Economic Conference (1933), 59
Lorre, Peter, 93
Lubbe, Marinus, van der 36
Lübeck, 40
Lublin, 134
Ludendorff, Erich, 168
Luftwaffe, failure of, 137, 200, 202–3
Lutze, Viktor, 20
Luxemburg, 115

Madagascar, 134
Madeira, 81
Magdeburg, 146
Maidanek death camp, 127, 134

'malicious practices', 82; 107; Decree
against (1933), 3
Mann, Heinrich, 34, 62
Mann, Thomas, 34, 95
Marburg University League, 17
'March Fallen', 46
marriage, 73, 130; law on 'healthy', 120;
in SS, Himmler on, 178
'Marxism', 8, 32, 35, 39, 43, 51
Marxists, 10, 42, 49; executions of, 115;
factories purged of, 158; Political
Police surveillance of, 103
mass media, 34, 44, 63, 64, 73, 91, 153;
see also press; radio; film; cinema
Mauthausen concentration camp, 105
May Day ('Day of National Labour'), 52,
84, 156, 170
Meissner, Otto, 166
'Meldungen aus dem Reich', see 'Reports
from the Reich'
Memel region, 110
Mennecke, Friedrich, 186–90
'Metallurgical Research Society' (Mefo),
74
Mezger, Edmund, 181, 182
middle class, 48, 56; and KdF, 81
military expenditure, 112
military service, reduces unemployment,
73; increases women in workforce,
114
Ministerial Council for the Defence of the
Reich, 113, 181
Ministerial Office, 32
Mitchell, Margaret, 95
Mittelfranken, 68
Mittelstand, discontent within, 4; see also
middle class; petite bourgeoisie
Mjölnir, 64
Modernism, 63, 96
modernization, 2, 151, 153, 155
Möller, Eberhard Wolfgang, 169
Moltke, Count Helmut James von, 144,
194–5
monarchists, 19
Monowitz (Auschwitz III), 127, 128
Moser, Hans, 93
Mosse Verlag, 130
motorways, 73, 97
Müller, Heinrich, 190
Müller, Ludwig, 66

Müller, Robert, 188, 189
Münchener Neueste Nachrichten, 22
Munich, 9, 20, 21, 22, 38, 40, 41, 73, 86,
96, 131, 144, 169, 182; Agreement
(1938), 110, 143; beer-hall putsch,
84
munitions production see armaments and
munitions
Münsterland, 25
museums, 65
music, 63, 64, 91, 94, 95, 96; the German
'hit' 94; songs to boost morale,
192–4; and youth nonconformity, 94
Mutschmann, Martin, 167

national community, 52, 54, 65, 71, 76,
77, 83, 94, 99, 104, 107, 138; and
draft 'Community Aliens Law', 182–4;
decay of, 147, 149; economic basis
for, 78–9; Hitler on, 171; and the
individual, 180; Jews excluded from,
129; and Nazi leadership, 203; Ley
on, 180; primacy of monopolized
politics in, 151; propaganda, 82, 83,
153; racially defined, 119, 123; and
social policy 118; totalitarian nature
of, 151; and Volk, 52, 196; and youth,
186
'national comrades', 81, 82, 88, 95, 100,
106, 112, 183; and defeat, 196, 198,
201, 203; and propaganda, 201–2
National Labour', 'Day of see May Day;
Law for the Regulation of (1934), 54
National Political Educational Institutes
(Napolas), 87, 176–7
'national revolution' see 'national uprising'
National Socialist Craft, Trade and
Commerce Organization (NS-Hago),
3, 56; boycott of department stores, 7
National Socialist Factory Cell
Organization (NSBO), 4, 50, 51–4
National Socialist German Workers Party
(NSDAP), 8, 42, 158; and agriculture,
57, 75, 161; aims 32, 44, 84, 98, 160;
anti-Semitism, 47, 109, 123, 129; and
big business, 50, 55, 61, 74, 76, 160;
Boycott Committee, 47; and Catholic
Church, 65–6, 67, 85; in coalition
government, 31–2, 35, 44, 70;
congresses, 61, 75, 84, 130, 163, 169;

consolidation of rule, 70; controls members, 158; cultural hegemony as aim, 84; and DAF, 54; defeat and members of, 196; dictatorship of, 159, 161; different from other parties, 84; disillusionment within, 3, 42; divisions within 161; and DNVP, 59; economic policy, 49–50, 71–5, 78, 142; education policy, 87–8; election propaganda, 50; electoral progress, 31, 32, 33, 38, 39, 44, 68, 159; embourgeoisement of, 89, 167; employees of, 89; employment policy, 50, 71–3, 78; foreign policy successes, 1; and *Gleichschaltung*, 41–2, 157; health policy, 123, *and see* German Labour Front; hierarchy, size of, 89; intervention in economy, 7, 71–3; ideology clashes with reality, 161; ideology, development of, 161; labour movement, persecution of, 50–2; and *Länder* Parliaments, 41; leadership as charismatic following, 161; *Lebensraum*, 109–11, 125, 160, 192; 'left wing' of, 17, 33, 50, 138; and local government, 89–90; looting by members during 'Crystal Night', 132; lust for power of lower ranks, 61; as mass movement, 152; and mass organizations, 88, 157, 159, 203; mass spectacles, 96; growth in membership, 46, 57, 159, 167; and *Mittelstand*, 48, 56; omnipresence of, 90; organization and leadership (1936), 244–5; Party Chancellery, 181; and personal unions, 89; phases of rule, 2, 70; as a political order, 159; Political Police surveillance of affairs of, 103; population policy, 123; power struggles within, 87; pragmatic attitude to research, 97 *and see* universities; primacy of politics, 49, 50, 74; programme claimed as original, 160; propaganda, 72–3, 152; and Protestant Church, 66–7, 85; Protestant support for, 66, 68; public opinion monopolized by, 159, 163; race ideology and 'Sauckel campaigns' 139; Race Policy Office, 126, 186; racist policies, aims of, 109,

122, 123, 126; rallies, 202; and Reich Concordat, 45, 59, 60, 65; in Reichstag, 59; rewards stalwarts and members, 158; social policy, 80–3, 117–20, 122, 154; SS: independent organization of, 101; and state administration, 35, 61; -state relationship, 84, 89; view of state, 170–1; status in NS state, 61, 89, 161; stylized image of, 83–4; symbolism, use of, 157, 160; terror and surveillance, development of system of, 100–8; totalitarian and populist traits characteristic of rule, 69; violent methods, 25, 43; war aims, 111, 123, 125, 126, 142; in Weimar Republic, 89; *see also* Party Organization; 'period of struggle'; SA; SS
National Socialist People's Welfare Organization (NSV), 83, 88
National Socialist revolution *see* 'national uprising'
'national uprising', 43, 47, 68; bourgeois fear of, 156–7; coalition partners, attitudes of towards, 7; end of, Hitler proclaims, 9, 157; resistance to smashed, 158; right-wing opposition, attitude of towards, 16; and social mobility, Ley on, 181; sociology of, 156–63 *passim*;
'natural decline', 191
'natural selection', 191
Natzweiler concentration camp, 105
Nazi Civil Servants League, 88
Nazi Community of Culture, 88
Nazi Drivers' Corps
Nazi Lawyers League, 88
Nazi League of German Technology, 88
Nazi Lecturers League, 88
Nazi movement: calendar of festivals 83–4; discontent within, 9; dynamism of, 34, 110; and economic crisis, 158; old elite, links with, 39; and monopolization of power, 61; nature of, 137; popular appeal of, 152; power and violence as an integrating element, 48; radical methods, 40; unique identity in Weimar, 83–4; violence, 32, 34

Nazi People's Welfare Organization, 119;
    Germanization of abducted children,
    127
Nazi Physicians League, 88
Nazi regime: and academic freedom,
    162–3; anti-Jewish policies, 129, 133,
    134; barbarism of as modernity, 155;
    bourgeois society maintained by, 157;
    'carrot and stick' methods, 52, 151;
    chaotic internal structure of, 152;
    collapse of, 203; competing elites in,
    117, 152; conflicts within, 161;
    consolidation of, 70ff. esp. 107;
    defeat blamed on leadership of, 200;
    disintegration of, 146–8, 149;
    stabilization of hegemony of big
    money aim of, 160; integrative ability
    of, 150; internal changes 1939–40,
    115; leadership and *Volk*, 196, 203;
    limited influence on culture, 91–5,
    151; limited influence on everyday
    life, 151; limited influence on
    religion, 151; limited influence on
    science, 151; military defeat, reaction
    to, 150; modernity of 152–3; and
    national community, 203; nature of,
    32, 34, 44, 49, 61, 67, 69, 70, 110,
    120, 131, 137, 150–3; normative and
    prerogative state, 120; occupation
    policy, 125, 142; popular opinion
    during defeat of, 200–3; popular
    support for, 44, 152; professional
    political class emerges in, 161; public
    opinion monopolized by, 159; racial
    reconstruction in East, policy of, 128;
    'racial and social hygiene' policy,
    aims of, 122; radicalization of
    policies, 110; sensitive to popular
    opinion, 150; separation of legislature
    and executive abolished by, 161;
    social and economic policy, 155;
    technical rationality and efficiency
    absolute value in, 155; terror,
    increased use of, 114, 150; in war,
    second half of, 137; *see also*
    individual policy areas
Nazi Students League, 62, 88, 97
Nazi Teachers League, 88
Nazi War Victims' Welfare, 88
Nazi Women's League, 88

Nazism: anti-Semitism, 48; and arts,
    63; death of, 148; 'German path',
    155; ideology, 56, 70, 77, 83–90
    passim, 116, 137; imperialist aims
    of, 74, 109–11; inconsistency of
    Weltanschauung, 89, 91; and the
    individual, 183; performance ethos,
    80; pursuit of by NSDAP, 8; racial
    ideology, 2, 74, 88, 111, 117, 154;
    reality and propaganda, 201; and
    Social Darwinism, 154; social
    planning, aims of, 154; state, concept
    of, 62; as substitute for religion, 162;
    totalitarian claims of, 62; women,
    ideology on, 114
'Nero Order', 146–7
Netherlands, 115, 133
Neubabelsberg, 21
Neudeck, 18, 27
Neue Zürcher Zeitung, 26
Neuer Vorwärts, 58, 59
Neurath, Baron Konstantin von, 32, 46, 110
New York, 46
Nierentz, Hans Jürgen, 169
Nitsche, Hermann, 190
Nolde, Emil, 96
'Nordmark', 14
Norway, 81, 115, 177
'November Republic', 62
'November Revolution', 112
NSBO *see* National Socialist Factory Cell
    Organization
NSDAP *see* National Socialist German
    Workers Party
NS-Hago see National Socialist Craft, Trade
    and Commerce Organization
Nuremberg, 61, 75, 163
Nuremberg Laws, 48, 109, 130, 131
Nuremberg rallies, 71, 84, 130, 131

Obersalzburg, 148
occupation policy in Eastern Europe, 126,
    127, 128, 142, 150, 200
Occupied Eastern Territories, Ministry for,
    126
Oder, 196, 198
Ohlendorf, Otto, 141–2; office in RSHO,
    195; opposes Speer, 142
'Old Fighters' of the Nazi Party, 22, 42,
    90, 155

'Old Party Comrades', 157
Olympic Games (1936), 71; causes restrictions on anti-Jewish measures, 131
'one-pot Sundays', 83
Opel AG, 50
opera, operetta, 95
'Operation Thunderstorm', 146
'Operation Valkyrie' (Stauffenberg bomb plot), 144
opposition, 15; arrests amongst, 46; decrease in popular, 107; fear of civil servants', 146; graffiti, 159; growing, 144; hopelessness of, 99; intimidation of, 159; isolation of, 143, 194–5; military, 143; open terror against recedes, 99; Political Police surveillance of, 103; right-wing, 157; in Stahlhelm, 159: verbal agitation by workers, 159; see also resistance
Oranienburg, 21, 87, 189
Ortsgruppenleiter see Local Party Leaders
Ossietzky, Carl von, 62

Pabst, Georg Wilhelm, 93
painting see arts, fine
Palatinate, 4
Palestine: 'Jewish Agency for', 133; Jewish emigration to, 133; 'Trust Company', 133
Papen, Franz von, 17–18, 21, 25, 32, 33, 41, 48, 68
Paris, 131; World Exhibition, 169
Party Organization (PO): and Army, 12; and 'Führer-principle', 89; and SA, 11; separation of, 159
'Pastors' Emergency League', 66, 67
peasantry, and agricultural policy, 76–7, 161; attitudes towards Nazism 6, 156, 158; attitudes towards regime, 152, 202; and Bavarian Peasants' Convention, 6; and defeat, 197, 202; discontent, 6, 77; in modern economy, 158; and 'national community', 77; and Nazi assumption of power, 37; and Reich Entailed Farm Law, 5; and Reich Food Estate, 76, 164; unrest within, 5; during war, 138
Penal Code, Reich, 181
pensions, 64; DAF policy on, 117–19

'People's Court of Law', 107; death sentences, 144, 145, 147, 212 n. 43
performance, 180
'period of struggle' (Kampfzeit), 10, 137, 161
Perlitius, Ludwig, 33
personal unions, 102
petite bourgeoisie: attitudes towards Hitler, 9; dissent within, 3; in modern economy, 158; Ohlendorf's economic policy towards, 142 see also middle class; Mittelstand
Planck, Max, 98
plebiscites, 33, 69; Nov. 1933 67–8, 159; 1934; Hitler on, 172–3
Pleiger, Paul, 179
Pohl, Oswald, 176
Poland: abduction of children from, 127; bogus border incidents, 112; deportations from 125, 127; Einsatzgruppen in, 134; forced/slave labour from, 127, 138; invasion of, 115; Nazi occupation policy, 125–6; plans for invasion of, 111; post-war internment in, 147; see also Generalgouvernement
police, 34, 35, 177; in Bavaria, 41; commissars, 40; and habitual criminals, 185; popular ignorance of different types, 106; 'preventive custody', 105; reports of, 3–4; SS takeover of, 102, 107, 115; traditional thinking in ends, 103; compared with Wehrmacht, 108
Political Police: development of and takeover by SS, 101; in Länder, 101, 102; responsibilities, 103
political prisoners, 37, 43, 104, 105
political violence, 34, 35
Popular Enlightenment and Propaganda, Reich Ministry of, 39, 169
popular opinion: accusation of defeatism rejected, 199; towards Allies, 202; 'big-shots', discontent about, 90, 202; bombing, discontent about, 203; towards coup against SA, 24, 26; towards 'Crystal Night', 109, 132; and defeat, 149, 197–203; discontent, 7, 15; disillusionment, 147, 201; early victories, enthusiasm for, 115; and

'euthanasia', 120; foreign policy
success, enthusiasm for, 71, 90;
Gestapo feared by, 106; towards
Goering, 203; towards changes in
health care, 123; towards Hitler, 9,
24, 38, 51, 90, 100, 107, 111, 116,
158, 162; ignorance of different
branches of police, 106; ignorance of
terror, 99; increasingly open, 201;
jokes about Nazi leaders, 158;
towards *'Jüd Süss'* film, 211 n. 28;
towards Luftwaffe, 200, 202; Nazi
employment policy, enthusiasm for,
78; towards Nazi movement, 6;
towards NSDAP, 8, 26; post-war
period, hopes for, 117; and
propaganda, 201; towards regime
8–9, 15, 107, 149, 152, 200–2;
towards resistance, 143; secrecy of
genocide of Jews caused by, 135;
secret weapon, hopes for, 198;
self-deception about victory, 137,
143; sense of complicity, 149;
sensitivity of regime to, 150; towards
Stauffenberg plot 145; war aims,
identification with, 116; war, fear of,
11; *see also* Bavarian Political Police;
Gendarmerie; Gestapo; Prussia;
'Reports from the Reich'; situation
reports; *Sopade*
population policy, 73, 119; and eugenics,
122, 124; motivated by racism, 115;
and sterilization, 122; vision of
renewal of *Volk*, 123
Portugal, 82
Posen, 26
'Potsdam Day' (March 1933), 44, 51, 52
Prague, 58, 59
Preminger, Otto, 93
Prenzlau, 146
press, 7, 24, 64; bourgeois, 34, 64;
censorship of, 3, 24, 25, 34, 63, 65,
95, 159; foreign, 46, 47, 160, 168;
Hitler on, 167; law on, 168; Nazi, 7,
24; non-Nazi periodicals, 91;
propaganda, 73; fall in sales, 160;
takeover of 64, 159; *see also* Amann,
Max
preventive detention, proposed for
'community aliens', 184

prices: control of, 76; food, 4; policy in
agriculture, 77, 164
prisoners of war, 77, 138; distinction by
nationality, 139; English, reward
offered for capture of, 179; Soviet,
139
propaganda, 34, 38, 39, 49, 73, 76, 81, 83,
91, 151, 152; films, 93; breakdown of
monopoly of, 201–2; mass events, 95;
at outbreak of war, 112; reality
contradicts, 201; about secret
weapons, 198; about Theresienstadt
concentration camp, 135; wartime,
138
Protection of German Blood and Honour',
'Law for, 130
'Protection of the German People',
emergency decree for (1933), 34,
35–36
'Protection of the People and the State',
decree for *see* Reichstag Fire Decree
Protection of the Republic, law for (1930),
36
'protective custody', 43, 53, 104, 105;
Political Police department for, 103
Protestant Church *see* Church
Prussia, 11, 32, 35, 37, 38, 39, 40, 41, 43;
Gestapo in, 101; *Landtag*, 59; reports
from, 26
Prussian Academy of Arts, 34
psychiatry: and 'euthanasia' 121–2, 186,
187, 189; psychoanalysis, 98; youth,
189
public opinion: abroad, 46; censorship of,
69; monopolized by NSDAP, 163
public spending, 50, 74, 121
publishing, 62
Putbus, 176

racial 'quality', Ley on, 180
racial policy: in concentration camps, 124;
overlapping competencies in, 90; and
population policy, 115, 123; Race
Policy Office of NSDAP, 126, 186;
and radicalization of policies, 109–11;
and Second World War, 111, 122; in
SS, 177; *see also* anti-Semitism; Jewish
Question; Jews; Jews, genocide of
radio, 14, 24, 34, 62, 94; 'collective
reception' of broadcasts, 88; death

sentence for listening to 'enemy broadcasts', 115; foreign, 160; Goebbels and Hitler on, 167

Raffeisenverband, 57

Rastenburg, 144

Rath, Ernst von, 131

rationing, 113, 138, 163

Ravensbrück concentration camp, 188

raw-materials: business group for, 76; oil production, 179; plundered from occupied territories, 115; saved in non-strategic sectors, 141, 164; shortages, 7, 75, 180

'reactionaries', 8, 16, 20, 25; Political Police surveillance of, 103; *see also* right-wing opposition

rearmament, 50, 53, 55; and big business, 74–6; inadequate for long war, 112; primacy of, 74, 75, 164; social cost of, 77

Red Army, 147

'Red Orchestra', 144

referenda, 33; of 19 Aug. 1934, 27; *see also* plebiscites

refugees, from East, 147, 153, 196; Jewish children, 133

Reich Association of Jews in Germany, 132

Reich Bishop, 66, 67, *see also* Müller, Ludwig

Reich Central Office for Jewish Emigration, 133

Reich Chamber of Culture, 64

Reich Chamber of Fine Arts, 64

Reich Chamber of Music, 64

Reich Chancellery, 23, 56, 137, 148; and draft 'Community Aliens Law', 181; and 'euthanasia', 187, 189, 190

Reich Chancellor *see* Goebbels; Hitler; von Schleicher

Reich Church, 66

Reich Commissariats of the *Ostland*, 126

Reich Commissars, 32, 40, 41, 42

Reich Commissioners, 50

Reich Committee of German Youth Associations, 85

Reich Complaints Office, 16

Reich Concordat, 45, 59, 60, 65

Reich Confederation of German Industry (RDI), 55

Reich Entailed Farm Law (*Reichserbhofgesetz*) 5

Reich Estate of German Commerce, 56

Reich Estate of German Craft, 56

Reich Estate of German Industry, 54–5

Reich Food Estate (*Reichsnährstand*), 5–6, 75, 76, 163, 164

Reich Governors, 7, 11, 17, 41, 42, 60, 61, 177

Reich Land League, 57

Reich President, 18, 27, 33, 34, 69

Reich Representative Body of the German Jews, 132

Reich Security Head Office (*Reichssicherheitshauptamt*) 115, 125, 142; and 'Final Solution', 134, 135, 190, 191; Ohlendorf office, 195

Reich Union of Jews in Germany, (*Reichsvereinigung*), 132, 133

Reich Vocational Contest, 80, 180

Reich Youth Leadership, 80, 85, 87

Reichenau, Walter von, 17, 19, 32

Reichsbank, 50, 74

'Reichsbanner', 58

Reichstag, 33, 44, 45, 58, 59; *see also* elections

Reichstag fire, 36, 38

Reichstag Fire Decree, 36–37, 40, 43, 46, 59, 105

Reichswehr, 9, 17, 50, 69; disillusionment within, 3; and Hitler, 14, 27; and right-wing opposition, 16, 25; and SA, 12, 14–15, 17, 19, 25

Reinhardt Programme, 72; and *Ehestandsdarlehen*, 73

'Relief of the Suffering of the People and the Reich, Law for' (1933) *see* 'Enabling Act'

religion, *see* Church; Jews

Remarque, Erich Maria, 62

'Reports from the Reich' ('*Meldungen aus dem Reich*'), 106, 115–16, 196–203, 211 n. 28; *see also* 'situation reports'

resettlement, 126, 160; *see also* Germanization policy; *Lebensraum*; occupation policy in Eastern Europe

resistance, 59; Communist, 100, 116; conditions of, 195; conservative-nationalist, 145; elite, 194; flares at end of war, 147; Hitler's life, attempts

on, 116, 143, 145; isolation of, 194–5;
Jews helped by, 135; Kreisau Circle,
143–4, 194–5; military, 116;
'Operation Valkyrie' (Stauffenberg
bomb plot), 144–5, 181, passive, of
working class, 157; popular reaction
to, 145; 'Red Orchestra', 144;
repression of, 100, 107, 158; roots of,
151; 'White Rose', 144; see also
Church; Sopade
'retinue', 54, 180, 198
Rheinmetall, 74
Rhine-Ruhr region, 145–6, 198
Rhineland, 172
Ribbentrop, Joachim von, 110, 148, 169,
189
Riefenstahl, Leni, 92
right-wing opposition, 15–16; aims of, 16;
and Army, 16–17; and coup against
SA, 21, 27; lack of distinction from
Nazis, 16, 157; Nazis condemn, 19;
desires restoration of monarchy, 17;
young conservatives, 16
right-wing political parties, 33; dissolution
of, 59
Röhm, Ernst, 9, 11–15, 17, 19–24, 41, 42
Rökk, Marika, 93
Rosemeyer, Bernd, 96
Rosenberg, Alfred, 67, 85, 126, 167, 168,
178
Rote Fahne, 100
Rowohlt Verlag, 94
Rüdin, Ernst, 122
Rühmann, Heinz, 93
Ruhr region, 35, 86, 198
Rust, Bernhard, 97

SA (Sturmabteilung), 9–10, 15, 40, 45, 88;
and anti-Jewish boycotts, 47–8; and
Army, 11–14, 17; and assumption of
power, 34, 35; in Bavaria, 41;
'beefsteak Nazis', 11; class distinctions
eliminated in, 160; commandos
'execute' citizens in last days of
regime, 147; commissars, 7, 10;
Communists join, 159; composition
of, 10–11; coup against, 30 June
1934, 1, 18–23; consequences of
coup against 23–7, 69, 101;
discontent within, 3, 9; and

employment, 39; French attitudes
towards, 8; homosexuality within, 11,
21, 23; independence of, 69;
influence declines, 10, 61, 69;
intervention in economy and
administration by, 7; and labour
movement, destruction of, 51–3; leftist
sentiments, 11, 17; looting during
'Crystal Night', 132; lust for power of
leaders, 61; as male community, 10;
and NSDAP, 10–11, 13; paramilitary
activities, 10; and 'Party revolution
from below', 42; permanent posts in
as reward, 158; second revolution
and, 13; special jurisdiction, 13,
205 n. 22; and Stahlhelm, 15, 59,
159; system of control of members,
158; unofficial concentration camps,
11; violence, 10, 13, 34, 35, 36, 40,
43
Saarland, 58
Sachsenhausen concentration camp, 101,
104, 187
Salzgitter, 75
Sauckel, Fritz, Gauleiter, 1; 'campaigns',
139, 141; 'Plenipotentiary for the
Deployment of Labour', 139
Savigny, Friedrich Carl von, 16
savings, 113
Saxony, 4, 40
Schacht, Hjalmar, 50, 74, 75, 131
Schaumburg-Lippe, 40, 101
Schiller, Friedrich, 95
Schirach, Baldur von, 85, 87
Schleicher, Kurt von, 21, 22, 25, 32, 50,
51
Schleswig-Holstein, 156
Schmalenbach, Curt, 188
Schmeling, Max, 96, 169
Schmid, Wilhelm, 20, 22
Schmid, Willi, 22
Schmitt, Carl, 26
Schmitt, Kurt, 55
Schneider, Carl, 189
Schneidhuber, August, 20, 22
Scholl, Hans and Sophie, 144
schools: Church influence abolished, 87;
and Hitler Youth, 86–7; importance
of sport, 87; Nazi education policy,
87; see also education

Schuhmann, Walter, 53
Schultz, Bruno Kurt, 178
Schulze-Boysen, Harro, 144
Schweitzer, Hans, 64
Schwerin von Krosigk, Count Lutz, 32
science 97–8; and Catholic Church, 163;
    limited Nazi influence in, 151, 163;
    see also universities
Science, Education and Adult Education,
    Reich Ministry of, 97
'scorched earth policy' see 'Nero Order'
SD (Security Service), 18; executes
    dissidents, 115; takes over Gestapo/
    Political Police matters 101–3;
    Ohlendorf as head of in RSHO, 142,
    195; departments of Security Police
    Head Office, 103; spies inside Party,
    103, 106; and SS mentality, 107; and
    Wannsee Conference, 190–1; see also
    'Reports from the Reich'
secret weapons, hopes of, 198
'seizure of power', 3, 8, 43, 84, 161
Seldte, Franz von, 32, 52
'selective breeding', 122; see also
    'Lebensborn Foundation'
sex: and foreign workers, Himmler on,
    178; offenders, castration of, 186
'Shooting Decree' (1933), 35
'Siegfried Line', 73, 187
Siemens AG, 50, 74, 142
Silesia, 23
Silverberg, Paul, 55
'situation reports', 26; responsibility of
    Political Police for, 103; see also
    'Reports from the Reich'
slave labour, 126; see also forced labour;
    foreign workers
small businesses, 56
Sobibor death camp, 127, 134
'social courts of honour', 54
Social Darwinism, 80, 154, 191; and
    eugenics, 124
Social Democratic Party (SPD), 32, 186;
    election results, 33, 38; and Enabling
    Act, 44–5, 207, n. 26; and Kreisau
    Circle, 144; members join Stahlhelm,
    159; persecution of, 37, 50, 58, 59;
    takeover of press by Nazis, 64;
    publications banned, 36–7, 40, 64;
    and trade unions, 51; opposition of,

/8, 82, underground activity almost
    ends, 107; violence against, 34
social expenditure, 4
'social hygiene', 122
social mobility, 80, 86, 174, 180–1
social planning, 154
social policy, 54, 73, 80; DAF, 117–20;
    destructive potential of, 122; and
    Lebensraum, 119; overlapping
    competencies in, 90; performance,
    selective breeding and, 119–20;
    Political Police surveillance of, 103;
    and sense of social equality, 82; skills
    training, Ley on, 180; welfare centres,
    90; and working class status, 153
social relations, uncertainty of, 162; see
    also class; social mobility; social
    policy
socio-economic trends, 77–8, 152–5;
    consumerism, 77
Sonderkommando, 134
Sonnenstein, 190
Sonthofen, 170
Sopade, 4, 58, 59; 'Germany Reports' of,
    4, 6, 9, 27, 82, 99
Soviet Union, 162, 166, 167; Einsatzgruppen
    in, 134, 142; post-war internment in,
    147; prisoners of war from, 139;
    victory of Red Army, 196, 197, 198,
    202; war of annihilation in, 127
Spain, 166
'Special Courts', 107, 115; death sentences
    in last days of regime, 147
'Special Penal Law and in Special Cases',
    Decree on, 114
'special treatment', 177
Speer, Albert, and big business, 140–1;
    and building projects, 84, 97, 167;
    and 'Central Planning', 141; flees
    Berlin, 148; Himmler and Ohlendorf
    oppose, 141–2; as Minister for
    Armaments and Munitions, 137, 140,
    141; as Minister for Armaments and
    War Production, 141, 146;
    mobilization of last reserves, 146;
    opposes 'Nero Order', 146
Spitzweg, Carl, 169
sport, 86, 87, 96
Sportpalast, Berlin, 8, 14, 137, 138, 202
Spreti-Weilbach, Count Joachim von, 22

SS (*Schutzstaffeln*), 15, 18, 20, 42, 99;
    Adolf Hitler Bodyguard Regiment, 20,
    102; and anti-Jewish boycotts, 47;
    armed brigades of, 102; concentration
    camp labour sold by, 128;
    concentration camps, 101, 106, 128;
    Death's Head Units, 101; Economic
    Administration Head Office, 128;
    Einsatzgruppen, 107, 125, 127, 134,
    136, 142; and 'euthanasia', 186, 188,
    189; 'executes' citizens in last days of
    regime, 147; to realize 'Führer's will',
    106; and genocide, 107, 136; and
    Gestapo, 25, 106, 107; Head Office,
    Administration and Economy, 176;
    Head Office, Department Heissmeyer,
    176; independence from NSDAP, 101,
    102; and destruction of labour
    movement, 53; marriage rules in, 178;
    mentality; 107; 'new heathenism'
    criticised by Churches, 85; -owned
    enterprises, 105, 128; permanent
    posts in as reward, 158; occupation
    of Poland, 125, 127; police controlled
    by, 102, 107; Race and Settlement
    Office, 177–8; racial selection as
    educational aim, 88; Reich Criminal
    Police Office, 181; rise of 101–8; SA,
    conflict with, 19, 21, 22, 26; 'social
    reconstruction' as task of, 106; special
    SS and police jurisdiction, 115; and
    Speer, 142; surveillance and terror
    institutionalized by, 101; and state
    bureaucracy, 25; state, foundations of,
    101; *Verfügungtruppe*, 102; violence,
    35; vision of völkisch new order, 88;
    war aims, 126, 142; and Wehrmacht,
    102; 'Yuletide' celebrated by, 84; *see
    also* Himmler; '*Lebensborn*
    Foundation'; Reich Security Head
    Office; SD
'*Staatsschädlinge*', 8
Stadelheim prison, 21, 22
Stahlhelm, 9, 15, 32, 35, 59; as reservoir
    of opposition, 159
Stalin, Joseph, 112, 142
Stalingrad, 136, 142, 201
Stampfer, Friedrich, 58
Stark, Johannes, 98
state; Hitler on, 170–3; *völkisch*, 171

state administration *see* bureaucracy
Stauffenberg, Count Claus Schenk von,
    144–5
Stauffer, Teddy, 94
Stempfle, Bernhard, 22
sterilization, ordered by 'Eugenic Courts',
    122; law on, 120; proposed for
    'community aliens', 183, 186; *see also*
    population policy
Stettin, 133
Strasser, Gregor, 11, 21, 22, 25, 33, 50
Strasser, Otto, 10
Straub, Erich, 189
Strauss, Richard, 64
Streicher, Julius, 47–8
'Strength through Joy', 81–2; KdF-car, 82;
    and theatre, 95–6
students *see* universities
Stürmer, Der, 47, 130
Stuttgart, 12
Sudetenland, 110; crisis, 116
suicides, 199
Supreme Court, 36
surveillance, 99–102, 106, 115, 156, 158,
    168, 184, 203
Sütterlin, Rolf, 177
synthetics, 6, 75, 76
'*Systempolitiker*', 40

taxation, 113
teachers, 87, 88
Tegel, 181
Tegernsee, 20
Tempelhof airport, 22, 52
Terboven, Joseph, 19
terror, 194; recedes during consolidation,
    99, 158
Thälmann, Ernst, 37
theatre, 65, 95–6, 168
Theresienstadt (Terezín) concentration
    camp, 135, 191
Thingspiele, 95, 168
Third Reich, historiography of, 149–55;
    nature of society in, 153; questions
    raised by, 149–55; social trends in
    152–5; *see also* National Socialist
    German Workers Party; 'Nazi regime';
    socio-economic trends
Thuringia, 11
Thyssen, Fritz, 7

Todt, Fritz, 73; as Minister for Armaments
and Munitions, 137, 141
Toller, Ernst, 95
'totalitarianism', theory of, 151
tourism, 81–2, 96; see also 'Strength
through Joy'
town planning, 97
trade unions, 10, 33, 34; Christian, 53;
destruction of, 42, 50, 51–3, 58, 62,
69; General Federation of German,
51–3; Hirsch-Duncker Trade Union
Ring, 53; leaders in Kreisau Circle,
144
training, industrial, 180
Transport and Post, Ministry of, 32
Treblinka death camp, 127, 134
Trepper, Leopold, 144
Troost, Paul Ludwig, 97
Trustees of Labour, Reich, 53, 54, 78; Law
on, 53
Tschirsky und Boegendorff, Fritz Günther
von, 16
Tucholsky, Kurt, 62

Ukraine, and 'General Plan East', 126
Ullstein Verlag, 130
unemployment, 4, 50, 51, 71–3, 146, 157,
165; caused by bombing, 198; Second
Law for the Reduction of, 72
united front, 34
Unity of the Party and the State, Law to
Secure the (1933), 14, 61
universities, 62, 97–8; academic freedom
in, 156, 162, 163; emigration of
academics, 97; 'German science', 98;
higher education policy, 97;
humanities, 98, 163; lecturers, 88,
144; scientific research, 97–8, 163;
social sciences, 98, 162, 163; students,
behaviour of, 157, 162; students in
'White Rose' group, 144; surveillance
of, 156; vice-chancellors as 'Führers',
97
Universum-Film AG (Ufa), 92, 93, 168
Upper Silesia, 198
USA, 94, 114, 133, 143, 160, 169, 197
USSR see Soviet Union

Vatican, 59–60
Vereinigte Stahlwerk, 50

Versailles, Treaty of, 8, 67, 109
Vertrauensleute, 106; see also 'Reports
from the Reich'
Vice-Chancellery, 17–18, 32
Vienna, 110, 203
Völkischer Beobachter, 15, 19, 163
Vogelsang, 170
Volk, 26, 61, 64, 181; and coup against
SA, 24, 25; and national community,
52, 196; in defeat, 146, 197, 201, 203;
and Führer, 137, 203; and Goering,
203; and leadership, 201; loyalty of,
197; and state, Hitler on, 171, 172
Volksempfänger, 63, 115
Volksgemeinschaft see national community
Volksgenossen see 'national comrades'
'Volksschädlinge' ('elements harmful to
the people'), 104, 118, 171; see also
'community aliens'
Volkssturm, German, 146
Volkstum ('Folkdom'), 171
Volkswagen, 82; 'Beetle' (KdF-car),
82
Vorwärts, 58
voting patterns see elections

Wagener, Otto von, 55
wages, 5, 53, 78–9; bonuses, 79;
deductions from, 78, 83; freeze,
78–80, 113; and productivity, 79–80,
119; and status, 80
Wagner, Adolf, 7, 41, 42
Wandervogel, 85
Wannsee Conference, 134
War Economy, Decree on, 113
War, First World, 181, 186; Hitler's lessons
from, 112
War, Second World, 2; aims 110, 126;
beginning of, 110; Blitzkrieg, 111,
112, 114, 115, 117, 138; 'Community
Aliens Law' not passed because of,
181; concentration of enterprises,
141; constrains domestic policy, 70;
course of, 136, 139, 147, 181; crimes,
127, 142, 147; defeat of Germany,
195–203; economy in, 138–9; effects
of defeat, 150, 153; end of, 146–7,
150, 195–203; evacuation, 147, 196;
everyday life in, 197; and genocide,
128, 136; German occupation policy,

126, 127, 128, 142, 150, 200;
leadership blamed for defeat, 200;
reality and propaganda, 201; plans
for, 98; popular opinion, 111–12, 115,
117, 145, 197–203; refugees, 147, 153,
196; 'Sauckel Campaigns', 139; and
social differences, 138; 'total', 114,
136–148, 198, 201; unequal suffering
in, 144; *Volkssturm* 146; as war of
extermination, 111, 127; as
Weltanschauungskrieg, 119, 150;
see also bombing
Wartenburg, Peter Yorck von, 144
Wartheland, *Reichsgau*, deportations from,
133; 'special treatment' of Poles in,
177
Wehrmacht, 74, 75, 82, 108; and draft
'Community Aliens Law', 181; and
Four-Year Plan, 76; and foreign
policy, 110; genocide, role in, 134;
High Command, 110, 181; and
leadership of regime, 143;
modernization of, 153; opposes 'Nero
Order', 146; resistance, failure of, 116,
143; and scientific research, 98
Weimar, 101, 183, 188
Weimar Republic, 32, 35, 38, 39, 41, 48,
52, 63, 70, 74, 94, 98; constitution of,
36, 43; foreign policy of, 110
Wels, Otto, 45, 58
Werner, Ilse, 93
Werwolf, 147
Wessel, Horst, 92
West Germany, 80
Westphalia, 20, 85
white collar employees, 4, 152
'White Rose' resistance group, 144
Wilder, Billy, 93
Wilder, Thornton, 94
Winter Aid, 78, 83, 160
Wittenberg, 66
Wolfe, Thomas, 94
Wolff, Karl, 179
Wolfsburg, 82
women: abortion, Political Police
surveillance of, 103; discontent, 200,

203; employment policy, 73–4;
massacred at Babi Yar, 134; wartime
labour of, 114; Nazi view of, 74, 165;
as *Volkssturm* auxiliaries, 146
'work-shy', persecution of the, 104–5;
and draft 'Community Aliens Law',
184
workers, 4–5, 52; absenteeism, 80; change
in, 77; labour protest, 80; verbal
agitation by, 159, 203; in wartime,
197, 199, 200; see also working class
working class, 4, 51, 52, 62, 68, 77–8;
passive resistance, 157; sense of
status of, 153; and KdF, 81; see also
workers
Workplace Representation Law (1933), 51
'works community' 54
works councils, 54; elections (1933), 51
Woyrsch, Udo von, 23, 26
Württemberg, 38, 40
Würzburg, 146
Wüst, Walther, 179
Wüstenrot Building Society, 114

young conservatives see right-wing
opposition
young offenders, legislation on, 186
youth: and draft 'Community Aliens Law',
186; 'euthanasia' of, 189; influence of
HJ on behaviour, 87; lack of
resistance to indoctrination, 85; Ley
on, 180; nonconformity, 86, 94;
promotion of, 158; psychiatry, 189;
reaction against individualism, 162;
religious and other non-Nazi
organizations, 85–6; see also
Arbeiterjugend; Bündische Jugend;
children; Church; Edelweiss Pirates;
education; Hitler Youth; Jews;
Jungvolk; League of German Girls;
schools
Yugoslavia, 115, 147

Zähmungskonzept, 32, 59
Ziegler, Adolf, 169
Zyklon B, 134